Grace under Pressure

Grace under Pressure

Passing Dance through Time

BARBARA NEWMAN

LIMELIGHT EDITIONS
NEW YORK

First Limelight Edition November 2003

Published in the United States by Proscenium Publishers, Inc.,
New York

Manufactured in the United States of America

Library of Congress Cataloging-in-Publication Data

Newman, Barbara.
   Grace under pressure : passing dance through time /
Barbara Newman.—
1st Limelight ed.
      p. cm.
   ISBN 0-87910-995-5 (pbk. : lg print)
   1. Dancers--Interviews. I. Title.
GV1785.A1N49 2003
792.8'092'2--dc22

                                    2003019294

Designed by Mulberry Tree Press, Inc.
(www.mulberrytreepress.com)

Acknowledgments

ITHOUT THE PARTICIPATION of the artists whose insights grace this book, I would not have written it. My intention from the outset was to honor their dedication by building a platform on which they could discuss it, and in my own mind the result is as much for them as about them. Having interrupted their work and borrowed their time to record their experience, I offer them my deepest gratitude for their generosity and the hope that they too, like the readers who will meet them in these pages, might discover something here to intrigue and delight them.

The following people responded to my requests for names, dates, facts and figures with scholarly precision and unfailing good humor. I appreciate their patient assistance and their helpful contributions in equal measure:

Barry Alterman, David Amzallag, Sofie Rask Andersen, Philip Back, Amy Bordy, Annik Coatalen, Phil Crewdson, Rob Daniels, Katharine Darst, Elizabeth Fawcett, Frank Freeman, Richard Glasstone, Heather Heckman, Jean Herbert, Majbrit Hjelmsbo, Vanessa Hurteloup, Mette Wolf Iversen, Kyra Jablonsky, Ellen Jacobs, Niels Michael Jacobsen, Diana Kolnikoff, Diane Kounalakis, Laurajane Lavender, Beverly LeBlanc, Dan Levans, Chris May, Sharon McCormick, Alexander Meinertz, Rebecca Nettl-Fiol, Marleen Nicolai, Ricki Ostrov, David Pratt, Siân Pritchard, Odile Reine-Adelaide, Nancy Reynolds, Kelly Ryan, Andrea Snyder, Margo Spellman, Susanne Steffensen, Michelle Sweeny, Nora Van Dessel, Francesca Vanelli, Sharon Wagner, Carole Walsh and Julia White.

My warmest thanks go as well

to Maggi Gordon, Ruth Klippstein, Dorothy Koehler and Ayşe Saraçgil for their memories,

to Julia Kokich and Olga Vetchtomova, the Russian translators and interpreters of Irina Kolpakova's interview,

to Genevieve Carpenter and Diana Davies for their invaluable knowledge and particular support,

and especially to Joan Brandt, Andrew Hewson and Mel Zerman, whose steadfast encouragement and belief in this book enabled me, finally, to realize it.

For my teachers
Stephen and Dickie

I asked the commander how to get to the TPP office, 1–138.

"Turn left at that building up there—that's Building 13; then go back up to the infinite corridor and turn right into Building 6 . . ."

"What's the infinite corridor?" I asked.

"It links all the main buildings, has glass doors on either end, and is about 319 paces long. On November 12 and January 31 the sun shines directly from one end of it to the other."

The Idea Factory
Pepper White

Contents

For the sake of clarity, reported speech is presented in double quotes and thoughts or unspoken comments in single quotes.

Photographs

Every effort has been made to obtain permission for the use of the photographs listed above.

Grace under Pressure

Introduction

*L*ISTEN, THIS IS TRUE. One night in 1977, I came home from a New York City Ballet performance and immediately picked up the phone and called a friend. I starting talking as soon as she answered, and our conversation for the next few minutes went something like this.

"I can't believe it," I began without preamble.

"I know. I can't either."

"It seemed impossible. I never thought it would happen."

"Never's a long time, but I guess it did look pretty unlikely."

"Did you hear anything about it before tonight?"

Pausing for effect, she said, "Maybe just the tiniest rumor."

"Well, everyone in the theatre was jabbering about the details during intermission. You should have been there."

"Who's everyone?" she asked. "No one knows."

"What do you mean, no one knows? Everyone knows. It's the biggest news in town."

"Wait a minute," she protested. "What are we talking about?"

"We're talking," I said, slowing down for emphasis, "about Misha joining City Ballet."

"You're kidding," she laughed. "I thought we were talking about the fact that I'm going to have a baby."

Twenty-five years later, she and I are still friends, still going to New York City Ballet when we can and still talking about it when we meet, but we don't meet quite so often, because in 1981 I left New York and moved to London. The dance scene I discovered here was smaller than the one I'd always known and more self-

17

involved—as if the rest of the world didn't matter, it focused inward, on itself—but I figured my experience as a critic in New York should help me decipher the action and my track record might enable me to work myself into it. With my first book already under my belt, I wrote a second, then a third, did some interviews for one magazine, began reviewing for another, and gradually I found a way to remain professionally involved with dance in my new home. It didn't happen quickly—this isn't New York, nothing happens quickly—but by networking a little, seeing a lot and reviewing as often as I could, I managed to make a place for myself.

People still wrote letters in those days, before e-mail came along, but a dialogue is always more fun than sequential monologues, so whenever I spoke to that New York friend on the phone, we would trip over our tongues in the rush to bring each other up to date. We talked, as ever, about dance and music, performers and choreographers, new productions and revivals, and after a while I noticed that very little of the information we swapped so eagerly made us laugh as we had laughed that night in New York, when all the news was good news. Instead, many of our stories ended with an exasperated sigh that traveled down the line like an audible shrug, as if to say, 'What can you do?' and many conversations in London echoed with the same unspoken perplexity.

By the time the '90s rolled around, I was hearing that bewildered sigh everywhere, and I also heard more bad news than good and more dire predictions than enthusiasm. At the ballet, I saw joyless dancers, sketches for the artists I believed they could be, in productions that resembled richly robed skeletons, all shape without body. The new modern works seemed to represent a branch of politics, more attitude than art, to which movement was incidentally attached—one spanking new studio I visited on a university campus had been built without mirrors. Although I maintained my optimism resolutely in print, I couldn't deny that dance was in serious trouble when the most loyal viewers I had met gave up on it and disappeared from performances, not because they couldn't afford the tickets, which would have made sense, but because they weren't enjoying what they saw, which didn't.

It's one thing when the general audience loses interest and quite another when critics begin to talk about reviewing as if it were a chore, yet that happened too. Of course we were all getting older, which meant the dancers became younger every year, like the policemen in the street, but that had never interfered with my enjoyment before. Now, suddenly, my heart sank at the prospect of attending two or three performances a week, and I had to corner myself into writing positively about them. What was going on? I didn't want to stay home as some of my friends did, watching videos and trading memories like baseball cards, so I blocked my ears to their complaints and struggled not to look back, hoping I could protect my eyes from the the real or mythical glow of the past. Yet even as I fought to remain objective, I noticed that the disappointment infecting my pleasure wasn't exclusive to me and it wasn't exclusive to dance. Knowledgeable observers everywhere were bemoaning the scarcity of pianists, classical actors, pitchers, orchestra conductors, boxers and musical comedy belters who could dominate their art and our imagination at once. "When I was growing up," Luciano Pavarotti said, "there were thirty great tenors, not three. I don't know why things are now the way they are."

I didn't know either, but the more helpless I felt as dancing became inescapably ordinary, the more I thought about an English joke of the early '90s, cast as a riddle: The queen, the prime minister, and the entire cabinet were sailing together in the Channel when a violent storm capsized their boat and drowned them all. What was lost? The answer was, Nothing. Nothing was lost, and Britain was saved. Did dance need saving? I wondered. Had it really hit the rocks or cast away some vital part of itself, or was I just burning out and losing my ability to adapt?

There was no point in tearing through town like Chicken Little, predicting doom and crying, "What's gone wrong?" because the world might simply have shifted on its axis and thrown off the artists I longed to see. Instead, I decided to find out what had changed, and as soon as that question fell into place I realized that the performers couldn't possibly provide the answer. They already occupied a dubious position in my thoughts somewhere between culprit and victim, and their perspective, by virtue of their relative youth, had to be even shorter and narrower than mine. I couldn't ask my colleagues to comment either, because they had their own fish to fry, which so far had kept them from volunteering any plausible explanation of our shared distress.

"Nobody's got the answers you want," my friends insisted. "The subject's too big. Forget about it." But I couldn't stop circling my confusion until I stumbled on Lenin's claim, that the most fundamental question of all is who does what to whom. Then, without hesitation, I went in search of teachers and coaches, directors, choreographers and stagers, the dancers who had turned the focus of their own experience on someone else. As the invisible authorities controlling the artists and channeling their effort, they alone could stand objectively between intention and achievement, drawing on both while they created both, and I believed they could see what the rest of us were missing. Look back, I urged them, assuming they knew the risk, and tell me about the guides you followed. Then turn around and look forward, from your current vantage, and tell me what you find in the dancers you encounter every day. I asked them how and why they had come to their present position, and how they learned to do what their job required. What do you need from the dancers, and what do they need from you? How have they changed since you were a dancer yourself? When does tradition become a burden? Who is responsible for the future? Why revive the past? Whom must the repertory satisfy? What is choreography beside steps? How do dances die? Why not quit?

Out of curiosity and to convince myself I was on the right track, as I was starting my search I posed a few of these questions to a Russian coach who spoke no English. When the translator fell silent, the coach turned to me with the most peculiar expression on her face, almost as if she pitied me for my ignorance, and began an answer that lasted several minutes and involved her hands, eyes, head and torso. She pointed to the stage—we were sitting in a dark theatre, waiting for a rehearsal to begin—and tugged my arm and rearranged her feet. The fact that she had never met me before didn't seem to matter. If I couldn't understand the significance of her work and her reasons for doing it—so obvious, her patient smile said, so simple—she was happy to explain them. I felt privileged to be listening and slightly ashamed of imposing on her good will, but the translator whispered to me later, "She loved those questions. She said those are the only things she really cares about."

It took me a long time to understand exactly what I wanted to know about the dancing that was troubling me, and nearly as long to realize that I didn't have to be impartial. Nothing obliged me to speak to every artist, or even the most famous artists, who had stopped performing and accepted a share of the responsibility for others. I was entirely free to choose my subjects according to my private preference and to question only those people whose work I knew and respected, which naturally makes for a biased selection. This book is also biased toward ballet, mostly because modern dancers do not share a common language. Evolving by constant disavowal, their discipline has flourished as a rejection of continuity and tradition, and the artists who defined it built its history out of swinging doors, turning away from their predecessors to explore uncharted territory of their own devising.

Of course, a limited selection of potential subjects is not necessarily a small one. Before common sense kicked in, I considered talking to every artist on my initial list, which would undoubtedly have taken the rest of my life. It would also have produced a manuscript the size of a house, and I had never forgotten delivering my first book, when my editor asked if I would cut it down to a manageable size myself or if he should do it for me. In the end, I needn't have worried. Many people were too busy to meet with me, and one of them, as a London producer gently informed me, probably never saw my letter. "If that choreographer responded to every question and every request," he said, "there would never be time to make another work. How would you feel then?"

So the list grew shorter without my help, but I also established some ground rules to control it. I decided not to contact anyone I had interviewed before or anyone involved with a company I never got to see. I eliminated anyone entangled in a public dispute on their home turf, because my concerns exceeded individual domestic issues. At the same time, I wanted to look beyond the activity in London and New York, with which I was most familiar, because the changes I could observe locally were clearly not local at all. So I deliberately approached artists of varied backgrounds and professional affiliations, hoping to collect as many viewpoints as possible from a limited number of sources.

But however broad the sample, I had no intention of writing a comprehensive survey of the last 20 years or an academic treatise on teaching methodology or arts administration. Except for the interviews, all the material I needed lay within easy reach, in my own observations and experience with dance, in my library and notebooks, in the publications I regularly read and the clippings my friends sent me. I wish I were as perceptive as the physicist Richard Feynman, who used to look at an impenetrable mathematical problem, think about it very hard, and then write down the solution. Lacking his gift or any professional role in the inspired drudgery that produces art, I thought of my own resources as the basis for some educated speculation.

It's easy to take everyday statements for granted without bothering to examine them, and it's easy to report plain facts, but they don't tell the whole story. Fact: A group of pupils studies at a certain professional school. Yes, but where do they come from, and what most concerns that school about their training? Fact: Stager A teaches Dance B to Company C. Fine, but what makes it Dance B, and why does Company C want it? In theory and fantasy the answers to who-whom questions can float around like balloons, complete in themselves and independent of reality. But the dancing that interests me is not an aesthetic abstraction, and the people who answered my questions were not speaking theoretically. Ideally, their responses and my speculation will together bring an elusive subject down to earth.

This book is about the craft of passing dance through time, about the transfer of experience and knowledge from one generation of artists to another. I wrote it as a tribute to the hidden artisans who choose that craft and in an attempt to document their work before they, and the standards they value, are gone for good. You have to remember that what we see onstage is merely the visible tip of a process we never see, which takes place in classrooms and studios, in rehearsal and creation, in the bank, the boardroom and the mind. The process reaches back into history and forward to a world no one can imagine, and the authorities who guide it fasten the past to the future every day. Here's what they said.

B.N.
London, November 2002

In the Classroom

*B*LUEBERRY, RASPBERRY, RHUBARB and sometimes peach. Every summer I eat the best homemade pie on earth at a luncheonette in Delhi, New York, population 4,629. I stopped there for a sandwich 15 years ago, and I've been going back for the pie ever since, though Delhi—that's Dell-high—hasn't got much else to recommend it. A block from the luncheonette, the county record office faces a tidy village green at one end of Main Street. A gas station and a supermarket pin down the other end, maybe 250 yards from the green, and there used to be a ballet school in the three-story building opposite the supermarket. Fading black and white photos of student recitals curled in the sun behind the front windows, and if you peered through the screen door you could just make out a mirror along the side wall, its silver surface gleaming like water in the shadows. Though the building hasn't changed much, free weights and exercise mats have cluttered the room since the school closed, so it looks as if jazz and aerobics have taken over. Every year I think the pies will disappear too, or the baker will retire or move away or the luncheonette will become a pizza parlor, but so far my luck has held.

Nothing connects the two ends of Main Street except coincidence and irony—you can't get that pie anywhere else but you can find a little dancing school anywhere, well, anywhere but Delhi, on any main street in any small town, and the studios are all the same, cool and expectant. Thousands of children pass through them every year, if not by choice then by chance. They stand at the barre trying to flatten their back, hold in their stomach, tuck in their bottom, push their knees over their toes and breathe, all at the same

23

time. Thousands more roll and stretch in the school gym, bravely bouncing toward the supreme triumph of a full split. I started dancing in an overheated studio over a jewelry store in downtown Cleveland. My teacher, a former member of the Chicago Lyric Opera Ballet, wore a white tunic and a fringed cerise shawl and somehow earned enough to pay a pianist. Years later, in suburban New York, I took class above a barbershop, and years after that, over a shoe store in Manhattan, in the studio where Balanchine had choreographed *Agon* with Stravinsky sitting beside him, on that bench with their backs against that mirror.

Many of my friends remember circumstances that were the same as mine only different. A child in the late '40s, one of them began dancing in Greenwood, Mississippi, then a town of about 20,000 people, where one local teacher met her pupils in the kindergarten after lunch, when it was empty. Around the same time, a friend who is now a librarian in Virginia was learning "Graham technique for ten-year-olds" on the top floor of a mock-Tudor office building in a New York commuter town, and another friend, who runs a cattle farm not far from Delhi, was starting out in a Catholic church hall in Carmi, Illinois. "My mother taught," she told me, "and after catechism class upstairs the nuns would come down to watch. She taught in all the little towns, Norris City, Shawneetown, Eldorado, as she followed Dad's teaching jobs around Illinois. The last Illinois studio was in Kewanee—it was the Dance, Modeling and Charm School, with classes in tap, ballet, acrobatic, toe and jazz. Her love was working with the little ones, getting them started and giving them their basics. They stayed with her 'til about the eighth grade.

"Her last school was in El Paso, Texas. She closed it in the early '80s, sold it to one of her pupils, and now the kids of her pupils are the students. When we went to her, the kids in the class hadn't seen any dancing except in the movies, and the closest places for musicals were Evansville and St. Louis. It was just something to do."

For most kids dancing is only that, just something to do. It's a way to let off steam or run around in your own imagination. It's dressing up to music. As a child, Mark Morris used to wedge his feet into a couple of plastic cups and pretend they were pointe shoes, so he could imitate his sister when she was practicing at home. Classes came later, after he saw José Greco's company when he was eight and decided that he could have even more fun dancing that way. Year after year children just like him wander into dance accidentally or for some short-term, sensible reason that has nothing to do with a future career. Margot Fonteyn was enrolled in a local dancing school because her father mentioned casually that she might need deportment lessons. Suzanne Farrell climbed into the car and went along for the ride every time her big sister went to class—the Cincinnati conservatory was 45 minutes from home and the family budget wouldn't stretch to include a baby-sitter— and eventually it made sense for her to try dancing too. Natalia Makarova signed up at 12 for an amateur ballet group that met three times a week at the Palace of Pioneers in Leningrad. At the time, all young children had to join the Pioneers, the youth organization of the Communist Party, but she could easily have opted for literature or painting classes instead. She picked dancing only so she could spend the time with her friends.

Theatrical families sometimes toss their children toward the stage almost automatically, not because the kids are talented or even interested but because it's convenient. Donald O'Connor joined his parents' vaudeville act when he was three days old and danced for the first time at thirteen months. "I was paid $25 a week to dance to the Black Bottom," he reported years later. "I couldn't actually dance, but they held me up by the back of my skirt, and I moved my feet like crazy!" Galina Ulanova followed her parents into the Maryinsky Theatre, where they were both employed as dancers, because they couldn't leave her home alone when they went to work. Despite protesting furiously, "I don't want to!" she became a boarder and a ballet student, and took her first classes from her mother.

Anything can happen. What would you do if a child acquired a broken nose during your son's first judo lesson? Angel Corella's mother grabbed her seven-year-old and sent him to watch his sister's ballet class instead, never dreaming that planting him outside the studio would root him in dance for good. Another mother, Mrs. Frederick Austerlitz, left Omaha, Nebraska, in 1904 and headed for New York, grimly determined to install her two children in a serious dancing school and launch their stage careers. Then only four, her little boy made his professional debut a year later, by which time she had changed his name to Fred Astaire.

Psychologists now condemn the practice of uprooting children from the stable, familiar environment of their home and overloading them with unrealistic expectations, and you don't often hear of parents schlepping their youngsters halfway across the country in pursuit of dance lessons, at least not before they can stand up. In the sporting world, on the other hand, ambition smothers common sense with frightening regularity, and the sports pages drip with juicy stories of parental obsession masquerading as cheerful confidence and hope. Look at women's tennis: Jennifer Capriati was taught to do sit-ups in her crib. Venus and Serena Williams' father describes himself as "a master planner—no one is going to outplan me . . . There was a plan in effect two years before Venus actually was born."

Or look at gymnastics or figure skating, both of which can transform a responsible parent into a monster far faster than they can change a prepubescent girl into an international star. "There's a rush that comes when you have a competitive skater go into a rink . . . ," conceded the mother of two such girls. "That's your prized possession. That's your showpiece. And when they do well, it's easy for a parent's need for recognition, for filling unfulfilled dreams, to surface . . . We all became junkies for our kids' success . . . You want more and more, and you push your kids, and you push yourself. And you spend money you don't have." When her daughters were competing, during the late '70s, about $20,000 a year covered their combined expenses. Nearly twenty years later, coaching, travel and equipment cost each competitor around $30,000 annually, but the game was well worth the candle.

In the 2001–02 season, each winner, male and female, of the World Figure Skating Championship pocketed $55,000 in prize money before they even started adding up their sponsorship fees. The same season, Reebok handed Venus Williams a five-year promotional contract attached to $40 million, which is chicken feed compared to the salaries that dominate major league baseball: the New York Yankees' payroll that season came to $109,791,893. But even a measly five-figure sum can soothe the sting of parental sacrifice, and of course all these earnings leave dancers' wages in the dust. After 10 to 15 years of training, in 2000 corps de ballet dancers at New York City Ballet pulled down $842 in base pay for each week of performance or rehearsal, and first- and second-year corps dancers at the Royal Ballet in London earned about £373 ($530) weekly. Although the English dancers were paid every week of the year, salaries like these might crudely be classified as chump change in the wider world of earning a living with your body.

The children who pack the high-school stage for the spring dance recital and the children who glide daintily across the ice or somersault from the parallel bars in international competitions wear the same wide smiles and grown-up makeup, no matter where they stand along the continuum of disciplined effort that begins at fun and passes through profit. At the far end of that line, beyond ruffled tulle and television cameras, desperate children take to formal training with greater resolve. Where everyday life is too harsh for them to indulge in aimless pastimes, they exercise to survive, and their parents and teachers present discipline to them as the tightrope they can walk to a safer future.

Nepalese parents sell their daughters to Indian circuses for about 5,000 rupees ($107), because in Nepal investing in a girl is considered a complete waste of time and money; an old adage compares it to "watering a neighbor's field." Trained as acrobats and contortionists but paid little or nothing for three shows daily, the girls are rewarded instead with security, a skill and friends of their own age. The life that enslaves them also protects them from a grimmer sentence in prostitution or in Kathmandu's carpet factories, where they would earn less than $10 a month.

In Mongolia parents push their sons into wrestling because wrestlers are as highly respected as doctors and lawyers, and in Ethiopia, children run from the pervasive poverty by running. The illustrious names of Olympic medalists draw them on, and the full weight of deprivation pushes them from behind. A world champion many times over, Haile Gebreselassie trained for years by running barefoot to and from school every day, a round trip of more than 12 miles. In 1998, he established the Global Adidas running team in the hills outside Addis Ababa, where he now coordinates the training of dozens of young athletes. One 18-year-old hopeful explained his dedication by declaring flatly, "In Ethiopia there is a money problem. When you have money, you get food and a true life . . . Haile is a hero: he comes and advises us on what we are doing, he gives us his experience."

Occasionally, young people turn their own experience to advantage, even without such an inspired guide. Early in the 1990s, to kill time that dragged like dead weight, a gang of defiant youths in their twenties began climbing the monolithic apartment towers in Evry, 25 miles south of Paris. They carefully confined their dangerous antics to the early morning, when the fewest people were on the street, to avoid tempting less responsible athletes into taking the same risks. After years of increasingly daring games, hand-standing on ledges and jumping the chasms between the concrete slabs, in 1996 the men decided to play for more precious stakes than excitement. They named themselves the Yamakasis, choosing a Zairean term that means "strong spirit," and began a disciplined regime of training that involved eight hours of intricate maneuvers and meditation every day. "The art of locomotion is not a circus; it's a philosophy," one of them commented. Without abandoning their aggressive motto, "Eat the concrete before it eats you," the self-taught acrobats have transferred their talents onto the movie screen and the world's stages, climbing hand over hand out of a life without prospects.

Rudolf Nureyev used to say he made his own luck, a sentiment the Yamakasis could honestly echo, but youngsters cannot always motivate themselves as those daredevils did or find a hero like Gebreselassie to guide them or pay the one they can find. Fortunately, many who tumble into dance do so purely for recreation, but even for them training is a bit like murder—anyone who takes a stab at it needs some combination of means, motive and opportunity. For years, only middle-class and more affluent parents sent their children to dancing school, because they alone could spare a few dollars every week for the lessons, and some of those who could afford to pay shoved their cash to the bottom of their pockets rather than support an activity of such dubious moral value. Fifty years ago some parents still believed the stage was only one step up from the gutter—an antiquated attitude even then—yet for most little girls in Cleveland and Greenwood and Carmi dancing was considered harmless entertainment, as long as nobody was making any serious plans or harboring any great expectations. Better than harmless, it might even do a child some good. A Turkish friend remembers that "in 1966 or '67, when I was about 13 years old, a private dance school called the Red Shoes Ballet School opened in Ankara, and I was immediately put in the school because my mother was terribly concerned of the way I was carrying my body. She used to say, 'You aren't very feminine anyway, and as you walk and stand in that horrible way you make things much worse.' I frequented that school for about six years, witnessing its growth every year. I was quite bad, as my legs never got apart in a satisfactory manner nor could I enjoy a proper equilibrium, but all the same I loved it. When I left it there were other schools of the same sort in Ankara, and almost all young bourgeois girls were attending some dance courses."

It's not so easy for little boys, who stand a good chance of signing up for lessons only in countries like Russia and Denmark, where dancing is a respectable occupation. When I was a child I didn't know a single boy who took class—even today I only know one— and Christopher Gable never forgot the fierce opposition he faced in 1951 when, at the age of 11, he wanted to try out for the Royal Ballet School. "My parents, like most people then, associated the ballet with effeminacy. In fact, when we went for my audition, my mother practically fainted with horror. You know the headbands that Bjorn Borg wears for tennis? Well, in those days fellows just didn't put bands around their hair, and I remember her saying to my dad, 'The boys all had ribbons on!'"

I'm talking about theatrical dancing, of course, what my grandmother used to call "fancy dancing." In the long-gone days when children were taught ballroom dancing, it served a strictly social purpose and bore roughly the same relation to stage dancing that thank-you letters do to sonnets. The adolescent girls in the suburban classes I attended during the '50s wore white gloves and horsehair petticoats, and learned not only to rumba and foxtrot but also to keep smiling when no partner crossed the floor to claim them. "I am an advocate for dancing," wrote a proper Bostonian in his 1802 dance manual, "because it has a tendency to refine the manners and behaviour of young people, and I am persuaded that if the art is kept under proper regulations, it would be a mechanic way of implanting insensibly into minds, not capable of receiving it so well by any other rules, a sense of good breeding and virtue."

Today, Finnish children can learn tango at school right along with geography, and folk dance flourishes within the Chinese education system during normal school hours. Almost everywhere else, folk dancing, square dancing and all sorts of ballroom dancing belong almost exclusively to adults, who dip into them for fun in the same way they encourage their children to try swimming or photography for fun. Despite his conviction that dancers are aristocrats whose nobility springs from their art, George Balanchine knew perfectly well that the social graces of an aristocratic upbringing had disappeared with engraved calling cards and ivory fans. Rather than leaving any effect to chance, when he choreographed *Vienna*

Waltzes for New York City Ballet he made a point of waltzing with every member of the cast to demonstrate the fluid, gliding quality he wanted. "The man doesn't turn around the girl, the girl turns around the man," he explained patiently. "The problem is using two legs in three-quarter time. It would be easier if we had three legs." For most of the cast three-quarter time automatically meant either a balancé or a mazurka, steps from the discipline's academic lexicon which, as it happened, the eight principals who created *Vienna Waltzes* had acquired independently in America, France, Denmark, Iceland and Germany.

Not that it mattered to Balanchine where his dancers came from. By then, as professionals, they all spoke the same physical language fluently, albeit with different accents, and experience had prepared them to adopt any dialect their work demanded. As beginners, scattered around the globe, they'd started out the same too, because of the one boon that fledgling dancers everywhere enjoy: the only tool they need to bring to class is their body. In that respect if no other, dancing is easy to learn, certainly easier than building a tree house or knitting a sweater. Back in 1874, when the Japanese Imperial Household began training pianists, nearly every student had to practice on a paper keyboard because there were only 12 pianos in the entire country. Luckily, dancers come equipped with portable instruments that allow them to study and practice wherever they can stretch their limbs, so kids can give dancing a whirl almost anywhere, just as kids can whip up a soccer game anywhere as long as they've got a ball. Beginners can dance to CDs or tapes or a resounding drumbeat, so classes can meet in sports centers and garden sheds, grange halls and church basements, and some housewife or volleyball coach can always be roped in to choose the music and concoct a few exercises. In a pinch, even another student will do—the local recreation department hired me to teach ten-year-olds when I was 16.

The opportunity exists, that's the point, and the basic steps and rudimentary concepts that beginners tackle are always the same, whether five or five thousand children are trying to master them. Consequently, life outside the studio has no direct bearing on what happens inside it. Waltz time is never march time and it never was, neither yesterday nor in the court of Louis XIV, and a knee is either straight or it's bent. Tap dancers have to learn to make specific noises with specific parts of their feet. Ballet dancers have to learn to put their feet down silently. It could be raining or Halloween, you could have a new haircut or a loose tooth, but the rules would not change and you couldn't avoid them.

Outside the classroom, the world never stops changing. I don't know how many neighborhood studios have opened since World War II or whether any of them still teach baton twirling and military toe tap. However, in 1961 *Dance Magazine* published a directory of colleges and universities offering dance—as a major, a minor or in a special program—that ran to 68 listings, and 30 years later a similar list included 261 academic institutions. So unless some cartel of big-city schools had cornered the market with a powerhouse schedule of classes, little towns like Delhi must have been quietly churning out dance students all the time. The supply of degree programs wouldn't have increased unless the demand for them had grown, and it's unlikely that teenagers would be trying to continue their training if they hadn't already dabbled in dance long enough to know they wanted more of it.

But the size and geographic distribution of their schools seem incidental to me beside the fact that every year a fresh batch of children begin to study dance, not always enthusiastically, and no one can predict anything about them. Inevitably, some will get bored and some will get fat. Some will shoot up like bamboo, which will nudge the boys toward the basketball court and scare off most of the ballet girls, who know they will one day stand six inches taller in pointe shoes and need a still taller partner. As the beginners stumble into adolescence, some will dump the sameness of the weekly class for more sociable forms of fun or to take a part-time job, and many will quit as their schoolwork eats into their free time or when they go to college. Those who have stuck doggedly to dance until then will probably keep an eye on it all their lives, even if they never set foot inside a studio again, and the public, unlike the stage, will always be ready to absorb them. If their original enthusiasm turns to appreciation as they grow older, it will transform them into the receptive viewers that professionals crave, and with luck they will pass a little of their interest to their kids and encourage *them* to take class too. The adults who love dance the most may even attempt a few classes themselves, as Lincoln Kirstein did after he graduated from Harvard. "I was too rich and too tall to become a dancer," he admitted years later. "I just wanted to have the experience."

Picking their experiences more haphazardly, children who

loathe dancing from day one quit on day two, and those who prefer it to sitting down might play around with it until something else comes along. The beginners who find dancing more engrossing the longer they study immerse themselves in it zealously, cramming in as many classes as their academic timetables and their parents will allow and then, more often than not, they quit too. Most dance students, even those who reach a relatively advanced level, disappear without a trace. Don't forget, it's murder out there without means, motive and opportunity. The only consolation is that as idle recreation loses its casual air and acquires a purposeful edge, those distinctions start to fade and all three become curiously interchangeable. For a dedicated pupil, means can refer to money or a car pool or physical coordination or a steady flow of encouragement, and motive can mean doubt, injury or a dare as well as tantalizing fantasies of stardom. Any of these can push a student toward greater effort and deeper concentration, but so can a parent or a teacher, who might also provide the opportunity. A Bulgarian immigrant in Paris with a dance-mad eleven-year-old, Sonia Arova's father sold his stamp collection to pay for his daughter's classes, and Pauline Koner's father supplied Michel Fokine with free legal advice in exchange for her lessons. When John Cage wanted to study music with Arnold Schoenberg, the older man inquired whether he could afford the usual fee. Cage responded "that there wasn't any question of affording it, because I couldn't pay him anything at all. He then asked me whether I was willing to devote my life to music, and I said I was. 'In that case,' he said, 'I will teach you free of charge.'" Were they discussing means, motive or opportunity? What were the means? Whose motive created which opportunity? How can you tell them apart?

If it's murder to satisfy those fundamental demands, imagine how tough it is to acknowledge that all dancers are not created equal. Students with plenty of money for classes, dozens of schools to choose from and determination to spare can still end up pushing exercises around with their muscles if they haven't got some kind of natural aptitude for dancing. Steps are merely the lowest common denominator of the art, the simplest way to distinguish one level of proficiency from another. But aptitude—call it innate opportunity— emerges as mental alacrity, physical agility, musical sensitivity or rhythmic security. Aptitude can't guarantee a student's future but it won't hurt his chances either, and it's a clearer hint of things to come than naked hope or consuming passion. The pianist Vladimir Horowitz once said he was playing the window at the age of three, long before he sat down at a keyboard, and Stanley Kubrick, who began snapping photographs when he was a boy, was selling them to *Look* magazine before he graduated from high school. The American artist Reginald Marsh used to take a sketchpad to burlesque shows and fill it with perfect anatomical figures while he admired the girls, without ever taking it out of his pocket.

Were it only a question of practice, you and I could eventually learn to do that too. But aptitude can't be learned at any age, and the skills young dancers can learn are only the start of what they will someday need to show the public. "You can teach somebody steps," Tanaquil Le Clercq insisted, "you can teach them how to hold their head, but what you cannot teach is whatever it is that makes a person step onstage and look interesting." Fanatical effort cannot produce fluidity or quick responses, and a beautifully proportioned body may hang from a pair of tin ears. At one reputable school that combined professional dance training with a high-school education, the audition panel would quickly and crudely grade the applicants' musical sense with the labels "Ahead," "Behind," or "Can't count."

With nothing at stake but their own amusement, small children skip blithely past such criteria, which don't really bother earnest beginners either. But by high school, dancers are nearly formed, and if they're serious about their training they've learned by then that every day of their dancing lives someone will be judging them, maybe against each other, maybe against some real or theoretical standard. Florenz Ziegfeld looked for soulful eyes, a straight nose, teeth like pearls, small feet and "a buoyant walk" in his showgirls. "On days of inspection, the girls pass through my office in long lines. As they pass I say 'Yes' or 'No.' That is all." He had it easy. Since he was convinced that only 5 percent of American women were truly beautiful and he wasn't remotely interested in hiring the other 95 percent, his decisions practically made themselves. The basic requirements for the dancers at today's Moulin Rouge are even simpler: they must be beautiful, at least five feet eight inches tall, and capable of smiling convincingly for 90 minutes.

Pinpointing the dance students who may one day meet more elusive artistic criteria is not so straightforward, because potential has surprisingly little to do with weight, height, shape or anatomy, the very factors that seem initially to provide all the resources any youngster needs. The elements that endow a dancer with promise are not only incalculable but also largely indefinable, and talent, which is only promise with enough experience to act grown-up, has a stubborn habit of emerging from an artist in its own good time. The examiners who auditioned Olga Preobrajenska for the Maryinsky Ballet school rejected her repeatedly, seeing only a short, thin child with a slightly curved spine and one hyperextended knee. Nikolai Legat called her "lopsided," and when her dedication and hard work brought her finally to Christian Johansson's advanced class, he described her as "a hunchbacked devil." Nevertheless, she entered the Maryinsky Theatre in 1889 and remained there for 25 years, rising to the rank of prima ballerina and mastering an astounding repertory of 35 leading roles, and her artistry inspired critics to praise her as a "poetess of dance."

If there were a sure-fire way of spotting talent, don't you think someone would be peddling it by now? Bookies would have shut up shop forever if every winner could be predicted, and your money would be as safe in a Broadway show as in the bank. Forget it—a sure bet is as hard to find as a free lunch. The wise and wary gamblers who do their homework to protect their investments also cross their fingers, hoping to minimize their risk with luck as well as preparation, and they readily concede that they could play the odds for years without beating them. The stud fee for a horse named Storm Cat soared to $300,000 in 2000—at one auction, someone paid $430,000 for his services—because his progeny had gone out on the racetrack the year before and earned more than $12 million, nearly one-third more than the offspring of any other stud. But it just doesn't work that way for artists. You can't breed talent in them, so bloodlines don't count for much—how many performing dynasties can you name?—and their enduring success can't be calculated in prize money or trophies. The dancers who eventually command the highest fees aren't always the best dancers on the stage, no matter how extravagantly they can maneuver their bodies, and even the wisest judges can't tell you what "best" means anyway.

They also can't explain where talent comes from or exactly what it is. Maybe it's charm—I mean, a quality that charms or enchants the viewer—plus skill plus refinement. Maybe, in dance, it's some aspect of a performance that everyone can see but no one can photograph. It's got to be more than a matter of subjective opinion, because gifted artists can grab and hold any audience that turns up, regardless of how much it knows about their art, but that ability doesn't nail it either. In fact, no one knows the first thing about talent except that it can bloom anywhere. Students long for it as if it were true love, the magical solution to every problem they cannot solve alone, and parents squint at their children's familiar bodies and try to discern even a hint of something special, maybe lurking just out of sight, that would finally justify all the work and expense of discovering it. Hanging around until the lesson ends, they drink their coffee and wait and watch, only skimming their newspapers in case they miss a glimpse of that mysterious quality and wondering what will happen to their kids if it never appears.

When the ballerina Alexandra Danilova toured America with the Ballet Russe de Monte Carlo during the 1940s, most of the reporters assigned to the local arts pages were flying blind. Since the work she did and the world she inhabited made no more sense to them than Chinese opera, they pestered her in town after town with one of the few names they knew. "Tell us about Anna Pavlova," they begged. "Did you ever see Pavlova dance?" Personally insulted and professionally mortified at being overshadowed by another star, and a dead one at that, one day Danilova retorted tartly, "Who is this Anna Pavlova, whom everybody talks of but no one has ever seen?"

Talent is like Anna Pavlova: everybody talks about it but only rarely will they get a chance to see it plain. And when they do, they may not recognize it. Which is why the most determined students leave home, even if they're not sure how far their skill or will or talent will carry them. What's the point of being the best dancer in Delhi if no one's ever going to see you? You might as well be an angel dancing on the head of a pin. So as they struggle through their early training, polishing every step to ready it for use at any time, they make up their own path to the future as they go along, and gradually two ideas take shape in their minds without any conscious effort on their part. Distinct as neon signs beside a dark road, their thoughts point them away from anonymity, away from the classroom they've always known and the teacher whose corrections they've learned by heart, and toward the rest of the world. Their thoughts say something like this: Find a place where dancing matters. Find the people who understand what they see.

The first idea will coax them into summer schools or university programs, opening their eyes to more styles and disciplines than they have ever encountered, and ultimately to cities, where trade and learning and money and leisure and aspiration and disappointment rub against each other like a bundle of twigs, and creativity flares up among them from the friction. Art burns brightest where there's room for the unexpected to draw breath and expand, and where people can make the time, if they're curious or interested, to examine it. So cities sparkle with theatres and their potential public, and consequently with stages on which dancers might one day dance.

The second idea may pack a heavier punch, because dedicated students who remain meekly at home often face worse threats than invisibility. Recalling her childhood in England during the Second World War, Valda Setterfield told me, "There was an amazing woman who taught tap dancing who used to put her knee in the small of our back and yank our shoulders back and say, 'Stand up straight!' . . . When I was about 14 I began to study . . . with [another] teacher . . . . And I think she was not scrupulous—maybe she didn't know any better—about bodies. It was all about height and turnout and pirouettes, and toe shoes immediately regardless of . . . whether you were strong or placed. I didn't have very much to go on, but I thought it was wrong because I couldn't move from any of those positions."

If staying put means subjecting the only instrument they've got to unnecessary danger, common sense alone can propel students out of town. If this situation is not right, somewhere there must be another situation that is safer and more productive, where someone can train and strengthen them without damaging them at the same time. Find the people who understand what they see also means, Go where experience gathers. I don't think I did those trusting ten-year-olds any harm with the simple exercises I made up for them over the course of eight weeks, but the serious students would eventually have needed better instruction than I could give them and then better training than my teacher over the barbershop could give them too, and the chance of their finding it in a converted garage or a suburban basement is so small you could put it in your eye and it wouldn't hurt you.

Everyone who wants to learn does the same thing. Tadao Ando walked away from a professional boxing career and taught himself about buildings by wandering all over Europe and America to look at them before opening his own architectural practice at home in Japan. John Cranko left Johannesburg for Cape Town and Cape

Town for London in pursuit of better teaching and bigger opportunities, and Kenneth MacMillan got out of Great Yarmouth, on the coast of the North Sea, by writing to the Royal Ballet School to request an audition and signing his father's name to the letter.

Nobody asks young artists to leave home and nobody is waiting for them to show up, yet they are expected just the same, because the teachers they discover will have made the same journey themselves, from a small town to a larger one and from the only available lesson to the finest instruction they could find and afford. Ignoring the odds and the risks to their body and peace of mind, eager students turn their back on Greenwood and Carmi and pour into cities like fish swimming to their destiny. Intent on conquering the current, they offer themselves innocently to the great, established dance schools, the name brands with the longest histories, most of which operate only a short step from the company they were founded to serve, and if the students are lucky or gifted those schools will reel them in. When shad travel like this, pausing only to muster the strength to continue traveling, the waters they pass through mark them so clearly that knowledgeable fishermen can trace their desperate progress by examining their scales. The students who reach the company schools will be indelibly marked too, and their training will stamp their minds as well as their bones forever.

Perhaps they don't think about forever while tomorrow is still uncertain. The long-term results of their choices are still a long way away, and the short-term effect may be harder to swallow than the hook that grabbed them in the first place. What the hopeful youngsters learn immediately is that coming this far to stand right before the acclaimed face of experience represents a minuscule triumph in a battle that stretches endlessly ahead. The giant step of leaving home has brought them only an inch closer to their goal, and once that brutal truth snaps into focus, the significance of their decision, which in Delhi seemed so logical, so desirable, may suddenly hit them with the sickening thud of a door slamming on their fingers. No longer the star of their local recital or the teacher's favorite, they look around the new studio, at the unknown faces of their new classmates, and realize they are again anonymous and probably no more promising than anyone else. Having come to the same place for the same reason, all they share with those strangers is the knowledge that the window of opportunity through which everyone hopes to pass is the size of a keyhole and will only admit a select few. Naturally the new students start to make friends—with the only people, in fact, who will ever completely understand the excitement and drudgery of their effort—but the longer they remain at the school, the more urgently they need to distinguish themselves from the pack, so they invariably end up competing even with their friends for the only prize that matters.

The most painful surprise is yet to come. Despite all the newcomers' romantic plans and sober sacrifices, the nature of a professional school guarantees that as they start to become more proficient they will also start to fail, many of them for the first time. Talk about irony! Natural selection will continually narrow the field, eliminating the indifferent or mediocre pupil and the scatterbrain who doesn't concentrate and the lazy one who can't distinguish between working hard and working hard enough. Puberty will condemn some of them to a body they never anticipated, and others will amaze themselves by discovering that chemistry or Greek fascinates them even more than dancing.

At the turn of the last century, the Imperial school in Moscow occupied a new building in which opaque glass fogged every exterior window. To catch a glimpse of the dashing officers in the street below, the girls would deliberately break the windows and then insist that their clumsiness was accidental. Since the administrators knew all their relatives personally and permitted no one else to visit, the girls' young suitors would disguise themselves as chimney sweeps to sneak into the hallowed cloisters of learning. If that sounds archaic, listen to this. When the students at the Imperial school in St. Petersburg left their dormitories to perform at the Maryinsky Theatre, they traveled in carriages supplied by the tsar, with a pair of liveried coachmen in attendance. Inside that school, according to Tamara Karsavina, "The windows of the studio were too high to see the outside world, so there was nothing else to do but practise our ballet, and this we grew to love."

One hundred years later, serious students no longer have to shut themselves away in honorable seclusion to learn to dance. Even those who consider themselves the most privileged students on earth live ordinary lives in everyday society. They travel by public transportation and flirt on their cellphones. They eat at McDonald's and smoke and drink beer just like every other modern child of their age. But at the same time they are not at all like other children, because their principal indulgence is restraint. As soon as they're free to make their own choices they throw away their new independence with both hands and lock themselves into a discipline that offers them physical dexterity with limitless interpretive applications while demanding their obedience, dedication and courage in return.

The students at professional schools who grow to love their practicing enter voluntarily into a pact with their teachers that is far older than computer technology and imperial largesse. Quite unconsciously, they mimic the roaming tribes of the Sahara and the settled tribes of the expansive savanna that borders it, who regularly enact a stately ritual of silent trading, exchanging measures of salt for measures of gold without a word of negotiation. When students and teachers face each other in bright, featureless rooms, they do exactly the same thing. One brings sweat to the studio, the other brings experience, salt and gold, and every day they begin again the patient, unending barter that defines their only purpose in meeting.

Suki Schorer

School of American Ballet

THE SCHOOL OF AMERICAN BALLET (SAB) was established in New York in 1934 by George Balanchine and Lincoln Kirstein, because they both wanted to build a ballet company. Unemployed at the age of 25 when Serge Diaghilev died and the Ballets Russes collapsed, Balanchine had been living hand to mouth in England, France, Denmark and Germany, accepting any work that came his way. So Kirstein had little trouble persuading him to abandon Europe and seek his fortune in America, particularly since the young choreographer was eager to find or develop dancers for the ballets he hoped to create. A restless idealist with towering, inchoate plans for America's artistic future, Kirstein intended to nurture the classical tradition in the new world, and on a hunch and the slightest acquaintance he invited Balanchine to help him do it.

They modeled their school on the professional academy attached to the Maryinsky Theatre, the Imperial St. Petersburg Theatrical School to honor it with its full name, where Balanchine had trained as a dancer. For their teaching staff, they engaged Russian artists, raised in the same stylistic tradition as Balanchine, and enthusiastic young Americans from Philadelphia and Chicago. The curriculum focused intensively and exclusively on ballet in technique, adagio, character and variation classes; it followed the pedagogic guidelines of the Imperial school but constantly adapted them to Balanchine's requirements. As the two men had intended, the school slowly and surely produced the basis and backbone of a new company, which since 1948 has been called New York City Ballet.

Founded to create dancers uniquely suited to the ballets Balanchine imagined, SAB fulfills exactly the same purpose today, but its curriculum has expanded to include pointework, music, social dancing, mime, contemporary partnering techniques and, for the men, weight training and gymnastics. Because SAB requires its students to pursue a high-school degree but takes no responsibility for their academic education, the ballet school must plan its class schedules around ordinary school hours until the students are old enough to attend the few high schools that tailor their academic schedules to accommodate professional training. SAB's interest in artistic education, however, has developed into an intensive program of auditions: these are held every fall and spring; weekly during the school year because, depending on the class size, a child can be admitted at any time; and in 22 cities across the country in January and February. A process of constant assessment and evaluation winnows students out at the end of each year, and, after consultation with the parents, the school can dismiss a pupil at any time who cannot meet its standards.

It can also demand increased attendance as the students progress through increasingly difficult classes. After the beginners class, boys and girls are taught separately, except for adagio class and ballroom dancing. The youngest students, age 8 or 9, must take two classes weekly during the nine-month winter course, for which, in 2000–01, they paid $1,120 annually. Advanced students, age roughly 15 to 19, must attend an average of ten classes weekly, which in the same year cost $3,462. Younger pupils can apply for financial assistance and more advanced ones for scholarships; however, boys pay nothing at all until they reach the intermediate class when they are roughly 13 years old.

Supported by its own board and its own budget, SAB is entirely independent of the company it serves, but the two operate in tandem, complementing each other like carefully matched partners. They occupy different floors of the same building, only a block away from the company's performing home, the New York State Theater, and each feeds personnel to the other in a steady stream. The students perform in the company's productions and lecture-demonstrations as required and enjoy free access to performances whenever tickets remain unsold. The company's dancers, both active and retired, teach at the school, and every spring the students exhibit their talent and training in ballets that are often drawn from the New York City Ballet repertory; launched in 1965 these annual Workshop performances have become an important public showcase for potential employers.

Except for those living in the 64-bed dormitory that opened in 1991, the students must find their own local accommodation, but developing that self-reliance forms part of their professional training. Warned that she might not qualify for promotion unless she strengthened her feet, one determined SAB student I knew spent a year picking up pencils with her toes. Perhaps unconsciously, she had absorbed Kirstein's deepest conviction, that the ideal training for classical dancers should fuse spiritual dedication and rigorous discipline. In 1982, nearly 50 years after conjuring SAB out of his own dreams and Balanchine's needs, he commented, "We always wanted to call this the West Point of dance. I visited West Point during my army years; I was amazed at the thoroughness with which they pursued a single goal. Dance is like that . . . Rule one here is 'There's No Justice.' Rule two is 'No Complaints.' Rule three is 'Shut Up.'"

❧

Suki Schorer. b. Boston, 1939. Trained San Francisco Ballet School and School of American Ballet. Joined New York City Ballet 1959, promoted to principal in 1968. Retired from dancing 1972 and immediately joined faculty of SAB, where she remains. International guest teacher and author of *Suki Schorer on Balanchine Technique*.

I THINK I LOVED THE PHYSICALITY OF DANCING. My mother started me in it when I was five. I didn't choose it, and at one point I wanted to stop, I think because I couldn't hang out in the drugstore after school because I had to go to my ballet lesson. And then we kept moving cities—we were in Berkeley, then my father taught at Harvard so we went to Cambridge, but I had ballet, ballet was constant. Then we moved to Italy and I was in another new school, in Florence, with nobody my age, and I went to a ballet teacher there and they said I was very talented. At one point my parents took me to Sadler's Wells and I auditioned and they took me into the school, saying I could probably never dance in the company there because I was American but I had all the makings for a dancer. I was 12 or 13. I had good proportions, nice feet, everything . . . I could make it.

When we came back from Europe I went back to Berkeley, and instead of going to Berkeley High my parents sent me to a private girls school, so again it was all new people. I think it was then that I said I didn't want to go back to ballet, because I thought all the ballet students I had been with would be more advanced—I had been taking ballet on and off, and they'd been more consistent. But I don't know, something just happened, and I thought, 'I'm going to work hard,' . . . something to do with the competitiveness and the physicality of it. I said, "I'm going to be a dancer. I want to be better than all these other people that got better than me. I want to be the best I can."

The first teacher that made an impression was Harold Christensen. He was sort of Cecchetti-trained, with a little bit of Bournonville thrown in, and he was very involved in exact placement, very correct positions, not rolling in. He used to say, "Don't move, little lady. Don't travel. Keep your hips down." So I learned how to straighten my back, how to turn out from my hips, to be very proper and correct and small. I mean, my développé à la seconde was about calf-high. Then there was Lew Christensen. Those were my early teachers.

I was trying to go to college at the same time, I did half a year at the University of California, but then I had to drop out of college because San Francisco Ballet went on a tour. I think if I had stayed in San Francisco I might have tried to continue with college and dancing, because there wasn't that much dancing, it wasn't that demanding. As long as I got across the bridge and to the city by 1:00 in the afternoon I would make company class, and I had rehearsal and I was in the new ballets. But the classes were not that inspirational, I didn't feel as if I were changing day by day, and it was very hard to move up the ranks. Lew Christensen was trying to build a company and he was worried that if he gave roles to younger dancers the older ones would leave and go somewhere else, and that was already happening.

So when I came to New York . . . I auditioned here thinking that I would go back and say to Lew that if he didn't give me roles, Balanchine liked me and I was going to leave. I was going to use that, but I never did, because Balanchine said my contract was upstairs and to go sign it. And then . . . the classes here . . . I wasn't sure I was going to like it, but I loved it. The dancing on the stage was so beautiful and so big and lush and interesting. The dancers were interesting to look at, the Melissa Haydens and the Allegra Kents, Jacques d'Amboise and Eddie Villella. And *Agon* and Diana [Adams], Arthur Mitchell . . . it was so alive and electric. And I couldn't believe how the women could all do entrechat six at the end of *Stars and Stripes*, and the men were all doing double tours. I mean, I couldn't believe that many men and all those women could do such high kicks and développés. I remember looking at Melissa, who made a high arabesque with her hip up, and thinking, 'My God!' because Harold had said to me, "Don't move your little leg. Don't budge your hip." I could dance a little—it was just that I couldn't lift my leg very high and I couldn't jump very high. But now that I was there I wasn't about to stop. I had a very very strong work ethic, no matter what I would do, it didn't have to be dancing, it was just the way I was brought up.

When I first got into the company Balanchine was not teaching a lot, so I took classes at the school. Very soon Balanchine started teaching classes, so from then on he was really my teacher. It was totally different, because, number one, he was very active in class mentally. I mean, we were always working for a goal, there was always something to work for, we knew what we were trying to do. He wouldn't just give a class. Sometimes my teacher, Lew, was kind of depressed. I mean, he'd give the combination and look at the floor—it was not very inspiring. We didn't know what he wanted or why he was feeling like that, and we all took it personally. I guess he was just having a hard time with his life. But Balanchine was very involved with us, and not only was he involved but he would ask us for things and then say, "No, I don't see it. Do it this way, let's see if you can get the result this way." Some people didn't come to Mr. B's class. A lot didn't come—it was hard. If you were older or set in your way, it was hard to come, and if you didn't want to change or if you wanted a predictable barre, it was unpredictable.

I really think that if Balanchine didn't choreograph he would never have taught. He said that if women weren't on pointe, if it wasn't for the pointe shoe, he would have been a musician. He didn't say that to me, but I've read that somewhere. I think it's because he choreographed and wanted his ballets to look a certain way that he got involved in teaching people how to dance, and everything he taught would get onto the stage in some way or other. He might be working on different kinds of turns, off-balance turns, for example, and all of a sudden Suzanne Farrell would have it in *Don Quixote*. Or chassé on pointe, and all of a sudden he did the birds, Alouettes [in *Harlequinade*], and all the girls chasséd around on pointe.

In all his ballets, he always wanted our legs strictly front, side or back, so in class he worked directly on tenduing front, learning where . . . memorizing where front was. He wanted us to be able to move very quickly, so he taught us always to have our weight over the balls of our feet, and he gave us fast steps in class. He wanted us to

be able to change direction, so we often went one way and then instantly the other, like a zig and zag, so we had to be ready and able
to move. He wanted our pointework to become second nature to us,
so we were on pointe the whole time, we didn't put on our pointe
shoes just to do a pointe step. He wanted us to be able to land slowly
from jumps and be able to land quickly, but always with control. So
we worked on everything that we needed, so that when we came to
dance, we had it. He wanted pirouettes from a beautiful extended line
in his ballets, so we did that in class. I wasn't there when he made
Agon or *Four Temperaments*, but I'm sure that he didn't give a lot of
pelvis stuff in class. But he might have given off-balance work, forward and back, for tombé, to get the hips going.

I also took class a lot with [Felia] Doubrovska. I took a morning
class, every morning, before Balanchine taught on the layoffs, to prepare
for Mr. B's class, because you never knew what you were going to get—
sometimes he gave an extra-short barre or something. And I also needed
to catch up. I felt so far behind, I had to get strong fast. So I took from
all the teachers at the school for that morning class, and then
Doubrovska . . . I think I took mostly with her for two reasons. One, because all my teachers had been men. When I said to Leon Danielian,
who had guest-danced with the San Francisco Ballet, "When I come to
New York, who do you recommend I study with?" he said, "I think you
should study with a woman, because you've only had male teachers."
Now that I'm all grown-up I know what he meant. It's interesting, because, really, Lew and Harold didn't know how to make a woman dance
in a feminine way. The second reason I studied with Doubrovska is that
Balanchine thought . . . I'm not sure if he directly said it, but he implied
that she was worth studying with. Balanchine took the most talented
girls from the top divisions, the most advanced girls, for a class that met
three times a week, and only Doubrovska taught it. I went to it and a
few members of the company went too, Allegra and Jacques. There was
always something to be gained and learned.

Those classes Balanchine taught during the layoffs were special
because they were endless. It wasn't called "the special class"—it was
company class on the layoff, for those that wanted to come and take
class, anybody in the company could come. They could go on for up
to four hours if Balanchine was free and decided to keep on working.
The studio was free from 12:00 to 4:00, so they could go on a long
time, and people left when they had to go. He just covered detail after
detail of every step. Some days it was working on tendus, some days

it was working on plié, some days it was working on extensions, some days it was beats, some days it was épaulement, some days it was hands and arms, some days it was a combination of those things.

The reason that he did this is that . . . After the Ford Foundation grant came through [in 1963], he invited teachers from all over the country to come for a week's seminar to study with him. I think the Ford money helped those teachers with their expenses, but I believe he gave his knowledge and his time to them for free. He wanted to raise the level of ballet training in the United States, and he used some of the company dancers, a few of us—we weren't paid either—to demonstrate and to talk to the teachers about teaching and about why he did certain things and why it looked a certain way. One year, it was just Balanchine, me and the teachers, for a week. Those seminars for the teachers went on for quite a few years.

In the beginning, with the Ford Foundation money, Balanchine took me on the road with him, and we looked for talent to bring to the school for the summer school. I think he saw that I was fascinated by what he had to say and his way of working. I think he thought I had a mind, that I was bright, and fascinated, not just in trying to get another role from him but in the mechanics of the technique and how it worked. And he probably knew really early on that I might like to teach and might be really good at it. So I think that's why he said, "Come." I went with him several times, and he said, "What do you think of this one? Why? This is the one I think is the most talented. This is the one I'd bring. What do you think?" So we would talk a little bit, what he saw, what he didn't see. At that same period, with the Ford money, a school could invite a teacher down to their community, and that person would teach, so I went out and taught in Florida a couple of times. This was in about '64.

Meantime, I was still dancing, and very early on, Balanchine had me teach. I think one of the teachers was sick or went on vacation, so on a company layoff I started teaching some late Cs [advanced evening classes] at the school—the students were roughly 15 to 17 but company members could take this class too if they wanted to. I think he had observed me in his class, where . . . A lot of dancers won't listen to any correction unless the teacher says, "You, Mary, tendu front." But I listened to everybody's corrections—no matter what Mr. B said to anybody, I listened, because I needed to improve rapidly and I wanted to know what he wanted. And then, dancers used to come to me and ask me to help them—"What did Balanchine want?"—because sometimes Balanchine would say, "Well, if you don't know how to do the step, ask Suki or Jacques." So already, he knew I knew. And he could see by my effort that I was trying to get it—even if I couldn't do it, I had the right approach to the steps, because I'd been listening and trying to do what he was saying. So already, before I was actually teaching, I was teaching.

I loved it, I loved it. First of all I had to teach myself, in a way. I had to listen to a lot of corrections and then apply them. I remember looking at other dancers, watching Melissa and Violette [Verdy] as they were doing their warm-up, and then figuring out what they were doing and why they were doing it. Why did they do that step? and What did they get out of it? And then I would try it. Balanchine always said, to anybody who'd listen, "Work a lot by yourself." He said, you know, the teacher was there to suggest, but it was up to the dancer to do. And the best way to do it—there was never time in class—was to go into a studio by yourself and work on whatever it was that you needed. If you could, take one step and work on it at a slower tempo, and next week build that tempo, and do that same step for a month. Then next month you take a different step and you work on that, slowly, 'til you get it, and then increase the speed until you can do it very quickly. Work alone. So I used to work alone. I used to always warm up slowly, an hour and a half before performance . . . I mean, I worked hard. And I love to work, so it was fun, to see my body be able to change and adjust and fit and make it all work out. And it was all so logical, what he said to me, it made such good sense. And it was so beautiful to look at.

I started teaching . . . On one layoff, Balanchine formed a class for talented young men, 15 to 17 years old, who included Paul Mejia, John Sowinski, the Sackett brothers [Francis and Paul], and a couple of others. I also taught a Children's 2 class, little children, they were 9 or 10—he said he knew I would get down on the floor and fix their feet. And it became . . . During the season he started to have morning appointments sometimes, he'd be late for class, and he said, "Suki, if I'm not there or if I'm five minutes late, you start class." Sometimes he wouldn't even show up because the appointment would go so long, and I would teach company class. And sometimes I would just do part of the barre and he would come in and I would say, "We did blah, blah and blah and we're ready for this," and he would take over.

In the late '60s it evolved that I was teaching about four times a week at the school and I had to work that out around my rehearsal and performance schedule. And then, I guess by 1970, Balanchine asked me to teach a newcomers class. In other words, new members of the company would take my class in the morning three times a week in the practice room at the theatre. He said the company was so big, and with only an hour to teach company class before the rehearsals and the performances, he didn't have time to teach the way he had taught before. There was hours and hours of other work to do, and the company had grown. I mean, when I first joined there were 30 dancers, and now there were 80. So he asked me to teach the new members of the company. So I started doing that and I was still performing plus I had about four classes at the school. So I was teaching maybe six, seven classes a week.

Meantime I was dancing a little bit less, because he was not putting me into the new ballets that he was choreographing. I was a principal dancer now, so I was out of all the corps parts and all the demi-solo parts. I only had my old principal roles to dance, so I wasn't dancing as often as I had been at one time. Sometimes I had had three ballets, three principal roles a night; now I was on about three times a week. It just got to the point where I needed to dance more if I was going to dance, because I got too nervous only dancing two or three times a week. Then he asked me if I would reorganize the educational lecture-demonstration program, and there were so many other things that I was needed for. The students needed me because they didn't really have a teacher at the school that knew what Balanchine wanted. They had older Russian teachers, but not the new Balanchine. All the stuff he had taught in the last ten years was not being taught at the school, because he had just developed that even further from where it had been when he had left Diaghilev.

So I decided to leave the company—I stopped dancing in '71 or '72—and I started teaching full-time at that point. I guess the most important thing for me to teach was everything that Balanchine had taught, which was a lot. Balanchine didn't talk much about placement, so it was as if my early training could come into play, because that was really all it was about, how to stand up straight, how to keep your back straight, how to turn out from the hips. Balanchine took us way beyond that, because he said, you know, every body is different and each body has to be worked on individually, and therefore you may have to adjust. But I just think that young children need to know the basics out of which they're going to adjust. The ballet vocabulary is so limited that you must articulate each step, movement, everything, to make it absolutely clear. I don't think you can start teaching to third-year ballet students or second-year ballet students what Balanchine taught his company. You can teach some of the principles he taught us, but not everything.

In the beginning I had a couple of very young children's classes at the school, Division 2 and 3s and Children's 5. Now I'm just teaching intermediate through advanced girls. It's basically the same for different classes, but the corrections are a little bit different. In the intermediate class they still don't know how to stand up straight and turn out from their hips and things like that, which you don't have to deal with in a more advanced level. You can ask them to move faster, and slower, in a more advanced level—I mean, you can make the combinations faster and much slower. And in the intermediate level, you're pushing them at a slower rate. Some of the people in our intermediate class come into that level from . . . not all of them are coming through the school.

But I travel to teach now, so if I'm in California teaching at Christmastime, I may stay an extra week and audition. I'm looking for proportions and a possibility, not so much at what's there right now but if inside that body something can be made. If there's proportion, flexibility, musicality, intelligence . . . Say a student's 16 and not advanced enough for their age but I can see the potential, I will invite them to SAB for our summer course. But if they really don't know anything at 16, it's just awfully late to start the basics. They have to know something at 16. We take them into the summer course as young as 12, and they can know a lot less at 12 if they have a wonderful body and facility to work with.

In the case of Balanchine and in the case of how I teach, I think that the technique is the style. I don't separate the technique from the inner spirit, because it all has to go together from the beginning of class. So even if you're doing a plié or a tendu at the barre there has to be a life in the whole body. Basically what Balanchine taught us and a lot of what I teach is just beautiful dancing. So I think that's how dance should look, and it can look that way whether you're dancing *Sleeping Beauty* or *Napoli*, sure.

The students' bodies are better now than when I started teaching. Better extension, better turnout, better feet—they point, they have a bigger instep maybe. Previously, if Balanchine needed three tall dancers for the company, he just had to take three tall dancers, and if their legs were bowed out a bit or they had gnarled feet or no extension or if they were turned in, they still might get in. Now you can get three tall dancers from the school and they'll have a better physique, they'll be beautiful. The technical level is much higher, and the attitude is very good. Our dancers basically want to dance and they work hard and they listen well. And it's so competitive that if they don't really want to dance and they're not striving, they get out or they're asked to withdraw. For some reason there's maybe less individual personality than before, it's a little blander, more similar, the people and the personalities, the way of moving.

But I guess I want more from the students than I used to—I want a lot. As a teacher I've developed a little bit more sense of musicality and phrasing and timing of the steps, and I might have changed the ways to get to a result. I think I've developed as a teacher over the years, I hope so. I hope I'm not the same as when I started. But I don't think you can teach teaching, because as a teacher you have to be able to look at something and know where you want that step to go and what's wrong with what you see and what you might suggest to get it to happen in a certain way. And then, somehow you have to get the dancer motivated enough to want to change or to go where you want them to go. On the other hand, if you look at a dancer and see something that works and that you like, you have to be able to figure out what they're doing and get that to work for somebody else who doesn't have it. If you read different things that Mr. B said, sometimes it says, "He learned from his dancer." All of a sudden he'd see somebody doing something and it looks beautiful. Then he could use it on them, because they did it naturally, but if he wanted somebody else to do it, he had to figure out what it was that he liked.

Basically, it's harder work teaching away from the school because it's all new to them and they don't have any models to look at, they haven't really seen people move that way or work that way. But my approach to the class is the same because of what I said, that working in this Balanchine way is really just beautiful dancing. So I think everybody should be able to dance that way, and then maybe if they want to do less, not cross their arms so much or not dance with their heels slightly off the floor, that's fine. But at least they should know how to go through their feet. I'm not teaching them *not* to put their heels down or anything like that. I'm teaching them to be in control of the descent, from the air or from pointe, and to place their feet on the floor, to be aware of their feet.

And you can teach them to do more. "I want to see you jump higher, dear, you're not moving. And don't flap your arms around like that, and don't get a fixed grin on your face." You have to say something, you have to bring out whatever's there. "Jump, let's see you jump now. That's a jump. It's not just nothing or a pretty thing with your arms." I thought the best thing in *Western Symphony* last night was Maria [Kowroski] in fourth movement. She was beautiful, elegant, witty. First of all, just standing there before she even moved, she looks good. She had her chest held up, she had a glamour about the way she did that role. When you looked at the first movement, nothing happened. Violette used to do that and the stage felt hot, you could feel sparks flying.

I think partially it's the way Mr. B brought things out of you, and how he cast whom in what, and what he valued. Well, what did he value? He valued dancing in time, he valued looking interesting when you danced in time. He valued making it interesting by the technique he worked on in class and by showing the steps and doing them big or as big as time allows, and then with some sort of a jazzy, beautiful, feminine look, personally. Everything is very level now—I'm thinking about the first movement of *Western* last night. She didn't have the attack or the phrasing. And then, she didn't have enough life in her whole persona. Rehearsing that first movement, Mr. B would probably demonstrate a little bit and show the accents and fall over the log . . . There's one step, you're supposed to be falling over the log and it doesn't look like that now. They're too straight, the emphasis is not where it always was. Yes, things do change and should change but still, basic things aren't there.

At the school now a lot more dancers are teaching that worked very recently with Balanchine. Although Doubrovska worked with Balanchine, she came from a whole different generation. That era of a slower way of dancing, with more time, bringing out more perfume, more soul, that kind of thing is finished. Things happen more quickly now. The tempos are faster, the ballets are faster, a lot of them are more athletic than they used to be. You have to see the current repertoire to see what I'm talking about, but I think that speed and athleticism are very important to some choreographers now, more than they were to Balanchine, who also liked femininity a lot and glamour and chic. That essence of it was nurtured and he was attracted to people who had that innately, people like Tanny [Le Clercq] that had a little wit or something more than just the speed.

Are we ever going to have dancers like we had in the past? They had something else, equally good but different. When Tanny stopped dancing, did we have Tanny back? No, but then there was something else, Suzanne Farrell or whoever. And now that Suzanne Farrell's finished, maybe . . . We'll see. But I think it's the teacher that's going to help bring out the qualities in each person and nurture them, first of all, in the classroom. And some things are unteachable—you can't teach them. You can only try to bring them out, but they have to be in there, inside. You're not going to nurture Suzanne Farrell out of somebody else, and you can't squeeze water from a stone. So you have to know who you're dealing with, and you have to teach very personally, to the person who's in front of you.

It's hard for me to leave the school for two weeks here or there to do staging, and it's not my forte. I don't have a photographic memory as some stagers do, and if I didn't dance the ballet, learning all the steps requires lots of effort. But I understand the essence of the ballets and the impetus of the movements, so I can bring out the qualities that Balanchine wanted, the nuances and dynamics and emotional undertones—that part I'm strong in. I don't have a big repertoire of ballets that I know, and I have to review and sometimes relearn them every time I stage them—I do it mostly for the school [Workshop]. They're not 100 percent with me. When I stage *Serenade*, I know a lot of it, but then I look at the video to see who goes where and on which count. And then I've worked with other principal dancers in the principal roles and I asked them to come to rehearsal to help me when I first staged it. So I know what Conrad [Ludlow] said about dancing the waltz and I know what Nicky [Magallanes] said about the "dark angel" part, so I can go back to that. When I don't have people like that, I mostly teach it off a video, and I always have five or six videos, not of the same people dancing. Because you don't want to teach them the mannerisms or that person's personality. And then you take the video away from them, so they don't all of a sudden look like whoever was on the video. And then I bring somebody in that's danced it and, if possible, worked with Mr. B or learned a lot of ballets when he was alive. Like Karin [von Aroldingen] learned *Liebeslieder* [*Walzer*] when he was still living, all of the roles, so he probably showed her the quality he wanted and they talked about it.

I try to teach them the phrasing and the perfume, the soul, the artistry. The music, obviously, is in the steps, or the steps are in the music. Well, it's one thing in my mind, because the music is obviously the platform for the steps. In class I work on making them do the steps technically correctly and on time—so if it's fast, pointing their feet quickly, all that technique—and looking beautiful and making it exciting. In *Valse Fantaisie* they run fast so it becomes exciting, and when she does the slow part, making it look romantic, beautiful, and making the man be as exciting as he can. At the school we talk about showing, model yourself, offer yourself. When a student is injured they're still required to come to class and sit and watch. As a dancer, whenever I was injured I learned a lot by watching the performances. Balanchine used to say, "Why do you like a certain dancer? Why does your eye go there? Figure it out." So I do the same thing with the students who are watching now. I say to them, "I want you to watch this and say who you like and why. Say it out loud, so everybody hears. Why did you like to watch her? Who looks like they like to dance?" I think they need to be very aware of all that.

And they want to dance, they're hungry, certainly I think they're as hungry as I was when I went to the school. I don't think the kids that I taught in London in '95 worked hard or in the right way. They weren't developing and growing and getting enough results. The younger, intermediate level kids work very hard but they were so contained and ordered, and the classes weren't challenging. They do the same thing daily, 'Monday we do this, Tuesday we do this,' and the same music for each combination, and the same accents for each combination! They have a sort of syllabus that they work on, and it seemed to me it produces boredom and just going through the routine, instead of making each moment count. They're lacking a little bit of life, and the advanced people don't put out much effort. I don't think they understand how much effort needs to be put out. I think they think they're working hard, but it's not in the right way. They might be tense, but they're not attacking the steps with the kind of energy that you need.

When you put that energy into a ballet, it's exciting, and that's what will happen in the Workshop, they'll dance beautifully. You'll see all those daily tendus and those daily pliés coming out, and the dancers look alive, so it's exciting to watch them. Sure, we have a lot of time to put it on, but their life depends upon these performances in a way, because if they do really well, maybe they'll get a job tomorrow.

With Mr. B you always felt that if you were in his class working hard, he knew, because he was teaching those classes as the director. So if he saw that you were working like mad or if you improved a bit, even if you weren't going to get the Swan Queen, he might give you a little something, just to say, 'It's worth it to keep on working, because you've changed and I see it and you're going to have this little demi-solo.' If he saw you just sloughing off and not coming to class and getting more and more lazy, you wouldn't get anything, you'd be in the back row of the corps. So the work, in a way, could pay off. You would get better, he would see it, and he often gave you something. He also watched all the time, and as he stood in the wings, even if you were in the back row of the corps, you thought, 'Maybe he's watching me.' Who know who he was watching, but you could feel, 'It matters, and my life may change if I do well.' That's what I think these kids think in the Workshop. And it does matter, because any director might be out there.

What's important for me is to help them develop a strong technique while moving in a beautiful and musical way, and to teach them to think for themselves and to be proud of themselves and to enjoy their dancing. This is basically what I learned from Mr. B and what I like to look at. I believe in that look and I like that look, so I teach them as much as I can how I learned to dance from him. Balanchine taught you how to present yourself, how to present dancing for the stage, not just the tendu but how the tendu was going to build to the next step. In class, we were already standing up and actively participating in the movement, and that's what you do when you're onstage, you participate, it's not just your legs moving. He didn't necessarily say, "Be aware of the public." He said, "Participate in the movement," and if we looked vacant, he said, "You look dead." And then sometimes he was teaching you how to live: Go after what you want. This is what you're doing now so do it as much as you can, 100 percent, and then when you finish this, do something else. If it's having a good meal, have a good one.

I try not to get relaxed as the teacher, because if I get relaxed, the class will get more relaxed and work less hard, so I try to be active. I might say, for a single step, "Well, I didn't see it, dear. Can you do that a little faster? Get out of fifth—bang! I don't want you to get there slowly. No, it's not good enough. You've got to get there faster." I have to be involved—otherwise, nothing's going to happen. I find it very rewarding to see change and to see students develop and grow and to see their appreciation of what they accomplish—I find that rewarding. And when you see one tendu done correctly, or one well-executed plié, going down and coming up with energy, it gives you such joy.

Kathryn Wade
English National Ballet School

*A*s in America, anyone in Great Britain or Ireland can hang out a sign and open a dancing school. When the Irish government urged everyone involved in agriculture to diversify during the 1980s, one dairy farmer applied for a European Community grant and converted his grain storage into a dance studio. Having built a dressing room in the calf shed and a dormitory in the hayloft, he established a residential ballet school, from which in 2000 he earned roughly half his annual income. Operating on a considerably larger scale, a company called Stagecoach Theatre Arts manages a franchise network of 386 performing arts schools, 355 of them in the United Kingdom, for students age 6 to 16. In 2000–01, the business cleared a profit of £500,000 ($710,000) on income from fees totaling £10.4 ($14.77) million.

Dance life in Britain expanded organically through the 20th century in a logical cycle of cause and effect—schools engendered companies that, once rooted in the country's cultural landscape, set up their own schools. The English National Ballet School is the newest kid on the block, a relative newcomer to British dance training and still small compared to its older competitors. Founded in 1988 and first housed in Markova House, the London headquarters of English National Ballet (ENB), in 1995 the school moved to the upper floor of an adult education center, where it converted ordinary classrooms into studios and offices.

Initially a band of 12 pupils, the school now accepts 20 to 30 students annually, either by audition or, in the case of foreign students, on the basis of a videotape of the applicant in class; the 16- to 19-year-olds who fill the two-year intensive course must have completed their secondary education to the level of GCSE (General Certificate of Secondary Education). Although primed by a vast range of teachers, most of the British students share a surprisingly similar dance background, because most British ballet schools adhere to a formal syllabus, devised either by the Royal Academy of Dance (RAD) or by the Cecchetti Society. Each organization uses a specific teaching method and a series of graded classes to train and assess students systematically.

To prepare its charges for the erratic demands of professional life, ENB's school deliberately offers a more flexible approach to training. The small permanent staff and an assortment of guest teachers draw on performing and pedagogic experience in England, France, America, Russia and Belgium. The curriculum, which concentrates primarily on classical ballet, includes contemporary and character dance, tap, jazz, pas de deux and repertory classes as well. The students also study for an academic qualification, called A level (Advanced level) Dance, with a syllabus featuring Benesh dance notation, choreography, dance history and anatomy.

Geographically separated from the company by a few miles of city streets, the students work in dedicated isolation, dancing for a minimum of four-and-a-half hours daily, and live either in supervised hostels or in housing they find and arrange privately, which can add considerably to the expense of their education. Tuition fees alone came to £9,600 ($13,632) for the 2000–01 academic year, when the estimated cost of accommodation and living expenses reached roughly £5,000 ($7,100); scholarships may be awarded at the director's discretion but the funds for them have to be raised first. Aside from the annual end-of-year program for which choreography is often created, the students perform only when the company needs them.

In the last ten years, dance has repeatedly hit the headlines in Britain, and not just because most dancers—65 percent of them in 1999—were reported to be living below the poverty line. The director of a leading ballet company publicly attacked British teaching standards, and a teacher at a respected ballet school accused its staff of bullying and intimidating the pupils. Dancers' fitness came under fire in a five-year study of their overall health, which discovered that 82 percent of the 658 performers polled had sustained an injury during the previous year. Carefully modulated voices argued politely in print and over the airwaves about the unimaginable effort and the intolerable difficulty of producing art and opportunities for artists. And all the while, in studios across the country, teachers went quietly about the everyday work of transforming teenagers into professional dancers.

～

Kathryn Wade. b. Bombay, 1945. Trained at the Royal Ballet School and performed from 1965 as a soloist with the Royal Ballet and London Festival Ballet (now English National Ballet). Retired 1975 and immediately joined the staff of the Royal Ballet School, remaining there until appointed director of English National Ballet School in 1992.

I THINK I GOT INTO DANCING BECAUSE . . . I was born in Bombay but then we moved to Calcutta and I was at school with Indian children, doing my schoolwork in Hindi, and my mother wanted me to have some contact with culture of my own country. Like all little girls I went along to dancing school, which happened to be in somebody's garage—we danced on a concrete floor.

Then we moved to what was then Ceylon, and I went to an extremely good dancing school there. At the same time, my mother started getting me trained properly as a swimmer, because she'd been a swimmer. So dancing's all tied in with high diving off an Olympic board when I was about five or six. I think swimming and diving made me very aware of having to get things technically right, because you've only got to belly-flop once from that high board . . . you learn your timing. Diving made me relatively fearless, and I discovered that actually I preferred the dancing, because you stayed dry. Oh, it was fun too and it introduced imagination—there's not much imagination in swimming. So it gave you a chance to have a fantasy life.

The next teacher I had was in Pakistan. She'd been a pupil of [Adeline] Genée, and her name was Madeline Watson. She was just a wife out in Karachi and she'd had this training, so she'd started doing ballet classes. She was a huge enthusiast who was very correct in her teaching. I mean, she taught with affection, but having been a professional dancer, she didn't give gratuitous praise if you weren't coming up to her standards, so her approval was worth diamonds. She had very good connections with the RAD through the Genée connection, so she had RAD teachers that came out to teach. I learned technique from her, hanging onto a dining-room chair on

a slippery ballroom floor, and learned from an early age one's physical limitations. We're talking about somebody nine, ten years old,
but I was already on that wavelength because of the training I'd had
as a swimmer . . . and there's something in your nature that makes
you want to go back the next time. So I did an RAD exam, and the
examiner asked my mother if she'd ever thought that I might or
should be trained professionally—I had visions of spending the rest
of my life wearing white net and flowers in my hair. My father was
dead against my training as a dancer, he wanted me to have an academic career, but after this suggestion I did a deal with him that I
would continue to work hard at my academic subjects if I was allowed to go to the Royal Ballet School. I had to come to England
anyway, because I was going to boarding school, and en route to
Edinburgh they believed that I could go and do the audition. My
mother was extremely laid back about it. She didn't think I would
get in and what's more she didn't care.

So my audition . . . I was wearing a swimming costume and a sun-
tan which was rarely seen in England in February. At the end of the
second audition we were invited into [the school director] Mr.
[Arnold] Haskell's office for the interview, and when they said to my
mother, "We're going to accept your daughter to this school," I nearly
died of shame, because my mother said, "Are you sure?" I think most
mothers burst into tears of joy. Then they asked me why I wanted to
dance, and I said, "I don't want to, I just have to," and they all
thought that was terribly funny. I felt a bit put down that they laughed.
I was just 11, and for me it was such a totally different world, coming
to England. My mother went out to India again, so I was in England
on my own from September 'til July, and I was at White Lodge [the
Royal Ballet junior school] for five-and-a-half years.

There was a most amazing art teacher called Molly Zambra, a
very enlightened woman. The first time I'd ever been to an art
gallery, we went to the Tate Gallery to see a Picasso exhibition. I
was back with her in about five minutes, and she said, "What's the
matter?" and I said, "I don't like them," the Picassos. And she said,
"Why?" Well, it wasn't literal enough for me, I don't see people
with three eyes. So she was very astute, and she said, "Go and find
a painting that you like, bring me there, and I'll tell you about it."
This was a fantastic revelation to me, because until then people had
always told me, "You should like . . ." or "You must like . . ." She
was interested in finding out what I liked too.

So she was a huge influence on me and in later years on my approach to teaching. Students come to me sometimes and say, "I've decided I don't want to do ballet." And I say, "Right, that's a very mature decision. If you don't like it, what do you like?" I think that's a responsibility that I have to have, because . . . You take them away from home, you've introduced them to a whole world, possibly different to their background, you can't abandon them just because they say they don't want to do ballet anymore. You have a responsibility to get them to find out where their talents lie, whether it's going into arts administration or contemporary [dance] or musical theatre or just out the door.

I was very happy at White Lodge and I was very lucky—I was in with a nice class, and they became my family. But I didn't find much joy in my dancing teachers there—they were very correct—and I didn't find much joy of dancing, partly because we didn't do enough of it, sadly. It was a great disappointment to me I had to do maths. But I had a wonderful teacher in Nora Roche, who'd been a student of Margaret Craske. She taught the RAD [syllabus] although she was a Cecchetti-based teacher, and in later years, I absolutely adored her. When I went into teaching, I went back to her and did the Cecchetti syllabus, because I'd done all the RAD at the school, it was part of the curriculum. She was wonderful to me, but one day I got cross with her when I was having a private lesson and I said, "Why didn't you tell me this when I was in your class?" And she said, "Oh, I did, but you were too busy hurling yourself off the walls. You didn't listen."

I'd already started teaching then, but I went back to her so that I could do the Cecchetti exams. When you're going into teaching as a profession, it's just like driving a car. You pass your driving test and then you promptly forget most of the rules. I really would be terrified to take a driving test now; having driven all over the world, I'd probably fail. It's the same thing once you've been a professional for many years: you need to go back to find out *how* to do a pas de bourrée and how many different pas de bourrées there are. It doesn't matter if you don't remember what they're all called, because everybody's got different terminologies, but it's good just to reevaluate 'Why do you do it like that?' when for so many years you've just done it. I had a whale of a time with Nora, going back to the fundamentals and the roots, and ended up a far better dancer once I'd stopped than I ever was as a professional.

She had a fairly feisty group of 16 girls at the school, and it was a bit like being a lion tamer. She was special, but it was different from having that affinity, that informality with teachers that is current now. You can't just impose now, and I think you learn more and you're not frightened of people if there's a dialogue and somebody actually says, "Do you understand why we're doing this exercise after that exercise?" It's important that you teach people to teach themselves, as a survival technique. Because when you get into a ballet company you're the lowest form of human life, and there isn't time to put in that one-to-one coaching for the corps de ballet. So if you can teach people to work things out for themselves, if they understand their own bodies, then they can look after themselves a bit better, rather than just feeling abandoned.

The school was very strong on academic work, apparently; we were in the top 25 schools academically in the country at that time. We had lovely Arnold Haskell, who I absolutely worshiped, and he insisted that we do our academic work, but we had to go to see things. We saw Klemperer conducting a rehearsal at Festival Hall, Malcolm Sargent . . . And I saw amazingly important, historical dress rehearsals when I was a child in the school—I'm talking pre-16, when we were incarcerated down at White Lodge. We all used to go up [to Covent Garden] in the week, so I saw Fonteyn in lots of things and when the Bolshoi came, [Nikolai] Fadeyechev doing Blue-bird . . . the first dress rehearsal of [*The Two*] *Pigeons*, the first production of *Fille* [*Mal Gardée*], and the dress rehearsal when Rudolf [Nureyev] did the first *Giselle* with Margot. It was a very creative and exciting time, and I always felt, 'I've got to try to do that.'

We didn't do a lot of dancing, funnily enough. Thursdays we danced all afternoon, but the rest of the time at White Lodge it was like an hour and a half a day. And then at the upper school we danced a lot more, we had pas de deux and things like that. Because we were so deprived of actual dancing, your ballet classes were that much more important, because you only had that hour and a half of doing what you really wanted to do. Beryl Grey has said that when she was a child she only used to have one class a week, but her mother made her practice. She made the most marvelous analogy, that if you take a child to piano lessons, they have their lesson and then they go home and their mother makes them practice. But that doesn't work with dance teachers. You take the child to the teacher, and it's almost like the teacher is having to make the child practice instead of the students applying that information to themselves.

So we had one class, and the rest of it was academic lessons. And quite honestly, we had people who hadn't really learned to teach—I'm talking about before Nora. They taught and we all learned somehow, but they hadn't done any formal teacher training. I don't think an awful lot of thought went into what you do at what age or what follows what. Maybe I'm maligning them, maybe I had very little understanding of what they were all about. They gave us great standards because they had worked with great people themselves, and I think that rubs off, and there was the discipline. If you were told to do something, you did it. You weren't expected to debate about it, and you were not going to be psychologically scarred if you wore a school uniform. It wasn't stamping out your individuality—what I could do to a school uniform was nobody's business! Those were the rules, those were the standards, and if you want to get on and have a relatively straightforward life, you abide by the rules. And that's very helpful when you get into a ballet company, particularly for a girl, because the discipline is extraordinary.

The person who taught me the most about standards and values, because he was the ultimate professional, was Henry Legerton, who I spent a considerable amount of time being absolutely terrified of because he was so direct. It was right or it was wrong—he was ballet master [of the Royal Ballet] and he used to teach the odd class—and there was nothing to argue about. It was quite simple, you were on the music or off the music, you were in the right costume or "What on earth are you doing wearing *that*?" And, a great thing with Henry, if he knew you were a worker, you had all the sympathy in the world for a cold or whatever. But he was a very good judge of character, he knew who was going to be swinging the lead and he was very fair. I was lucky, I only had one injury in all of ten years, but I can remember one day . . . I was just starting to get really nice things to do, so I had Blue Girls in the afternoon in *Patineurs* with Peasant pas de deux and Queen of the Wilis [in *Giselle*], yes, in the same performance, and in the evening I think I had Red Girls or Brown Girls in *Patineurs*, peasants and then leading wilis, so it was a pretty hefty day's work. And I went along to Henry and said, "Oh, Henry, . . ." Actually it was "Mr. Legerton" for a long time. You got permission to call him Henry and you thought canonization was shortly coming your way. So I said, "Do you think it would be possible if whoever did my peas-

ant place in the afternoon could do it in the evening? Please, please."
And he said, "Why?" and I said, "It's quite a heavy day, actually."
And he said, "Yes, I can make the day lighter. I can take you out of
Queen of the Wilis in the afternoon." "Oh, I'm fine." Never com-
plained about my rep load again! So he taught you to be grateful for
what you've got and get on with it. He was a great, great man.

My last year at school I had Madam, Dame Ninette [de Valois],
as my teacher every day—*that* teaches you standards and a joy of
dancing, along with everything else, and how to deal with the unpredictable. And at Baron's Court, we were not far away from
Leicester Square, and Errol Addison used to teach two open classes
there every morning. I was stuck in London, obviously, during
school holidays, so I used to go up and do Errol's first class, which
was four shillings and sixpence, and in that class would be John
Gilpin, Nadia Nerina, David Blair, Anya Linden, Svetlana Beriosova,
occasionally Margot, Galina Samsova, André Prokovsky, Maryon
Lane . . . and he used to let me do the second class for free if I hung
onto the piano. It was amazing to be a social equal with those people in class, and there was this lovely camaraderie. They were all
principals in the company, and I was at the upper school, I was 17
or 18. You weren't allowed to do classes outside. I just shot off and
did them, and all these stars were very kind, they didn't let on. Oh,
I'd have been expelled. But I wanted to dance more, and Errol was
so exuberant. He had great sensitivity, but he had this persona of
being a rough diamond. He'd been on the boards, he used to do an
act doing pirouettes on a drum. He had also been a pupil of [Enrico]
Cecchetti's, so what he had to say . . . well, it was Moses and the
tablets. He set the most sublime *adages* . . . he used to teach pas de
deux to us on Saturday mornings, when I first went to the school.

I was ambitious, I suppose, if I'm honest about it, and I had very
good advice from Barbara Fewster when I was at the upper school.
I was put into a class originally that was far too hard for me and I
was going downhill. They shifted me sideways into Barbara's class,
and she understood better than anybody else about this energy that
I had to get rid of and control. Now, all my year were ravishingly
beautiful . . . Lynn Wallis, Geraldine Chaplin, Jenny Penney with
those legs up to wherever . . . and Barbara said, "You're not the type.
You've got a brain," which I thought was very nice, because nobody'd told me that before. "So," she said, "what you must do is to
learn everything of every ballet. If you're in the middle"—because

being medium height I was in the middle three—"learn the three in front, learn the three behind, learn the other side. When you know the shape of the ballet, then learn the next one up, like the leading wilis or the Big Swans. Learn it, learn it, learn it, never waste time." And that stood me in the best stead, because—we're talking about ambition—I got all my work, I think, by being quick to pick up. And once you'd established a reputation for being quick, then you get chucked on. Once you've been chucked on, provided you haven't made a complete Horlicks of the whole thing, then it's only common decency to give you a rehearsal the next day. With Queen of the Wilis, Henry came and found me at 5:30 and said, "Do you know Queen of the Wilis?" I said, "Yes." So I was on. That night. I didn't cover it. So I think that's one of the best bits of advice you can ever give anybody: Don't just sit on the floor complaining in a rehearsal—in those days we used to sit on the floor and smoke too—use the time. It's such a short career, so use every moment.

I was told when I was at the school that I would never get into the Royal Ballet. So I went hell-bent for getting a job, and I ended up with three contracts, two in Germany and one in Canada, before I was told that the Royal Ballet would take me. So now, dealing with kids, I say to them, "OK, if you're not wanted in X company, don't keep banging on the door. Go and find a company that wants you. Go and find a director that really believes you're going to enhance his company. Don't eat your heart out, don't get bitter. It's such a waste of your energy. If you're not happy, there's an answer, there's a door, and as long as you don't slam it behind you, you can always go back."

I did that when I left the Royal Ballet and went to Festival. Having done a lot of principal work at Covent Garden when I was a coryphée . . . *Pigeons*, the Blue Girls, major roles . . . I found that I had no performances at all for months. So I thought, 'I can't be bothered to sit around here and grumble,' and I picked up the phone and rang Beryl [Grey, then director of Festival Ballet]. When I went to see the lovely Henry Legerton about it, he gave me a very sound bit of advice. He said, "Never forget that all companies are the same. They are the same people, but their names are different." In every company there's the totally reliable group. There's the resident bitch, who never leaves despite her grumbling—always threatening to resign and everybody from the management down, including the stagehands, would be immensely relieved, but they never go. And if they do, they reincarnate themselves—somebody always rises up to take their place.

Then I did two years with Festival, dancing my socks off, and I grew up. I still think it was the best thing I ever did, to go away. See other things, get to know other people, and it was a different repertoire. They had people from [Grand Ballet du Marquis de] Cuevas, so if I wanted to know what the gossip was I had to learn French. The only thing to do was invest in *Paris Match* and read it on the train. I had a ball, but then when I was asked to go back, I did go back. The Royal still had this immense security, and Festival was always a gypsy company, which I liked, and it was the sort of company where you had to prove your worth.

I did ten years of touring, the whole of my dancing career, and I think sometimes there's more appreciation outside of London. In those days there were not so many companies touring around, so it was an occasion if the company went to Wolverhampton or somewhere. I always believed, whether the public taught me that or not, that a good performance is a good performance and it doesn't matter where. I don't think that you can dance down to any audience. You have to do the best you possibly can on that night, whether you're in . . . what's now the regions, in my day the provinces . . . and whether there are 20 people out front or 2,000, for your own satisfaction, if you're going to sleep at night. One night when I was doing *Pineapple Poll*, I came on for the fouettés, did double pirouette, and it was like somebody pulled the plug out. The orchestra was fighting with the conductor and they stopped playing. This poor sod was conducting in the pit, I was doing fouettés in total silence, and the only thing to do was to keep going . . . they joined in at the end. Then we were going to the pub afterwards, and I cleaned the orchestra. I was so angry, because the public comes first, and I don't think they should be brought into whatever argument is going on.

They will recognize when people are doing it flat out and all for them, and they'll come back. And it's less exhausting to go flat out, because you get that feeling of being on a real high. If you hold back, then it just becomes a job, and for me that wasn't enough—I had to enjoy it. And then you've *got* to go back the next day to see if you can get it better, you've got to have that drive to drag yourself in at 10:30. We had wonderful examples when I was first in the company—Svetlana, Margot—and they were always immaculate for class. How could you possibly turn up looking like an unmade bed when you had those megastars who took such pride in themselves? It wasn't false pride. They knew their value. In those days, when you saw people leaving the stage door, it was still part of the magic, and they had a responsibility. Their performance didn't end when they went back to the dressing room. I feel sorry sometimes for children standing at the stage door now who don't have the cloud of perfume and the bouquets and the immaculate artist.

When I stopped, I had done a tour where I had danced a principal role every time I walked on the stage—I was a soloist, not a principal—and I hadn't had a rehearsal in eight weeks. I was reaching 29 and . . . I keep going back to the physical side of things, but I was always aware that once you'd passed a certain age, the bloom is off and you're starting to become almost a caricature of your own physical self. You can go through all the physical things that you don't like about yourself . . . they're not going to change. So I had a long chat with Kenneth [MacMillan] and Peter [Wright], and they said, "You're fine," and I said, "But I think I could be so much better if I was rehearsed." You need to have that input as a dancer. Maybe I was giving the impression of being too self-sufficient, and there wasn't much time for rehearsing. We were touring, the corps was being rehearsed a lot, but for the Waltz and Mazurka in *Sylphides* and *Concerto* third movement and all those things, I was on, I was doing it. And I was healthy and robust, there was no way I was going to go off with an injury. But I felt rather neglected, rightly or wrongly I don't know, and I remember saying, "I don't want to be bitter. I'd rather get out now." People say to me, "Oh, you were very young when you left," but I always think, 'No, I got out half an hour before I was pushed.' I had one of those "What are you going to do?" conversations with Kenneth, and I said, "I don't really know, but I've spoken with Barbara Fewster," who was then principal of the school, "and I think I'd like to teach." I left it all open, and then Barbara rang me up and said, "There's a vacancy in the school for a teacher." I didn't even think about it. I just said, "Yes."

So that's how I started: I finished with the Edinburgh Festival on a Saturday night and I started teaching on Monday morning, with the whole intention of just seeing if I liked it. And I absolutely adored it. Intellectually I think it's more stimulating to teach, because you're coping with people with totally different physiques to your own. You have to use your intelligence to imagine what it must be like to have a pair of God-given legs that you can't move, or try to understand why people can't turn or can't jump and try to get it through to them that they *can* do it or at least give a good impression of doing it or of overcoming their fear.

When Barbara Fewster was my teacher she was generosity itself with her knowledge—a very remarkable person. And when I went in as a junior teacher, people like Pamela May and Julia Farron and Valerie Adams were there, who had taught me in the school, and Nora Roche was still teaching. The first day of going into the staff room to change was just as nerve-wracking as the first day of going into the corps de ballet dressing room—all of a sudden you're the new girl again. But they were all so much part of that Royal Ballet continuity of handing on, and they didn't make me feel like I was totally ignorant, which they were quite entitled to, because I was. When I told Rudolf I was going to start teaching, he said, "What do you know about teaching?" and I said, "Nothing," and he said, "Remember that. Every day you find new things." Well, it's true—teaching isn't just a matter of going in and slinging the steps.

Initially I had to fall back on . . . I think everybody that teaches plagiarizes a bit, you're a magpie. I've been very lucky with the guest teachers I had, [Natalia] Dudinskaya came to the company for a while when [the Kirov] were in London, and when I was with Festival people like Matt Mattox taught class. A teacher I've neglected to mention, Erling Sunde, a Norwegian . . . He had worked with [Vera] Volkova a lot. He taught me very briefly at the school, and I always used to call him the Scandinavian Depression, because he was very lugubrious. He had . . . not an enormous range of fancy steps, but such well-constructed *enchaînements*. I could still give . . . I still do. If I have to suddenly rush in, because somebody's stuck in the traffic, and teach a class, I give an Erling Sunde barre, because it really gave you everything, soup to nuts—you were ready to jump when you came off the barre. He was tremendous.

All those [Royal Ballet] teachers were very open and very enthusiastic about taking on new ideas. If Barbara got in guest teachers, they couldn't wait to go and watch. When I was first teaching, Erik Bruhn came more than once, and it was wonderful for me to sit in a class with this childhood hero. He stayed at a friend's house near my flat in London, and I used to pick him up in the morning. I was very reluctant to sell my tin Fiat—it should have had a blue plaque on the top saying "Erik Bruhn was in this car." So it was fabulous to learn from those people, and all the teachers had a great common interest in good ballet. We all know there are several ways of doing anything, but in the end it's good ballet that you want to see on the stage. I'd been through their hands, but now I was able to discuss with them Why do you do it like that? which one certainly didn't in my day as a student. In the ballet class, some things were not for negotiation. Ballet is not a democracy. In the classroom the teacher has to decide what they wish to see done and what they are aiming for and what gives maximum training value for the students at that time. The obligation is also on the teacher to keep an open mind, which is why I think it's very healthy not to have a didactic syllabus. Yes, there is a vocabulary of movement that has to be covered for an understanding and a mastery of the technique. But if you only teach in one specific way . . . You can always ask for different ways of executing, just so people don't get into a rut. We were always, in the Royal Ballet School, trying to find different ways of doing things thanks to Madam, who had an inquiring mind. Some of her classes were extremely choreographic. They weren't just repetitions of glissade, assemblé, glissade, assemblé. She always had wit in her *enchaînements*, there was always the twist in the tail.

I went to the Royal Ballet School [staff] in '75 and left in '92, so it was a long haul. But I was very fortunate inasmuch as every couple of years I changed jobs within the organization. I spent two years shadowing Barbara Fewster, and when she knew she was coming up for retirement, she and Merle [Park, the school's director] asked me if I would be interested in doing her job. I had already spent some time helping them do the schedules and timetables—they discovered that I could cope with a pencil and an eraser, it was pre-computers—and it seemed like an interesting thing to do. Try it, try it. And also at that time two very good people arrived at the school: Nigel Grant, who was deputy director to Merle but had responsibility on the financial and academic side, and Maureen d'Alberthanson, who became head of White Lodge. They were important for me because for the first time I started learning about the academic responsibilities and government funding. I was in on staff meetings . . . they could have been speaking Mandarin for all the sense it made to me, because I had only ever been exposed to the dance side of the organization, and it was not really for the teachers to worry about funding. The great advantage for me was zooming up and down between White Lodge and Baron's Court [the upper school] with one or both of them in the car, so staff meetings just continued. I was able to pick their brains, through curiosity, and would almost get a tutorial on why things were done as they were. I owe them a great debt.

I was invited to come here by Ivan Nagy, who was then director [of ENB], and his deputy, Lynn Wallis. The school was started by Peter Schaufuss, when he was director, with the intention I think of having more of an apprentice scheme for the company. Which in theory is a great idea but in practice is almost impossible, because if you're going to get grants and apply for public funding, you have to have a more formalized school. He started off with 12 dancers, I believe—there's very little documentation—and then rather like Topsy, it grew.

It started with Kerrison Cooke in charge, and then when Kerrison was dying, Lucia Truglia took over the school and helped to build it up. Then I was invited to take on the directorship. I was given a blank sheet of paper—absolutely terrifying—by Ivan and the board. A lot of people said to me, "I suppose you want to make another Royal Ballet School," and I kept saying, "Well, why? There's a perfectly good Royal Ballet School down the road." It's quite funny—you always get branded as being "a product of." When I left the Royal Ballet company and went to Festival, I was always accused of being "so Royal Ballet." When I went back to the Royal Ballet, they all said, "But of course you're so Festival Ballet." I used to say, "Well, make your mind up! What am I? Perhaps I'm just me."

Mainly my brief was 'Get it up and running and make it an international school. The place is yours.' It was a very large blank sheet of paper, but I've got broad shoulders so I had a go. We had very little space or time in the studio, because we were then at Markova House and the company was usually there at the same time. We had 18 students, they were 16 to 18 or 19 and they were with us all day. It was a separate organization under the same roof, so we had to have two timetables, one for when the company was in and one for when the company was out. One of the first things I did was to get a staff together. We were trying to get visiting teachers, like for contemporary and character work and tap and jazz—it was a logistical nightmare. The school already had some contemporary work going and some tap; it was where one put the emphasis that was important. And also I was very keen that the students did Pilates work. Alan Herdman was marvelous with helping, and now we've got one of his people who was a dancer with the company, so she's coming at Pilates from a dance angle.

I believed very firmly that one should try to get some sort of academic program going as well, so they weren't just dancing and then sitting and watching the company do rehearsals. So the school started Dance A levels . . . I mean, the woman with no A levels to her name imposed an A level, because . . . well, I felt they must have some sort of intellectual stimulation. They're not going to dance all their lives, they need to be able to write things down. And I thought, 'What would I want to do, if I was a student now?' The only thing I would have wanted would have been to find out more about the subject I was obsessed with, which was dance. So to do history of dance and Benesh notation and a bit of anatomy and music . . . the Dance A level incorporates all those things. And the syllabus is so video-orientated that even if somebody doesn't have English as a second language, this was one subject that the whole school could do together. We have students from all over the world, and I'm delighted that last year we got the highest and the second highest grades in the country for A level Dance, which is a great tribute to the teachers. But we don't put unnecessary pressure. If somebody's going to get stressed out about doing an exam, let's be real about it, they are not here to get an academic qualification. If they want to and if they can . . . This is the paper generation, they're going to need all sorts of certificates. Please God they're going to have a hugely successful career as a dancer, but should they need it, they've got that piece of paper in the drawer.

So that's what we did on the academic side. On the dancing side . . . One of the things I had to do was to meet with the parents. And I knew, from previous auditions at the Royal Ballet School, that parents whose children had been doing a particular syllabus from primary [level] up to elementary and intermediate are always very keen that their young follow it through to its ultimate conclusion. Again, it's the paper generation—maybe you won't dance for very long or if you want to do a teachers course, you've got that certificate. So we kept going with mainly RAD syllabus because, sadly, few people seem to be coming to us with the Cecchetti background, but we've never used it as an actual syllabus. I feel it's a way to an end, a tool, but it's no good going along to a director and saying, "This is my X Society of Dancing certificate"—they want to see what you can do.

Six or nine months after I joined, Ivan left the company and Derek Deane joined [as director]. Similar background to mine and

Lynn Wallis' and to Antony [Dowson], who came to the school from the same background—Royal Ballet School, Royal Ballet company, all the rest of it. So we had very specific expectations, and we sat down and talked it through. We're all for fast, neat footwork, I suppose with a great admiration for the French-Danish-Balanchine style, the quicker style, bourrée in the fast lane, so that was a good meeting of the minds.

I love the Paris Opéra school, I love that French training, it's so specific. So we have tended, in the last four years, to incorporate a lot of the basic French training into this school. We got Dominique Franchetti, whose father, Raymond Franchetti, was such a wonderful teacher. Fabrice Maufrais came for two years, and Francesca Zumbo and Marc du Bouays come as guest teachers. What's so valuable is that the French are not extreme in any way. They are relatively un-forgiving, inasmuch as 'This is the position' and 'This is the look,' but they don't do anything to achieve it that is physically detrimental. If the student is physically incapable of ever getting there, then they don't take them into the school at all.

Of course, they've got a vast nation to choose from and they can choose what might appear to be perfect bodies. Inevitably we don't have the range of bodies to choose from in this country, in a way be-cause it's smaller. But we do all right, we get nice bodies and good physiques. It's a difficult age too—we get ours at a later stage than Paris. Here they're 16 going up to 18, maybe 19, and people's physiques change enormously. What looks absolutely enchanting at the audition, maybe at 15, might turn out to look like Auntie Lou or Uncle Bert. You can't even tell from the parents. But in many ways auditioning and accepting is guesswork based on your experience. We get the whole of human life coming to do a class at our auditions, we get people from Japan and Australia . . . Out of 52 students we've got 14 nationalities this year, which I think is wonderfully healthy. They all rub along very well, and I think that's very good training for when they join ballet companies, where you have to live in the same dress-ing room as somebody who might not be your first choice as a com-panion on a walking holiday.

I wonder sometimes how much they really want to dance to the exclusion of everything else. There's a fine line between the arche-typal ballet mother, who's pushing her child to realize her own am-bitions, and the mother who says, "I want little Susie to have three A levels and university entrance [qualifications], in case she fails."

And I think, 'Why are you already considering failing?' You know, you either get the one that's telling you, "She's mega-talented and it's all she's ever wanted to do," or the one who's almost demoralizing the teenager by wanting her to have a second career prepared for the inevitable day of failure or retirement. And parents do a lot more research nowadays. There's been a great burbling and murmuring that "it's a short career, it's a high-risk activity, you can get injured," you know, all that undercurrent of negativity, instead of people saying, "Right, yes, I'm going to go for it and be positive about it." My father said to me, "If you don't want to do it, it doesn't matter. You can do something else." So I wasn't pushed. But nowadays I wonder whether so much emphasis is put onto "You can do something else" that it's never that vital. Some people *need* to dance to live a happy and fulfilled life, and you never know until they're actually in the school.

You can sense which way the majority of the class is. It's very hard for them when they come into a school like this at 16, because they've probably been relatively cosy in their last school. They've known where they are in the hierarchy and they've probably been close to their teacher. We have to recognize that and deal with it, because you can't, the moment people walk into the school, say to them, "No, the way you've been doing it is not right," because you're insulting their previous teacher. What you have to say is, "That's very good" or "That is one way of doing it, but this term we're going to establish this particular way. We will come back to that way, so you'll already be ahead." They're away from home, they're having to cope with living in a hostel, looking after their own financial affairs . . . it doesn't matter whether you come from Surrey or Sydney, you can be desperately homesick. So we have to tread carefully in the early stages, with quite a few egos and quite a few people who are very apprehensive. Sometimes the talented ones are more sensitive to not wanting to get it wrong, and you have to say, "It's not wrong. It's a different way. We're going to try to bring you together into a cohesive group to make you look like a corps de ballet. Because that's what you want to do, isn't it, you want to go into a corps de ballet. And *then* you become a principal."

Our mission, if you like, is to enable people to train as ballet dancers, but we would be very shortsighted if we didn't include other disciplines of dance. Many people dance for three or four years and then decide they want to go into musical theatre, so if they have never worn a pair of tap shoes or jazz shoes, they are disadvantaged. Also, nowadays there is no such thing as a purely classical ballet company. When you see the Paris Opéra company dancing Pina Bausch, they've got to have that much more ability and mentally they've got to be more open, and I think being adaptable is so much more exciting than being eternally stuck as Aurora's friend. I remember taking the students to Adventures in Motion Pictures' *Swan Lake*, and they were somewhat puritanical about the fact that it really wasn't quite what they were expecting. So that's also part of our obligation. We've got to open up all kinds of dance for them. Whatever company comes to London we do everything we can to take them, because they might, if they're fortunate, have longer careers by not being blinkered in their opinions, and they might actually see something that they think, 'Wow. That's what I want to do.'

I don't know how much they've really thought this through. They want to dance. They go to the ballet or they see it on video, and they want to be able to do that. I don't know how much the reality has sunk in of how much they have to submit themselves to hard work in order to achieve what looks so utterly effortless and full of joy and exuberance on the stage. What we're trying to do is train the students to train themselves, because in the end when you're in a ballet company, for a lot of the time you're teaching yourself. So unless you understand why you're doing something and what it's for, you're just going through the motions.

And we try to educate them into being responsible for themselves. So we do quite a lot of work with the physiotherapist, so they know you are as good as the care you take of yourself. Your body *is* an instrument, you have to make sure that when you put it away for the night it is ready to play the next day. Rather like when you go auditioning, it's up to you to make sure that you have your tape. They're teenagers, they are going to goof up from time to time, and they're mortified if they go wrong, or you hope they are. But you can only check them and say, "Have you written to Mr. So-and-so about your audition? What time is the class you're going to be seen at?" In the end it becomes almost like a parental nagging. And hopefully, once they've gone through the process, they're going to turn into responsible dancers.

It's incumbent on teachers to develop their own skills of communication in order to extract the best from the students. You can't, any more than a parent can, impose yourself on another individual, but you can give them standards, values—as a teacher, you always have to offer. I think of the old days, when a teacher stood there with a stick and thwacked you . . . you can't do that anymore, and quite rightly, because I don't think you're going to get artists on the stage unless they really are striving. You have a big obligation to give it your best every night, and the only way you can do that is if you've tried your best in every class or rehearsal, even in a placing rehearsal where you're not doing the steps flat out . . . well, for God's sake, just be in the right place at the right time. There's no point in being the star of Miss Whoever's Dancing School if you're not coming up to the standards required of you at this particular moment.

I don't want to sound like I'm blowing our trumpet, but we do have very strong pastoral care in the school. When I first arrived, I got in touch with the local crime prevention officer, and the local police do a lecture for young girls coming to London for the first time. We've done that every year for the students, like in the second week—you don't want to frighten the living daylights out of them as they walk in the door. It's informal, the police come along in bomber jacket and jeans, and they show a video on living in a big city that's practical and down to earth. We're lucky here, it's a very good area with lots of shops. That was one of the nightmares of finding a place—there were some fantastic buildings, but you wouldn't send your girl to a school in an area like that.

We've been here for five-and-a-half years now, and the building still looks good. We respect the students enough to give them a nice place to work in, and they pay back the respect in bucketfuls by treating it nicely. They look after it, they're pleased to be here. Everybody said I was crazy to make the place as smart as this, but I resented the fact that there was a wall halfway across Errol's studio. It was two rooms knocked into one, so there was a big archway that you had to jump through, and there was a grotty little cubbyhole that you changed in. But then, I desperately wanted to go to him and it wasn't a full-time training. That was when you followed a teacher and wanted to work with that particular individual. But if you've got a school and you're responsible for young people's lives, you have to give them decent accommodation and a hygienic dressing room. These are the standards by which we expect them to live and comport themselves.

I also got the local health authority to come in and do an HIV/AIDS awareness lecture with them, and they also get the smoking and drugs lectures, but these are done by experts in their fields, so the person who nagged you about your battement tendu is not going to nag you about not smoking. It's virtually impossible to stop somebody who wants to smoke, but they don't do it in these premises and that goes for everybody, staff, students, the lot. And my father always said, "In this profession it's too easy to fall over. Never have a drink 'til you've stopped working." But the students are normal human beings, they are going to kick over the traces, it's all part of growing up. So the various lectures are just part of making them realize they've got to be responsible for their own work.

We have a nutritionist who comes in, and I always say to the students, "You've got to be like a Ferrari, and there's no point putting in rotten petrol." There have been very, very few cases of not eating—we've been fortunate—and I think that's partly because the staff are involved in the pastoral care. We have a weekly staff meeting, so we can pool that information. It's a small school, you're seeing students the whole time. We've got a wonderful general practitioner in the area who is extremely supportive. When I first met him we auditioned each other, and we came to the conclusion that anorexia is a problem that would concern the parents—they wouldn't want to be not involved. You cannot exclude the parents. Sometimes I feel like the church steps, as if they're saying, "We've had this one for 16 years. Now it's your problem," but these are not our children. So if we are concerned about anybody having an eating disorder, we get the parents here as fast as we can.

There are times when I feel immensely sorry for parents: they're not here on the spot, they probably know nothing about the dance world, so they're slightly lost. We encourage them to call if they're worried. I would rather a parent ring up because they were concerned than sit around and worry at home, because that worry conveys itself to the student. And then you've got a worried student who doesn't quite know why the parent's worried, and you're on a downward spiral. I think we were told to "Put up or shut up," but that's not the way education is anymore, the world has moved on. In this school there's a lot of dialogue between students and teachers. We hope they can come in and talk, and the door's always open. But even so, it's a daunting thing to go to somebody and admit you can't cope on your own, and it's a mature thing to decide you need help, so you don't need to be brushed aside. They deserve time.

We've got a wonderful hostel, which doesn't belong to us but it's on the other half of the company building, Markova House, just by the Albert Hall. About 25 of them are there, and it's very well run and secure. You can't claim to have a strong pastoral policy if you abandon them as they go out the door. We've got a red-hot attendance system, so that if anybody hasn't rung in here by midday, we ring the hostel. And if they're not there we ring the parents, and I don't care where the parents are. If they're in Australia and I wake them up, that's fine, because the parents can impose that discipline on them. I never want the responsibility of having a student who hasn't shown up for a couple of days, and then I discover there's been a mega-disaster.

And again, discipline is part of your training. If you miss the train, if you've overslept, if you've got the flu, whatever it is, you have to let the ballet master know ASAP, because you're a part of the whole. We keep them fairly active with a varied day, and we don't have much absenteeism . . . I mean, somebody might hate doing tap or contemporary or have a temporary falling out with their teacher, but you do the whole course or you don't. We try to make them realize that all the disciplines are contributing . . . It's like cooking. You've got to have the various flavors in order to get the full result. Otherwise, if you're just on pointe, you're going to be a dancing meringue-head.

Now, my job . . . This is a private school and a registered charity financed by fees, which means that every student has to be underwritten in one way or another, either by the parents or part-parental and part-scholarship or, in the case of the really talented and needy, by a school scholarship alone. All the scholarship funding has to be found, and part of it comes from government funding, which has been much trumpeted. In principle it's very good that it's coming from central government rather than from local education authorities. In practice, however, I think it is too thinly spread over a wide range of schools, though I couldn't ever say, "This school or that school shouldn't be funded"—that's a terrible thing to say. But it should be recorded that the government isn't picking up the whole bill. We are grateful for the funding we receive, but it is not enough to cover the cost of the training.

The present scheme basically leaves us with a shortfall for each government-funded student, and within their training period those students must also achieve a qualification which has been set by Trinity College, London—there is a large fee for the Trinity qualification, but they have to do it. Now, to fulfill that qualification the students have to keep diaries on what they're learning and files on everything they're doing, which is very different to the way most dancers are really trained. Dancing is a doing skill, it's not a paper skill. And it's slightly ridiculous, because the Japanese can't . . . I say Japanese simply because it's such a totally alien language to English, which is so difficult for them . . . they usually can't write sufficient English, so they wouldn't be able to complete all the paperwork. There's an immense amount of paperwork involved. What value is it to them? None.

The bureaucracy cuts enormously into my time as well. In order to get government funding, we have to complete the documentation and criteria for six different organizations, none of which have the same format for their questionnaires. In '01–'02 we have the DfES [Department for Education and Skills]. We have the Learning and Skills Council, which assesses the quality of our provision, delivery and results as an educational institution. Then we have Trinity College, London, who assess the students for the qualification and award it. Then there is the Centre for Educational Development, Appraisal and Research within Warwick University, which monitors the whole system. Then there's Manchester City Council, which organizes the Further Assistance Fund for students who can't afford the £1,075 [$1,548] to come here in the first place—every student in the country must now find £1,075 annually to pay to their university. And then there's one more, PricewaterhouseCoopers, which is assessing how government funding actually affects the schools that receive it.

We do keep asking, politely but so far without success, could they please just get together to allow us the time to get on with what we're supposed to be doing. We should be accountable if we receive government funds, but if there was one form each year, no matter how long, with all their queries, we could complete that for each student and get on with the job we love. But we're now called the dance "industry," every student has to have a number, and we have to do the same documentation for 45 students that the college surrounding us in this building does for 15,000. People told us that our 37-page self-assessment report in 2000 was too short, but you can't make a regatta out of three dinghies. I wanted to say, "We put our time into the studio, not into envelopes," but my staff wouldn't let me. The latest thing is that we should all go off and get qualified as teachers—after all this, I've got to get qualified.

The staff too have to keep files of their lesson plans, their aims, objectives . . . In many ways it has nothing to do with the actual teaching of ballet, which we all know is very repetitive. You are still teaching people to tendu properly when they are 24. You are still coaching pirouettes. There must be very few careers in which a professional is still a student, but a dancer can do Odette-Odile one night and return to the studio the next morning. It's partly responsible for a lot of dancers' insecurities, because the next day you're back to the beginning. You could be the greatest dancer in the world, but even the ones who seem totally in command of the situation and really rather arrogant still crave that recognition from their teacher that they are doing their best. And also they have to match up to their own standards. You know, even if you did a good performance, you go in the next morning and you can be all over the place and all over the floor too. It's very hard to explain this to somebody who's a politician and a bureaucrat.

I never really think about why I keep going. Maybe my reason is what I said at my Royal Ballet School audition—I have to. I believe in good training for dancers. I love being with the students and I love the age group that we have, because they're still discovering new things. But there's more. I was always very aware that my parents struggled financially to put me through school and through my training, and there was nothing for them at all, no education authority or any kind of charitable foundation, to which they could have applied. Maybe because I haven't got children of my own I feel you should try to do what a parent does, which is to make life easier for the next generation . . . not easier, but make it more possible for people to carry on the tradition of ballet. I do feel passionately about it, and I'm surrounded by a team that feels passionately about it, and the students do too. I mean, how lucky can you get?

Marc du Bouays
Paris Opéra Ballet School

*T*HE PARIS OPERA BALLET SCHOOL traces its artistic lineage all the way back to a stagestruck king. Louis XIV so adored performing at court that in 1661 he instigated the creation of a Royal Academy of Dance to protect the French style from the influence of the foreign ballet masters who were teaching in France. Although the academy survived almost until the revolution in 1789, Louis assigned the task of developing professional dancers to the Conservatory of Dance, established by his royal decree in 1713.

Having fallen under the authority of the director of the Paris Opéra in 1860, the ballet school moved in 1876 into the Opéra's home, the Palais Garnier, where it was still ensconced when its present director, Claude Bessy, took charge in 1973. A tiny fiefdom in a large, complex kingdom, the ballet school consisted at the time of 60 children from Paris, squeezed into cramped quarters at the top of the building and studying only ballet; until the 1960s, academic education had to be completed elsewhere. Within three years Bessy introduced classes in adagio and repertory, folk and character dancing, modern and jazz dance, mime, music and the history of dance, all of which entered the curriculum for the first time. In 1987 the school left the Garnier for the suburb of Nanterre, where a brand-new building had been built expressly to house it, equipped with ten dance studios, an auditorium with seating for 300, a video library, a gymnasium, 12 academic classrooms, and 50 residential rooms. Any French child can now apply for training, and roughly 95 percent of the students are French citizens.

Entering the six-year graded course today is an arduous

process. At the first audition, a group of candidates is selected, largely on the basis of their physique, health and dance experience, for a term of preparatory study called the *stage,* which lasts six months for younger applicants and one year for slightly older ones. After completing the *stage*, the applicants audition again to enter the lowest division of the school. To call the competition fierce and the standards rigorous is putting it politely: in 1990, more than 600 children attended the initial audition, of whom 120 were chosen for the *stage*; five months later, 40 girls and 20 boys were permitted to enter Division Six.

Girls begin their studies age 8 to 12, boys age 8 to 13, and each group follows a clearly defined syllabus year by year, joining forces for folk dance, mime, pas de deux and repertory but refining their technique separately. The faculty consists exclusively of former members of the Paris Opéra Ballet, and every three months the pupils' current teacher and their teachers from the previous year and the coming year submit detailed written assessments of each child. As in all national ballet schools in France, an end-of-year examination determines whether a pupil shall advance, remain in the same class or leave the course. The decision rests with an examination jury made up of the directors of the school and the company, two members of the Paris Opéra Ballet and two members of the school faculty; for complete impartiality, the boys' teacher votes only on the girls' advancement and the girls' teacher votes only for the boys. The school now provides a general academic education as well, and no one may enter the corps de ballet without first earning the Brevet des Collèges.

To strengthen the ties between the school and the company, the dancers in the Paris Opéra Ballet act as *petites-mères* or *petit-pères*, like friendly godparents and professional advisors, to a student of their choice. The students perform in public demonstrations, both at home and abroad; in a repertory performance that is their annual showcase; and with the company as required, and they attend ballet performances when tickets are available. And the state pays for everything but the *internat*, the fee for boarders, which in 2002–03 cost French and European Community students 1106 euros ($1,106) for each of three terms lasting three months.

Traditionally, the Opéra celebrates special occasions with a *grand défilé*, for which the back of the Garnier stage opens to reveal the Foyer de la Danse behind it. To the solemn strains of the march from *Les Troyens*, the full company flows from the glittering depths of that hidden jewel in waves of ascending hierarchical order, ending with the *étoiles*. The students of the ballet school lead the procession, dressed in the same pristine white as the artists and already alert to the demands and delights of appearing on the stage they hope to inherit.

∾

Marc du Bouays. b. Aulnay-sous-Bois, near Paris, 1950. Trained at the Paris Opéra Ballet school, member Paris Opéra Ballet 1968–81. Appeared with English National Ballet, Pittsburgh Ballet and Northern Ballet Theatre before retiring in 1985. Freelance teacher worldwide from 1982 and member of the Paris Opéra Ballet school faculty since 1997.

ONCE I SAW A DANCER ON TV and I said, "Oh, that is liberty." Even when I was small I always wanted to be free, to leave my parents very quickly . . . I loved them but I wanted to be free. And I liked planes because that's like a freedom, and for me the first thing to be free is with the body. So I said to my parents, "I want to be a dancer," and my parents said, "Why don't we try the Paris Opéra?" We were living in the suburbs.

My very first class was in the Paris Opéra—I was 8 at the *stage*, it was '58. I went to one class and the teacher asked me to do first position and I did it. I did only one step for the *stage*, that's all. I just saw what the other people were doing and I tried to do something like it. I stayed for like 15 days of class and after that I was burned with hot milk, so I stayed for two months in bed. My father went to see Mr. Harald Lander, the director of the ballet school, and he said to my father, "Go away. I want to see him at the exam." They just picked me like that. Mr. Harald Lander had seen me two or three times, and maybe he saw a quality in me, I don't know, maybe not. But I didn't know one step. I didn't know what first position was, I didn't know everything. I just saw a TV dancer and thought, 'Yeah, that is liberty.' That's all. And I was alone of my generation to stay, the only boy. First we were thirteen, and after the *stage* ten went to the regular class, and then year after year . . . I was the only one of that year to stay.

For me the school was fantastic. At that time we had only two divisions, two levels. We began with Mr. [Robert] Le Blanc, *stage* with Mr. Le Blanc, like 15 days for me, and after with Mme. [Uguette] Devanel for three years, and after that we had Mr. Franchetti—I had him for six years, every day, every day. He was for boys—we had a boy class and a girl class, always separate. I stayed a long time, nine years, in the school because I began very young, so I stayed two years extra. For all those nine years we had just one class a day. Everything was there in the Palais Garnier; in the morning it was school and then dancing. After I finished the writing school at 14, in the morning I took a class with Mr. Franchetti plus another one in Paris Opéra plus one in the evening, so I had three classes. With Mr. Franchetti it was very wonderful, because he made an *ambiance* that we were in good competition, not in bad competition. Everybody tried to do the best of himself, and sometimes we made a *concours* together, after two pirouettes we had to do four, then we had to do five, just for each other. And even now, as older dancers, we are always happy to meet and we speak about Mr. Franchetti. I think he was the first to bring placing into Paris Opéra, maybe not the very first one, but he brought it to the feet, he took care about the arms . . . Mme. Devanel was good, but she was not so careful about placing. She was more about technique, not really about the body. Or maybe I didn't understand at the time—maybe she explained to me, but I was not clear enough in my head to understand what she said. So after three years maybe I understood Mr. Franchetti better.

Mr. Franchetti was not really a classical dancer, he was a character dancer. And what is very important is that he himself was very *en dedans* [turned in], I realize now he was *en dedans* when he showed, but what we saw was him turned out. All his students were turned out, because he showed the right step to do to become that way. A tendu like this to the front, he would oblige us to pull back this way, with the heel forward and the little toe moving first, and it showed the shape of the leg and we were obliged to be on the vertical. We did that every day, every day. He understood turnout very well and he wanted us to be turned out. I only realized he was *en dedans* because one day he said, "Don't do it like me."

Of course I had some models. I wanted to be like Franchetti wanted, not like he showed but like he explained. That was the model—it was not a physical model, it was a model of what he said and his experience, and since it was in our mind the body would follow. After that I liked a lot Attilio Labis for natural placing, he was at the Opéra, and I liked a lot Flemming Flindt, who came from Denmark. He was very placed and very cold, not a lot of expression, but I liked that. I don't like expression, I don't like emotion. I liked placing, so also I liked Pieter van Dijk, who died two or three years ago, he was a very good dancer. I liked to beat and to turn also, but I liked more the position in the air or on the floor, to use the spine, to use all the body. At that time we did not have Kylián or Mats Ek or that kind of choreography. If we could have had that, I would have done it happily. But I only wanted to be at the Paris Opéra—when we were children, we based everything on that—and just to dance, to be the best of myself, with the most placing I could have, to destroy everything *plus*, too much. That's why I don't like people who make so much emotion—for me it's better to take away.

At school we did only ballet. I did jazz, from the Studio Constant in Pigalle, for two years, with an American, one of the first dancers to bring jazz to Paris. I was in the company then, I just went by myself to take class. And later, for six months only, I did a Spanish class with José Torres in Paris. But until I was 17 years old I just studied in the Paris Opéra. After I was 17 I found another teacher, Mme. Lilian Arlen, who was very important in my life, because with her I could learn really how to move the body with coordination and rhythm, and how to place the spine. She rented a studio in Salle Pleyel, and she died in '92 when she was 80 years old. She showed me a therapy class based on Hatha yoga but formed for dancers and even for people in the street. With her I really learned how to put my body in the vertical, and that was very important. It was completely different from Franchetti, but it was very complementary. With Franchetti we also had that verticality, the placing, the rhythm, and with her we had rhythm also but a different way, more modern. She taught a method of therapy and sometimes with dancers she would make a therapy exercise and then she would say, "So now, do that on classical dance," so whatever you did in the therapy exercise you had to put into the dancing. She tried to do the same thing for people in the street, in life, when they didn't know how to walk or to breathe. We tried to put the therapy into dancing and into our life, and sometimes we worked for people in the street and dancers together, because it is important to understand what those people are trying to do and what we are trying to do also, and it is also very interesting.

I grew tall very late, at about 16, so my body had no coordination at that moment and all the bones were not in place. One day I looked in the mirror and said, "No, I'm completely *en dedans*. I feel bad to make my arabesque. I can't stay like that. There must be something to do." I spoke about it to a dancer in the Paris Opéra, and he said, "Oh, I know a woman . . . ," and he brought me to Lilian Arlen. She was from Vienna and she was a Jew, so she had to leave Austria because of the Nazis. She explained to me what she had done. The Nazis broke her arms so she couldn't use them to dance, so she wanted to kill herself. The doctor said, "Yes, you can dance, but use your arms the way they are," and in fact later, she did cabaret and the *gitane*, gypsy dancing. She made the choreography for herself, and nobody could see that she had those broken arms.

And what was good in the same way, but completely different also, was that I learned to fly a plane. For me flying was really liberty, because there is a verticality, there's a horizontal, there's pushing, exactly like dance. I was speaking once with a pilot of Air Afrique, and he said to me, "Oh, I don't know if I like dance." And I said, "But you are a pilot. You make ballonnés with your feet, there's speed, it's exactly what you use in dance. To fly a plane is the placing of dancing." I began to do that when I was 17 also, and I did it for about six years. I was dancing then too, yes, but the first year I was engaged for the ballet, the Paris Opéra closed because they had to rebuild. So for one year we took classes in the morning but we were preparing for nothing. At that time we had to wait . . . Fortunately it's not like now: when you are engaged for the ballet, you dance at once. But at that time, no, even when the Opéra was not closed. You just watched and you learned the roles and you stayed with your arms folded for maybe one year, two years. After the *concours* we had to wait—it was terrible. We did class at the Opéra and then we went to rehearsal, but every afternoon I did two or three hours flying and I did my therapy class. In that case I was lucky, I had a lot of time to do that, but I didn't want to lose my time at the Opéra.

With Mr. Franchetti all that changed—he was the director of the company for four years. He was very fair. He did not advantage somebody to another. Even when we were children he was always fair, there was no preferring people. He explained to the class the people who were good, and he tried to give young people the possibility of dancing. With him, when you went into the ballet you could dance at once, even a small role, but at least you were onstage, you learned something. At first I had *le trac*, I was a little afraid to go onstage sometime, and anyway I knew I had to work more. Because while you wait, you have to make a . . . how do you say? . . . *remplacement* . . . substitution, sometimes you have a small role, and I wanted to do more. I didn't think I was ready, but you go onstage and little by little you will be ready. Of course now I realize, which I didn't at the first performance, that I'd made a lot of mistakes, of course, but you have to learn onstage.

I wanted to show, of course, the best of myself, but also the *propreté* [neatness], because the more we are correct and *juste* in the step, the more we can be sincere. That's why I don't like emotion, because emotion for me is not always sincere. I'll explain it better. The first thing, you have to be very clean with your steps and no emotion, the first thing, and the public has not to see your steps, it has to see your sense, what you feel. If it sees your steps, it's not good. You have to feel something inside of yourself that the public can feel. But first you have to work a lot on your steps, to make them clean, to bring to the public your soul . . . I don't know if it is the soul, if the soul exists or not, but what you have inside. If you want to give that to the public, there is a big work to do before, to find yourself. I think the body can show emotion . . . it's difficult to speak about emotion. We can't use words for emotion. Our body is our words, and every part of the body can show our emotion, every cell of the body, I think. Even in the street, when people walk, we can see if they are sad or happy or foolish. Maybe we don't realize it, but there's some part of the body, if we analyze it, that shows it.

I did the pas de dix in *Giselle*, on the music of the pas de deux but we were ten, five boys and five girls, it was quite difficult at that time. I didn't do a lot of ballets but I did also a small pas de deux in *La Sylphide* by Pierre Lacotte, in Act I, and also in the *Orfeo* of Balanchine, the Gluck [*Chaconne*], I did the pas de trois with two girls and one boy, I liked doing that. And later of course I did Bluebird and *Grand Pas Classique* of Auber, and after that I left.

I was dancing, so I should have stayed—I had an operation for my knee, but I retrained and it was OK. But my wife, Evelyne Desutter, was going to Roland Petit and then she went to London Festival Ballet. So it was difficult for me to be in Paris Opéra with her in London, so I decided to go with her to Festival Ballet, where

I stayed for two years. In Festival Ballet it was of course a different way. I left my country and I had to adapt to English people, who were completely different. And then I went to America, with Patricia Wilde in Pittsburgh—it was very difficult because it was class at 9:00, and with her it's good American work. She was with Balanchine, of course, and she had a lot of steps that she learned from him. And that was very interesting, because we could learn the speed that at that time we were missing in the Paris Opéra. The first month I had to learn a lot that was very different, but I liked the speed . . . for me it's complementary, because I know the steps. For one month of the two years it was very difficult, but as we had the tradition and the *base* in Paris Opéra, we could adapt very quickly. With the school of Paris Opéra, all the teachers in the school are from the Paris Opéra, so we have the same way of working. It's like a tradition. Now we have [John] Neumeier and Pina Bausch coming to choreograph so we can see something else, but for the school we have one way to work—there is no name on that, but we work very square and we are very careful about the cleaning of the step—and we are preparing them to be in the other styles later. In Paris it's not a style, it's a way to work, like in Russia they have [the method of Agrippina] Vaganova and then they can go elsewhere to learn something else.

I adapted very well with Patricia Wilde, and also I found here in England Elena Mordvinova. She was a Russian, she was teaching at Urdang [Academy]. It was the Russian style and it was also very difficult, a lot of demi-pointe and a lot of difficult steps, simple but very difficult to do it right. When we were not in shape we went to see her for strength. And I liked also in England Vassilie Trunoff, who was very artistic. Even if he did not do a lot, he explained a lot of things for my wife. Mme. [Nina] Vyroubova was also the teacher of my wife. Evelyne and I worked together with Mr. Franchetti and Mme. Marie Tatalia. But I wanted to find an artistic woman for my wife, who could really show the role, and I knew Vyroubova was very *artiste*. I saw a film of her in *La Mort du Cygne*, a small piece . . . the film was very old, but she was wonderful. She rented a studio at Salle Pleyel, so we took her class, and from her I learned a lot about rhythm. I was rehearsing the *Grand Pas Classique* of Auber with my wife in Paris Opéra, and I had a lot of difficulty for the style. And the first thing Vyroubova said to me, "You are not on the music." So she put me on the music, and that way I was more on my body and I could find more my style. We did not learn music at school, no, nothing. Now they do it, but at the time we just learned "La Marseillaise." That's why when she brought me on the music, it was something like an awakening for me.

And of course we learned a lot from Nureyev. First he came to Paris but not as the director, as a guest dancer and he brought his ballets, and later he danced with my wife in *Nutcracker* so I could see the rehearsals. We learned in each minute from him, the styles, the way to do the steps, and the force, to give a lot of force. You couldn't say to him, "I'm tired," because he did more than us, so we were obliged to do it. And of course he came a lot to London Festival Ballet, and he showed *Les Sylphides* also very, very well. And I realized that all the people like Nureyev, Patricia Wilde, Vassilie Trunoff, Elena Mordvinova, Franchetti, Vyroubova, Yvette Chauviré also, Lilian Arlen . . . all those people were very sincere and very simple inside. Some of them are not diplomatic, but I think it's very difficult to be a diplomat and sincere.

I stopped dancing . . . My last performance was with the Northern Ballet [Theatre], *Sleeping Beauty*, in Manchester. We were guests. I did Bluebird and my wife was dancing with Rudolf. And I decided—I was 35—that now I want to teach, first because I wanted to teach and not because it was difficult to teach and dance together. My wife was dancing some parts, and for me it was difficult always to find work with my wife and we wanted to be together. So I decided to stop, and I said to Rudolf Nureyev, "You know, tonight I stop dancing." "If you stop dancing, I don't want to speak to you for six months." I said, "OK, you will not have to speak to me." Of course, he spoke to me at once.

And then we were guests. When my wife was a guest with Northern Ballet or Australian Ballet I taught at the school. Maybe people felt that I could teach, maybe I'm wrong, I don't know. But, you know, the first time I saw Patricia Wilde . . . I knew her past was with Balanchine, I never saw her dancing, I never saw her teaching, but just looking in her face, I said "She is a good teacher." I don't know why. When you see Violette Verdy, you know she's a good teacher. It's something in her—I don't know why—they are teachers. We can feel the people . . . when I'm not dancing, people don't feel me like a dancer.

I began to teach in fact when I was 18. When I learned the therapy class with Mme. Lilian Arlen, a friend in the suburbs had a bad back, and I said, "You can do this for it." And later, my teacher of therapy had to go to the hospital because she had a problem with her hips, and she said, "You have to give class for me." I said, "No, I can't. It's not possible." "Yes, yes, you give class for me. Go ahead." I said, "What do I have to do?" "You will see yourself." It was with people who were not dancers, so I was pretty afraid, but she said, "If you can do something with people on the street, you can be a teacher for dancing." Because as they don't understand the movement, you have to make an understanding of movement for people who don't know. The class was that kind of people, and they all had a lot of problems with the back and the legs. So I had to make a therapy to shape the legs, the arms, the head, the eyes, the breathing, so I was already learning to make the shape for dancers. I liked doing it, but for me it was difficult because I was anxious. But when I was in the room, I don't know what happened, I found the way to explain. For some people I explained with pictures, for people who were doctors I explained with anatomy—because I learned anatomy from a book. In school, at the Paris Opéra, we had a teacher for design and painting, Mme. Georgette Bordier, and she made a book of anatomy for dancers, an anatomy for turnout and for the *axe*, yes, the vertical axis. So we could learn anatomy with movement, not only from the book, and as dancers we could feel where the position is. I had learned a little anatomy on my own, but from her I learned a lot. I had not the chance to study with her—I was already in the ballet when she taught at the school, but I could read the book and sometimes I saw her, so I could ask her things, because it was sometimes difficult to understand. So when I began teaching the therapy class, at the same time I was learning. Sometime if I didn't explain to somebody how to do it, in the evening I tried to find a way myself and then to work again with that person. So like that I could learn anatomy with people who were not dancers, and afterwards I taught people who were dancers, and it was more easy, of course.

I gave my first ballet class with Roland Petit, in '76, because he asked me to give the class, and I gave also private class in therapy to Zizi Jeanmaire, because at that time she wanted to dance *Carmen*. And then at Pittsburgh Ballet, Patricia Wilde asked me to teach for the school, and I taught in the school for Australian Ballet also. When you explain something, you know if it is right or not right. You know. So then, if you know if it is right, it's easy to teach. With some students, if I don't manage to do it one way, I say to myself, 'Oh, I have to change my language. To explain this exercise I have to do it another way.' Or you can show it better, like Mr. Franchetti showed you good things, or if you can't show, find a way . . . For every person you have a lot of ways to teach, and it depends also on the character of the people and the moment—everybody, in two seconds, can change his mind. He can have anger, he can be quiet . . . the same person, in two seconds, can change, so you have to feel that feeling and change your approach. I don't think it's intuitive. You look at the person and you know if she's here, if she has the attention, if she has the concentration, and first you have to get her attention, to bring the concentration and so she has confidence in you.

Of course I had a lot of influence from Mme. Lilian Arlen and Mr. Franchetti. But I had influence of some other teachers we had also, like [Alexandre] Kalioujny, at Paris Opéra Ballet. He had a balance . . . his steps were very dancing, and all of the steps had an *équilibre*. And also, a long time after, I learned a lot of things from Marika Besobrasova in Monte Carlo—she was a Russian, Vaganova—and from Rosella Hightower. I went there to teach. I taught two years with Marika Besobrasova and three years with Rosella Hightower. Rosella Hightower left people free to teach, and that is very important, to be free when you are teaching and there's not somebody who tells you, "You must not do this, you must not do that." You can't teach like that, and sometimes Marika Besobrasova did that—that's why I left, because you are not free, it's difficult. But it's good to control, I need that also. Mme. Claude Bessy sometimes comes into the class now and says, "Oh, careful, you don't do that enough." Sometimes we are going one way, because that way is very good, and we forget the other way, and you need somebody to remind you, "Careful." Leave me free—just remind me.

Now when I teach, before my class I always prepare—I need to know what I'm doing. And I'm always scared before every class, even for small children of people in the street, the same fear that I have for professionals. I always have the same hope in each class, that they find something for themselves, not for five minutes but for all of their life, forever. So with my students I always think, '*Pourvu que je ne sois pas faux*, I hope that I don't say something wrong.' For me that's very important, because if you don't say anything wrong, people can make an evolution and reach a verticality. I think the first man was like this [slumped over] and he tried to find the verticality. Evolution for me is the verticality, and verticality has to be flexible, not rigid—that's why you have to be open to a lot of things. To be teaching the dance is to bring the student on the verticality. Not only the dancers, but even when I teach therapy for ordinary people, for anyone, I try to put them on the verticality. That's the most important thing for me—I think it is like a light inside of yourself. To go on the verticality, I had to learn with Mr. Franchetti, with Mme. Arlen, and I had to learn to fly a plane, also that made me understand it.

I don't give the same class as Franchetti, not at all. Of course it's an inspiration, but . . . you have not to do it the way you have learned. You learn one thing, but if you feel something of one teacher, you have to feel it as yourself, because nobody's the same person. You have your own *entité,* so with that you make a construction and you have to be yourself. It's like . . . My wife worked with Nina Vyroubova and Yvette Chauviré, but she doesn't want to dance like them. Here you have Margot Fonteyn, and Margot Fonteyn was fantastic, but you have not to dance like Margot Fonteyn. You have to learn about her, but it is not right to want to copy her. I don't think it's good to make a copy. It's an *impasse, cul-de-sac.* And I don't want to be like my teacher. I love Lilian Arlen, Mr. Franchetti, but I want to be myself. I learned something from a lot of them, but I make my own construction, because I'm somebody else. I change always my teaching. There is a *base*, but I don't teach now as I taught ten years ago. Each day we learn something in the studio, of the way to speak or to explain.

Today I think the school is quite the same as for us, but we were fewer people. And we had fewer facilities in our time, so we had to be more responsible with ourselves. But now it's more dangerous in the street than in our day—we have to follow the children, because we are afraid about the people who are outside, so the students have less responsibility. But at the same time, we have to take more care of them for the dance, we have to tell them more, and so they think less. Of course dance has an evolution also; before you danced to express yourself, now the technique is different, we ask for more technique, more placing. This is fine, and yet at the same time I think we have to find a way to make the students more responsible. We help a lot—"Do that and do that and do that"—and it's too much, because if you say too much to a student he will do nothing.

When you do an *équilibre*, a balance, it's your brain that decides to go down from it—it's not your body deciding. That's the way—*you* decide, not your body. And that reminds me . . . Sometime Mme. Arlen told us once what we were to do, and again, twice, but not three times. After she told us what to do twice, she would say, "You are wrong." "I'm wrong? But what is wrong?" "It's wrong." "But *what* is wrong?" "*You* are wrong." Then you begin to make yourself responsible for doing something. So a student is a teacher for himself. Otherwise, you tell him what to do and he will do it when you tell him, but when you leave he will do anything. So you have to teach so that the student can do it by himself. That is very important, that the student doesn't need you, that he can tell you, "Go away. I don't need you. Now I'm free." I will be happy to hear that. We have to ask them to work alone. Some do, but very seldom. I don't think it's the ambition that is different from our day—it's because they maybe have too much to do. When you have too much to do, one class, another class, you have no time to mature in your mind. You have to grow up in your mind, and your body has to absorb the brain.

I started teaching at the school in Paris in 1997. I left Paris Opéra, and when you leave it's very difficult to come back, but . . . I was with Rosella Hightower in Cannes, and Claude Bessy just phoned me, "If you want to come . . . ," so of course I said yes. I give a classical class, but I give a therapy class for the two older classes too. We have a whole class for all the year—I teach Division 4—and each teacher also has the class over and the class under. We have eight classes a week, so we have six classes with our students and two with the other students. Normally it's technique for the class under and the class over, but I have those two classes, with the third division and the second division, of therapy and not technique.

The way we work is very important, and always to have the same students all the year is also important, because first they are . . . not weak, but at the level of the year before, and at the end they have to be at the level above, and we can see the difference—each class can see it. I know that at the end of the year my class has to know the brisé volé, they have to do entrechat six, they have to do one turn and a half en l'air, not two—if they can do two, OK. So I have to plan, because if they are doing anything too difficult in the beginning, it's not good. But then it is difficult for us to brake, not to go too fast. At the beginning of each year I think, 'Oh, I have to do it all again.' But when I have the children in front of me, it's fine, and every year is not the same because you have not the same children or the same characters. Some children are like this, some are too much like that, and you have to make a middle way. They are between 13 and 15, so they are growing. Once I had one boy who understood very well, and in the holiday, like in 15 days, he grew tall and he couldn't move, so I had to reshape everything.

But, you know, if you put them in the right position, even for one second, they will feel it, and after that . . . they may not succeed to do it, but I think everyone knows the good position because we all have, inside of us, verticality and rhythm. So the first thing I always do is to put them on that verticality, so that it's a shock for them, and then they try to find again what they have felt. When I come to another school, they don't know me. When someone doesn't know another person, he's always obliged to be good, because he wants to show himself well. So for one week it's easy for me to work, but after they know me, they can be themselves. That's why you have to show the good verticality right away. You don't know if maybe it will be too difficult, maybe not enough, so in the first class you have to discover. In Tokyo they have a lot of attention, maybe too much, but I think that is their education also. What I have seen in America, in England, in Germany, they have good attention; in France and Italy, less—you have to bring more for them to get it. For me, the first three classes are the most difficult with new people, and that's why I'm always afraid in the first three classes. When they understand the way I want, then I can work. When I'm in class, I'm confident. When I'm out of class . . . if I don't teach for three days, I say, "I don't know how to do a class," and I'm lost. That's why I say I make class in my head and in my notebook.

Because we have a tradition, we have a *base,* with that *base* they can learn something else. The therapy class gives you something else that makes you think about your *base.* It makes you aware about your work, otherwise you sleep on what you have learned and you stay there, resting. When you feel comfortable, it's not good. I think when a dancer begins to feel comfortable, the company has got to be careful. Even in our life, even with a man and woman, when you feel comfortable, there's a danger. So of course the teacher has to feel when the students are more comfortable, and then "Careful!" because otherwise you sleep and you can have accidents and you can make no evolution.

As a teacher, I want always to have the possibility to explain—always, always—and until I'm free of my movement, to show. The day I can't show I want to have the possibility, like Mme. Arlen, to explain something and always to bring something to people. I don't need anything else. For myself I don't need anything—just to teach. I like to bring people to their whole liberty, their whole verticality, because I think even if they can't succeed to be a good dancer, they can make an evolution for themselves, for the body and for the brain. If I succeed to do that, for me I'm happy. It's not for me—they listen to me, but they do something for themselves.

Anne Marie Vessel
Royal Danish Ballet School

$\mathcal{T}$HE ROYAL DANISH BALLET SCHOOL began as a gleam in the eye of a Frenchman, Pierre Laurent, who was chief dancing instructor to the Danish court in the 18th century. In 1771, Laurent took the initiative for establishing a proper school for dancers, tucking it into the Court Theatre at Christiansborg Palace in Copenhagen, where he taught six to eight pupils for two hours every day. Four years later, an Italian dancer and choreographer, Vincenzo Galeotti, settled in Copenhagen and quickly became ballet master at the Royal Theatre, where he launched another, competing school that gradually took over the work Laurent had begun. Drawing on his experience in Italy and England, Galeotti led Danish ballet away from the decorative dances preferred at court and introduced it to the theatrical *ballet d'action*, in which mime and dance together relate an expressive, dramatic narrative. His pioneering efforts to develop a professional company with its own national character led him to support the artistic education of Danish children and fill all the important positions under his control with Danes. Fortunately for history, he made an exception to his own rule by engaging a single French dancer, Antoine Bournonville, whose son August, a native Dane, would later rule as ballet master of the Royal Theatre from 1830 to 1877.

Through his teaching, his choreography and his own example as a performer, August Bournonville shaped the company's artists and repertory so thoroughly that the effects of his work far outlasted his life. He created about 50 ballets, a handful of which are still performed today, and because he danced the leading parts himself, he composed male roles as interesting and challenging as their female counterparts.

Although Bournonville concocted his company's class spontaneously every day—he seldom taught the students—after his death in 1879 his successors organized his classroom exercises and variations from his ballets into the Bournonville Schools, a structured series of six lessons, one for each of the week's daily classes, that completely defined the dancers' training through the first half of the 20th century. Then gradually, as more varied choreography entered the repertory, the training became more varied too. Vera Volkova, an AngloRussian, arrived in Copenhagen in 1951, bringing with her a thorough knowledge of the syllabus formulated by the pedagogue Agrippina Vaganova, with whom she had studied in Leningrad. From Volkova, who taught the company for 24 years, and Edite Pfeifere Frandsen, a Latvian teacher who was invited into the theatre in 1961, the school absorbed a Russian approach to technique, and American and Canadian teachers later joined the faculty and broadened the training.

An active member of the extensive family that occupies the Royal Theatre today, the ballet school shares the building with the ballet, opera and theatre companies. Like them it is completely supported by the state, so the ballet students pay no fees for their dance training or their academic education. Out of roughly 300 children of different ages who now audition every April, 25 to 30 are accepted and assigned to ballet classes according to their age and their academic school schedule. Although the school does not house them, the children virtually live in the theatre; they attend ballet class every morning, then "reading school" and rehearsal, and finally, on many evenings, apply their own makeup and join the professionals onstage in opera or ballet performances, returning home only to sleep. The youngest pupils are seven years old, and if they finish the ten-year course they will have simultaneously completed their professional education and the same state education as every other child in Denmark.

Their stage training embraces ballet, modern, character, jazz and ballroom dance, mime, dance history, music, Pilates, makeup and language classes, and because the school is so small, only 63 students in 2001–02, the children study in enviably small groups. Except for the girls' special pointe classes, the boys' gymnastics and the oldest pupils, boys and girls study together and, regardless of their attitude or ability, can only be dismissed at the end of an academic year.

Until the 1960s, the school would accept only Danish citizens for training, and until quite recently all the pupils it did accept had no choice but to live in Copenhagen or move there if they wanted to enroll. In 1996, however, the Royal Danish Ballet school Holstebrø opened in Holstebrø, Jutland, about 185 miles from Copenhagen. This branch duplicates the parent school's program of professional and academic education and offers an additional preschool class that meets three times weekly. In 2001–02, this outpost comprised three teachers from the Copenhagen faculty and 28 students who, at the age of 14 or 15, just prior to their final year, could choose for themselves whether to finish their training in Holstebrø or at the parent school. In 2002, a second outpost opened in Odense, with an inaugural class of 19 students.

The proscenium arch at the Royal Theatre bears the admonition *Ei Blot Til Lyst* (Not for pleasure alone), a cautionary notice for the public that probably reduces the students to giggles. A friend's 11-year-old son, who began his training at the School of American Ballet in New York, entered the Royal Danish Ballet school in 2001 and within months was playing Fritz in *The Nutcracker* and appearing in *Napoli*, *Romeo and Juliet*, *The Whims of Cupid and the Ballet Master* and *The Red Balloon*. The dancers he could observe at all the dress rehearsals, even when he wasn't performing with them, were his colleagues and friends as well as his teachers and idols. Not for pleasure alone? What would you call it if you were 11 years old and wanted to dance?

ॐ

Anne Marie Vessel. b. Copenhagen, 1949. Entered Royal Danish Ballet school 1956, joined Royal Danish Ballet 1965, retired 1992. Director of Royal Danish Ballet school since 1988, with sole or shared responsibility for staging and reviving Bournonville ballets for Royal Danish Ballet and Royal Swedish Ballet.

IT WAS THE FORMER DIRECTOR, Kirsten Ralov, who asked me to teach first. She had a private ballet school outside of the theatre, with Fredbjørn Bjørnsson, before she became vice-ballet master. She said, "You have a good eye and you're interested in the steps, the syllabus," and then she asked me to teach there. I was only 22. That was actually the way I started, because she saw I had an eye for teaching and I was very interested, especially in the Bournonville, building up the steps. And then in '79 Henning Kronstam asked me to go to Canada. We had a very good relationship with the Canadian ballet because of Erik Bruhn. When Erik was in Stockholm and Henning Kronstam was director here, Henning Kronstam was suddenly a little confused which language should be here. Of course we have our Bournonville, but which other language should we take? It's always a problem in any company; you should have your own, but . . . To get the teachers along one line and not confuse the students and, later, the company, Henning phoned Erik and said, "What can we do to try to arrange things?" And Erik said, "Why don't you send the teachers on a course in Canada?" because he had a very good relation with Betty Oliphant [at the National Ballet School].

Because she had a bad back she was very interested in this . . . what do you call it? . . . the shin and how your legs are built. Here in the school we never really thought so much about that. Here we work on the natural movement, teaching from . . . I always say from foot to foot, eye to eye, and that's our old beautiful tradition that we all love. But of course you have also to learn how to teach and how you break steps down. So that was actually the beginning. All the teachers teaching the children went to Canada, and we had teachers from Canada coming here. Then—not so much now. Now Vivi [Flindt] has come back, she has never been in Canada, and Adam [Lüders] has never been in Canada.

We didn't take the style from Canada—we took the way they teach the teachers to teach. That doesn't mean we are not doing our own style—I just learned how to break steps down to correct them for a small student. Here I never was taught that, because it was more "Do what they do in front of you, watch Hans Brenaa," and that's also good, but that was what we learned in Canada. And also there we learned that you should have an assistant for a group of children when they're small—they're very small here, we take them from seven. You have a teacher and an assistant. I think it's worth having a lot of assistants, because that's their way also of learning how to teach. So you still have a line, instead of suddenly having new teachers who don't know what it's all about. I think that's very important.

I started in 1980, teaching here, and I actually started as an assistant to one of the teachers. But then I was teaching Bournonville, and my specialty was to teach all the Bournonville classes. Now I'm working out a little more of a syllabus, written down, for teaching small children Bournonville. I know the steps so well that I can teach them easily, but it's for others, you know, you have to go on with the tradition of having some teachers here that know Bournonville.

I feel, of course, that I am teaching the style, the phrasing of the music is very important for Bournonville—I mean, that's the whole thing—and the épaulement. And I teach what I learned from Hans Brenaa and Kirsten Ralov, they were my teachers for Bournonville. But of course today you analyze things a little more. I go into it more, down into the details, so it can be a tiny bit cleaner. When you teach children, you have to really tell them what all this is, what is a tendu actually doing. The only thing that's dangerous with that is that you can analyze so much that you cannot move. In Canada they couldn't believe how we could jump and fly around, and we would say, "Sometimes you analyze too much." The most important for me is that they move but they have to know the style, and I think that's what makes a good teacher. It's exactly explaining the style so they're not getting confused, but also don't forget to dance and move. But you have to get it into the right order, because if you just put steps as if the children were grown-up, professional dancers, they couldn't do it. You have to explain what it is, how to prepare, and then go for the dancing. I mean, a lot of teachers stand for one-and-a-half hours at the barre doing tendus.

I started with the small ones and I've been teaching all the groups here, the company, everything, during all these years, and you have of course a big difference with each age you are teaching, depending on how much Bournonville they've had. When Frank Andersen first became director [in 1985], there was a whole group who didn't have the tradition for Bournonville, and there was a big gap in the regular teaching for Bournonville. I had it when I was a child, because every morning we had Bournonville class with Hans Brenaa, born in the theatre. And that was good, because as we always said, "If you can dance Bournonville, you can do everything." And then when I was 13 I had Fru Edite Frandsen, the Russian technique, so I got to see the difference, and I had Vera Volkova, also Russian, and I could learn a lot from that. But if you teach the small ones, as I'm doing now, you have to tell them about the style in an easy way. Otherwise they will get so confused, because we have the Bournonville style and of course the Danish style, but that is a little mixed. It's a little Russian, English, Danish, a little of everything I would say, and that's from Vera Volkova.

Here in the school we have a lot of discussions, because otherwise we would be dying, about how to teach. We don't always mean the same thing, and I don't think any group of teachers will always agree with each other. I've been visiting a lot of schools and they all have a syllabus, and I'm trying to make a syllabus here, because Peter Schaufuss came back [to Copenhagen, as director of the Royal Danish Ballet, in 1994] and people were maybe a little confused about which line he wanted to follow. I mean, even we who have been here . . . Vivi is from the house, Johnny [Eliasen] is from the house, from the school—who else is teaching?—Adam, but they have been away, and sometimes you forget something. I have my opinion about Bournonville and I agree with most of the teachers teaching Bournonville. But I don't agree with what all the Danes are doing, because I feel they have been so influenced being away from the Danish tradition for so many years.

When I got to be director of the ballet school in 1988, I had a lot of wishes. The students could have a little more modern and they could have ballroom and they could have flamenco and character, and I put those subjects into courses. Every morning they have the ballet class and they are also going to grammar school. We must have a good grammar school, of course, because you will say good-bye to three-fourths of the children. It's the same in every ballet school— only one-fourth will do it as a dancer. That's the way it is, and we can only be happy that we have from them a very famous company in this little country. So we have to think about the ones we have to say good-bye to, but we also have to think about educating the dancers here—I mean, they also have to be educated if they're going to be dancers. That's important for me. So in the afternoon I put all those courses, we use the whole day. They have pointe every week or the boys have gymnastics. This year we have a little more choreography and a very good modern teacher. Then Saturday I mix the girls and the boys so they're all together and doing modern choreography. When Stephen [Pier] was here he did José Limón [technique] with the apprentices, and I think that's a good idea, because when suddenly one day they have to do José Limón or Paul Taylor or whatever, it's nice that they have a feeling of what it is.

Now we have a big repertory in Denmark. It's not only Bournonville, it's not only *Sleeping Beauty*, we have everything, and I think it's a gift. I mean, if you go to New York City, it's Balanchine mostly, Robbins and Arpino and that's it. You go to Germany, it's Neumeier, only Neumeier. Royal Ballet . . . I don't think they have such a big repertory as we have. Sometimes we have I think 15 different choreographers, and actually it's a gift for the dancers. I know it is, because I also had all these different styles, and it was lovely suddenly to do Alvin Ailey. I mean, I loved the Bournonville really in my heart, it's fantastic to do, but to do other things . . . I loved it. Of course we're a classical company and we have to be very aware about the Bournonville ballets because they are our treasure, it's where we are coming from. But we have to be open-minded to do some other things, and that's why I've been making a lot of courses. We're going to have an anatomy course and then we have Benesh notation . . . maybe we'll learn about film.

Of course they need to have technique, so you can use them in the company, and you have to teach them some rules, because small children want to have rules or they'll be so confused. I teach them self-discipline. They should have their own responsibility, and I think they have. They shouldn't be afraid of me or the theatre. That's not the way you educate people. They should have respect for the theatre, they should have respect for the art, for their friends, but they shouldn't be afraid to ask me or the director of the theatre about anything.

They start learning the repertory when they are apprentices, when they're 16. Then they also do pas de deux and special mime. Of course we do repertory sometimes in the lesson, and I've done a little mime from Bournonville sometimes on Saturday, for the small ones. But they have so much time onstage. That's the best education they can have, to be onstage in a lot of performances, and they're not only in ballet, they're also in opera and plays. So they see all the Bournonville mime and they're in the Bournonville ballets—*Napoli*, *Conservatoire*, *La Sylphide*—and that's their education, to do all of that. That's the whole tradition, to learn it that way. If they were not going onstage, we'd have to do a lot more lessons to teach that. And we make time for them also to go down and watch what is going on on the stage, to see all the dancers there during the day. It's a treasure, and I think they feel this too. I'm completely sure, because . . . Sometimes we have to say no, for example when they ask to have our children for an opera performance that goes very late. You know, it's a balance for us to say, "Now it's too much for our ballet children. You must find some from outside." One year the parents said, "They have too much to do," and that we must stop some of the performances, and then I had a big letter from all the children, "Please don't take us out of the performances." I thought it was very sweet. But of course it's our decision whether it's too much or not.

We have no guest teachers for the children, but the apprentices take company class, whoever the teacher is, whether the director chooses a guest teacher or is teaching himself. And Vivi and I have been teaching Bournonville, but it's a little bit difficult for some of them in the company to pick it up, and I think it's because some of them didn't have it when they were children. You know, we have these six daily classes [the Bournonville Schools] and then Vivi made the book of Bournonville *enchaînements,* and some of the steps are the same as in the six classes. If you go through all the week's schools, you have all the steps. Because I thought they needed a little more training, when I started as director of the school I planned that they would have all the schools in special Bournonville lessons—I had the Saturday morning and one after-noon—just like they had the technique in the Anglo . . . English . . . Volkova tradition, I will call it. Peter [Schaufuss] decided that this extra Bournonville should be in the morning on two days. And I said, "Well, that's OK, but it shouldn't be less teaching [of technique]. I mean, they only have one-and-one-half hours."

Now it's 40 years since I was a student here, and of course the students have changed a lot. They are much more open, they are not afraid to ask why are they doing this. We were afraid. We didn't ask about anything—"just do it." That was the old-fashioned way, and the parents weren't allowed to go in and see a class. Now we open the classes three times a year so they can see what we do with the children . . . you have to do it like that today. But also, some of the children seem much more motivated to dance. Yes, more, because in the old days, maybe some of it was the parents' ambitions. The worst thing is actually parents to be ambitious for a child who isn't really interested in doing ballet. Somehow I feel the children we get are here really because *they* want it—it's not because the parents want it. Fifteen years ago there were a lot of parents and it was *their* own ambition to be a dancer, and when they couldn't do it, then the child had to do it.

When we hold auditions I always ask the children, "Why are you here?" They've seen television, with a lot of ballet, and I do some matinées, where I tell about the school and show a little piece. Last year we actually had 200 students auditioning for the school— it was 100 more than we used to have—because we did a lot of PR, we put a lot of money into saying, "We're having an audition now." We even take children from other countries, but they must have somehow a relationship to Denmark. We had one Italian boy one year, we had a French boy—he's still here—and right now we have two from Iceland and a Russian boy. The only thing is, it's difficult for them in the grammar school. But we only have one classical company in Denmark, so this school is actually made to make dancers for the Royal Danish Ballet. When we cannot use them we have seen a lot of them go to other companies and do very well, and I think that must be a compliment to our school.

I would actually like to do a little more teachers courses. I planned that for many years and it could be interesting, but right now we are a little off it because three years ago we changed the pension age for the dancers so that now you have to stop when you are 40. I think this was the only place where you had to be a dancer until you are 48, a very, very high age. It was very hard to change that, but we are lucky now—you can give the older dancers a special contract as character artists, year by year. And I think that's the way to do it, because a bunch of old dancers, my age, were sitting on all the places [in the company] and we didn't have money to take all the young ones in too. So we changed. The pension age came down, and they have a very good policy that the ones who were around 40, 43—that's my age—got full salary for three years whether they were here in the theatre or not. So then they could get some education and find out about themselves, because they had their money for three years.

We had a lot of dancers who started teaching. I think they opened four dancing schools around Copenhagen, and four of them I have had as assistants in my school. They know already the life we are in, so I know they can teach it. You know, when you are in . . . I can call it an amateur dance school where the children are coming once a week, you have to teach in another way. I mean, they can't sit on the floor to do feet exercises for half an hour—then they would scream and run away. But if those teachers have some talented children they want to tell me, and they wouldn't spoil the children. I've seen many times that teachers who don't know are teaching ballet, and they spoil the children. Sometimes we have people audition here who say they have taken ballet classes, and we think, 'Oh, my God!' It would be much better, much better, if we could do some teachers courses. I've thought about that many times, and maybe we can do it. It's all to do with having the space here and the time to do it.

You know what we are going to do? We are going to open a school in Jutland for our children, a branch of this school, and I have been working since '88 to have a boarding school here. That was my whole heart, because I thought, 'We have a famous company, we have a ballet school, and there are a lot of students from Jutland and Fünen who will never come here if we don't have a boarding school.' I applied to the minister, and we actually got the money. And then we were discussing where we should place it and how it should be, and then we had a new [administrative] director who was not so much interested in making this boarding school.

Of course it's difficult, I agree. I go every once a month to do some courses or teaching in Jutland, and I found a little girl. She's so talented. She came here to the audition and we took her, but of course her parents said, "No, we can't allow it." I mean, they're living out there, five or six hours from here. But if we had a school with our teachers, maybe three or four places around Denmark, and teaching every day, not only once a week, then you could make some good dancers. That would be a beginning, to maybe open their eyes, and maybe they would be so talented and so motivated that the parents would say, "OK, now you can go." So if we can get a boarding school here, where we could take care of them, really they would have the last, very important education here. So I hope it will work. We only have to think about finding the right teachers.

If you have the right teachers or instructors, coaches, I think the style can remain. We have to be very keen on keeping our own style, our own tradition here, but we have to be very careful how we do it. We have a lot of dancers and teachers, going from this school out into the world, teaching Bournonville, but I feel if you have been too many years away from the teacher who has done it, from the work that's here, you forget. I see it often. We can always discuss what is the right style, but it's a delicate question. I think you have actually the same problem in Balanchine's company. All the old ballerinas are discussing, How was it? What did Mr. Balanchine say? Now they have this problem, but we have had it for many, many years, because Bournonville died in 1879. But what we did, we had these Bournonville courses a long time ago and we're going to do it again, hopefully, maybe in another form, to discuss the whole idea of building the style. "Where are the arms, the musicality?"—it's so, so important—and "It's not on 'And,' it's 'One and . . .'" If you forget about that and do it in another way, or the head direction in another way . . . Keep the style clean. Every style should be clean, Balanchine, Bournonville, even Cecchetti. Try to keep them.

That's my heart's love that we're talking about, and the teachers here have it too. Vivi and Adam are children from the house, and then I have Petrusjka Broholm, she started teaching last year. I think we have so many good dancers here who can be good teachers and know the whole Bournonville tradition. I wouldn't say I wouldn't take one teacher from outside for the children, but mostly I would prefer that they are from here. If the company has a guest teacher, our apprentices will take that class, and then they have me for Bournonville and Palle Jacobsen doing pas de deux—he is also a child from the house. They will get what else they need when they are in the performances. When we did *Sleeping Beauty* with Helgi Tomasson—it was Petipa, more or less—the kids were in that, and they learned on the stage to do whatever he wanted.

When have you seen the company the last time? Don't you think we have a lot of good artists? But that's the Bournonville mime tradition, I think. We educate artists. It's difficult for me to say, but when you see the [British] Royal Ballet, also when I saw it when I was a little child, I could already see it was another style. For me, it wasn't the big, mime, artistic thing, but we have a very big tradition here for mime, so we are acting as much as we are dancing, and that's what gives a good performance. We're not only doing steps. I feel myself that maybe when I was younger we had some more personalities, but I'm not saying we were better dancers.

The funny thing . . . When I was watching the Peter Martins' ballets, actually they made a bigger, better performance than what I sometimes see in New York [City Ballet], because I think our dancers are much more interesting to watch. I shouldn't say that, and maybe that's my own taste, a Danish taste somehow, but I think they did a beautiful, interesting evening. Maybe they are better dancers, some of them, and more into Peter Martins' ballets today. But think, in the last years we had the Bournonville festival. Then we had the Balanchine festival, and then we had a lot of whole-evening ballets. We had Peter's [Schaufuss] *Sylphide*, we had his *Giselle*, where the dancers were standing in the back. Now, in Peter Martins, they move, and you can see they really were going for it. And that's what I mean—they did it in their own, Danish, personal way, and I think that's still the tradition at work. You know Peter Martins' choreography . . . it's dances for the steps and for the music, like Balanchine said, it's not to make a history. But I think our dancers somehow make a history, and that's what *I* like. It was interesting to me to watch them making their own history even if it was not a drama ballet.

But I don't think you ever could learn the talent of being a dancer, never. You either have the talent or you will never have it. It should be inside you. That's it, so small. Then as a teacher you have to make it grow, press on the right button at the right moment. Of course you could be a good dancer if you don't have a talent. We have many good dancers who are not big artists. They learned how to do this. Maybe they are fabulous technicians, technically they can do everything. But it's very, very seldom you really see one who has everything. Even the big dancers—there was something they didn't have but they were very good at hiding it, intelligent. But if you don't have *the* thing inside you, it will never enter there.

I teach now because I love it. That's my whole life. This is my home, and I still feel that I could do a lot here and I still have so much to give. When I started teaching, I became a much better dancer myself, and its companion is to give away. Today I really think it's the most beautiful thing to do, to give away and teach and think about all the children. Of course for me it's very important that they learn the right way to do the thing. But if I'm not here, somebody else maybe could do it, and I think it's very important, with a special school, that we stay, the people who really love it.

In the Interim

FOR THEIR 1987 MOVIE *Raising Arizona*, the Coen brothers auditioned 300 babies. They made it clear from the start that they didn't want a child who could walk—they needed a crawler, so walking automatically lost you the job—which prompted one mother to put her baby's shoes on backward to guarantee he got his fair share of attention.

By the time dancers are ready to leave school and start to dance for a living, they're old enough to put on their own shoes and it's too late for their parents to give them any help. But some companies ease their passage to the new world by allowing certain students to keep one foot in each camp, at least for a while, or by accepting them into the profession on probation. Selected by the New York City Ballet director while they are still officially SAB students, New York City Ballet apprentices work with the company for no more than a year, performing in a maximum of eight ballets as often as those ballets are danced. Provided they perform at least five times per week, they earn the same wage as the corps de ballet dancers or collect a pro-rata share of that wage depending on the number of performances they actually dance. Although the company has first call on their time, for class, rehearsals and performances, the apprentices must still attend their SAB classes whenever possible and continue their academic education. If the company does not offer them a contract, they can complete their training at the school but must look elsewhere for a job, as do the other advanced students who have not served as apprentices. Once the apprentices join the company, only their skill and talent can insure their security. "I don't hold auditions for the company," Balanchine said matter-of-factly. "Only for the school."

Of the handful of students who graduate from the Royal Danish Ballet school, a few are invited to become ballet *aspirants*, apprentices. As *aspirants*, usually for two years, they are required to attend company class, which is voluntary for the company, and to study pas de deux and repertory for the first time. When their apprenticeship ends, the company may extend the trial period by offering them a yearly contract that is renewable three times, after which the dancers may finally secure a life contract that assures their employment for the next 20 years and awards them a state pension on retirement. They are free to retire at 40, but the law permits them to remain with the company as guest artists until they are 67, and it is not uncommon for a "child from the house" to end a performing career of 60 years on the stage where it began.

The students who survive the annual examinations at the Paris Opéra Ballet school graduate at 16 or 17 and, if there is room in the company, proceed straight to the Paris Opéra Ballet, initially as *stagiaires* or apprentices. Following a few months of scrutiny, they may be signed to a full contract as *quadrilles*, the rank roughly equivalent to the corps de ballet, from which they begin the daunting process of promotion all over again by means of a revered competition called the *concours*. It works like this: The dancers who want to advance to the next rank—from *quadrille* up to *coryphée*, *sujet* and *premier danseur*—appear at the annual *concours* having prepared an assigned solo selected for their current rank and a solo of their own choice. Wearing identical practice clothes for the obligatory solo and appropriate costumes for their chosen piece, they dance on a bare stage to piano accompaniment before the impassive jury and an invited audience, all of whom are forbidden to applaud. After an entire day of solo presentations—first the *quadrilles* compete, then the *coryphées* and so on—the jury grades each dancer numerically so that when an artist at the next level leaves or retires, the position can be offered to the highest-ranked competitor from the level below.

In Britain, young dancers have no choice but to fend for themselves when their training is over. No time-honored tradition escorts even the best of them from their final school performance to the back row of a professional ensemble, and no provision exists for a single day of their future in their country's companies. So as soon as their formal studies end, they're back where they started, better equipped than before but still forced to throw themselves repeatedly into the unknown on the off chance that someone will want exactly what they have to offer. Yet they're not that much worse off than the lucky apprentices in Paris or Copenhagen who apparently have a head start, because everyone's in the same bind when they finally land a job. Whether they've just hopped off the bus from Delhi or emptied their locker at a prestigious training academy, the young dancers who manage to secure a professional contract plunge proudly into their glistening new life and sink like stones.

Overnight, the stars of the annual performance, heroes to the younger classes and darlings of the weary faculty become the company's foot soldiers, useful bodies whose immediate purpose is simply to make the numbers come out even. Insignificant unless they make a mistake, they disappear into a routine even more dispiriting than their first days at a new school, because the company that supposedly wants them can scarcely afford to pay attention to them at all, not as individuals anyway. Their genial colleagues welcome them with a warm smile and then go back to work, leaving them dangling in their own minds somewhere between indispensable and superfluous. And although the schedule pushes them implacably from class to rehearsal to performance to class again, no one in a big company can spend a lot of time with them, because, let's face it, there are more important things to do.

So the newcomers crank up their concentration and learn faster than they ever have before, stuffing their muscles with steps and their head with musical cues, trying to keep up and fit in and stay out of the way without completely dropping out of sight. "You just want to get through class in one piece and hopefully show them that you deserve to be there," one young corps de ballet dancer explained. "You don't want anyone to be watching the other girls, even if they are, like, all of your friends." As they teeter between audacity and caution, first pushing themselves forward, then holding themselves back, it doesn't take long for two unsettling facts to slice through the tangle of detail like daggers, not the old enthusiastic suggestions that encouraged them to try their luck away from home in the first place but sharper ideas that cut the wrapping off the prize they've finally won.

One says, Never forget you are expendable. Plenty of dancers can balance longer and jump higher, and any one of them could turn up tomorrow. They could be here already, standing right beside you. You think you're all set? Don't kid yourself.

The other says, One person controls your future. One. The director is the boss. The director is God, and God sees everything. So it's up to you.

It's not as if these ideas arrive out of the blue, because one way and another their teachers have been bombarding them for years with demands that add up to the same thing. On a daily basis, "It's up to you" sounds more like "Listen to me. You're not listening. Well, then show me. No, not like that. That's not what I asked for. Listen to the music. No, look at him. Do it again." But the impatient comments don't mean much until you've actually got a job to protect and a real live director judging every move you make, any more than drowning means much when you're splashing around in knee-deep water, and teachers know that perfectly well because hypothetical undertow never scared them either. So they do their best to fortify their students against the dangers the students can't yet recognize, and they repeat, over and over again, that in the end every dancer must believe in himself, rely on himself and accept the responsibility for his own progress. If they are completely honest, they find a way to give their pupils the same warning Thomas Beecham gave his orchestra the day he began a rehearsal by saying, "You may find it a matter of some difficulty to keep your places. I think you might do well to imagine yourselves disporting in some hair-raising form of locomotion . . . My advice to you is merely, Hold tight, and do not let yourselves fall off. I cannot guarantee to help you on again."

On the Job

REMEMBER THE STORY of the three blind men trying to draw an elephant? One of them strokes its hide and says, "An elephant is a worn, wrinkled bag made of heavy canvas." The second man grabs its tail and says, "An elephant is a vine like a rope with a stiff tassel at the end." The third guy feels its trunk and says, "An elephant is a giant snake, much bigger than a python, with a thick, rough skin."

Each of them is telling the truth as he perceives it, yet none of their definitions is correct, which is how dance companies resemble elephants. Well, think about it. Would you say a company is a bunch of artists with a single purpose? No? A gang of dancers performing the work of a single choreographer? United by a single style? Any way you slice it you come up short—no single definition quite captures the entire beast. Not that you need definitions to enjoy a performance, but dancers don't develop in a vacuum any more than children do, and artistry isn't a cold they can catch in the street. They need something a lot bigger and stronger than they are individually to support their effort, frame their talent, sustain their initiative and cut a clearing in the jungle of everyday events so that they and their public can find each other. OK, maybe that something is not an elephant, but it needs an elephant's memory, thick skin, patience and stamina. Hundreds of people depend on it for their professional survival, thousands of people turn to it for entertainment or enlightenment, and its nature defines the experience they can only complete together.

When I started collecting material for this book, I made a file called Companies that ended up stuffed with notes and articles about stars, opening nights and business administration. There's remarkably little in it about creativity or abstract ideals, which is not at all what I expected, but I suppose it makes sense. If a journalist can hang a story on a new production, you'll read about its size, overall cost, and the buzz in the rehearsal studio. Accidents and disasters appear on slow news days—"Baked potato explodes backstage" is worth a line or two, and "Black Swan Vanishes in Blackout" might generate a few paragraphs—and cool soloists on hot motorcycles will always sell more papers than incisive comments about art and inspiration.

The Companies file is also bulging with clippings and comments about money, which makes sense too, because nothing affects a company's fate quite as much. One article mentions that the Joffrey Ballet cut its budget from $9 million to $5 million and lost 25 percent of its dancers when it moved from New York to Chicago in 1995. Another describes San Francisco's Hotel Tax Fund, which, for a given period in 1999, supported 724,000 members of the local arts community at a per capita rate 41 times larger than the National Endowment for the Arts' spending in the same period. In 1998, Kevin McKenzie, the director of American Ballet Theatre (ABT), laid his company's needs on the line by acknowledging that "new [board] members are expected to give a minimum of $50,000." Two years later, the Houston Ballet raised $1.7 million at its Nutcracker Market in the Astrodome; when that annual event was first organized several years earlier, it was held in a church hall and brought the company a paltry $11,000.

The most succinct reports of a company's birth, growth or demise boil its history down to cold, clear figures. New York City Ballet released statistics during its 50th anniversary celebrations in 1998 documenting its employment of 589 dancers to date and its production of 386 ballets, including 112 that Balanchine had created for the company. In the anniversary year, it was spending more than $500,000 on pointe shoes and paying 90 performers; 74 of them had to be onstage at once for *Union Jack*, and 84 roles needed filling in *The Sleeping Beauty*.

Computers now crunch the numbers that used to tax the patience of accountants, tallying box-office receipts and comparing attendance figures as if those laborious tasks were child's play, so the figures attached to dance activity come at you in a hail of decimal points and bar charts. But the money is only one way to sketch the elephant, and following the money only leads farther and farther from the animal I'm trying to define. Still, it's tempting to think about companies in terms of finance, because figures are comparatively polite. Budgets and balance sheets tend to lie neatly on the page without wriggling away, unlike, say, a company's artistic identity, which is almost impossible to define . . . now. It used to be easier.

The companies I saw first and came to know best when I was learning about dance emerged straight from their founders' imagination, and most of those founders were choreographers. Through the 1950s and '60s, Martha Graham, José Limón, Merce Cunningham, Paul Taylor, Alwin Nikolais and Alvin Ailey charged into the vanguard of modern dance, each of them trailing a company that danced their work and nothing else. After them came Twyla Tharp, Lucinda Childs, Murray Louis, Pearl Lang, David Gordon, Meredith Monk and Trisha Brown, whose respective troupes served their founders just as faithfully.

New York City Ballet was Balanchine's playground and cathedral, expressly created to fulfill his choreographic needs, and both American Ballet Theatre and the Joffrey Ballet made their name as repertory companies, exactly as their founders intended. In the initial season alone, ABT's repertory included Fokine's *Carnaval* and *Les Sylphides*, Agnes de Mille's *Black Ritual*, Anton Dolin's abbreviated *Swan Lake* and Antony Tudor's *Dark Elegies*. Lucia Chase and Richard Pleasant had made up their minds to display American dancers in an international repertory, an ordinary inclination now but a bold ambition during an era when, as Lincoln Kirstein pointed out, most of the American dance audience considered "Russianballet" a single word.

The company Robert Joffrey launched in 1956 consisted in its entirety of six performers and four pieces by its founder. As it grew, it also collected classical, neoclassical and demi-caractère ballets, yet never for a single moment could you confuse it with ABT, despite Joffrey's passion for reviving the historic repertory of the past. In 1967 his company made the cover of *Time* magazine with *Astarte*, his hip, multimedia creation that brought strobe lights, body paint and film projections to ballet for the first time and drove it straight into the arms of the Swinging Sixties. His dancers were young, brash and about as natural and un-stagey as ballet artists could be; by comparison, ABT's performers seemed wholly mature, artful in their theatricality and deeply imbued with tradition.

During the 1960s and '70s, you went to ABT for the distinctive artists—Erik Bruhn, Carla Fracci, Royes Fernandez, Lupe Serrano, Sally Wilson, Ivan Nagy, Cynthia Gregory—an international galaxy of stars who populated the theatre with three-dimensional characters and colored every role with personality. You went to Joffrey for the choreographic smorgasbord, to feast on exotic delicacies like Kurt Jooss' *The Green Table*, Leonide Massine's *Le Beau Danube*, Jerome Robbins' *New York Export: Opus Jazz*, Tharp's *As Time Goes By*, and Flemming Flindt's *The Lesson*, many of which you couldn't see anywhere else in the world. Don't worry if these titles don't instantly bring music and movement to your mind. It's probably a function of your age, or I should say of your youth, because it's even harder to locate them on a stage today than it was 30 years ago.

Sometimes the world came to New York, usually traveling from abroad under the banner of Sol Hurok, an impresario so captivated by ballet that he occasionally rouged his cheeks and ambled onstage in *Petrouchka*, leading the lumbering bear. But you always knew where you stood with the foreign companies. The Royal Ballet brought us home-grown treasures by Frederick Ashton and Kenneth MacMillan, plus what were then, for America, the definitive productions of *The Sleeping Beauty* and *Swan Lake*. After its first appearance in 1959 at the old Metropolitan Opera House, the Bolshoi regularly treated us to outsized emotions and bravura technique in *Giselle* and *Don Quixote*, Leonid Lavrovsky's *Romeo and Juliet* and Yuri Grigorovich's *Spartacus*. These days it's hard to imagine that *Giselle* has not always surfaced periodically in every city that can field a ballet company, but I had never seen it, or any of those works, before the Bolshoi introduced them to me, and I had also never seen dancing of such physical power and dramatic intensity.

On the few occasions when the Royal Danish Ballet crossed the ocean, it naturally made the most of its Bournonville repertory, which then, as now, lived almost exclusively in Denmark, and although the company performed several modern creations, we thought of it as perpetually buoyant and essentially charming, just like the characters in Bournonville's magical romances. After its triumphant opening engagement at the Met in 1969, the Stuttgart Ballet returned frequently to show off the literary narratives of its director, John Cranko, and both Roland Petit's Ballet de Marseille and Maurice Béjart's Ballet of the 20th Century splashed us with provocative theatricality and chic flamboyance. The Paris Opéra

Ballet was languishing in temporary obscurity at that time—I first saw it in London in 1982—and although the Kirov Ballet reached New York in 1961, I don't remember laying eyes on it until the 1970 London season, when the 22-year-old Mikhail Baryshnikov consistently stole the show and a young ballerina, Natalia Makarova, closed the tour with a bang by defecting.

So the question of identity never arose in my mind as long as every company seemed to occupy its own distinct territory. The troupes that performed only one choreographer's works maintained nearly exclusive access to them, whether intentionally or by default I had no way of knowing. For example, aside from a few scattered stagings, during the 1960s and '70s no one danced the Cunningham repertory but the Cunningham company, so if you wanted to see those dances, that's where you went. Except for the occasional commission, Twyla Tharp choreographed solely for her own dancers, as did Taylor, Ailey and Graham. The ballet choreographers kept their work close to home as well, and only a tiny portion of their catalogue ever turned up anywhere else.

We could also recognize each company by the signature style it wore onstage no matter whose work it was dancing. Every other winter, after the Royal Ballet announced the details of its spring tour, a line would form in the tunnel beneath Lincoln Center at 3 A.M. on the day the box office opened. Armed for the nine-hour siege with coffee and the Sunday *Times*, we would put our heads together over the casting—someone always had a friend in London who had a friend at Covent Garden who fed us that vital information before we parted with a penny—and pass the night debating the relative merits of the performers. Many of those devotees saved for months in order to be profligate that morning, and like all cognoscenti they could cite chapter and verse to defend their favorites against equally experienced opposition. But the amicable bickering didn't alter our overall appreciation of the company as a particular compound of elegance, lyricism, lightness and fluidity. We thought of English dancers as poised, refined and equally capable of comic wit and dramatic depth. Any viewer coming to them fresh, whether from New Jersey or the far side of the universe, would quickly discover these qualities by watching them dance, and the artists who hadn't been raised in that company grew into its style by performing its repertory.

In the same way, whether or not they'd trained at his School of American Ballet, everyone who danced for Balanchine acquired speed, precision and articulate phrasing, because that's what he wanted to see. Both curbed and propelled by the musical dynamics, the performers often seasoned their delivery with contradiction, darting through a boisterous reel like a dragonfly or rumpling a sleek classical variation with a jaunty swagger. At New York City Ballet, choreography and music ran over the dancers like water, smoothing and polishing them until they glowed within the movement like the beating heart that made it move.

At ABT, it was the other way around: the dancers rode each piece like surfers, adjusting their skill and shape to balance triumphantly atop the choreography, secure in the knowledge that it would reward the risks they took by supporting their individuality. They were a different breed entirely from the City Ballet dancers, because their repertory required it. The men in Balanchine's *Western Symphony* are fantasies, American cowboys filtered through Hollywood and Broadway and then remodeled by a Russian, and the frilly women they partner embody nothing more substantial than their silken desires. But at ABT, the men in Eugene Loring's *Billy the Kid* are villains and killers, with long pasts and short futures, and the cowhands in *Rodeo* are hunting for sturdy women and stable marriages, not dance-hall flirtations. So instead of a recognizable house style, what unified ABT's dancers was the range of their authority. Trained for the classics, they were prepared for anything, and they inhabited the repertory like chameleons, reveling in their ability to adapt.

But you could never completely define a company in terms of its style and today it would be lunacy to try, mainly because no one can put his hand on his heart and tell you what constitutes *that* elephant either. In the last decade or so, style has turned into an incredibly loaded subject, a minefield of relative erudition and absolute professional pride. Hanging their reputations from its fraying form and snarled history, academics and in-house experts argue about exact steps and their precise shape, about the dancers' attack, about linguistics, about music, about fractional pauses and minuscule discrepancies of execution. Everyone has an ax to grind, and without an acknowledged authority as the point of universal reference, the axes have gradually become sharp enough to split hairs.

After three years as director of the Royal Danish Ballet, Maina Gielgud concluded that "one of the problems . . . in propagating the Bournonville inheritance was that all the people who are trying to transmit it are desperately trying to prove that what they're saying about it is right. Before, the debate in itself was almost fueling the activity, and it wasn't that somebody had to be right or wrong. But now, you would get two or even three of the Bournonville experts coming onstage and telling someone who was playing Gurn [in *La Sylphide*] that this mime was not right and that they should be doing it this way rather than that way . . . And then another person says, 'No, no, that's not right,' and two minutes before going onstage this poor dancer is like, 'And what am I supposed to do now?'"

For their part, the companies would probably prefer to conduct this family argument in private. You can't afford to squabble publicly when your box office is full of tickets and your city is full of competing attractions, so ideally you keep the debate to yourself and resolve it as best you can behind closed doors. The viewers don't really care about stylistic niceties anyway. They choose a program, come to the theatre and expect to have an enjoyable evening, and believe me, they don't give a damn whether Aurora's arabesque points straight up or into the wings.

Nobody else used to worry much about style either, certainly not out loud where strangers could listen in, not only because fewer people were dealing with dance as an academic discipline but also because for many happy years we felt close enough to the choreographer's intention to believe we were getting the real thing. When Ashton was rehearsing his own ballets, absolutely nothing stood between his creation and your perception of it but the capabilities of the interpreters he had just prepared himself. As long as the choreographers were in charge of their own output, style didn't present a problem, and after Fokine's death and Jooss' and Massine's and Bronislava Nijinska's, even Bournonville's, a clear line of descent and dedication enabled us to see what they wanted us to see.

Or so we thought, sitting out front. Anyone who was there, out front, during those singular decades worried only about finding the time, money and stamina to check out all the available dancing. We didn't try to define one company's style or another company's nature because we didn't need to. The elephant was standing right there before us, and every time the curtain went up we could see it with our own eyes. What we couldn't see was the machinery that made each company tick, and since for many of those years it gave us no cause for concern we simply didn't think about it.

While time and distance always lend enchantment to memory, just about everyone agrees that dance in America boomed in certain ways from the early '60s until sometime in the mid-'80s. Companies grew larger, busier and more numerous; between 1965 and 1994, the number of professional dance troupes increased from 37 to 400. In 1963 the Ford Foundation announced a ten-year plan that allocated more than $7.76 million in nine portions: to New York City Ballet and its School of American Ballet; to regional ballet companies in San Francisco, Washington, D.C., Philadelphia, Salt Lake City, Houston and Boston; and to nationwide support of local dance instruction. Created two years later, the National Endowment for the Arts quickly kicked in with federal funding, and by 1976–77 more than half of its $3.6 million dance budget was specifically tagged for touring. As a result, and thanks also to massive state and local assistance, 92 American companies took to the road that season and gave a total of 432 weeks of performances in 56 states and territories.

The audience was obviously growing too, but the taste we were developing in New York for choreographic daring did not travel as easily as dance itself. Because the wider public was generally less exposed to innovation than the big-city audience, it was naturally inclined to be more cautious, so while more and more people attended dance performances, most of them wouldn't venture very far into the unknown. By 1992, you could see ten versions of *The Nutcracker* within 80 miles of San Diego or select one from 230 productions across the country; out of 281 ballet companies operating in the States by then, only a handful were trying to survive without it.

In New York, however, many of the century's pivotal choreographers were still active in the '70s, if not actually creating new pieces then overseeing the staging of their old ones, and every branch of the art was flourishing simultaneously. I remember a group called the Lockers, sassy dancers from Los Angeles whose limbs rippled like eels—that was my first electrifying encounter with break dancing in 1975. I also remember the tap dancers Raymond Kaalund, Isaiah "Lon" Chaney and Chuck Green, headliners from the golden days of the Savoy Ballroom and the Apollo Theatre in Harlem, showing off their slickest tricks in friendly theatrical competitions, and young enthusiasts like Jane Goldberg and Brenda Bufalino harvesting their steps and memories against the day when they'd hang up their tap shoes for the last time. Of course, it was all a glorious accident, a historical fluke. All those artists simply happened into the right place at the right time, and so did we. If you were lucky enough to be caught up in that whirlwind of creativity, it was easy to ignore the possibility that it would ever end. When I arrived in London in 1981, I found three companies that roughly paralleled the three I knew at home. The Royal Ballet revolved around Ashton and MacMillan as New York City Ballet revolved around Balanchine and Robbins, proudly displaying its hoard of familiar gems while mining their still fertile imaginations for fresh treasure. A youthful, lively troupe that married respect for ballet's history with avid curiosity about its future, Sadler's Wells Royal Ballet, now Birmingham Royal Ballet, could have been the Joffrey's twin, and London Festival Ballet, now called English National Ballet, looked to me like a slightly more staid version of American Ballet Theatre. Founded in 1950 by Alicia Markova and Anton Dolin to carry popular ballet at affordable prices far and wide, during the '81–'82 season Festival Ballet staged *Romeo and Juliet*, *Swan Lake*, *La Sylphide*, Ronald Hynd's *Rosalinda* and *The Nutcracker*.

Modern dance was another matter entirely. Coming from a city where experimental events had spread to rooftops, parks and churches, I was astonished to discover that modern dance had barely scratched the surface of public awareness in Britain; except for the critics, none of the people I met at the ballet ever went to see it. The only established contemporary companies in London were the Rambert Dance Company, which had been founded as a ballet troupe but had changed its spots in 1966, and the London Contemporary Dance Theatre, which also ran a school in a small theatre, well off the beaten track, called the Place. In 1978, Val Bourne had launched the Dance Umbrella festival to showcase modern choreography and provide a sturdy platform for young British dancemakers like Richard Alston and Ian Spink. Her perseverance kept the enterprise alive through its shaky early years, and by 1981 she had offered Britain its first glimpse of American innovators like Douglas Dunn, Remy Charlip, Simone Forti, Steve Paxton, Bill T. Jones and Arnie Zane, and Karole Armitage. "I suppose we had been rather isolated, too insular, even in-bred," she conceded on Umbrella's 20th anniversary. "We didn't know [in 1978] that this sort of work was going on across the Pond." The funding agencies didn't know about it either, nor were they particularly interested in the talent emerging at home. "The powers that be had decided to fund us," Bourne continued, "but not because they believed in us. Oh, no. They took the view that if they gave us enough rope we would hang ourselves."

She was laughing as she spoke, and with good reason, because just as she started poking holes in Britain's parochial dance scene, stabbing intently at it from the inside, visitors from abroad decisively smashed the nation's artistic complacency. During the 1980s Sadler's Wells Theatre alone presented Pina Bausch, Erick Hawkins, Sankai Juku, Pilobolus, La La La Human Steps and Paul Taylor. The Arts Council funding for Dance Umbrella, to take a handy example, increased from £4,265 [$7,818] for the inaugural season of 38 performances to £64,750 [$115,579] for the six-week season ten years later.

It looked like a win-win situation everywhere, especially with figures like those reflecting more ambitious schedules and fatter budgets. In 1990, Americans forked out around $4.31 billion to attend live, nonprofit performing arts events, which sounds spectacular until I tell you that in the same year they spent more than twice that amount on potted plants, seeds and flowers. If we believed the good times were here to stay, perhaps we simply lacked the incentive to put the numbers—$4.31 billion!!—into some reasonable perspective. Or maybe we were standing too close to the big picture to see it clearly. Unwilling or unable to back away and focus on the splendor from an objective distance, we missed the fact that the dance scene was changing even as we watched it, and by the time we noticed, the boom was over.

Today, standing closer to bust than to that legendary boom, we're still trying to comprehend and assimilate the fallout of all that success. If you follow the money, which is unavoidable, you find a new pattern emerging, which nobody foresaw. When the government funding agencies in America and Britain began tightening the purse strings and urging the ensembles they had supported to stand on their own feet, the companies were forced to enlist private and corporate sponsors to help them remain upright. Because the sponsors naturally expected to see some return on their investment, programming gradually shifted to attract the public with the deepest possible pockets. So during the 1980s, as the world economy soared to unimagined heights and corporate entertaining grew increasingly lavish, the audience changed and dance became fashionable. After all, if Jacqueline Kennedy Onassis and Diana, Princess of Wales, could be seen at the ballet, so could anyone who longed to drop their names. At Covent Garden, the business executives squiring their international counterparts around town sank into their seats with easy minds, knowing that the performance would conveniently sidestep every language barrier.

These were not the old, loyal viewers, who came to dance year after year because they loved it, but a new crowd that wouldn't come back, and might not come at all, if choosing that diversion saddled it with a chore. Having extricated themselves from the office, the kids and rush hour, most people wanted to switch off their brains and their cellphones in the evening and relax. If they didn't like the look of your program, they could always spend their leisure time and disposable income on some competing attraction or, for a fraction of the cost, kick their shoes off at home and shove a movie into the video machine. The new audience would not sit still for electronic music or rigorous abstraction, but you could often lure it to the theatre with a dramatic narrative, the sexier the better, or with a short modern work decorated with nudity or film or outlandish costumes by some recognizable name. So Issey Miyake, Gianni Versace, Jasper Conran and Christian Lacroix were invited to embellish new dance works with their designs, and anyone who paid top dollar to attend the premiere and the party that followed it could rub shoulders with those celebrities too.

With their opulent decor and lilting tunes, fairy tales like *The Sleeping Beauty* and tempestuous romances like *Manon* and *Onegin* fared best of all with tired businessmen. Houston Ballet's director Ben Stevenson ruefully declared, "If Fanny Brice choreographed *Cinderella*, people would come to see it because it was *Cinderella*," and Balanchine once remarked, "We should call all ballets *Swan Lake*. People will come." Without commenting on the evident irony, even his New York City Ballet finally gave in and opened the spring season of its 50th anniversary year with its first complete staging of that ballet. A year later American Ballet Theatre mounted a new production as the highlight of its 60th anniversary schedule, and artistic director Kevin McKenzie didn't hesitate to say why: "To be crass about it, if you don't speak in artistic terms, it's one of the very few ballets that sells at the box office."

By then, creeping recession had gripped the funding agencies, and both corporate sponsors and private donors were funneling their donations into social problems rather than artistic ones. According to Dance/USA, a nationwide service organization, 60 percent of the companies it surveyed reported a profit at the end of 1990; a year later, only 40 percent could make the same boast. While the business managers gobbled aspirin for their headaches and repeated John Maynard Keynes' warning that "markets can remain irrational longer than you can remain solvent," the ballet companies kept battling the odds, ducking and diving to pay for this year's blockbuster while laying plans to top it the following year with some event even more dazzling that would satisfy the dancers, the public, the critics and the accountants all at once. The modern choreographers were suffering too, trying to scale the same obstacles with even fewer resources. In 2000, Elizabeth Streb described her situation with painful clarity: "Ten years ago I thought of myself as someone who had a dance company. Today I think of myself as someone who creates wild actions and movement moments in a show that I sell."

In itself, the tireless search for a winner represented business as usual, since even the dance companies that draw their entire budget from government coffers have to balance their books. But now it wasn't enough to find a winner; the winning attraction also had to be sold to the public and sold hard, and the pressure increased in direct proportion to the art's overall success. As more and more regional companies put down roots and dance became a staple of the cultural diet, it lost some of its fascination and excitement—the girl next door can never be as alluring as a glamourous guest—and each troupe had to work that much harder to grab and hold its audience. The viewers had their problems too, because their money didn't stretch quite as far as it used to. Back in 1980, a $100 ticket to New York City Ballet's spring gala bought you a seat, a souvenir booklet and an invitation to the pre-performance buffet. By 2001, you needed ten times that amount just to walk through the door for the same festive occasion at American Ballet Theatre.

In England, the three leading ballet companies gave 293 London performances during the 1973–74 season, which turned out to be the high for the next 20 years; by 1993–94, the total had fallen to 189. To spread the artistic wealth around the country, the government agencies required ballet and modern dance troupes to tour domestically if they wanted to qualify for certain funding. Although touring started to drop off in America, hobbled by the demise in 1983 of the National Endowment for the Arts' Dance Touring program, in Britain the companies traipsed diligently from city to town, all but stepping on each other's heels—England alone is roughly the size of New York state—and fabricating every ploy they could imagine to fill the houses. Not a single work, old or new, could pay its own way. When David Bintley transferred his *Edward II* from Stuttgart to Birmingham Royal Ballet in 1997, the press officer reported using "S&M flyers in gay clubs" to drum up business. Far from its Halifax base, Northern Ballet Theatre promoted its *Dracula* in London by winding a chain of garlic through the local streets and straight to the box office, and the effort paid off handsomely—40 percent of the *Dracula* audience at Sadler's Wells was attending a ballet performance for the first time.

Even *Nutcracker* came in for the hard sell, largely because so many producers had their eye on the same slice of the public's income. In 1998, for the first time, New York City Ballet ran local television ads for its celebrated staging and boosted the box office significantly. At the same time, Pittsburgh Ballet Theatre was bidding for an audience that could easily have gone down the street instead to catch *Anastasia on Ice* or the national touring company of *Sunset Boulevard*. *Riverdance* was coming to town after Christmas, and so was *Footloose*, whose marketing budget for the Pittsburgh dates was roughly twice the size of the ballet company's for its *Nutcracker* season.

But you couldn't run a company year after year on one or two works, not even on *Nutcracker* and *Cinderella*, and "the people who think we should have preservation," Robbins pointed out in 1984, "will find that you don't have an audience unless you have what Mr. Hurok called novelties." While the companies and the audience were young and growing up together, every work was new to almost everybody. During its first seasons at the New York City Center in 1948, New York City Ballet's repertory was so small that balancing an evening posed more of a problem than finding novelties to fill it. "We had certain guidelines," company manager Betty Cage remembered. "Since we had very little scenery, we'd try to have at least one ballet that had something on the stage. We tried to have one ballet that had real costumes and not leotards. We'd try not to have more than one ballet with string music or a piano solo and at least one ballet with a full cast, instead of a pas de deux. There had to be one ballet to blast the audience with the full company, which was only 50 dancers."

Fifty years later, balance was the least of the companies' worries, since by then the public was treating older works like refried beans, rejecting them impatiently as it waited for spicier fare. So the active list of revivals dwindled, and the short vivid pieces that had hooked the 20th-century audience on theatrical dance in the first place began dropping from sight. Between the flocks of swans and the birthdays of princesses, the choreographic landscape bristled with harsh, deconstructed movement and edgy emotion that caught the dangerous atmosphere of aggressive times. For novelty, ballet companies borrowed the talent or output of contemporary choreographers who often welcomed the fresh crop of viewers and the helping hand. When Twyla Tharp submerged her troupe in ABT in '88, after maintaining it for 23 years, she was devoting so much time to fund-raising that she had not made a new piece for two years. Along with Paul Taylor's work and Limón's, ballet companies slowly took on Graham's dances too—by 1999 Dutch National Ballet had acquired five of them—and since 1991, commissions or existing pieces by Tharp, Lucinda Childs, Maurice Béjart and the stage director Robert Wilson have become the novelties of the Graham repertory.

The crossover phenomenon and the stark, jarring creations that dispensed effect without affect suited the restless energy of the hard-nosed '80s down to the ground. Beside those bold efforts, the colorful confections of the past looked frivolous and their painted characters merely insipid. As recession began to bite in the '90s, dwindling subsidy crowded out courage—no one could afford not to play safe. Once the proud guardian of Tudor's distinguished ballets, in 2001 ABT's repertory included none of them at all, and not only were Tudor's works gone but Tudor was gone too, and he wasn't the only one. Limón died in '72, Massine and Cranko in '73, Marie Rambert in '82, Balanchine in '83, Lucia Chase in '86, Tudor himself in '87, Ashton and Joffrey in '88, Ailey in '89, Graham in '91, MacMillan in '92, de Mille in '93 and Robbins in '98.

It's cruel and somewhat misleading to list those names together as if a single cataclysmic event provoked all 14 deaths. The world lost those leaders one by one, and as long as tears for each loss filled our eyes, we couldn't see a connection between one death and all the others. I mean, I couldn't. Instead, during the course of 10 or 15 years, I noticed a trend I had never anticipated, which made me consider, for the first time, whether dance in general and individual companies in particular might be navigating without a compass. When dancers started playing international hopscotch, as if they too were looking for a winner, I realized that some factor just as powerful as the economy was transforming their art. Not that performers hadn't felt bored, overlooked or underpaid before, not that they hadn't ever abandoned a safe, familiar situation to investigate fresh challenges among total strangers, but that suddenly everyone was on the move at once.

I'm not talking about artists who retired because of injury or to choreograph or run a company. I'm thinking of the dancers, mostly of the ballet dancers, who simply upped sticks and went somewhere else, and the English companies alone supplied more evidence than I could comfortably absorb. During my first ten years in London, 1981–91, the Royal Ballet lost Alessandra Ferri and won Sylvie Guillem and Irek Mukhamedov. In the next ten years it acquired Johan Kobborg from the Royal Danish Ballet; Carlos Acosta, a Cuban, who arrived from Houston; Inaki Urlezaga, from the Teatro Colón in Buenos Aires; Johan Persson from Sweden via the National Ballet of Canada; Tamara Rojo, a Spaniard, from English National Ballet; and Alina Cojocaru, a Romanian, who had trained and danced in Kiev. During the same period Viviana Durante and Adam Cooper decided to freelance, and Tetsuya Kumakawa absconded to Japan with Michael Nunn, William Trevitt and several other men. By 2001, only five of the 18 permanent and guest principals had been trained predominantly in Britain and raised on the so-called English style that had evolved with the company's reputation, and foreigners filled the ranks in Copenhagen and Stuttgart as well.

The hopscotch made slightly more sense wherever a wheeling constellation of international names regularly shared top billing with the repertory, so it didn't surprise me that in the decade before 2001 ABT scooped up Nina Ananiashvili, a young star of the Bolshoi; José Manuel Carreño, a dashing Cuban who slipped away from the Royal Ballet; Paloma Herrera, an Argentinian; Maxim Belotserkovsky, Irina Dvorovenko and Vladimir Malakhov, all from Ukraine; Angel Corella, a Spaniard, and Giuseppe Picone, an Italian.

No leading dancer from Balanchine's stable had abandoned New York City Ballet for another company, and not returned, since Gelsey Kirkland left for ABT in 1974, so when Ethan Stiefel did just that in '96, his decision stuck in my thoughts like a burr. Yet I couldn't understand what that decision meant, and watching the dancers swing from one affiliation to another with the apparent nonchalance of gymnasts didn't help me unravel their reasoning. To be honest, all we civilians know for sure is that dancers are students or amateurs until someone pays them to dance for the public, preferably for extended periods occurring at regular intervals. Most of us can only guess at the fate that befalls them as professionals, because we've never done

anything remotely like their job. Athletes know a little about it because they follow a similar regimen of physical discipline and inex-
orable repetition, but they don't need to hide their effort and they can
conceivably attain their goal—one of them, finally, will win. Who else
spends their days as dancers do? A renowned chef contends that every
kitchen staff is, "confined for most of their waking hours in hot, airless spaces, and ruled by despotic leaders," which sounds like it has
"dancers" written all over it, but I'm guessing.

Each performer who walks through the stage door disappears
into an experience we never witness and can hardly imagine. From
out front, we see only what we're meant to see, or, as Muhammad Ali
slyly taunted Joe Frazier, "You'll see what your eyes will allow you to
see." Antoinette Sibley told me that she and Anthony Dowell talked
to each other constantly while they danced, and I've stood in the
wings during *Les Sylphides* and listened to the motionless ethereal
sylphs onstage making plans for the evening with the boys who stood
beside me. Watching *Taming of the Shrew* one night from the same
spot, I saw a man play two characters in the same scene to cover for
someone who had fallen asleep in the dressing room, and I'd bet very
few people noticed.

But as the '80s passed, no one could avoid noticing that stage illusions were starting to crack and that the distinct artistic vision that
had once saturated this company or that one was beginning to evaporate. And then, almost as quickly, we sensed that a turbulent current
was carrying us into ever deeper confusion. That's when I started to
think about the bewildering issue of identity, because I suddenly realized a lot of companies were adrift in that current too. They were
bustling with activity that, from a distance, seemed vigorous enough
to keep them afloat, but they were flying different flags every season
and their repertories were flapping between timidity and desperation.
Having lost their choreographers or founders—remember those 14
names—they had apparently lost their anchors and rudders, and what
looked from out front like a continuous celebration—New works!
New stars!—could just as easily have been the flurry of hands grab-
bing for an elusive mooring.

When I turned from the ballet companies to the modern troupes,
hoping for some reassuring indication that performing the work of
one person could generate stability for the artists and continuity for
the public, I found anxiety and anger. "Look at who's saying dance is
dead. Dancers. And that means something, . . ." Mark Morris cried

in 1995. "There's no work for anybody—no work for companies, no work within companies for dancers." He must have been speaking metaphorically or about someone else's situation. Surely *his* dancers didn't believe dance was dead, and neither did any other performers I met. Even allowing for the fact that dancers complain as reflexively as they swear, those I talked to grumbled more about their rehearsal schedules and bruised feet than about the imminent death of the art to which they were still devoting their lives.

Maybe they voiced their fears only to each other or, even more privately, at home, where no one could possibly take advantage of their uncertainty. Or maybe, and this seems much more likely, my fears and theirs simply didn't coincide. If I were a 25-year-old dancer, I'd probably worry about my health, my roles, and whether I was spending more time in the canteen than onstage. Sitting out front as a middle-aged observer and working critic, I was worrying instead that characteristic styles were fading, that form was strangling content and that performers were cramming themselves with skill and losing sight of their art. I heard these same concerns from friends and colleagues, though it's safe to say that critics can compete successfully even with dancers when it comes to complaining, and I heard similar remarks about other arts as well as dance. When the Royal Shakespeare Company decided, early in 2001, to split into six or more smaller troupes, which would either concentrate on a single production or tour several, an experienced drama critic protested that "the RSC may become so little a company, let alone an ensemble, that it will end up with no distinct identity at all."

As the '90s advanced, more and more arts pages and television programs told me less and less about the issues that were troubling me; instead of the explanations I needed, at the core of all those earnest discussions I heard thunderous silence, like the emptiness at the eye of a hurricane. When performers were interviewed, they naturally spoke about their own circumstances, and choreographers inevitably wanted to discuss their new work. Occasionally, a sharp young manager or a distinguished board member would hold forth about a company's finances, but I didn't expect those businessmen to address aesthetic issues and most of them never did.

Why should they? It wasn't up to them to steer a company through the tides of supply, demand, creativity and commerce. In the end, that job belonged solely to the artistic director. He was the fixed point in the turning world, the one individual whose position obliged him to imagine a destination and aim for it, so his voice was the only one that counted. The public didn't care where these leaders came from, as long as we could trust them to deliver the goods. Whether they started out as dancers or choreographers or both, the job changed them into a completely different animal, a solitary creature who, all alone, represented the entire organization massed behind them—as the conductor Eugene Ormandy used to say, "the Philadelphia Sound—it's me." Each director was the company's mascot, figurehead, and public face. If his decisions eventually merited praise, it fell on the dancers, choreographers, designers, even the wise guy who thought up the advertising campaign. If things went wrong, the boss alone stood up to take the blame. So directors became sleight-of-hand magicians, wheedling hucksters, dapper hosts and wily negotiators. As adaptable as Plastic Sam, the old cartoon character who insinuated himself into one situation as a lamppost and into the next as a stack of dollar bills, directors learned to be whatever they had to be.

"Poor things," Violette Verdy said to me sympathetically, some years after holding down the job herself in Paris and Boston. "They use the most improvisation you can think of. Many of them are such respectable people and such good people. They become directors, and they still don't really know what they are in for. Then they find out, and the job they thought they were going to get is not the job they get, and they cannot do, with the job they have, what they should be doing with it. Most of the people that want to be or are directors have what it takes and could offer it, if they were only allowed to."

Watching them operate, listening to their upbeat pronouncements, you have to applaud their bravery—since most directors today have grown up in one artistic world and taken charge of another, it's a wonder they can find their bearings at all. The daily routine of class, rehearsal and performance remains inviolate, and so does the absolute demand for a single authority before whom all disputes can be argued and settled; for the stage director Martin Charnin, this judicial role boils down to knowing "when to say, 'Now,' or when to say, 'Later,' or when to say, 'Never.'" But beyond that, the director of a dance troupe can count only on his wits and his fingers. It's as if anyone who accepts the job starts out holding all the cards in a deck that's already stacked against him.

For a start, he can never win a hand when there's serious money at stake. Live musical accompaniment costs more than tape, touring costs more than performing at home, and staying home can prove expensive, and sometimes impossible; when the fabric of an old theatre becomes threadbare and its machinery archaic, the resident companies often hit the road. During the 1990s London's Royal Opera House and Sadler's Wells Theatre closed their doors completely while they were renovated and modernized. Having shut down as well, the Place christened its new studios in October 2001, and Birmingham's Hippodrome, which houses Birmingham Royal Ballet, emerged from its scaffolding the following month. In New York, the Metropolitan Opera House and the New York State Theatre—home to American Ballet Theatre and New York City Ballet respectively—are due for refurbishment along with the rest of Lincoln Center, and Milan's La Scala has recently gone dark for renovation too. With luck, more attractive, efficient premises will replace the old familiar ones, but nothing is certain. The theatre buffs who claim that the world's finest opera house is in Australia carefully point out that the exterior is in Sydney and the interior in Melbourne.

A company that wishes for new facilities and gets its wish must then justify the shiny new box by keeping it full. No one builds small theatres because it's hard to make them pay, although the Joyce in New York, which rose from the ruins of a fleapit movie house, has become the most active dance house in the world. Seating only 472 spectators before a stage measuring 43 feet by 36 feet, it has presented more than 300 different dance troupes since it opened in 1982. Unlike the Joyce, big theatres with big stages demand big productions, which naturally generate big bills, not only for steel gantries and beaded bodices but also for rehearsal hours. Because the working day can't get any longer, the only way to prepare for a big production is to construct a rehearsal schedule as intricate and fragile as lace, knowing that once it's stretched to its limit, the slightest extra strain will tear it in a dozen places. Push the dancers too gently and they'll never be ready. Push them too hard and they break, and broken dancers cost the management just as much as healthy ones.

One hundred years ago, every dancer at the Maryinsky Theatre was expected to be so well schooled that any coryphée could replace a soloist and any soloist could take over for a ballerina without compromising the performance or disappointing the public. Having joined the Royal Danish Ballet at the age of 18, Henning Kronstam proudly recalled that at 20, "sometimes I did Stanley's [Williams] children's class at a quarter to 9:00. And I did Vera's [Volkova] men's class, quarter past 10:00 until 11:30. I rehearsed, and then I did

Vera's afternoon class from 4:00 to 6:00." But now that the public must be wooed and won again and again and the repertory must revolve constantly to keep it coming back, no one has time to work like that. Dance has become like major league baseball where every season, as one ESPN commentator pointed out, is "like seven years, like dog years," for the players. "We used to have longer layoffs," Suki Schorer reminded me. "We used to have time to take two weeks off and then have a month to study, to take class before you went back into rehearsal. Now there's not much time to take time off because you're going to start the rehearsal season again. They lose the chance to come back eager to begin again."

As for expectations, even the dancers' sense of what it means to be a dancer has gradually shifted. Birmingham Royal Ballet launched a new scheme in 1997 to enable its artists to earn a bachelor of philosophy degree from the University of Birmingham; during two years of part-time study, they could fit their lectures and tutorials around their performing commitments. The Joffrey Ballet School in New York joined forces with the New School University in 1999 to create a bachelor of fine arts program so students could prepare simultaneously for success or disappointment onstage. In 1992, a foundation called Dance On began awarding scholarships to New York City Ballet dancers to help defray the cost of their academic education during their working lives. By 1998, 316 dancers had benefited from these scholarships, and for several years before that, one-third of the company's roster was enrolled in some sort of academic program. And when the closure of the Royal Opera House pushed the Royal Ballet out on tour in 1998, five members of the troupe had babies within months of each other, and two more became pregnant.

Any director who worried about the distractions that might claim his dancers' attention might also have worried about the public, which increasingly treated live performances as if they were televised—a 1999 cartoon of a couple leaving a concert hall bore the caption, "The music was so loud I couldn't hear myself talk." At one ballet performance in London, a woman adamantly refused to turn off her cellphone despite polite requests from the ushers and ruder suggestions from her neighbors. Flicking the remote control at home allowed viewers to indulge their own impatience—channel-hopping bred window-shopping—and food, drink and the tinkle of cash registers splintered their concentration during every intermission.

Unfamiliar with conventional behavior in theatres, intimidated by the form and puzzled by the purpose of what they saw, many viewers simply didn't know how to respond to live performances, and they increasingly wanted the critics to do their thinking for them, which didn't necessarily help the directors. Although by 2001 dance reviews featured regularly in nine national broadsheets, four tabloids and three weekly magazines, not counting trade publications and broadcast or electronic coverage, some British reviewers were neither interested in educating the public that might want to learn nor equipped to do so. One of them casually mentioned to me that she had never read *Romeo and Juliet*: "I've been in love with ballet since I was a child, so basically I think the ballet of *Romeo* came first and everything else followed afterward." I've known writers who sleep through performances or compare current dancers to artists they never saw. Some critics became media performers in their own right, fixing their eyes on more glittering prizes than a few column inches, and others fell headlong into the marketing machine, promoting an event one week and reviewing it the next.

While guides like these may unwittingly have shortchanged their readers, the audience had no alternative but to rely on their judgment. The artists, however, could turn elsewhere for guidance—to their director, teachers, coaches and colleagues—but they still read reviews hopefully and they still flinched when a journalist mounted his hobbyhorse and rode roughshod over their effort. Loitering backstage before a rehearsal in London, I saw two dancers from the visiting company scanning the opening-night reviews on the bulletin board. One article wiped the color from their faces and the light from their eyes before the local press officer told them to ignore it. "He likes Ashton and Balanchine," she explained. "He was put on this earth to destroy ballet wittily."

Like the rest of us, dancers have long memories when it comes to criticism, and they gladly review their reviewers if given the chance. "The critics make a difference," Sorella Englund murmured to me thoughtfully, "but I have been surprised so many times. When I thought 'This is no good,' they thought it was fantastic. And sometimes when I thought . . . not when I was performing but about my colleagues . . . 'This was just wonderful,' the critics were like, 'It's tired, and it wasn't what I expected.' It sounded like they hardly could put the pen on the paper.

"If I read a criticism where I can see that he's right about the weak points, I really try to learn from him. But if I'm completely of an opposite opinion, I can be shaken, but it doesn't affect me. It's something like a nose taking a wrong smell—you think, 'No, this is the wrong way.' Criticism is usually something to listen to to get honest in yourself. You sometimes stand by yourself and you hear the noise of other people—'Oh, wonderful'—but you can't be fake."

When I asked Irina Kolpakova about critics, she responded with more animation. "We had wonderful critics, like [André] Levinson, so it was always interesting to read their books and of course it helped us. When I read Théophile Gautier's comment after the first *Giselle*, when he was writing about Carlotta Grisi . . . it's phenomenal. He wrote, for example, when he saw Carlotta Grisi, he saw a young girl who opened the door and came out and ran across the stage as if her legs had been stagnant and she wanted to begin to move after sleep. And Levinson wrote that his ideal of a ballerina was a 'coquettish Aphrodite.' Here is immediately an image in front of you.

"Critics were always with us. I don't know if you know the name of Poel Karp? He was very close to us and to our generation. Every day he was there at the theatre, and he was also educating us. The language of Karp . . . his tongue was like a razor blade. I remember what he said when Natasha Makarova and I danced *Romeo*. [Tatiana] Vicheslova was working with us behind closed doors . . . difficult, difficult role. And after the performance Karp said—we were always very afraid to hear what he would say— 'Makarova knows better than you how to love, and you know better than her how to lose your lover.' He was talking about the last act. I wailed, 'Oh, oh, no, I don't know how to love,' but I was proud, because the whole last act in the Lavrovsky version I am onstage. I hold that last act, it depends on me. There's an example for you of a critic.

"Now I can't even read what is written about the ballets that I know. It is possible, but very difficult. About those which I don't know, the historical facts are so interesting. But when it concerns the ballets that I saw, when I read what others think about it, it's impossible to compare that with what I know."

Whether the companies assumed the extra burden of tutoring the public with eagerness or resignation, through the 1990s they conscientiously expanded to accommodate it, wedging entire education departments into their premises and onto their payrolls alongside their marketing departments. Necessity forced them to develop lecture-demonstrations, study days, community projects, regional workshops and schools matinées with printed information packs for the children.

In London the Rambert Dance Company's school and the Central School of Ballet, which is officially linked to Northern Ballet Theatre, offered open classes for adults with little or no dance experience. ABT resuscitated its school in 1995 and invited both amateurs and professionals to learn what they could from the company's ballet masters. At the time, ABT's executive director, Michael Kaiser, pointed out that "companies have typically marketed themselves in ways . . . that don't necessarily appeal to marginal buyers. When you are financially challenged . . . you tend to cut back on two areas . . . You can save on artistic initiatives and marketing. But those are the two things that are going to save companies."

Oh yes, artistic initiatives. I had almost forgotten them. If a director were calling the shots without interference in any corner of the kingdom he supposedly ruled, you'd think it would be artistic initiatives, where he could let his imagination run wild. You would think so, but you'd often be wrong. Long after the 1951 premiere of her *Cakewalk* at New York City Ballet, Ruthanna Boris remembered that "Lincoln [Kirstein] asked me to do a ballet: 'I don't care *what* it is,' he said, 'but please try to do it in costume. If we do *one* more ballet in leotards, they'll kill us.'" Directors lose sleep over the same concerns today, fifty years later, because there are more of "them" now than ever, more viewers, more competitors, more critics and, with costs continually rising, more at risk for a company too. On top of not enough time to rehearse, now there's also not enough time to fail, which limits the director's options and raises the stakes on his decisions considerably. "The whole concept of the journeyman artist has disappeared," declared the theatre director George C. Wolfe in 1997. "You are not allowed to go on a journey. There is no journey. You're either extraordinarily brilliant or you're dead." And what goes for entire companies and for individual choreographers goes double for dancers, who watch time passing as they labor for recognition and feel time passing as age corrupts their bodies. The Kirov ballerina Altynai Asylmuratova, who graduated from the Vaganova Academy in 1978 and is now its director, believes that time itself has changed for young dancers. "Before they were used to ripening slowly; now they tend to peak a bit too soon," she mused. "It's much easier now to be a ballerina. I was in the corps de ballet for five years; I worked my way up slowly and I had to prove myself at every stage."

The more you think about the director's situation, the worse it appears. Not only is he strapped so tightly to the mast of his vessel that it's impossible to tell which is propping up the other, but his ship is expensive to run, overloaded with cargo, buffeted by the winds of fashion, and regularly invaded by pirates. While some members of his hand-picked crew are diving recklessly past his eyes in a frenzied bid for attention, others may be slipping quietly away under cover of darkness, either in the fear that the whole vessel might sink or because they're convinced that paradise lies just over the horizon. Nevertheless, replacements constantly appear, both for the captains swept overboard by raging storms and the ships that fate has smashed to bits, because someone always wants to stand on the bridge and take charge.

The most obvious lure, especially for a former dancer, should be the power. Having served as Italy's prime minister seven times, Giulio Andreotti commented, "Power weighs most heavily on those who do not have it," and he must know the subject inside out. But, honestly, a dance company is neither the state of Italy nor General Electric, and a director's influence doesn't tip the global balance of power very far. The salary is not that munificent, the glory invariably goes to the performers, Christmas bonuses and stock options don't exist, and the title won't impress either *People* magazine or the *Wall Street Journal*. When Anthony Dowell left the Royal Ballet after 15 years as director, one broadsheet waved "*Au revoir* to the greatest British male dancer" as if he had simply decided to retire from the stage.

Be realistic. Except in novels, no one leads a dance company for power, money, security or fame, and once you eliminate those motives, the reasons for taking the job look remarkably like the impulses that motivate artists to do anything, you know, ordinary factors like imagination, curiosity, self-confidence and a passion for their art. "I am in service here," asserted Peter Martins, speaking in his office at New York City Ballet about his role as ballet master in chief. "When you come in here, you check your ego at the door. You have to forget that you performed. You have what you've learned, not what you are."

Along with the obligations, the meetings, the budgets, the glad-handing, the stultifying weight of deadlines and temperament, the administrative distractions of a gigantic support system and the crippling responsibility for infinitely valuable, infinitely fragile bodies, come extraordinary prerogatives to which no one else has the same access. The director can shape the dancers he wants to watch and program the works he wants to see. He can open the viewers' eyes and broaden their minds. He can preserve what he cherishes most. He can characterize the future. He is the arbiter of taste and the ultimate referee of every quarrel. He is the gold standard on which the entire enterprise rests, the backing that defines and validates it, and consequently he has the last word.

During the 21 years that Jiri Kylián ran Netherlands Dance Theatre, he invited, at his count, about 60 choreographers to work with it, in an attempt to inject the widest possible variety into the repertory. He also formed an experimental troupe for young dancers, NDT2, to help them bridge the transition from student to professional status, and created a small senior company, NDT3, "for dancers between 40 and death," whom he considered "libraries or encyclopedias of dance knowledge." His artistic policy, which eventually dominated all three companies, arose from his personal priorities. Another director might make a different set of choices. Why not? It's his privilege. In 1959 Robert Joffrey produced the American premiere of Tudor's *Soirée Musicale*, which marked his first raid on the world's far-flung repertory and his initial attempt to start a conversation between museum works of the past and viewers of the present. This curatorial task would eventually earn him universal acclaim, but revival in itself didn't satisfy him; he used to insist that "when you are director of a company, you don't own the ballet, you take care of it. If you feel you can't take care of it, then there's no point in doing it. It's better to drop a ballet for a season or two, until you have the right dancers to make that ballet live again."

Since no company can be great without great works and no work can be great without great dancers, the task of finding or forming "the right dancers" may constitute the director's most pressing need and the pinnacle of his achievement. Sally Gilmour remembered Marie Rambert saying, "We have a new girl coming. She has no neck, but she has a wonderful quality, and I will get that extra two inches of neck out of her." In a certain way, the teachers and coaches the boss hires and the ballet masters he entrusts with rehearsals and revivals function on two levels, as experts in their own right and as extensions of his mind. An exclusive band of artisans, they lend their gifts to the realization of his vision, arranging and shaping their charges like master carpenters and stonecutters following a meticulous blueprint. However generously they share their experience, they are working at the director's behest, constructing his privately imagined ideal for public consumption and, if his choices can either match or mold the times, to sustain the art itself.

"To be a [movie] director is very hard," Federico Fellini once admitted ruefully. "You wake up early in the morning. You impose your will on other human creatures. You are a clown. You are a general. You take the megaphone and scream like a crazy man in the middle of the street. You have to stop traffic. You must have tremendous enthusiasm to do this work." Fellini made art out of ordinary people. He cast them for their faces and filmed them speaking whatever language came naturally to them, routinely dubbing their voices later. But later has no meaning for dancers—if they don't produce right now, when the music cues them and only their movement at that moment can fulfill the choreography, the chance is gone, and no technology on earth can reclaim it. Standing in the shadowy wings or sitting out front, the director watches his artists helplessly as they make or break, instant by instant, the illusion they have struggled toward together every day. Unlike Fellini, he cannot immediately give them another chance, so each time they stumble, they inflict a little damage on his artistry too. Without mechanical tools or retakes, he can only create to the limit of everyone else's efforts and capabilities. He is eternally at their mercy, as they are at his. That's the deal, take it or leave it, and directors take it, every time, because they cannot resist reaching for the moon.

When Frank Lloyd Wright designed his utopian Broadacre City, he composed a set of requirements that would endow its residents with "A New Freedom for Living in America." His demands included, "No landlord or tenant. No traffic problems. No railroads. No street cars. No poles. No wires in sight. No headlights. No slum. No scum." Reading the list for the first time, I thought about the resolve with which a director charts his company's course, peering beyond probability toward a destination that is all the more tempting for being impossible to reach. The second time I read the list, its pie-in-the-sky optimism reminded me of a director's job description, which calls for one individual to be pragmatic, canny, numerate, sociable, tenacious, dependable and persuasive, and to possess the taste and intuition of Lorenzo de' Medici, the wisdom of Solomon and the business sense of Bill Gates.

It's a fairly tall order, and it only gets taller when a hopeful candidate steps bravely up to those criteria and tries to satisfy them, because however much you may want the job, you can't really prepare for it and you can't learn to do it except by doing it. So every director makes it up as he goes along, and if, miraculously, he can somehow meet its outlandish requirements, he earns the right to pull his own list of dreams out of his back pocket and find a way to set them dancing. "Nothing can be hurried," Fellini warned, "things must be allowed to fall into place little by little . . . Every detail is an opening on to a world of its own. You may see a tiny tail poking out through a hole, tug at it, and out comes an elephant."

Maina Gielgud

b. London, 1945. Studied with Tamara Karsavina, Lubov Egorova and Rosella Hightower. Performed internationally with Roland Petit, Grand Ballet du Marquis de Cuevas, Maurice Béjart's Ballet of the 20th Century 1967–71; Deutsche Oper, Berlin 1971–72; London Festival Ballet 1972–76; Sadler's Wells Royal Ballet 1977–78. Artistic director Australian Ballet 1983–96 and Royal Danish Ballet 1997–99.

[*Gielgud was director of the Australian Ballet when she made these comments.*]

*T*HE FIRST ANSWER is that you can't make artists. All you can do is develop the dancers' artistry if it's there in the first place—99 percent of the time the embryo's been there from their student days. It doesn't necessarily show in class, and often in the teenage years it disappears, when they become self-conscious. But when a dancer who's an artist appears on the stage, I think that little core is usually visible if it's there. It just varies so enormously from dancer to dancer; sometimes you get dancers who have a maturity at an early age in the stagecraft, a way of presenting not only their dancing but their personality. You find so many Australian dancers who have this instinctively. And you see it, you don't have to scratch for it, and it literally is a question of using what is there and just developing it further.

In a way, it's a lack of self-consciousness. Australians pride themselves on being laid back. I mean, they work extremely hard but they don't make a huge, life-threatening issue of every step, and that has advantages and disadvantages. They will work towards their performance 100 percent, very much with the idea that they are there to

141

enjoy it, which is absolutely right. They have started dancing because they want to dance and they enjoy dancing, and that business of not making it a life-threatening issue means that they actually keep that enjoyment. Whereas in a lot of situations in Europe and in America, that gets lost terribly quickly, because the focus becomes an obsession on the detail and the polish of the technique.

But the disadvantage is that they tend not to have a vision of how far they can develop both technically and artistically. So it will become a short-term vision rather than a long-term vision. In the ideal situation, the dancer will be working along two parallel lines. There's the immediate performance tonight, which is vital and they've got their audience to think about. But parallel with that, there's the vision of their long-term goal, of the perfection that one never gets to. If you're working only with this short-term vision in mind, basically you cannot fulfill your potential, because to do so sometimes you have to compromise a little bit now for later. And yet, it's possible to go too far and be thinking of the long-term and forgetting the audience that's there to see you.

Most of the company, about 90 percent, comes from the school, but it's only a three-year course, starting around the age of 15, 16, and they come to it from all over Australia—from some wonderful schools, some less good schools, some downright bad schools—and they come at all stages of training, so it's quite a problem. I occasionally teach, not very often because there's not a lot of time, but the third-year graduates of the school make up the junior company, which is under our umbrella but has a separate director. We also send dancers to it from our company to do principal or solo roles or perhaps the kind of role they wouldn't get to do in the company. So it's got huge advantages of all kinds and permits me to see the students onstage before I take them into the company.

What I've attempted to do in Australia, because I think the dancers have the potential for it and it interests me, is to have a schooling that is not particularly Russian, Danish, or Italian but a basic classical technique that you can't go, "Spot the style." When they come into the company they have a range of guest teachers from all the top schools—from Russia, Denmark, France, America, you name it—and I've found that that increases their adaptability. You don't then get the situation of people who've been trained one way and think an arabesque is only here. When you get to *Giselle* and you want a certain style, those are the dancers who look at you in amazement and have no idea how to adapt, because 'I was taught this way.

This is the right way.' I worked with so many different teachers as a student, and it helped me tremendously, because I didn't have this sort of blocked thinking, that there was only one way.

There's also the problem of refinement. There's beauty in refinement, but there's also danger in the fact that we're refining technique to the nth degree nowadays, sometimes, I'm afraid often, at the expense of artistry. If the audience sees an Alessandra Ferri or another real artist, they'll cheer much more loudly and they'll pay much more. I do think they can tell the difference, I do. Why are audiences falling off in America? This is frightening. I think it's because we're not seeing dance anymore, because the classics are being presented as feet and legs.

We actually don't have this problem in Australia. I wasn't faced with a company of exquisite feet and legs and nothing from the waist up. Now I'm sending them elsewhere, so that they see for themselves what they have in Australia and, interestingly, they notice. They usually do sort of a bird's-eye-view trip. Some of them go to a specific teacher or a specific school for a period of time. Ultimately it's my choice, having talked to them about what attracts them, but there's great interest in what goes on elsewhere, I think because we're so far away. In Europe or America it's much easier to get around and see things.

You know, students who have a great facility for dance can now and do now become professional dancers, and they are people who would not have got into the profession before. It's a very sad state of affairs, because it stems from what needed to happen, which is that dancers are being paid better, not wonderfully but better, when they're professionals in companies. They're paid for their rehearsal time and for their class time, and this means that they can afford, if you want, the basic luxuries. In Australia, for instance, they can afford to buy cars and certainly in their second year they get mortgages and buy houses. And they can do other things but dance. Hours are unionized, in some places in a way that almost isn't sensible. In Australia they've set union rules that I think make absolute sense, that dancers who are on at night shouldn't rehearse within three hours before a performance and that there should be 12 hours between the end of a performance and class the next day. Most of the rules are sensible and protective, but in a way it's sad because the occasional exceptions could be in the dancers' or the company's or the ballet's favor.

So there is this . . . species, if you want, and I will call them "people who dance." They don't last in the profession, but they have this natural physical facility and maybe a natural instinct for the stage.

They are not necessarily, and don't have to be, very interested in working in class or in rehearsal, but because of that facility they've been taken seriously as students and taken into a company. They may not have great ambition, but they can get on and they enjoy it while it's relatively easy. And you'll have a few dancers of the other species, the real dancer, who may not have nearly the same facility, who have had to struggle with their turnout or with their feet and work ten times harder than the others to get roles and promotions. And at the end of the day when they face injury or round about the age of 27 or 28 when things are not that easy for any dancer, they're the ones who are going to hang on, because they're interested in the whole challenge, not just in the performing. Whereas when the "people who dance" strike that age or strike injury, it's like 'Oh, shock, horror. How do I deal with this? I can't turn anymore. I can't jump anymore. What do I do?' And then it's over.

I think they're missing hunger, and this leads to great, grave problems. The artistic director may see the potential of the dancer and have an idea of where they could go if they really put their energy and their mind to it, but those dancers don't have that vision and they don't feel the need to. When they are very young, one tries to put a sort of conscience into them: "You've got your pot of gold there— don't leave it in the bank. Use it." But unless the hunger and that embryo are there in the first place . . . And then there's all the peer pressure to be like everybody else and not to specialize, to be all things to all people: Yes, I'm a dancer but I'm also going to be a wife or husband and a parent and have all these hobbies. All that takes time. And if we suggest that perhaps channeling would develop the potential further, we run the danger of being told that it's none of our business or that we're old-fashioned.

To choose your rep, you've got to take into account where they are technically, where they are artistically, what kind of principals and corps you've got, how good your male dancers are . . . We're doing *Bayadère* now, the Shades, because we've got the best female company I can ever remember and I think it's going to display them wonderfully. We also did *Bayadère* some years ago, when they weren't as good, and then I wanted it for the challenge more than the display. The public will come to it because of the tutus and then see beyond the tutus, because it's terrific. There is another public that is much more open to what we classical people call contemporary—Kylián, Tetley, Graeme Murphy in Australia—but it is still a very small sec-

tion of the audience. What has happened to the audience from the Diaghilev era, who flocked to the triple bills and wouldn't go to see full-
lengths? We don't know. Perhaps the public flocked to see the dancers
more than the ballets at that time?

I care very much about those ballets, but I haven't revived Massine,
for instance, because I've not felt there was anyone capable of staging
them up 'til now. I've now heard that the *Rite of Spring* of Massine was
just revived extremely well in Nice by people who worked with him I
think in the '50s. I've not seen the Massine ballets since we did them at
Festival Ballet. They went well then, but we had Massine teaching them
himself. There's still a public for *Graduation Ball*, which we do here,
and I hear ENB is doing *Les Sylphides*-new work-*Graduation Ball*—I
don't think there's a company in the world that hasn't tried that trick.
We all do it, we have to do it. The danger everywhere is that we're
going to be catering for the box office only. The public still wants the
classics—we all know that. But if one is intelligent about it, there is
good reason why the audience goes to see the classics and why they
have become the classics. The dancers need those ballets as well, for
their development and as a yardstick, for all sorts of reasons.

The advantages of video are incredible for the dancers who have
a good eye—especially if you're as far away as Australia—because of
being able to see a whole gamut of different swan queens, or whatever, without having to see them perform. But video is also dangerous, because it could give a feeling of many more possibilities than I
believe there really are. Well, what is the correct style for a classical
role? What is a classical dancer? Every authority you talk to will give
you a different reply, and what I feel is a classical dancer will probably be different from what Anthony [Dowell, then director of the
Royal Ballet] feels or what Kevin [McKenzie, director of American
Ballet Theatre] feels. There's a whole education process for a director
in relation to what is all right to change, in particular what steps in
the solos for male dancers, and what is out of style and out of character. And again, that varies according to the company, the director
and the coach. So in a way, if these dancers who come up into companies look around the world, they could say, "What the hell is it all
about? They're all saying something different," because we are. Our
ideas of what would be desirable for a Romantic ballet, the second
act in particular of *Giselle* or *La Sylphide*, might be different everywhere. Erik Bruhn came to us to put on *La Sylphide* a few months before he died, and even Erik disowned a certain amount of what I

would think of as the Romantic style, in terms of posture and arms and so forth. I suppose I inherit more of Pat Dolin's way of thinking about *Giselle*, because I knew Dolin very well because I worked with him a lot on *Pas de Quatre*. So when we do *Giselle* or *La Sylphide*, that kind of thinking about the Romantic style is what I'm trying to impart. I like the idea of doing those ballets in that way, I think that's the point, and then beyond that you get the dancers to characterize and to make it relevant to themselves and consequently to the audience. But those young dancers, who I'm trying to get to do an arabesque with the arms below shoulder level, may be looking at videos and seeing something different. I've seen photos of Giselle with straight, strong arms like this, which is very strange. Those elements still bother me, but they won't necessarily bother others of my generation and dancers nowadays won't necessarily know the distinction.

But it's very interesting, because we all go on about the necessity for coaching, and there is a certain section of the ballet world that believes it to be very important. But historically, it's actually quite new. If you talk to [Irina] Baronova or any of the dancers of the Ballet Russe, including the Diaghilev company . . . It wasn't because of their coaching that they were great dancers. My understanding is that there was no coaching. Literally none at all. The dancers learnt behind each other. There was no video, a ballet master didn't teach the role. You picked it up, and you weren't spoonfed. I hear that Marcia Haydée believes that coaching, and the kind of coaching that is done nowadays, is spoon-feeding, that it takes away from the individuality of the dancer.

But a lot of the time . . . When I was with Festival Ballet, for instance, we were struggling to pick up roles and having minimal rehearsal time. There wasn't enough space, there wasn't enough time, there would be a ten-minute Rose Adagio call for each Aurora, one after the other, and if you could get onstage and do a decent job, then you were on. That was it. I went to Denmark to work with Volkova on *Sleeping Beauty* and with Toni Lander for *Etudes*; everybody knew that Volkova was the greatest, and of course she had coached Margot Fonteyn. *Beauty* just seemed the obvious thing to work on with her. But that wasn't all the time—most of the time I'd hire studios by myself. I used to hire the Dance Centre for two hours on a Sunday and stay for six and hope that nobody noticed—it was expensive—and try and work out for myself how to do these roles, how to do them in style, how to build the character. I don't think it would occur to dancers nowadays to do that, except perhaps those who don't have tremendous facilities, if they ever got into a company at all.

There is much more coaching nowadays, whether it's concentrating on what one would consider the right aspects or the wrong aspects, and as a director it's a question of being the catalyst and of choosing the right coach for the right dancer at the right time. Ideally, it's a balance. Where would I send somebody for *Beauty* now? Probably to Gelsey [Kirkland], because I think she has acquired great understanding of the truly classical style with little decoration. And for the boys? It's so difficult, more than for the girls—and it's hard enough for the girls—because they're all gone. Dolin's gone, [John] Gilpin's gone, Nureyev's gone, Baryshnikov's not coaching, which is terrible, Erik's [Bruhn] gone. It's frightful, that situation.

But the dancer should also have the opportunity or the difficulty of working by himself sometimes. Again, it's a question of the right moment and whether the dancer is prepared to do that. If they're used to being fed material, are they actually going to take initiative themselves? Of course, even when they're coached there's a certain amount that needs to come from the dancer. It's a give-and-take situation, it's not just simply saying, "You put your arm there, you put your focus there, and this is how you think and this is when you should breathe." But then, some coaches do that—that's the other extreme, which is also bad. But sometimes you're encouraged to do that because the dancers don't take initiative, they don't give back, and you've got the responsibility of getting them on the stage.

❧

[*Gielgud had left both Australia and Denmark when she made the following remarks.*]

ROBERT JOFFREY USED TO SAY he knew at 12 years old that he wanted to be a ballet director That was his big ambition, and it became as wonderful as he thought it was going to be. He's one of the few directors I have ever met who said that he really loved it in the way that I did. It was put in my head by the then administrator of the Australian Ballet, Peter Baird, who just mentioned when I was a guest artist there, "You'd really make a good director one day." It stuck in my mind, and I thought, 'Maybe that's why I'm always going out front when I'm not on. I thought I wanted to learn as much as possible for my next performance.' So it occurred to me that perhaps it had something to do with wanting to direct at some stage.

When I did get the opportunity, I was very aware, having worked with many different directors, of what I treasured in the way they had behaved, mainly towards me as a dancer but also in general, and what I had felt was lacking and what were mistakes, and I tried to amalgamate and utilize that experience and at least try not to make the same mistakes. What I treasured most was when people really appreciated something good and let one know, because very often in the tumult of the whole thing, one gets so busy trying to make things better and consequently criticizing that one forgets to make it known how much one appreciates the good things. Dancers feel the caring of directors very much.

And then there's that awful business about what is fair. All the dramas, all the problems really come from the sense of 'I've worked so hard for five years and I haven't missed a performance even though I had tendonitis, and here comes this young thing, who's only been in the company for six months, and she gets the role. It's not fair.' In my time, I think there were more dancers like myself whose first tendency was to think, 'It's because I'm not good enough.' My way of dealing with things was, 'Maybe this has been done to challenge me. I'll show them. I'll just work that much harder and I'll show that I should have really been first cast.' That was my instinctive decision, but also it was a logical one in the sense of making the most of it rather than going, 'Ooohh, it's not fair! So I'm not going to work and why should I come to rehearsal if I'm not called?'

I've always been aware of that as a director, while being terribly sure that the most important thing when you're . . . engaging for the company first of all, and then casting and promoting, is what you're putting in front of the audience. Although you have to weigh the dancers' sense of what is fair to a degree, it's secondary. That is the director's tightrope the whole time. If you're literally thinking of what you're putting in front of the audience, you could be making some grave mistakes in terms of the future development of the company and of particular dancers, because to get the best performance to-morrow night, you might be putting someone on who is actually not ready. Then you're not doing a service to their career or to the company's career, even though *that* performance might be better than if you put someone else in. It's a tightrope or . . . it's like juggling. One is juggling the value of what one is putting on in terms of the developing standard of dancing. Juggling the entertainment side, the emotional side, the educational side of the choreography the audience is getting. Trying to introduce them to works that it wouldn't necessarily be apparent to them that they're going to enjoy.

I think they're controlling things more and more. I was pretty sensible as a director during my 14 years in Australia in trying to balance what the audience would like to see and what I might want them to see. But it was only in the last four or five years that the influence of the marketing department became apparent. "We really have to do a third full-length, as opposed to two full-lengths and three triple bills," they might say, because the mixed bills don't sell anywhere. They really did try to influence me, to a point where I was saying, "OK, I can understand why. But if we do that this year, within two years we're going to run out of the full-length, popular works." We're all desperately trying to get the message across that the mixed bills are usually more interesting than the full-length works, but we can't seem to get it across. And we're all saying to the marketing departments, "You're going to help us," and marketing are all saying, "There's only so much we can do." Surely this is a vicious circle, because the more we sell the ballets that sell themselves, the more popular they're going to become and the less there is for these wonderful mixed bills, and people will not know about them.

It matters terribly. I mean, a ballet like *Les Sylphides* has a huge importance. The public doesn't value it because the dancers don't value it because it doesn't take off. Rather than being more and more free, dancers are more and more restricted now by what they think they should be doing, a sort of visualization of "how it should be." They get stage fright stepping from the wings onto the stage, but it's about whether they're going to execute exactly, correctly, what they visualize. Rather than being what you start from, the ideal is set by the fear of making mistakes. I don't think dancers feel free to be interpreters. There's more and more work behind the scenes, and rather than setting them free it seems to be locking them into a box that they feel has been defined by their training, by their teachers in the first place and then by their coaches. And they are worried by all the people who have done these roles before, rather than approaching a work as though it was brand-new. But the purpose of all those rehearsals, all that coaching, all the research and whatever is that you're free. Having done all the preparatory work, when you go on the stage you should be prepared to receive inspiration—old-fashioned word—from a higher source than just you. To receive it and to transmit it. This is what I'm not seeing in dance now.

I'm saying exactly what I swore I never would when I was a young dancer, that the artistry is just not the same as it was. Where are the artists who really live on the stage and share on the stage, share with the audience and with everybody else? Thank God there's Tamara Rojo—she's the first one that I've seen for years, apart from mine in Australia, of course—and Alessandra Ferri. I think we're to blame also, the directors, for focusing so much on perfect positions that when they perform, dancers are still worrying whether their fifth is turned out enough and where their extensions are. I have seen directors go back[stage] after a performance and their notes will be that it wasn't exact, it was fuzzy. What one needs to know as an artist is what came across. Did something, some emotion, come across?

I made it a rule from the start that whenever the dancers are in the studio, I'm in the studio virtually all the time. So if I'm not in the office during the dancers' work time, I'm doing the paperwork with my coffee and my breakfast and in the evenings and mainly in the weekends. That's the programming and casting and latterly rehearsal scheduling as well, and also board reports every month. I suppose I really use the office for staff meetings and for interviews. I'm hardly ever behind the desk. You're not a director behind the desk. I ended up doing about nine years of rehearsal schedules while I was in Australia, as well as in Denmark where nobody wanted to take it on. It's almost a 24-hour job in itself.

I didn't know that dancers' injuries were going to take up so much time, I suppose because I was rarely injured myself. I wasn't aware of how much time is spent, by the ballet staff and the director, not only taking care of them but also amending casting, rearranging things . . . I had no idea. They're injured more than they used to be for a lot of reasons. Partly because of doing so many different styles, partly because maybe they're not as hardy, partly because things like stress fractures didn't exist in my time . . . and my theory for that is because they don't eat as much meat or protein as they used to because the fashion now is much more towards pasta and rice. And in some ways the demands on dancers are greater now, definitely greater in terms of what the men have to do in partnering.

But I was very lucky in Australia because I inherited a company where the wheels were wonderfully oiled and turned magnificently.

Within three or four months, Noël Pelly was appointed administrator, and then I had the best possible administrator-artistic director relationship, with someone who was *really* there to try and make the artistic dreams come true. I remember being on a plane with Noël in the early days and saying, "It would be great if these dancers could see how it is in the companies overseas," and he immediately said, "Let me see if there would be a way of getting scholarships from a few people." And from that came the Christmas scholarships, where every year during their summer holidays in Australia, up to seven dancers went to visit different companies, to take class, watch rehearsals and performances and so on, for three to four weeks. I thought the dancers could get so much from it, and we would be able to keep more of the talented ones because they'd be more aware of how privileged they are. They'd also see what is lacking in themselves and the company, whether technically or artistically, and get a view of what's happening in the dance world. They were absolutely fascinated, and that has happened every year from then on, that type of program is still in place.

The same thing happened with sending dancers on an exchange program to other companies and having dancers from those companies come to us. Peter Wright did it with Sadler's Wells [Royal Ballet], and I thought it was a wonderful idea. I mentioned it to Noël and said that it wouldn't need a great deal of financial support, because each company goes on paying its own dancer and the receiving company pays for their journey and their accommodation and per diem, and the exchange happens at a time that works for both companies. In my experience as a dancer, there were often times when the company's repertoire is not considered to be right for you and you're not getting enough work to challenge you. Normally, that's the time when the dancer still tries to work hard but feels that maybe they're not good enough, or they just get into a complete apathy or depressed. Even if you try and overcome it, you tend to be less than at your best, and it's a stagnating period. So I thought I could approach another company and say, "I've got this excellent dancer who is not doing much at this point. Do you have anything in the rep that they could do?" So they would go for anything from two weeks to two months or more. And in exchange, that company would look at which dancer was not busy in the forthcoming rep, not necessarily at the same time, and look at our rep . . . It's funny. Some directors found the thought of it so complicated and difficult, but it worked terribly well with a lot of companies, and rather than it being a depressing time, it's an excitement for that dancer. They go away, they get an experience that nobody else in the company has, they come back with that special something. And there's always a great deal of curiosity about somebody who's coming in. So you have all the advantages of a guest artist but without the feeling that they're taking a lot of money and also taking away roles from the dancers.

In Australia, there was a subscription system, with five new programs every year in Melbourne and Sydney, the same five programs, and normally some of those programs toured to Brisbane, Adelaide, Canberra and, once every four years because it's so far away, to Perth. That system was there when I arrived, and there didn't seem to be any reason to change it. Having five new programs each year was very exciting for the dancers, as opposed to taking the repertoire over from one year to another—here in England it's often the same programs over and over again year after year, the *Swan Lake*s and the *Sleeping Beauty*s, and maybe one or two new programs change within the year. But there in Australia it was five in a row, which I thought was terrific.

But what you didn't get was a continuity, particularly with the classical ballets. If you did *Swan Lake* one year, you wouldn't do it again for another four or five years, until it came 'round in the subscription system. But you couldn't do it less than once every four years because of the subscribers. So I worked out that the way to do it was . . . If you did *Giselle* in Melbourne and Sydney, then take something else on tour. Then the following year take *Giselle* to Brisbane, Adelaide, and so on, so the dancers would get a continuity of developing in the roles and the ballets. That was just common sense, I think. There are never enough performing slots, and, God knows, we had 187 performances a year in Australia. We didn't own a theatre. There were 21 performances of each program in Sydney, because of the opera house being so small, and 12 performances of each program in Melbourne. So that would be 33 performances, lots of opportunities for dancers to get their teeth into. But there's an expectancy now on the part of the dancers that everybody—the director, the teacher, the ballet master—is there to motivate them. There is less 'I've got the chance of doing this. How am I going to do it?' and more 'Nobody tells me how, what, why.' There's much less of this in America, maybe because the contracts are short term. I think that breeds an awareness of the shortness of the career and of the fact that they may not have the opportunity of dancing at all—never mind dancing certain roles—so they're more greedy and harder workers and much, much more self-motivated.

In Australia, the dancers are obliged to do four classes a week. Now, originally, in the Ballets Russes and from there in general, I believe, class was not necessarily given in the company, so dancers had to go and pay for outside classes. Then classes *were* given in the company, and then, presumably when the dancers were reprimanded for not always going to class, they said, "Oh, but we're not paid for them." In America they're still not paid for going to company class, yet because of the lack of security I suppose, there's no problem. The dancers are logical enough to realize that not only do they physically need to go to class, but they also need to show that they're in class, because the directors can release them . . . they don't need to renew their contracts for the following year.

In Denmark no class is obligatory through their entire career, and they have contracts for life after the first five years. Generally, that security seems to be counterproductive. There are always the exceptions; there are Danish dancers who are extremely hard-working and it wouldn't affect them one way or the other. But someone *can* take advantage of the system, perhaps without even knowing that they're taking advantage. It's only natural. A dancer can have 120 days off a year before anyone can do anything about it, and as long as they're odd days here and there, they don't have to provide a medical certificate. Now, one of the rules is that you can't have a rehearsal of the program that's being performed that same night. But in emergencies—and when you might have 23 dancers off every day out of 90 there's always an emergency—you can call a rehearsal during class, always using the last half-hour of the class, and you have to slot in whoever you can during that time—they're called emergency rehearsals or sick rehearsals. You're only allowed 2 hours 55 minutes of rehearsal on the day of performance, and 3 hours 35 minutes on a rehearsal day—that's all you have.

It leaves you, the director, basically incapacitated, because you can't insure that there's going to be a basic standard. And also, because of the lack of rehearsal time, there was barely time to rehearse the first cast in time for a premiere, and the second cast would hardly get a look in, let alone the understudies or any other cast. There *is* the possibility for another rehearsal, at the overtime rate while I was there of about $100 per person of any rank, but you couldn't call it for less than two hours. So you were using that over-time continually but basically for principals, maybe four people, who were going to work the full two hours, because you can't keep calling the soloists or the girlfriends in *Giselle*, paying $100 apiece for two hours, when you only need them for half an hour. And it was upside down, because the corps de ballet would work first, immediately after class, because they had to have their five-hour break between the end of rehearsal and the beginning of the performance. And you'd use the principals in the overtime slot because that was the fewest people, so they would work last, during the last two hours of the rehearsal day, which is topsy-turvy. And the soloists . . . The corps de ballet suffers but the soloists suffer most.

You see, in the Danish school they get virtually no repertoire. They have regular education and basically one ballet class a day, of an hour and 30 minutes, early in the morning, and that's it. Then as apprentices they work from morning to night—it's a complete shock to the system. Up to 16 they do one class a day and then the senior class does one extra class, which is Bournonville, and another extra class, which is a pointe class, in a week. When they become apprentices they take company class and they're supposed to learn all the corps de ballet work—they're not told what to learn, they're just supposed to learn everything—a big change from the school. Then they have a 4:00 class, a two-hour class especially for the apprentices, and then often they're in the performance. The school and the company are under the same budget, but the apprentices are not paid by their time so they can work all day, and what happens is that many of them get injured immediately. This is the shock.

Of course the ballet was sharing the theatre not only with the opera, as in all opera houses, but also with the drama theatre and to some extent the orchestra, and that made the planning far, far more complicated. I inherited a system there of program planning which was absolutely the opposite of what I had in Australia, in that the programs were presented in repertoire: half or more of the programs would go on the following season, and you'd bring in three, four, five new programs. From the point of view of developing dancers in roles, it would appear that this was a good situation, but it was not. You might have *La Sylphide* three times in September, then it drops until January when you had one performance, then in March you had a couple of performances and in May another one or two, and of course never the time to rehearse in between.

Sometimes programs went on after two months without any rehearsal in between. If you had a week in between, the principals might work, again in their overtime, and the corps de ballet would often have one full call for two or three works. If there was a creation, and the choreographer actually had in his contract that he had all the hours of the day for rehearsal, then there was no way the corps de ballet could work on anything else. Sometimes we would have five programs going in in the same month, which meant that none of them were adequately rehearsed and the dancers were just jumping from one to the other. So I asked that we do no more than two programs simultaneously over, say, a couple of months, and then go to the next program. And they did allow me to do that the following season, which did help in having some consistency of standard.

Video was utilized enormously for those going in in an emergency; after the half hour of sick rehearsal, some of the apprentices would spend the rest of the day trying to learn from the video. One was so happy if they hadn't bumped into anybody and didn't make too many mistakes, and went around to them all backstage saying, "Thank you for saving the performance," because performances were also cancelled because there weren't enough people . . . with 90 dancers in the company. The week before I started I said to someone, "How did *Swan Lake* go last week?" She said, "Oh, we had to cancel, we didn't have enough swans." So I felt that one of my big challenges was going to be a negative one, not to cancel anything, and I managed—we didn't cancel a single performance.

In the opera house situation, certainly in Denmark, there's an *intendant* as a general director, and repertoire was passed by him as well as being discussed at meetings, including marketing. A big headache is how to get enough creativity while at the same time working in the tried-and-true ballets that you know the public is going to come and see and that you know the dancers need to develop. So you're thinking of the audience, the dancers, the rehearsal time, the availability of choreographers . . . You can make up a lovely repertoire and then discover that people aren't available to come and stage the works when you or the company has the time, so again, you're a juggler.

A catalyst-juggler, because one of the most important tasks is to act as a catalyst, to put people in touch with each other at the right time, the dancers with coaches, choreographers, ballet masters. I thought it was really good for them to have visiting teachers in Denmark. They supposedly wanted a different repertoire and new inspiration, they wanted to work with different choreographers, and consequently I thought they needed to be exposed to different ideas and schools of the top standard. I brought in Boris Akimov, a fabulous teacher, and they did like him very much. I also brought in Aygol Gaisina from Australia, who's Russian and trained in St. Petersburg, and Timothy Gordon, an Australian, and I brought in Violette [Verdy], who generally speaking was appreciated. They had had a great deal of influence of Balanchine's school, dating back . . . I think they felt they could adopt Balanchine a bit, because he had been there in the '30s, and of course they have a love-hate relationship with Bournonville. They couldn't really show that they hated him or hated what that rep stood for, they had to pretend they really loved him, and that made my life very difficult. I think they felt that Balanchine was an antidote to Bournonville, and I felt they took their admiration to too great lengths and it was actually harming their Bournonville, in terms of the port de bras, the épaulement particularly, the not bringing the heels down . . . that's not Bournonville. Especially with the young dancers, the be-all and end-all was New York City Ballet.

But the Danish dancers do have a dramatic sense, and that dramatic tradition is handed down, visually and by osmosis. There are no mime classes, though people say there used to be. There certainly were none when I was there, nor just before I came. I brought them back. I got, I think, Flemming [Ryberg] and I know I asked Sorella [Englund] and Lis Jeppesen. Because although there's more dramatic flair and understanding than in most ballet companies nowadays, I do think they're going, even there.

There's a story I love, which told me a lot. I was in the wings at a final rehearsal of *Napoli* with a nice, professional corps de ballet man, and there was this crooked line in the finale. I said, "Has it always been like that with the corps?" and he said, "Oh yes, we're known for that." And he was quite serious—we're known for feeling that it's not important. What is important is that everybody dances and enjoys it, that it shouldn't be regimented. They do enjoy dancing Bournonville—as I say, the loving is on a par with the hating. I think the hating comes a little bit because of their dependence on it, which they're very aware of. The hate half also comes because Bournonville is difficult to dance, and Bournonville classes are particularly difficult. Generally speaking, the company did not enjoy doing Bournonville classes, and there was a feeling that it wasn't necessary to do them. Bournonville ballets—yes, of course, their heritage, et cetera, and no one could or should do them as well as they do, but not the classes.

I tried to balance four different strands in the repertoire: the Bournonville, the classics, important contemporary works and creations. First of all, maintaining the Bournonville, whatever that may mean, is absolutely vital. It's one of the few companies that actually has a hallmark, something unique that no other company has. We had a Bournonville conference at one stage, and I think the idea we came up with was the right way to go, which was not to erase anything. There should be a maintenance of the traditional Bournonville, that is, reviving, restaging, as far as possible in the style—as far as one can gather—of how it was meant to be presented in the beginning. And then side by side with that, a sort of innovative Bournonville strand, to experiment with some of his works, perhaps in another theatre, and do the equivalent of Mats Ek's *Giselle* or less radical things. It never went further than some papers, but that was the idea, and I felt strongly about it—maintain the traditional, and then you can do anything.

I don't agree with the newfangled notion that you need to be allowed to update the style of a *Giselle* or a *La Sylphide* so that it means something nowadays. Nonsense. The whole challenge of it is to do it as close as you can to the style of that period, but at the same time bring your own living experience, personality, artistry to it. This is the biggest challenge to dancers and coaches, to make the roles their own while respecting the tradition. If you just do *Giselle* like you do Balanchine or [a work by William] Forsythe, it's not *Giselle* anymore. If [Jean] Coralli was living now, wouldn't we want to try to do it as close as possible to what he wanted? If Ashton was alive, you wouldn't say, "Oh no, I don't want to do Ashton in the style of Ashton. I want to bring it up to date." You do of course have the problem that Balanchine and Fokine and others did change their steps according to the individual personality of the dancers, but I don't think the essence of the style or the musicality changes.

When I was in Denmark, everyone talked about Hans Brenaa and his tremendous personality, great love and great knowledge of Bournonville, and how that made it a living tradition. People all have their little stories of "Hans Brenaa said this" and "Hans Brenaa said that," while acknowledging that he probably changed some of what Bournonville had originally intended. And when Brenaa was alive,

I'm sure there were virtually as many detractors of the way he was expounding it as admirers, but there was a tremendous feeling about it, and its spirit was being passed on. Now there's a general feeling that there isn't anyone who can pass on that spirit. Henriette Muus is sort of thought of as the next person who understands Bournonville and could do it, but I think everyone is waiting for a tremendous inspirational person, who may or may not pass it on step for step or stylistically to the last fingertip but who will rekindle the desire.

Then the classics are of huge value, because they're always the yardstick, especially for principals and soloists, of where you are as a classical dancer. But again, maybe they're thought of too much in terms of the right way to do Aurora because such-and-such did it this way, rather than a concept of Aurora—who is she, what is her relationship to the other people on the stage, how can I bring that across to the audience? I saw some fabulous dancers in roles that I later danced, but it never occurred to me to . . . it's the wrong word, but to take the luxury of worrying about them as a burden. I've never understood that. I just had to get the role to a presentable standard and then have fun with it and see what *I* could do with it. Perhaps that was from not having been brought up in *a* single school with all that tradition.

In the great schools of the world, it seems that drama classes have fallen by the wayside. So much else has come in, from Pilates to contemporary dance at a much younger age than ever was dreamt of before. Mime classes hardly exist, and we've lost quite a bit of the character work. Looking around the schools, from Cuba to Paris and St. Petersburg, I've often asked, "What about drama classes?" And every time the answer's been, "We used to have a wonderful drama teacher," but they retired or they went to another city, "and of course there really isn't time." That is one of the reasons that we don't see it onstage, and perhaps because it's not been put into their studies at an early enough age, dancers are less interested in portraying roles than in doing *In the Middle, Somewhat Elevated.*

I always try to encourage them to go out front and see what the public sees. Quite a lot of them don't like to, I don't know why—as a dancer I wanted to have that awareness. Because you can't get everything right, prioritizing is often important, and . . . Well, I always found that rehearsal time was too short, so it was my duty to get across the most important things and try and deal with the less important things in my own time, maybe for the next performance.

Not that you would cheat as such, but if you have limited rehearsal time, you might spend less of it worrying about something which, if you were watching from the wings, you wouldn't realize an audience doesn't see. If you have their perspective, you don't necessarily think your performance was absolutely ghastly because of such-and-such. I always fell over, especially on first nights, so I simply had to get used to it. But I never understood dancers who felt it was almost the end of the world if they fell over. It means you've taken a risk, right? The public doesn't mind—they're usually for you.

With works new to the company . . . By bringing in works that one thinks are perhaps going to be the classics of the future or are particularly relevant to that country or company, one is training the audience to see and value diversity and exposing the dancers to a particular choreographer. Sometimes you don't get exactly the piece that you want, but one just can't overestimate the value of that one-to-one connection with the creator of the piece. In Australia, the dancers felt really nourished by it. When we had Jiri [Kylián] there . . . not creating, he never created a work there, but staging his own work, even just for a few days . . . that kind of inspiration was one of the most important things for keeping the dancers, because the choreographer is God. In most places dancers will accept almost anything from a choreographer. In Denmark, most of the choreographers had hardly been seen before, and the mixed bills didn't sell. The dancers who worked with Kylián and Mats Ek of course loved it, but the choreographers themselves felt restricted by the hours, and when I dared to mention the subject of creating something, it was "Well, how many weeks would I have to come for, if I have three hours a day and five days a week? What am I going to do—sit in my hotel room and twiddle my thumbs?"

But it's every dancer's dream to have a work choreographed on them, and obviously for ballet to continue it's absolutely vital for new works to come about. I feel strongly about not throwing money at choreographers before they've proved themselves, I don't mean in terms of paying them, but in terms of sets, costumes and general productions costs. The most vital thing is to find basic choreographic talent, skill . . . talent more than skill. It's a huge part of my job as a director to find new talent, because that's where the future lies. And you have a tremendous responsibility to the dancers to give them that creative opportunity but not to waste their immensely valuable, short dance lives, killing themselves for less than talented choreographers.

By talent I don't mean choreographers that are going to produce masterpieces every time but choreographers who have a respect for the dancers and a real need to express themselves.

Obviously, you want to find your own choreographers . . . I mean, one has a duty to find the next generation. Who else is going to find them? But also, you have to remember that the Mats Eks and Jiri Kyliáns are very unlikely to create new work on a company that is not their own. Before they've got to know the dancers, they will not do that, which nobody seems to understand when you take on a company and bring in choreographers who've not worked with that company before. Everyone's saying, "But why aren't there new works? Why are there old works by such-and-such?" Well, because the choreographers need time to develop a relationship which they can believe will be a creative one. So for that reason amongst others, it's important to discover and nurture and develop your own choreographers, and it's easier for all concerned, because they will know the dancers better than anyone.

But you can only plan so far. A lot of it is as though you're at the mercy of fate, so I think one has to be wise. If you are, say, in Denmark, make the most of your tradition, and then see whether there is the possibility of finding, so to speak, the next Bournonville. With a repertory company like the Australian Ballet, you try and see whether there is the possibility of finding your first Bournonville, but it's not a tragedy if it's not there. What is a tragedy is if you try and make a Bournonville of somebody who doesn't have it. You see a lot of companies that are trying desperately to develop their own choreographers, or they're intent on finding their identity through *a* choreographer, perhaps of a certain skill but not of genius. But you need genius for a real identity to come through—skill is not enough. Skill is enough to keep the dancers creating a bit here and a bit there, but not enough to throw money at. And then, while you're still delving, what is interesting is to encourage the dancers to delve as deeply, to really take on style and the concept of the choreographer, whether it's an old work or a new one.

I was freelancing and really enjoying a different sort of life, but there are many reasons why I wanted to take up a directorship and why I would again if the circumstances were right in the future. First of all, I love it. I love developing dancers and trying to put top-standard productions and dancers, most importantly, in front of audiences. It's a pleasure as well as a duty to use the experience that one has, but also I think that classical ballet is ailing. It's not by accident that audiences are not coming in droves as they did in the '70s. I think it's because a lot of the theatricality has disappeared, as I was mentioning before, the stagecraft, the dramatic ability of the dancers to tell a story, to portray characters and to connect with an audience. I love dance—stating the obvious—and I think that it has a great deal to say and a great power, and I'd like to help put it back on its feet.

Helgi Tomasson

b. Reykjavik, 1942. Studied at the National School of Reykjavik, in Denmark and at the School of American Ballet before appearing with the Joffrey Ballet 1961–64 and the
Harkness Ballet 1964–70. Joined New York City Ballet as a
principal in 1970 and choreographed his first ballet, for students, in 1980. Upon retiring in 1985 became artistic director
of the San Francisco Ballet, the position he holds today.

I HAD SEEN A PERFORMANCE of Soloists of the Royal Danish Ballet that had come to Iceland. At that time I was about five
years old and living in a fishing village called Westman Islands. My
mother brought me to the performance, and . . . I guess I was thrilled
with what I saw. I tried to imitate it, every time there was music on
the radio I was trying to do what I had seen. I was about five and a
half, and I still have images of those lights and color and movement
now. We moved to Reykjavik when I was nine or nine and a half, and
she enrolled me in a local ballet school with two Icelandic teachers,
women, and I never stopped from there.

Erik Bidsted would have to be the first . . . He sort of instilled in
me the idea of 'I could do this' and the joy. He was a very good
dancer, a strong dancer, and at that time he was still demonstrating in
class. Maybe it was the physicality, the athleticism, that made me
think, 'Wow, I want to do that.' He and his wife kept my interest
going, and maybe part of it was that they brought me to Denmark
when I was ten years old and again when I was 13, and I saw dance
and I saw the Pantomime Theatre. When I was ten years old I saw
practically every performance there for over a month. So in that way

163

I think the influence was there for me to keep the spark going. Basically my training was very much towards Bournonville even though it had a lot of French influence, because Bidsted had trained in Paris.

When I think back, later the most influential teacher for me was Stanley Williams. We arrived at the same time at the School of American Ballet, I on a scholarship and he starting there as a teacher, practically in the same month. He knew of me in Denmark, he had seen me dance. I did not know him, I just knew the name, and being that I was coming from Denmark, speaking fluent Danish at that time, we sort of struck up a friendship. I thought he was a wonderful teacher, so over the years, even after that one year in the school, when I went with Joffrey for two years and then with Harkness, whenever I was not away on tour I would most of the time just go back to the school. I was allowed to take [class] there, and it was fine.

When I came to him, I had learned to dance. I had already done two or three years, in the Pantomime Theatre. It didn't mean I was a finished dancer, but I was already dancing professionally, I was trained already. And what Stanley was really best at was to take people like that and say, 'OK, now. Let me make this better. Let me refine that. Let me show you how you can get more out of that movement.' I realized later on why Stanley would have all those wonderful dancers in his classes: because he made you aware of the little details, basically the perfection of classical ballet and the nuances. It's the refinement and the quality of movement that he instilled in you—it's not how many pirouettes you do, it's how you do them. He was wonderful that way, and you just believed in him. He was so into helping you.

Sometimes in his English he couldn't always describe what he wanted to say, but I had no problem with that because I spoke Danish. So a lot of times he would say something to me in Danish, and I just had this ability to really understand him. I don't know if it was because when I started my second year of dance in Iceland with the Bidsteds, they didn't speak Icelandic and at the time I didn't speak any Danish. So as a child, you tried to understand what the teacher wants however you can, without the language. So maybe in the strange way, when Stanley was not very verbal but he was trying to explain, I understood. When he used to say to the guys, "Oh, you don't understand," he would turn to me and say, "But you understand, Helgi," and I would say, "Yes."

When he first came he was teaching very much Volkova-type classes, with the influence of Bournonville, of course, but if my memory serves me right, I almost want to say his classes were more Volkova than Bournonville, because she had trained him to teach. That's what he always told me—he learned from her. But over the years, working with Balanchine and the School of American Ballet . . . Balanchine would say, "Well, I want certain steps done this way," so he would adjust. So he changed a great deal towards, quote, "more Balanchine technique," if you want to call it that. But it was more in the sense of how you executed certain steps—he never let go of the quality of movement and he tried to explain the excitement you needed and how to get it out of certain steps.

There's no question in my mind that Robert Joffrey influenced me. I was there just before Mrs. [Rebekah] Harkness came in to support the company, and Bob was just starting to branch out with bringing in choreographers from the modern dance community to make new works for us, choreographers who traditionally did not choreograph for ballet companies. I was there, and all of a sudden Alvin Ailey was coming in, and he himself was a great dancer and he was still dancing and had a small company. Bob went as far over to modern dance as Anna Sokolow, who we thought of as, really, kind of way out there. So he went into that . . . how can I say it? . . . entered that room, which was not a ballet room, he went in to look for something else in there. Norman Walker did choreography, he had just come out of Martha Graham's company, then Bob would maybe get a *Square Dance* of Balanchine and he choreographed a little bit himself, Jerry Arpino was just starting to choreograph and he was not doing classical things.

So there I am, in my first company in America and experiencing all these different styles of movement. And they were not easy to master, but they were fun. And that sort of continued with Harkness, particularly in the beginning, the same idea of infusing the repertory with something that was maybe not traditionally done, and I credit that to Bob Joffrey. But being, what, in my very early 20s, that had a tremendous influence on me, and I loved it. Also, I came with Joffrey and in the beginning I did two ten-week tours of one-night stands with them. Ten weeks—we danced every night in a different city in the United States. We traveled 2 . . . 3 . . . 400 miles sometimes a day, by bus, and danced. It gave me a lot of strength. There were only 20 or 25 dancers. There were no understudies, that's it, you were on. You danced every night, you danced two or three ballets, so you gained tremendous strength.

And Joffrey was probably the biggest balletomane that ever was, and you couldn't help being smitten by that. He loved dance of any kind, everything about dance, he loved dancers, and maybe his curiosity was why he tried to experiment. And there's no question in my mind that that has influenced me as a director, remembering those experiences. They were, in general, fun and it was interesting. We felt we were doing something special, something different. And that idea was sort of carried through with Harkness. A director like Brian Macdonald would try to get . . . [George] Skibine was there for a while, but he would tend to go more toward the classical, and then Larry Rhodes and Ben Harkarvy were co-directors—Larry had been with the Joffrey— and they tried to do a little bit the same idea. But what happened, of course . . . With Harkness I went through six directors in, what, six years. I think the sixth was coming in when I said, "Thank you very much, I'm leaving." But that was also right after I had won the silver [medal] in the competition in Moscow, so I just really wanted to make a change.

I hadn't discovered yet, like I did after the competition, that maybe my strength, my primary strength, lay in directing. But when I now sit here and direct, those things just come natural to me. I think, 'Well, that makes an interesting program. If I wanted to buy tickets and I went to the box office and said, "What's on tonight?" yeah, I would like to see that. There's a Robbins piece, there's a Mark Morris, there's something else.' I have brought choreographers out here and sometimes it has worked and sometimes it hasn't, but they have all had their chance. And in the meantime I give an audience a glimpse into . . . how can I say it? . . . Let me back up . . .

When I came here, I was coming out of New York, where you can go and see New York City Ballet, you can go to Merce Cunningham or Paul Taylor, you can go to Joffrey, you know, you have all these different things open to you as a member of the New York dance audience. And I felt from the beginning that it was kind of my responsibility here to expose the whole spectrum of dance to this audience, to show that it's not just *Swan Lake* but that dance is more than that. So we have had lots of different people, and the audiences come for it and they find it interesting. In many ways it was part of this company already—they did more Balanchine when I came than I do now. But I wanted to do more and other things beside Balanchine, and I maybe also was making a conscious effort not to have it look like I was trying to make another New York City Ballet.

This company had never done a full-length *Swan Lake*, so I did that in 1988. At that time the company needed it, they needed to be challenged by it, and also, for me . . . My vision was, 'If I'm going to make this a major player in the world of dance, then you have to be able to do those full-lengths and do them very well to be taken seriously.' *Swan Lake* was my first introduction to that, and there was some hesitation from people here at the board, but I said, "No, we need it." And after the fact, all of a sudden the level of the dancers rose. It's for them, absolutely. Otherwise they would not be dancing the style, and I think it also gives them a great deal of strength—it's necessary for them in their development as a dancer.

What has helped me a great deal when I have staged the full-length ballets and there is mime to be done is that I feel very comfortable with it. And I know I can speak for American dancers that it doesn't come easy to them, partly because they don't have many opportunities in the companies to view an older dancer doing those kind of roles, like you would have, let's say, in the Royal Ballet, where you have that tradition, or in Denmark. In America dancers come to a certain age, and it's sort of, 'OK, next one.' Companies here are not part of a theatre that has more drama-theatre-opera like in Europe, where they're exposed to other things. We tend to be just a dance company, so unless they see older character dancers or have somebody teaching them, they feel very self-conscious with the mime. They say, "I'm not doing glissade, assemblé, double tour." So you have to show them—it has to do with stage presence—and tell them why and you have to do every part. And you have to explain how to slow everything down so it can register to the audience.

I always felt I could show all the mime very easily—it was just something I had learned as a teenager. And, funny, when I went and staged *Sleeping Beauty* in Denmark in '93 . . . You know, for me, from when I was a little boy, the Danish Ballet had been always "Wow," and here I was showing them how to do a mime and I couldn't believe it. They do great trolls, but to make them do *Sleeping Beauty*, where there's royalty and there's an aristocratic behavior . . . I was surprised how it seemed a little bit awkward for them. Maybe not quite as awkward as for some of the dancers back in America, but . . . What I'm saying is that I could show everything, if there was a king or a lady and how they had to walk in their dresses, and it needs to be shown, absolutely, because that's how you learn, by watching. It's hard for young dancers to become someone like that, and there has been a lack of opportunities to do that, particularly, let's say, in this company until I started doing the full-lengths. And also what I have discovered, some people can learn it and do quite well at it, and with others it doesn't seem to jell. So I work around that or I say, "This part is not that great for you. Maybe you'll do something else." You have to use what you have.

There are only so many ballets that I feel keep the classical technique alive on a very high level. It's something like *Swan Lake*, *Sleeping Beauty*, *Giselle*, *Symphony in C*, *Theme and Variations . . .* we start going into the Balanchine ballets . . . to keep that technique. So it's important for me to bring in those ballets to make the level and the strength of the dancers rise and challenge them with those roles so they can also take on something very contemporary and modern and different. Forsythe is based on classical technique. He told me, when he came and did a work for us here in 1987, that to him Balanchine was, 'Wow, this is the one I've learned from.' It's amazing how many people you hear say that. Look at Robbins, he just thought that George was the top, and there are people in the modern dance community who admit it—listen to Mark Morris. But what I'm trying to say is, I brought these ballets in more to develop the company than because, 'Oh, I need to bring *Swan Lake* on for the audience.' The dancers need to grow and to develop and they need to become whoever they may be.

And I have to help them, in the best way possible, to have a fulfilling career, knowing that I cannot please everybody. It's a hopeless task—maybe I thought in the beginning that I could change the way some dancers dance, but it's very hard. You can help them do things, but you cannot totally change them, because you are basically changing the person itself. They dance the way they are inside. You can't say, "Well, if you do this it would look good," because they are still who they are. Dancers come to me and say, "What do I have to do to become a principal dancer?" It's not what you have to do—it's sometimes who you are. Meaning, There's nothing wrong with who you are, but maybe your maximum is a very good corps de ballet, and that maximum in the corps de ballet is very important to this organization. We have to have all the layers—I can't just have all principals and nothing underneath, that's not going to create a good company. Sometimes dancers have a hard time understanding that, they think they just have to do one thing and then all of a sudden they'd be promoted. Some have it in them to develop—whether there is more talent there or there is an ease for them to just come onstage and create and be what they need to be—and others are very held back and technically oriented or they are very mathematical in their dancing or something.

By far the majority of the dancers I have worked with over the 16 years have been very open and willing to listen. Not all. I'm there, I've offered it, if they don't want it, then there's nothing I can do about that, it's their choice. But I'm there, and I'm there to help. I think an artistic director of a ballet company is there really to give. I have 70 dancers and they all want something from me, so you're constantly giving yourself. It gets tiring, but that's part of it, and I think it takes sometimes a special person to be able to do that well. There are some directors who are very good choreographers and they just can't deal with that giving—there's nothing wrong with that—and sometimes very "famous" dancers might not be the best artistic director for that reason, because they were so used to taking.

I don't think any dancer, working in a company, has really a clue of what it takes to be an artistic director. Well, as a dancer, you look at yourself, one on one, with the artistic director, because all that's important to you is how that artistic director or choreographer sees you, uses you. Or if he doesn't use you, 'My God, what is happening? Am I no good? He doesn't like me or he hates me' or whatever. You know, all those feelings come into play. Being the artistic director, I have to care for 70 people. Each one of them looks at me one on one, but I have to see the whole, total picture, and I have to make decisions that . . . if I make this one happy, it's probably going to make the other one unhappy. But you have to weigh that choice against the other and deal with it.

I think and I feel and I say to my dancers, "We have an obligation to be at our best at all times. You cannot think of it as just another performance, because once you start that, something sets in and an audience picks up on it. You have to go out there . . . ," and this is when I talk about the passion, "You have to go out there and dance for them. They might not like every ballet that we dance, but my golly, you're going to make them feel so good about what they're seeing that they'll want to come back. Either through your artistry or through what you can do physically, which is not normal for people to do, they'll say, 'Wow, I want to come back. I really liked that.'" Hopefully, the programs will sort of do that too. "Gee, I didn't like that first ballet, but that second one! I want to go back, and I hear they're doing something similar next week. I want to go back." Nobody's going to like everything, but give them a repertory that is interesting, very well danced, with dancers who enjoy what they're doing . . . well, I think that's half of the battle.

And I also remind the dancers: Look at everything today. There are all those shows, and even Walt Disney has now gone into the traditional ballet rep. Now, we can't compete with Disney films or million-dollar shows, so we have to do something better. We have to do something different, we have to do something else, that they can't do, and we have to make the audience feel that. We have to make them interested in you as a person—that's why I want personality, not just a group of ten dancers, very well together, looking beautiful, and boring.

I was so privileged as a dancer. I've worked with Balanchine and Robbins—that's quite a bit. Of course I learned from Balanchine, who was instilling the respect and the love for music and the articulation of dancing those steps, which was not difficult for me because I always thought of Bournonville as being very articulate. Balanchine talked a lot in his classes. We would all stop and stand around getting cold, and he would start talking about a philosophy of dance, the meaning of it. And in a way . . . I'm not comparing myself to Mr. B, but at times I have sort of used that same idea. Images can say so much more than just trying to explain a step. I always remember Volkova telling me in class—and she said that she told Erik [Bruhn] the same—that when you do glissade, assemblé, "Think that you have a beautiful white dove there, on your wrist. And you go glissade, and you *send* it off." Well, you hear that and you don't forget it. Instead of, "Bring your arm to the side and aim it up to the corner." That's going to be gone in ten seconds. Once you're in the studio working with dancers, I think they're receptive to all those things.

When I was dancing . . . What can I tell you? I mean, to just put it bluntly, I knew I was talented and I knew I had something special, and I knew that this was my calling, this was what was meant for me, and so the question was, How good can I get? I think you always need people to push you. Dancing is so hard, not only just physically, but . . . it's very easy as a dancer to have doubts. You are so reliant on whoever directs the company, and you feel in a way quite vulnerable. So you have to be very strong inside and believe in yourself, and I think I did. Maybe I had my mother to thank for that, because she knew that this was something I was going to achieve and be very good at. There was no question in her mind, and maybe part of that spilled over to me.

I had not planned to become a director, I truly had not planned it. I had been asked while I was still dancing to maybe take over a small company in America, and I thought, 'Well, thank you very much, but I'm still dancing.' It was way too early, so I didn't give it much thought. I was teaching sometimes at the school [SAB], Balanchine asked me to give classes for the young men and also adagio classes. Then in '80 I did my first ballet, so that became an interest to me. I think in my own mind I thought, 'OK, I'm not going to dance much longer. Maybe I can stay with New York City Ballet and maybe teach at the school or do some choreography and still be part of it.' And out of the blue comes an offer from the Royal Danish Theatre for me to come to Denmark with the idea of directing the Royal Danish Ballet. I was absolutely floored. They were looking for someone, and maybe part of the reason was that they knew I had been there, I spoke Danish, many in Denmark think, or like to think, I'm Danish. I'm sure there was talk among themselves about who would be a good choice, and I know for certain that Erik Bruhn was very very much for it, so I thought maybe it was something I could do. But I wanted some changes to happen, and they were not willing to change, so I said, "Well, you change, and I come," and they didn't, so that was the end of it.

But during all this I got a call from Lew Christensen in San Francisco, also out of the blue, saying he would very much like me to come out and talk to him with the idea of taking over the company. And I said, "I'm still negotiating with Denmark," and he said, "Before you sign anything, please come out and at least give me an opportunity to talk to you and show you what we have." And I said, "That's fine, except I'm leaving the day after tomorrow for Denmark, and if everything works out I'll probably sign my contract there." I did go back to Denmark, things were still not worked out, so I said, "Well, then call me when you're ready." In the meantime, I go back and I read in the paper that Lew had passed away. But I didn't give it a second thought, I just waited for Denmark, and then I get a call from the head of the search committee, Tom Perkins, and he said that he knew that Lew had wanted me to come out here and would I come and talk to them. So I went into the whole explanation, but I thought, 'Maybe I owe it to Lew to go out and take a look.'

That's what happened. Denmark didn't want to change, so I said, "Thank you very much," so there I was. I did find out later from Lew's wife, Gisella [Caccialanza], that it was Lincoln Kirstein that said, "Get Helgi. It's the only one. You have no choice. That's it." It's always Lincoln Kirstein. And they had called Robbins—this I found out many years later—and apparently Robbins sort of said the same thing, "I don't know why you're hesitating. This is the right person for you."

Learning this job . . . it's trial by fire, definitely. You jump in and you roll up your sleeves and you set to work. The company needed discipline, it needed better classes, it needed better repertory, so I just went out and did that. They had always had Balanchine ballets in San Francisco, not danced as well as they should have been—that needed to be fixed. Robbins was very generous . . . I think we are the only company outside New York City Ballet or maybe the Paris Opéra Ballet who has been allowed to dance the number of ballets that we have. Again, it comes back to my experience, of having different types of works in an evening. My respect for the full-lengths . . . if we were going to be taken seriously, in America or anywhere for that matter, we had to be able to dance the full-lengths well, so I wanted a company of that caliber and size. There were 49 dancers when I came here and now there are 70, and I think that's about it, that's enough. I still remember everybody's name, but after that it gets a little too much.

Other than *Nutcracker*, which starts in the middle of December and runs for two-and-a-half weeks, our repertory season at the opera house runs usually somewhere from the end of January until the first week of May, with a few nonperforming weeks in between. And then that's it—there's nowhere else for us to go in San Francisco, because then the opera has the opera house, so I only have a winter season. So for me to keep high-caliber dancers—maybe I can accuse myself of being a collector of good dancers, that's maybe my hobby—they need to be kept dancing. If we want to keep them in San Francisco, which is far away from . . . well, touring-wise it's far away from the East Coast and Europe, it's far from Asia. So if we want to tour anywhere, other than southern California which we do also a little bit, it takes a great deal of undertaking and expense, but I have convinced the board how necessary it is. I can't just have dancers dancing for February, March, April and the first week of May and then say, "OK, come back in December." It's not possible.

And maybe, with those few weeks of touring, dancers in this company are just dying to get on the stage, they can't wait to get on the stage, they can't wait to dance for you. I think in some ways that has determined the way we dance, that energy level, the joy. Whereas some other companies, particularly the European companies, have a long season year after year, from September to the end of May or the middle of June, and they're very secure, so maybe there is not the same incentive to really be at one's best all the time. Maybe they think, 'It's a good job, it's a solid job, I'm here for my life as a dancer and I'm being taken care of.' I don't know. I just suspect . . .

There's competition in this company too, but I think it's on a friendly, supportive basis. If somebody goes out in a new role, you will find a great many dancers in the wings, urging them on and applauding for them. And you see principal dancers go down to the corps and the soloist level and say, "You need a little help with that. I could . . ." And it goes the other way too, "Can you help me with this?" There's respect for the great artists in the company, obviously, but that doesn't mean you can't go and talk to them, no. There's no fear.

I think there *is* a little bit of fear of me. I'm the artistic director, I'm their boss, I decide who dances what, I have a total control over their career basically. But if you were to ask any dancer in the company, they probably will tell you . . . that I'm fair. You don't have to behave like a dictator. You can get your point across and you can get what you want without humiliating people or making them feel insignificant. But there has to be only one person who decides. You cannot run a ballet company by lot or by committee. I have an extremely good board, very supportive, and I have total artistic control. If they don't like what I'm doing, then it's up to them to say, "Thank you very much, Helgi, goodbye," but there is no interference. It's in my contract, from day one.

One of the hardest things is the people part of the job. Not so much arranging for the touring or to find the repertory, but to deal with 70 dancers, who all look to me for guidance in their career and want me, hopefully, to promote all of them and give them everything to dance. To deal with that . . . That's hard. And also, in a way, you become a victim of your own success. My God, everybody is saying, "This last season in San Francisco . . . wonderful! How can you top it?" and I think, 'I don't know. What do I do next?' And you just go on, and you try. I basically go with what I believe in and what I want to do, what I think would make good programs to satisfy myself, the public, and the dancers. And for them I think it is very important to have new works created, because always having something brought in that has been done before . . . it just isn't the same.

Dancers feel that if they are part of the creative process, it's more special. It means that you, as an artist, are maybe also giving your talent into the work that is being created and hopefully influencing the choreographer. Without that, I think there comes some sense of dissatisfaction, that something is missing. They find . . . yes, so-and-so is a wonderful ballet, and I'm not saying they don't like to dance . . . be it Balanchine or Robbins or Ashton ballets. But in the end, if they only were to dance ballets that were created by other people, I think dancers would sort of feel, 'Gosh, am I missing something here? Those are wonderful works but they were not done for me. I could not look back and say, "Gee, I worked with so-and-so. I was in the studio with Mark Morris,"' or whatever. There is a pride of being with . . . anybody, for that matter, David Bintley, Helgi Tomasson, or whoever.

And in a sense it also creates a feeling of belonging to a company, maybe you could call it a sense of loyalty. Things are not the way they were before. I mean, years ago, when I was dancing, we stayed with one company, that was it. Now dancers change a lot more. There are a lot of them and they want to experience many different things, and if they feel they don't get opportunities right away, they say, "Oh, I'll go there." Particularly the men, because there's always a shortage of men. The women are much, much more patient. So I think if they feel that things are happening, new works are being created—this is what's going to keep a dancer happy.

But we are running out of time. Meaning, during the season it's so intense that we can't have anything created. So the creation has to be done in the summer and the fall, around the touring. And of course the more touring we do, the more it cuts into preparation time for the season. So that becomes a problem—how can we do it? Fortunately I have extremely good people—ballet master, ballet mistresses—but it is becoming more difficult to juggle things, to coordinate everything, particularly if people have to come in and stage ballets by different choreographers from outside or oversee them or take a look at them again. We always make sure there is a ballet mistress or ballet master there with the dancers, who knows the work. They might bring a video into the studio sometimes to give a dancer an idea, "OK, you go between so and so," but the step itself is being taught to them by the person. So it's not a question of saying, "Here's the videotape. Go and learn this." What is in the ballet that's not steps? Emotion. Passion. A feeling of . . . a total freedom,

freedom of movement. Maybe that's why I like my dancers to move, feel that freedom, cover that space, make you feel that the stage is not quite big enough for them. The intent of the step has to be behind it, there has to be, hopefully, a reason for that step, why do you do it, not that you just do it, especially in a work that either has a story to it or suggests a story or a relationship. So the gestures become a part of your inner being, rather than just a technical step.

And it's important that a director of a company also choreographs, because I think you have much better and closer contact with dancers than if you don't choreograph or if you don't teach. I convey to them how I want them to dance in the class—I teach company class—or in the choreography, so they get a sense of what I want, what I'm about, and in a way, indirectly or directly, it sets the style of the company. So however they dance, on the Royal Opera House stage or in San Francisco or whatever, it probably *is* a reflection of how I want them to look. If I want them to move a certain way in class or do a certain step that way or have a certain musicality or stress this and that, there's no question that it will affect everything else. This is who I am, this is what I like. How it looks to someone else on the outside, looking at what I'm doing, might not be the same that I feel. But this is what's true to me, and I have to go with what I believe in.

I used to teach about five times a week when I started, but that has trickled down, unfortunately, to maybe twice, sometimes three times a week. But I think it's very important, and choreography also ranks high. The demon of the job is that sometimes you don't have the time. And also, as the director, overseeing the whole repertory and all those dancers, I find myself at times creating something for somebody because they don't have very much to dance. It's very different from someone who comes in as a guest, who says, "I want this, this, this and this," and they choreograph and they leave. My choreography also has a practical purpose, of keeping the dancers happy as much as you can and making sure that they have enough to dance. You sometimes find yourself doing what's necessary—it goes with the job—whereas a choreographer who is engaged to choreograph is probably never going to be in that position. You're not telling them, "You have to do what's necessary"—you let them do what they want, because that way they will do the best work possible. But what do they say about the shoemaker's children? That they're the last to have shoes? It's a little bit the same thing. I'm the last one to have the time to do anything. I have to give my time over to someone who's coming in, because those are the only three weeks they can be here. Or all of a sudden they come with this music and they're so excited about it, and I say, "Yes, I know it," and I think 'Oh, shit,' because I have been thinking of that music too. What do you do?

My greatest obligation, I would hope, is to the integrity of the art of dance, to make sure that it keeps its artistic integrity. Hopefully, what we dance is interesting to see—and I know that not everybody's going to like everything they see—but what I mean is that I hope we don't fall into saying, "OK, but this is what the public wants." Or, "This is what the impresario wants us to bring, because that will sell tickets, so let's just do that." Somebody asked me, "Why did you bring this repertory to London?" and I said, "Because that's what we're about. This is who *we* are. Judge us by who *we* are." Yes, we also dance the full-lengths, but in London you get a lot of full-length ballets, and I'm sure they do them extremely well. But in San Francisco, six out of the eight programs we do normally are mixed repertory programs, so this is what *we* do.

I'm becoming aware that the way this company dances is something special. It's something interesting, something fresh. There's nothing jaded about it, and I feel that it will influence . . . maybe dancers and maybe the way companies look at themselves. They might rethink themselves, not to copy, but I think this company dances in a way that is very uplifting to watch. There's a spirit about the dancers that you don't always see. I want my dancers to show me a joy of dancing. It sounds so simple, but it's an enormous part of dancing. It's not just the physicality of doing everything correct and a good pirouette, but it's 'Take chances, go for it, don't play it safe. And if you fall down, OK, you fall down, you get up again. I would rather you did that and really have gone for something and made it exciting than playing it safe and cautious.'

Do I miss dancing? No, not at all. I have no desire to go back on the stage. At one point I was going to do Madge, but I didn't have time because I was staging it [*La Sylphide*] at the same time, so I didn't do it. Maybe what has replaced dancing is seeing my own work onstage. There's no need for me to go out there anymore. Yes, the dancers are my own work too, but that's different. How can I say this? Dancers come and go. There's always another . . . It was very interesting . . . I had choreographed a ballet, and two or three years later we brought it back, and it was the same thing. It was the same work, and it had the same success. As a dancer myself, I was only as good as what I danced last night, and three years from now I might be dancing differently or maybe not as well, whatever. But what I had choreographed was still there. It gives me a very nice, warm feeling, because I can't dance forever, but that ballet was what I did and it's still there. That was a new discovery.

I have been given the opportunity to do what I think I can do well, what I think I'm good at. This is what I know. I've received so much, and I feel I have so much to give. I have an enormous amount of knowledge in me that I can really help pass on to other dancers. And as long as I'm willing to do that, and the work of being an artistic director still gives me more pleasure than not-pleasure, I think I will do it. It doesn't mean it's an easy job, but when you have worked with a dancer it's great to see that dancer blossom. Something you might have said . . . you know something's clicked in their head and the light bulb has come on and there's a clear understanding and an enormous difference in their approach to what they've been doing, and all of a sudden they go on the stage and they become what their potential is. That is very satisfying.

David Bintley

b. Huddersfield, 1957. Trained at Royal Ballet School and choreographed his first work at 16. Performed with Sadler's Wells Royal Ballet (now Birmingham Royal Ballet) 1976–82 and with Royal Ballet 1982–92. Having spent 1989–93 as resident choreographer of the Royal Ballet and 1993–95 as a freelance choreographer, in 1995 he was named artistic director of Birmingham Royal Ballet, which he still leads today.

I WAS STAGESTRUCK VERY EARLY ON. I was onstage when I was four, in Sunday school concerts at the autumn bazaar once a year, just singing and a bit of movement. I did about three of those, and it was so exciting I just lived for it. My sister started going to a dancing class when I was about ten, and she was going to a local school, an evening thing, doing a bit of ballet, a bit of tap, song and dance, everything, and she was doing dance festivals or concerts or being in amateur dramatics, and I just thought that was the way to get onstage. I had two private lessons at home first, in the safety of my bedroom, with what must have been a 16-year-old girl—she appeared very old to me at that time. I learned to plié . . . no method in this teaching, I have to say . . . and I learned pas de cheval, in my bedroom. That was just to see if I liked it, and I said, "Yes, yes, I like it. Let me go to the proper place."

Going to Audrey [Spencer] was great because I really was onstage, doing everything from old people's homes to big amateur productions where I did song-and-dance stuff like *Music Man*, *My Fair Lady*, *Bless the Bride*, those kind of things. This was a lady who had something like 300 kids who all had six solos each, and after doing a lot of those dance festivals and winning medals with my set of solos, I wanted to change them because I was bored with them. So I said that I wanted to do different solos and would she do some new ones. She came up with some ideas and I didn't like them, so I came up with my own ideas. So I trace the beginnings of my choreography to then, when I didn't have the tools for making the movement but I had the ideas and I knew the characters that I wanted to get across. I saw *Cabaret* when I was very young, I saw it many times when I was much too young, but they let me in and I just loved Joel Grey in that film. And I said to my teacher, "I want to do this character, this M.C." and I showed her some of the things that he'd done. So that was important.

Audrey's forte was not classical ballet, so I had to find teachers that would get me into the school, because at about 14, I really decided, I don't know why, that it was going to be ballet. I just wanted to get to the Royal Ballet School. So that's why I went to several other teachers, the most important of whom was probably Dorothy Stevens. She was high up in the RAD, so you knew that you were within the system. It was good training, and all of those teachers were well schooled in what needs to be done. Then I got to the Royal Ballet School through them, and that was really where my training started.

The first male teacher I had was at the Royal Ballet School—that was Walter Trevor. Oh, he was one of the best teachers ever there, a great character and great for people like myself and for White Lodge kids [from the junior school] as well, he just knocked us into shape. You know, that first year at the Royal Ballet School—I didn't go to the junior school—it's a shock for the outside boys to arrive in a full-time training school. And Trev was great, because he was a no-nonsense, basics teacher and a bloke, a real man, and you need that when you're that age. You need somebody that's going to say, "Stop all that nonsense with the face," just basic stuff, and by the end of the year teach you double tours both sides, [entrechats] sixes, sauts de basque, basic. And despite all his down-to-earthedness, he was a very sympathetic man. I had a tough time at the school the first year, I had an operation pretty quickly, and Trev helped me along psychologically. Not a lot, he didn't baby me through it, but he knew what a struggle I was having.

The great thing about the school at the time, being right next to the company, was that you're sort of a professional apprentice. So you are learning about what it is to be a professional. I won't say you're learning the tricks but you see the tricks, you see the artifice. Although they are concentrating on the perfection of your technique, at the same time you become very aware that that, in a sense, is the laboratory, but the real world is where you have to do it. And when you were seeing the dancers with a range of technical abilities in the Royal Ballet company, which is the thing that you're aspiring to, it opens your eyes. It gives you confidence as well, because so few people are endowed with the kind of perfection that we all would like, and opportunities for somebody like myself arose every now and then. Well, such as . . . The very first time I met Madam [Ninette de Valois], we were doing notation class and we were learning the Satan solo [from her ballet *Job*]. It was the turning point in my life, really. It wasn't often that one had the opportunity to do that kind of dancing, to show that kind of ability. I remember three very key points in my life there, which was a struggle because most of the first year kind of revolved around the injury that I had, which didn't set me up too well for the second year. The Satan solo was second year, and certainly doing that solo and having Madam just happen to walk past the window at the time . . . She took my hand, and that was it. She took my hand to the exclusion of everybody else in the room . . . I mean, everybody else was doing the solo too.

And another key point was the Ursula Moreton Choreographic Competition, which I won midway through the second year, and the other one would be straight after that. Obviously some people had realized that I had some kind of talent and it wasn't a talent to become Anthony Dowell. And they heard that at the Christmas party I had done my M.C. solo from *Cabaret*, and Leslie Edwards asked me to repeat it at the Friends [of Covent Garden] Christmas party. It was just a sort of song-and-dance number, but suddenly, from being a kind of nobody with no chance in respect of what they valued, I had choreographic ability, I had a stage ability—which I had been developing since I was four years old, which one doesn't have much chance to show. Suddenly people were talking out of my earshot about me, and I had been somebody who was being asked to leave the school and go and audition, abroad preferably, which was way down the list of aspiration at the school. But given the criteria of the school at the time, it was not unreasonable, because I was not mild-mannered reporter Clark Kent. I had very strong opinions about certain things. They used to have a music appreciation class for children who didn't go to White Lodge, because apparently those children didn't know anything about music. Both my parents were music teachers, I'd passed all my music exams, top marks, and I had to sit and listen to a record of Beethoven's Pastoral Symphony. Well, I said, "I'm not going to do this. This is an insult." So I got off on the wrong foot with that.

I wanted to be a dancer in one of these companies, but I wasn't what they wanted. I mean, I've never been a top-flight classical dancer, I never had good feet and my legs didn't stretch as much as I'd like, I wasn't the right height, not good proportions, but I was still a good dancer, and there's an awful lot of people who have very nice technique who aren't good dancers. I don't think I got into the company because I could act and choreograph but because I had a whole range of these things which I could do, and you need dancers like that. You can't have a company of Anthony Dowells, especially back in those days, when Kenneth [MacMillan] was still working and Fred [Ashton] was still working. The British repertory still needed a lot of people like Jonathan Burrows and Alex Grant and Guy Niblett, people who could play roles. I think Ashton probably created more roles on Alexander Grant than any other dancer over the whole span, so you needed that kind of dancer—you still do. But also, Trevor was good, because Trev was . . . more a classical dancer, probably, than I was, but he was still my height, my build, did the roles which I thought were interesting, and also [the teacher] Terry Westmoreland, the same—fast, not very tall—so those were the people that I . . . I didn't have illusions about the kind of dancer that I was.

You kind of made your own way. They brought the assessments into the school for the very first time when I was there. We did a virtuosity class and we also performed a solo before a panel that gave marks. I did the Mercutio solo from [MacMillan's] *Romeo*, the ballroom solo, and did it with real character. I mean, I went into the room as Mercutio, I did the solo and went out as Mercutio. I didn't walk in as me, prepare in a corner, do a series of steps, bow and walk out, and that was one of the things those people were having to evaluate. At that time they gave like a performance mark out of ten and then a technical mark out of ten, and I know I got a performance mark of ten out of ten because my teacher told me.

Very soon I went to the [Sadler's Wells Royal Ballet] company, and I was lucky again. Because I was doing these kind of roles, I was doing principal character roles really quickly. I did Coppélius immediately because I'd done it at the school matinée—I was only 19 or something—and Alain and the Widow [in *La Fille Mal Gardée*] and stuff like that. And then Peter [Wright] asked me, within six months, to think about doing a piece. I suppose if I had been a little bit more sensitive I would have realized that that could create a little envy within certain circles, because I was very young and being given chances very young, whereas some older people, who were in the company already, had been asking for those things for a long time. That element was tough.

It never crossed my mind that I was having to do two things—it's always been so. After starting choreography right at the beginning, thinking up ideas to do as solos, the first ballet that I did was when I was 16, just a month after I went into the school. I did it for my old school, for Dorothy Stevens, but really I made this piece, *Soldier's Tale*, for myself, I was the Soldier. But the interesting thing was, I made the ballet for myself but I didn't actually choreograph the role. I choreographed everybody else and then realized that I had not thought about what I was doing or my performance or anything. And after that I realized that actually I was far more interested in the making of the piece than I was in doing the role. It had moved that way. The next piece I did was for the school, it was for the competition, and I was in that ballet because I was using 12 boys, and to get 12 boys together to make a piece at the Royal Ballet School after hours is kind of tricky, so I had to be in it just to make up numbers. But what I'm saying is, I got less and less interested in dancing. Come the first ballet that I made for the company, I wasn't in it, and I've never choreographed a role for myself, ever.

So very quickly, over a period of maybe five years, the choreography just became far more interesting to me. If I had ambitions as a dancer, it was to do certain roles which I just thought I *could* do and were wonderful roles, and I did all of those things except the one which I probably wouldn't have been that good in. I'd like to have done *The Prodigal Son*, and I didn't get it, which was fine. But everything else I did. I did the serious ones, and the comedy ones just all came my way anyway fairly quickly. I must say, I did like playing the serious roles, the Rake [in *The Rake's Progress*] and the Red King [in *Checkmate*] and Petrouchka, because for a character dancer there aren't that many. There are a lot of comedy roles, of course, which are wonderful, but there again, whenever I'm looking at a comic role I'm always looking for the tragedy in it, I'm always looking for the sad bits, the real person, not the clown, the mugger. Even in the Widow . . . there's a soft center there which it's nice to find if you've got the right leads.

Doing that first full-length ballet, *Swan of Tuonela*, was like beginning again. None of the short ballets that you do prepares you for what a full-length means, to have a paying public for an entire evening and not be able to run away after 25 minutes and let somebody else make their evening if I've spoiled it. With a full-length you've got to keep coming back, and the pacing of it is so different, the ingredients need so much more variety. So that was fairly traumatic, and immediately after that the company was going on a two-month tour of Australia and New Zealand, and the idea of being cooped up with the same people immediately after that experience was not something that I really wanted. I'd done those gigantic *Lac* [*Swan Lake*] tours, and the idea of standing at the side and doing the Czardas for that long was not something I felt I could manage. I just wanted to see things, I wanted to get around, and I particularly wanted to spend some time with New York City Ballet. I'd seen them when they came over in '79 and I really wanted to get back to something basic. That happens to me every time I do a full-length work now: I always go like back to basics, to pure things, music and steps and classical . . . just pure things.

So when I took that leave of absence, I went to New York, I went to Berlin for a bit, I went to Canada for a bit, and then that was it, because I'm not actually a traveling person. If I can watch classes and see performances, that's great, but if there's not much going on, I get very bored and frustrated. You've got to see things. You get such a false perspective of what things are by reading about them or hearing people say, "You've got to see this." And I think it's very easy as well, in a company like the company was at that time, schlepping around, working very very hard, turning out performances, to feel that you're not going anywhere. It's a wonderful job, it's a wonderful life and it's giving a lot of people a lot of pleasure, but you've got to think about 'Are we moving forward? Is there some kind of progression? Am I getting better?' And it's very easy when you live like we lived then, as much more of a touring company, to not have enough external influence and also to think rather poorly of oneself, you know, to think that wonderful things are happening everywhere except here. It's not as bad as staying in the same place and thinking that nothing else is happening anywhere, which happens in some companies, that's for sure. But there was just an air, in our company, that we were struggling along and very nice, but maybe not important.

When I went to Covent Garden, I danced quite a bit initially. I did *Cinderella* and *Enigma [Variations]*, which I'd never done, and it was nice to do Bottom [in *The Dream*] and *Fille*, the things that I had done, on that stage. Initially I found it very exciting, and the company at that time was full of people that I admired a great deal. And also, I knew them quite well through [making] *Consort Lessons* and *Young Apollo* and *Galanteries*. The reason that I went there was because I felt that it was a kind of a move forwards and also my family situation had changed, Jennie'd had the baby, and it just felt right. And I knew that I could still maintain my ties with the Sadler's Wells company. My dancing there had lessened a great deal just because I was an older member of the company. By that time I had a big problem with my knee, so things like Petrouchka were out. So I was much more of a resident choreographer there than when I moved to the opera house and started dancing again.

It was an enormous change, worlds apart. Just little things, you know, a man comes and puts your wig on. Now, I'd never gone on-stage in my life with somebody else sticking my wig on, and I didn't like it. I want to know that I have put my wig on and it's going to stay there, and that's got nothing to do with those guys, because they were great, sweet guys. But the amount of attention and all that was very different, and, I'll be quite honest, I preferred it when we did it ourselves.

Everything was very, very different. I didn't find that it was the same kind of family. This [Birmingham Royal Ballet] company, and I would say two or three companies that I know around the world, have a family atmosphere, and you only know that if you've been a part of it. You don't understand it otherwise, but the mutual support within a company like this, as opposed to some other companies, is tremendous, and that's always something which I've really valued highly. San Francisco, when I went there, was a tremendous company—it's a different family now. Stuttgart Ballet also has changed, it's different now, but when I went there Marcia [Haydée] was still there and there was a tremendous sense of unity, of anything internal being kept internal, sorted out internally. And there were no big, deep-rooted divisions within the company, which I do find in some companies. You get rifts which are never really healed, perhaps because the company's big enough to accommodate those rifts, but ultimately it damages them, in a way it makes them less secure.

I think dancers are pretty much the same everywhere, and how much they complain depends on which company they're in. That's what dancers do: they complain, they bitch about the management, I know that. But there is a different degree to how important that bitching is and how much it damages the fabric of the company, and how much it damages the perception of everybody who comes and works with that company. Everybody who comes and works with this company loves it, and I'm not being conceited when I say that, they love it, because everybody's helpful, everybody's working toward the same thing, everybody's pleasant, more or less, and if they're not, then I want to know why. Because if somebody gets invited to work with us, whether as a teacher or a choreographer or *répétiteur* or whatever, then they're important. They're there because we want them there, we want the best that they can bring us. The places that I went back to repeatedly were the places that I was happy to work at, and if I'm not happy somewhere I don't go back.

For the dancers . . . well, again, I think size matters. If a company's just too big and your place within it is capped or too small or not going anywhere, then it becomes a job. It becomes a job that you enjoy doing or a job that you don't enjoy doing, because everybody in dance, everybody in life, is frustrated at some point. You know, you don't get what you want—nobody does. I never got to do *Prodigal*, but so what? I got over it, and I'm not going to make the paying public suffer because of it. That's one of the things that I try to impress upon the dancers, that not everybody is going to stand in the middle. I couldn't run a company where everybody was good enough to stand in the middle. You've got to have levels, and at their level, everybody is appreciated. That's a hard thing to say to a young 20-year-old or something, but I think it's quite important, because you can get yourself into a position—and I was in that position when I was at the Royal Ballet—where you kind of realize that things are not going to be what you want them to be, but you pretend that they are. And you go on for a while, hoping that they are, and then something, if you're lucky, makes you realize, 'This is not going to change, and I am becoming somebody I don't want to be.' Which is exactly what happened to me. You hang around and you wait for it to change, the years go by, and you suddenly realize you're wasting time, you're running out of time, it's not going to happen. The best thing would be if somebody just said, "It's not going to happen," and then you could just go, "Right, now the choice is mine." That's basically why I left—I was becoming somebody I didn't like, because I wasn't able to do what I felt I could do, what I could offer.

When I had joined the Royal Ballet, pretty early on it was suggested to me that I might at some point become director of the other company [Sadler's Wells Royal Ballet]. Now, I had never thought of being a director in my life, ever. It never crossed my mind, it was not something that I had any ambition to do. And my initial reaction was exactly that: "No, it's not something I'm interested in at all." I'd made the move to the Royal Ballet and I was very excited by it. I'd done a couple of works that had really taken off and I was very happy there. And then of course as time wore on and things began to change, I realized that I was not being fully used. 'I've got stuff to offer, and that's not within the plan,' that's what I felt. That was when I actually started thinking that what I was lacking, what I needed, was exactly what a directorship might offer, in that you get to work alongside the dancers. You get to know them, you get to bring them on through a role when they're young, and that wasn't something that I was then able to do, because I hadn't got enough works going into repertory.

And also, in terms of my own ballets, I wanted to be in some kind of control over what they were presented with. Working as a freelance with the companies, especially with San Francisco, I was very keen that the works that I did were of use, that I would make a work for a particular program or that it would go into rep, rather than, "Oh, I'm coming along and I have a marvelous idea." Well, this is a resident choreographer's mentality—that's the kind of choreographer that not only I admire but I aspired to be, a gourmet chef and a short-order cook, as Balanchine said. And quite often it was difficult, because you're not familiar with a foreign company's repertory. In terms of the Royal Ballet, a couple of things had been programmed, I thought, wrongly, and I had said so, which was not received well. You know, I'm not trying to do the man's job, but ['*Still Life' at the*] *Penguin Café* was made to close a program, it wasn't meant to open, and anybody can see you've got to have something to bounce *Penguin Café* off. And I also knew that the audiences liked it so much that they wanted to go home after it. We had a program with *Penguin Café* followed by *Symphonic* [*Variations*]—now, that's doing *Symphonic* a disservice because . . . I'm not being conceited, but a lot of the audience would rather see penguins, they don't understand that *Symphonic* is fabulous.

So for things like that I just thought, 'This is the only way out.' And to be quite honest, I also thought, 'Do I want to stay in this country? I've left the Royal Ballet now, and there's nowhere else here for me to go. If I'm going to work in this country it can only be in this position and it has to be within the confines of a company, because that's the kind of choreographer I am.' I was seriously looking at going to America or possibly to Germany. Certainly some overtures were made to me about the Stuttgart position—I know I was sort of asked to go there because of the Cranko connection, because I did full-lengths, because I worked in a classical idiom and all that. I'd just resigned anyway from the Royal Ballet. I said, "That's it. I'm out of here," and they kept me to finish *Tombeaux*, which I'm very happy about, because it was an important piece for me and it was an important piece to leave the Royal Ballet having made and it was a piece about leaving the Royal Ballet. They advertised the [Birmingham Royal Ballet director's] job, and I applied. Kind of simple, but it's like all of these things, it's never as clear-cut as that. It was never a foregone conclusion, but I knew there were an awful lot of people that thought I was the right person for the job, and I was. I mean, I just had a history with this company which went back a long, long way.

On the one hand, the job is having an artistic vision, an artistic path which you stay on as long as that's the right path and nothing upsets it, like deciding to become a small contemporary company or something like that. The job is that path, which is a kind of summation of everything that you've learned and you believe in, and it's making everything fit in towards that. It's picking the dancers, it's training the dancers, it's picking the staff and the repertory, it's choreographing the ballets, it's schmoozing the right people, it's working with the education people, it's functioning within a specific city. And all of that is great, I love doing every aspect of that. But at the same time, the thing that you don't realize is that you actually are responsible for the minute details of every single person's life, like whether they've got a headache, whether they're having trouble at home, whether you have cast them in the right role, whether they've behaved badly that day, whether they are an unbalanced person, whether they have aspirations beyond themselves, whether they are not aiming high enough. You have to baby and nurse and care about and make feel important every single person. That's the hard part, and that's the part that there is no substitute for. In a sense, choreographing gives you a head start in that respect, you get a definite feel for the pressures of babying people through certain things, knowing when to shut up and when to have a thick skin and all that. It really does help, it does prepare you, although as a choreographer you have a specific ballet and a specific cast and you don't have to worry about whether the people who aren't in it like you or not. As a choreographer there are people I really like working with and there are some people that I don't, even within the company; perhaps they don't work that well within my pieces. But as a director I have to compensate and find work for them to do in other things, not to say that they're always not in my pieces, but I have to balance it out.

Overall your responsibility is to the public. In the end, you can be the nicest guy in the world and you can turn a company upside down and make it into a lousy company by being a nice person. If I feel sorry for somebody because they've not got enough work and I put somebody on who's not capable of doing the job, the public won't turn up in droves. I don't think they'll come, no. You've got to find a broad kind of level, a balance, between the public, the critics, the Arts Council, the board . . . Sometimes you can do a ballet which the critics don't like but the audience loves, so it stays in the rep. Sometimes you make a ballet or you put a ballet on that the critics love and audiences don't like, so it can just about stay in the rep. It's all a balance, isn't it? Money's in there too. We have a certain amount of money and we're not allowed to spend more than that unless it's for the right reasons. We go to the Arts Council and we bribe them. We say, "We need more money, because without it we have to lose those peripheral things which you find so important, like education packages. We have to keep our core activity. We still have to do this many performances, we still have to do this many premieres, so something else has got to go."

Actually we do most of the new productions that classical ballet companies do in this country, and we do the most interesting rep. We have to do this much new work, I believe, especially as nobody else is doing it. If we did rep like ENB or something like that, then the Arts Council is going to start bitching about ballet per se. I'm very happy to take that on board, as long as they recognize that new work is risky and new work costs money. The Arts Council has to balance that out as well. At some point they have to look at classical ballet and at the major companies and say, "There isn't enough new work being done." And if we took the route that other companies are taking, then I would feel that the Arts Council would be justified in taking money away from classical dance and giving it to contemporary groups, that make newer work and don't make as much money as we do.

Somebody's got to do the new work, because that's what the art has to do. We have to do it. We have to. Absolutely. What's the point if we don't make new work? No point. No point in doing *Swan Lake* if . . . You know, the reason that Madam did *Swan Lake* is because that would make the kind of dancers that she could make the new work with. And that's exactly why we do *Swan Lake*. I couldn't have done *The Seasons* if I didn't have a company that did *Swan Lake*. We couldn't do the Balanchine rep if we didn't do *Swan Lake*, if we didn't keep that training. What's the point of employing 60 people if you're not going to use them all in those ballets, which have a corps de ballet? The whole edifice comes tumbling down if you don't have new work. And the dancers fall asleep. Well, what they do is they all just dream of being Odette-Odile. They turn into . . . you know, kids come along at 15 and all they want to do is *Don Quixote* pas de deux. I've heard 15-year-old kids saying that, and I thought, 'God, what are we making here?' This is their life ambition, to be the ten-millionth person to dance the *Don Q* pas de deux. Christ!

The greatest thing, it seems to me, as a dancer is to have something written for you. Even if it's not very good, even if it's not going to be as good as something else or even as challenging, it's as memorable. It's something, at the end of your career, to be able to say, "I did *Swan Lake*," but I know who created Lise and Colas [in *Fille*], I know who created *Pineapple Poll*—I know about those people too. We found about 20 photographs in our archive the other day, the first photographs I've ever seen of Cranko's *Sweeney Todd* ballet—fantastic. And to me, the wonder of looking at those pictures and sorting out who those people were is much more important than finding some stack of old *Swan Lake* pictures.

But I'm not interested in seeing whole evenings of my work, of my pieces—all right if it's a full-length. That's not the way in which I personally would want my work to be seen, and that's not the tradition that I grew up in. It's not the MacMillan tradition, it's not Madam's dream, which was a balance, and I enjoy that balance. It's like the difference between going to see a one-man show and going to see the Impressionists, with the right painting hung next to the right painting. I am interested in programming—I think it's a great skill and maybe instinct and maybe what you've learned from the past, and it was done particularly well by the Royal Ballet over the years . . . and sometimes not. You never know until it's actually there in front of the public whether it works, but I get a real kick out of people saying, "What a really good program." It's just basic to do something for everybody, but not something where you're going to swing wildly and alienate people. I'm not of the opinion that if you put three different works on, well, they're going to like something. No, I try to put works together which have a contrast but they have . . . a theme, although I'm not desperate to theme things either, but there's something within them that 'If you like this, you might like this too.' And I like to do that musically as well, because things can be deadly dull if you're not thinking about music.

Certainly the competition that we have within what's euphemistically called "the leisure industry" has seen audience numbers dwindle a little bit, certainly on tour. We used to do a lot more performances in a lot more theatres, and it always seemed to be fuller, so it is trickier now. A lot of that has to do with pricing, which is a shame. In a place like Sunderland . . . what an amazing turnaround we made there, just because of pricing, initially, and they come back all the time. The first time we went there, in '95, we played 29 percent over the week, 29 percent, and that was with *Swan Lake*. The next time that we went there, a year later, we were around 90 percent, because we just charged £10 [$15.80] for every ticket, and now we're always around the 80 percent mark, which is brilliant. And the other brilliant thing is that most of the letters that I get about productions on tour come from the northeast. It's great. When we go up there, if you get in a taxi and go to the theatre, all the taxi drivers know the ballet's on and they know how much the ticket prices are and they usually have their girlfriend or their mother going. I always say, "Why aren't you going?" "Well, it's not for the working class," they say—I've had those arguments!

But I think audiences have become very lazy—that's probably television culture—and I think they're lazier in London than anywhere. Two practices I absolutely deplore in a theatre: You don't clap the conductor all the way to the podium and then stop as soon as he arrives. You clap him there, and he faces the audience and he bows, and then you stop. But the number of times I've seen the conductor get to a podium and take a bow in silence! And the other thing is, Just because the curtains are closed you don't stop clapping. Curtain calls are because the audience wants a dancer to come through. You don't just wait until somebody else comes out. I hate it. I hate it! And aside from that, the number of people that go to the theatre and just don't applaud, and they're even people who are having a really good time. People that are having a really good time will clap very enthusiastically at the end, but all the way through they just sit there like they're watching TV. So I do get angry about that . . . because I'm the person that has to keep the clapping going.

I think it's important that we get the feeling that we're part of an international community—it's easy to be isolated outside of London—so I like to work with international choreographers and I like not to go for the big guys. It's easy to give the big names a call and get them to come and do a piece, but I like to go for the people who are kind of breaking, the people who are hitting their stride, like Stanton Welch and Lila [York], who is doing really nice things, and James [Kudelka]. Those are people I think it's important to work with, as well as our people within the company. Now we have our second space, the Patrick Centre, where we're going to be able to do small audiences, so that's going to be good, and with that we're going to be able to do some serious, public workshopy type things. And then for the big stage we're already planning another evening with the £10 ticket deal, which has always been very successful, so that's back on course. For the rest of it, you just feel as you go along. The makeup of the dancers is changing at the moment. Some of the people at the top are beginning to leave. We have a lot of young people at the bottom, and a lot of them are coming through the [Royal Ballet] school, because we've been working with the school and trying to improve things there and [school director] Gailene Stock is making a big difference. I'm really trying to bring people from the school, get that as a proper feed for the company instead of this, 'Well, that one's not bad, let's have that one,' and then looking somewhere else.

I'm trying to think of the next few years in terms of what the company's going to be like and what its strengths are. And for me, the emphasis is going to be on lots of steps—I think that is where the company could move quite easily. Over the past couple of years, we've not been able to get the classics on as much as I would like. Now with things like this [performing at Birmingham's National Indoor Arena], I can get a classic on every year. We can afford it because it gives us more performances in Birmingham, and it means that I can give more performances of these things to more dancers. I don't want to lose all of the new work that we get nice reviews for and the Arts Council applauds, but at the same time I want to be able to still keep putting on *Swan Lake*, because it keeps the company in shape for the technique and for classical ballet. Over the next few years I certainly am going to make more work in that vein, and I want to make a company which is strong technically. People don't realize that we've been doing this [Peter Wright's] *Swan Lake* very successfully for 20 years— we have not done it as well as we do it now. I have a handful of soloists, and if you cannot do double lame duck [piqué turns] right every time, then I want to know why, and you're not going to keep your place because there are too many of them that can.

And all the rest of it we do better . . . well, not better but as well as any company in the world. I mean, we have the basic belief that dance is not just about steps, that dance is not just an abstract medium. In fact, it's not an abstract medium at all, I don't believe in abstract dance. There is still the spirit that comes out of your eyes and along your hand and into the distance. Most dancers these days are only putting their hand out, and that's as far as it goes. Well, that's an arabesque, isn't it, but I'm talking about spirit and soul and everything else. We've never lost that in this company. I think we've always had that, to the detriment at times of other aspects of our work, but certainly at the heart of our . . . This company is entirely run by people who come from that tradition and were trained by Fred and Madam. Marion Tait, Alain Dubreuil, Desmond Kelly, Denis Bonner the notator, even our executive director, we were all in this company 20-plus, 25, 30 years ago, and we still believe that that's the right way to do things. Some of the stars that were about, and indeed are about, have a great technical facility which is focused upon to the detriment of their performance as a whole. Certainly that has happened of late. I'm not denigrating that technique at all, but it is not a replacement for performance. This company was never a leader technically but in terms of performance and giving and role-playing, there was nobody better, ever.

We never put on any work without going as close as we can to the source that is available nowadays. We get the people from the past in, the people who have done these things, whether it's Peter [Wright] and Galina Samsova when we do revivals of their work or Jean Bedells or Pamela May for *Dante* [*Sonata*]. It's quite hard, sometimes, when you're making a revival of something like *Dante* or *Prospect*

[Before Us], to enthuse 17- or 18-year-olds, to make them understand why a piece like this is worth doing and what the peculiar challenges of it are. The important thing is that we keep that history alive in them and in our training of them, so that they understand that it is important to us. *Dante* is not a difficult ballet physically, and *Prospect* even less. You see, maybe this is part of this myth, that if you're not busting a gut, spinning 'round all the time, the work is not going to appeal to an audience. Now, the great thing about this company, regardless of what it may think or feel, when it gets on and does it, there's nobody better. The commitment that these kids bring to *Dante* is part of its great success, because they dance it with 110 percent belief. But not everybody's interested in it. I personally always was—I was a great history fan, ever since I was a teenager. The value of these revivals is simply that works which were obviously of some importance in the past don't just go away. *Dante* and *Prospect* were important works in the past and were danced a great deal—they don't just become unpopular and go away, "Oh, we don't like it now," it's gone forever. Things come into style, they go out of style.

I don't think *Dante* is so much of a problem to revive. I don't think there's some secret thing that we've lost, but *Sylphides* . . . *Sylphides* is probably one of the most difficult things you could have suggested. *Firebird* still is as dazzling as ever, and *Noces*, but *Sylphides* is a real problem because it's a period piece which is capturing a period, so even intellectually it's very removed. Already we don't understand what he was evoking . . . not even evoking. I think he was making some kind of modern comment on it; he was probably, in terms of his day, playing with the conventions very subtly. How are we to understand that? And it's hardly in the steps, because I've been there when Markova's taught it, and in the end I can see the dancers going, 'What are they talking about?? Do they really want me to mark this?' because that's what she's almost saying. You can't get all these girls, in a line, so alien, doing next to nothing . . . it is the most difficult example.

And each revival does represent something different. I don't think you can say, "What are the problems of reviving *Dante*?" and, because they were made at the same time, think that those will be the same problems as making a revival of *Façade*. You have literally got to look at every single piece and say, "Will this work now? Will the audience respond to this now?" Why do them? Well, why play Beethoven Nine? Why do *Marriage of Figaro*? They are great pieces. *Façade* is a terrific piece and needs to be revisited, and maybe it's not right for a particular time. I think *Dante* was just startlingly right for this time.

And you see, having a piece like *Dante* in the repertoire affects the rest of the repertoire because it affects your outlook—everybody's outlook, but particularly the dancers', that's who I'm talking about—on what the persona of the company is. The dancers cannot come on and do all that and not have it affect the way they would do something else, say, *The Seasons.* You can't just become a blob. Dancers won't stay with a company where they're bored or not being challenged or where they're not interested in what's going on. I wouldn't—I didn't. And the versatility and the broadness of our rep means that I can give something to everybody, because everybody has different gifts. We're probably not the best company in the world doing *Swan Lake,* in fact I'm sure we're not, because we don't have all those people trained all their life to do one thing. We have people dancing swans who are far more at home in *Dante Sonata* and can show much more in that.

What I'm here to do is to carry on the Royal Ballet, Madam's institution, the British ballet, what British ballet is, what it has to do, where it has to go. That's not something that we're going to reach and say, "Here we are." It just keeps going. That's my job. That is ultimately what it's all about, so that is the biggest pressure, and that is the biggest privilege as well. It's the same thing. In the very broad sense they are one and the same.

Francia Russell

b. Los Angeles, 1938. Studied at San Francisco Ballet school and with Vera Volkova, Felia Doubrovska and Robert Joffrey. Danced with New York City Ballet 1956–61 and with Jerome Robbins' Ballet U.S.A. in 1963. Appointed ballet master New York City Ballet 1964; ballet master Frankfurt Ballet 1973–75, its artistic director 1975–77 and, since 1977, artistic director of Pacific Northwest Ballet in Seattle, sharing all three positions with her husband, Kent Stowell. For the George Balanchine Trust she has staged more than 100 productions of Balanchine ballets internationally, including the first at the Kirov Ballet, 1989.

J LEARNED TO DANCE from Mr. B more than anything and from watching. I was lucky to be in a lot of places where there were great dancers to watch, so it shaped my mind's eye. Volkova was wonderful—she was the ultimate teacher. She loved dancing. In the studio it was the most important thing in the whole world, so there was a fire inside of her and she drew us all to that great warmth—she was incredibly warm and generous. She was a little bit awkward, you know, she'd stumble around sometimes—and I'm awkward too—but it never bothered her. She didn't have time to be self-conscious because what she was giving to the dancer was the only thing that was important, not what they thought of her but her love of dance and what she could see inside of them, drawing out and connecting the two. There was no performance in the class—it was all about the student and the importance of dance and that it's an indispensable part of life. I studied with her when I was 11 and

197

12. I lived in London with my family, and then when we had to go back to California because we couldn't get the papers to stay any longer in England, she and Hugh Williams wanted to adopt me. My father was so overwhelmed, he thought it was such a compliment, that I think he even considered it, but of course we didn't do it. I respected and loved her. I think she was the example for me of the kind of teacher I would really want to be, even though I had no idea I would ever be a teacher, it never entered my mind.

Mr. B's classes were the most demanding I've ever taken, especially the ones he taught on a layoff. We'd have three-hour classes, and I'd go down to the Village to Bob Joffrey to get warmed up, because I couldn't do Mr. B's barre unless I was warmed up. So at the end of this I was like a wrung-out dishrag, but I felt that my body and my brain had done the ultimate they were capable of. If it wasn't good enough, I really could feel, 'Well, that's it, I cannot do more,' and that was a wonderful feeling. He took everything apart. You think you know, say, a tendu—you think you know what it is. Well, there are about 80 billion things to know about a tendu.

I'd been in the company a while before I took his class. I was in the school [SAB] three weeks, went in the company, and I don't think he was teaching right then. And then, Tanny [Le Clercq] got sick right away so he wasn't around. So these classes were later, and by then I knew him. I mean, I'd been in the first cast of *Agon*, and that was around the time when he started teaching again. But I was obviously trying to learn from the day I got there. I had wanted desperately to be in ABT, I kept auditioning and trying, but Lucia [Chase] didn't like me, so that was never going to happen. So I thought, 'Well, I'll try New York City Ballet,' and Kent was the same, get in New York City Ballet or quit dancing. And fortunately for both of us, he took us like that, immediately.

Then . . . Well, I left dancing because . . . My father had really promoted my career and it wasn't my own and I had to grow up. And also . . . Partly because I didn't have enough good training or I had so much bad training, I knew I was never going to be the kind of dancer I had to be in order to satisfy myself. What I was doing wasn't enough to satisfy me. I was getting wonderful parts to dance—in *Apollo* . . . my God, all sort of great things—but I didn't have any confidence in myself as a dancer and I didn't think I could go the next step. And now I think I was right—I don't think I *was* good enough. I had a lot of problems with nerves, stage fright, and

I had a knee injury too, and in those days knee surgery was out of the question. But injury wasn't the primary reason I quit, I also had tremendous curiosity about the whole world. I wanted to learn other things, I wanted to experience the world—I'd been in the ballet studio all my life—and I wanted to use my mind. And the main thing was, I did not want to think about myself 24 hours a day. I couldn't stand it—my feet, my shoes, my hair, my energy, my diet . . . So I was bored with myself and I wanted to go out.

But I came back because I really love dance and I really respected Mr. B, and he kept wanting me to come back. The first thing I did was teaching in the school. [Antonina] Tumkovsky and [Helene] Dudin took me by the hand and I watched their classes and they told me, over and over and over, and that's where I learned the syllabus for small children. That's where it came from. The way I now teach a tendu I learned from Tumey and Dudin and Mr. B. We've shaped some things a little bit differently at PNB [Pacific Northwest Ballet], but the fundamental part of the way the children are taught is from Tumey and Dudin, who were from Kiev. Balanchine really trusted them for teaching children. Then he would come and watch my class, and it's the most nervous I've ever been in my life, oh, much worse than being a dancer, because not only was he analyzing everything I was doing but I had a responsibility to the kids too, and I was so inexperienced. He would take everything apart after class, everything I'd done wrong.

Then I met Kent, who was back with the company. He had come after I left. I met him actually when I was teaching at the school, I think, and then Mr. B suggested that I come back as ballet mistress. Well, it's more complicated than that, but it doesn't matter. What matters is that I was responsible for other people and *to* other people. I owed *them* . . . I mean, I had to know the ballets to help them, to teach them, to get them onstage, to prepare them. And then I was responsible for those little kids I was teaching in the studio. So that was really more frightening in many ways, but when it went well, incredibly more fulfilling. And then I just loved staging the ballets, because I loved the ballets and I loved going to a company that didn't know Mr. B's work and spreading out this incredible array of riches for them and seeing them realize that what they were getting was so wonderful, so interesting. I was teaching wonderful roles and the dancers couldn't resist them, they loved them. At first the roles would feel hard, and then they'd start dancing it, and your body . . . With a Balanchine ballet, it can feel completely uncomfortable in the beginning and then your body learns to love it from doing it over and over. It makes muscular and kinesthetic and musical sense.

When I'm staging a ballet, particularly for the dancers at PNB, it's not just about getting the ballet together and putting it on the stage. It's really about teaching them in a way that's going to make sense to them, that they're going to have to think about and that they're going to remember and that they can then pass on as well. I'm teaching them Balanchine's intentions, what made him put the steps to the music in exactly this particular way, as much as I can understand it . . . which is a lot, but of course it's not being inside his head. But he explained so much to me, particularly about the relationship of the movement and the music, and said, in a couple of instances, "Some day, Francia, you'll be the only person who re-members this spot. You must remember it." And so when I get to that spot in the ballet, I tell the dancers, "You have to remember this, because you're going to be the ones who are going to teach the next generation exactly what this is supposed to be."

The essence of Balanchine is the marriage of music and move-ment, so that's the most important thing to get across to them. And they're trained in the style . . . We don't teach Balanchine technique at PNB. We teach everything Kent and I have learned in our careers, in very eclectic backgrounds. Balanchine was the primary influence, but we don't try and mimic Balanchine in our teaching. It was ap-propriate to the time and place, but it wouldn't be right for our dancers, who have to perform in many different styles. They need to be trained in many forms of dance and they need to have real versa-tility in the repertoire. There are also some things I think have been exaggerated in the style since Mr. B died, and I don't like that. You see, when I'm staging a Balanchine ballet I feel it is my responsibil-ity—as I've said before, my holy assignment—to pass it on as faith-fully as it is in my power to do. When I'm training dancers in class, there are other things that I like to see. So I'm not just teaching a Bal-anchine class: I'm teaching a Francia Russell class, and Mr. B is a lot of what I know. But that's different from staging a Balanchine ballet. Then I don't say, "I'd like you to do it this way, because I like it bet-ter"—I never do that. I try and make it as much the way he would have wanted it as possible.

Sometimes I think that Kent and I were more influenced by Bal-anchine as artistic directors than almost in any way. We espouse his values for training and running a company, because we've found that they make sense to us, we believe in them. Mr. B said he always really wanted to be remembered as a teacher, that he felt that was his greatest contribution. The school was of huge importance to him, and ours is to us. As a director I think the school and the company are equally important, and Kent's very much the same . . . I mean, our personalities are different, but the basic values are the same. We're very demanding, patient, patient, patient, patient and when we've had it and we've waited long enough, then it's over, that's it. A lot of those things are very much like Mr. B.

Also, as directors we spend a huge amount of time doing administrative work and fund-raising and board and all that stuff, which he didn't have to deal with—Lincoln [Kirstein] did it all for him. We have to, but thank God there are two of us so we can divide it up. Otherwise I don't know what we'd do. People are on the board for different reasons, social reasons, business reasons . . . If only they were on the board because they love dance. There's a man on our board, Jeremy Jaech—he loves dance and he's a big supporter of the school. He's done wonderful things for the school, really intelligent grants. He gives us money, and he wants to know exactly what we're doing with it. He wants us to tell him what we need and then how we spend it. He's particularly enlightened. There are a few like that, but not many. Most of them are there because they love parties and they love to meet the dancers because they're curious about them.

We have the fight every year over different priorities. This year there is a young man at the Kirov, a dancer and ballet master, Yuri Fateyev, who helped me tremendously when I was there recently staging three Balanchine ballets. We're bringing him to Seattle for a month to give our dancers another view, to teach class and maybe stage some little things, and also because I want him to understand more of what I was talking about at the Kirov, because he's helping with more Balanchine ballets there. If we decide something like that is important, we find the money and allocate it, squeeze it from somewhere in the budget. But the board doesn't make decisions like that. They have to approve a huge expenditure, like a new full-length ballet with a big production, but otherwise we draw up the budget and we don't expect them to question line items in it—that's our business. If they don't like what we do they should get somebody else, but they don't interfere at all in what we do artistically. Sometimes they don't like everything or they disagree, you know, some like it, some don't. But they trust us overall, or we wouldn't still be there.

In Europe you have so much money that you have to decide where it goes. We were there for seven years, three in Munich—I was staging Balanchine ballets and Kent was dancing there and choreographing—and then we were in Frankfurt four years, two years as directors. And we didn't have to worry about money, at that time we really didn't. We were young and inexperienced and didn't know very much, but we had everything we needed. Now we don't have unlimited funds; we raise or earn every penny, but we like it better in America, even though it's so difficult to raise the money, because the community's involved. A lot of people in our audience give money, maybe $25 a year, that's all they can afford, and they write these wonderful letters, you know, "I wish I could give more," and I try and answer every one. But they're involved. They accost us out front, they call, we hear from them all the time. They're making choices about what they support, and the involvement of the community makes a big difference. It was just a sort of abstract audience out there in Frankfurt; in Seattle we know the community and they know us and our company.

I want dance and ballet specifically to be indispensable to the life of the community that we live in. That's it. Not 'Oh, it's nice to have a ballet company,' but 'We can't *live* without having a ballet company. We've gotten so much out of this company that we can't live without it.' That's one of the reasons we do a huge amount of outreach. We go into the schools . . . We raise the money to do all this stuff the public schools should be doing, and we're doing it for our community so that successive generations are going to feel that way. Not our audience now, but their children and their grandchildren—you know, we've got to keep it going.

We're obligated also to give them high quality and to raise their level of understanding. I think it's a terrible mistake . . . The minute you underestimate an audience, the audience is less smart. They're almost immediately less intelligent, less aware and less adventurous. When you hear that the Royal Ballet is doing *Tales of Beatrix Potter* and *Cinderella* over and over . . . I mean, what do they expect of the audience? It's not the audience's fault. We just did a 25th anniversary season celebrating the history of PNB, and all we did was new works. That was Kent's idea, and when he first told me, I thought, 'Oh my God, that's insane.' And our staff said it was crazy—in fact, we made a major change in staff because they didn't believe they could sell it. Our colleagues in America were all watching to see what happened, they all said, "Our board would never agree to this. We wouldn't dare do it. We need those ticket sales guaranteed." And we said, "OK, watch. We may fall flat on our faces." But we've been building up to it for years and years, and we sold it better than we've ever sold anything—we did new work after new work and we brought in choreographers from all over the world. The audience didn't know what to expect, but they've learned to trust us. So they know that if they come and see three or four ballets, they might hate two but there's going to be something they like. They know they're going to be challenged—they even love hating it—and they know the dancing is going to be great. So we've made the audience hungry for new work. We didn't do that overnight. Their appetite has grown; the better the quality product we've given them, the more they want to see. Sure, we have to do *Nutcracker,* and we do *Cinderella* and *Romeo and Juliet,* but we also do Donald Byrd and Nacho Duato and Billy Forsythe and Mark Dendy and, you know, a million people, and the audience love it, they love the variety.

I think I'm always teaching, whether I'm teaching class or teaching a ballet. In the school . . . We started out training teachers, because I didn't have teachers when we came. So I had to train some dancers in the company to become teachers or train the teachers that were available. We had to write a syllabus with the teachers—they were very involved, they were a part of it—for the early levels of training, starting out with the timing of every single step, so that we were all teaching alike. We have faculty meetings every two weeks where we hash out everything about every kid and parent and syllabus question. We go from five-and a-half years old for creative movement to pre-ballet at six and seven, and then they start ballet at seven and a half or eight and go right up to some of the kids who are here [on tour] being dogs in back of the court couples [in Balanchine's *A Midsummer Night's Dream*].

What I want the school to be has changed a lot over time, not fundamentally but we do so much more now, because I think it's incumbent on us to prepare a young person to be a dancer, not just to have a technique. So it means they now study classic flamenco, modern dance, jazz, they study character, they have conditioning, weight training, they have dance history, music, seminars on all aspects of being a professional dancer. They have counseling on college options, they have help with figuring out how to make their academic education work with their dance education, all sorts of correspondence courses and various programs through community colleges, things like that. One of the things Jeremy Jaech is funding is a complete program for helping them learn to write their résumés. We take videos of them, we have photo sessions, help them put a complete professional-looking packet together to send around to ballet companies, and help them plan their audition tour. Also they can apply for very substantial grants for travel money to go around to audition.

One thing we have not instituted yet, which I have down on paper but I don't have any money to do it, is a teacher training course, because I think teachers also have to be very wise counselors. They do tons of counseling with parents and students—our teachers do. There's always a member of the school staff in a conference and a teacher, who is in the studio with that child, who knows really what goes on from having that daily contact with the child. So the teachers are very involved in all that and they need to learn how to do that. They need to learn other dance forms, they need to learn about music, because most of us don't read music—so many dancers don't—and can't communicate effectively with the accompanist, there are a thousand things to learn.

Learning a syllabus is a complicated, long affair. There's knowing what a tendu should look like and then being able to present it for small children to get the timing that not only makes sense to them but also shapes their muscular reactions and their muscles. The science and art of ballet training is pretty good, but the dancer who's onstage now doesn't know how to achieve that tendu. They don't remember how they learned it. One of the reasons it's so important to me and to Kent is because we learned all over the place. Especially me—I just lived everywhere and had some wonderful teachers, like Volkova, and some terrible ones. And my dancing wasn't anywhere near as good as it could have been if I'd had a foundation. I didn't have one, so I want our kids to have it, so the teachers have to be really thoroughly grounded. Not to take away their personality in the classroom, but they need to be communicating all the time so that we teach in a way that doesn't confuse the kids. If they have two classes with Flemming Halby and three classes with Lynne Short, the training has to be consistent so at the end of the year nothing has been counterproductive.

This year we took five into the company, which is a lot . . . no, four—one is from SAB. We ask the teachers' opinions about how the kids have been working out, but I'm involved in the school all the time so I know everything that there is to know about them. The teachers and the ballet masters put in their two cents . . . We want them to feel good about it and share information, but we have to decide. And, you see, even the little kids in the school perform. We have performances for the tiniest ones in the studio. We have a big school performance with every child in the school, and half of that performance is what we call the Professional Division and they do excerpts from company repertoire. They all dance with the company in *Nutcracker* and various other things and they understudy company dancers in the biggest ballets so that they have a feeling of what it's like to be a professional dancer. The design of the building is based on our ideas for the organization: everything is windows. So the kids in the school are watching the company all the time. They couldn't know more about being a professional dancer without actually being one, which is always different, of course. And the company's also interested in the kids in the school, watching them grow up and seeing which ones they think have promise.

If there's exciting dancing for the students to watch, if there's a company right there that they desperately want to be in, and there's competition—hopefully healthy but not always, some of it's cutthroat between them—I mean, how much motivation can you want? They're tremendously motivated and if they aren't, we don't want them and we'd like to know that before we take them in the company. I think the dancers in our company believe that what we're doing is important, and I think they believe in the kind of dancing we want them to do. Sometimes it's hard, if they've come from another company or another country. The kids from our school have grown up in it, they're marinated in what we want. They know what we want better than Kent and I do—they know exactly what we're going to like.

Sure, there are always some in the company more ambitious than others. We have lazy people too, but not very many—they don't survive. They aren't interesting to us, so then it becomes uninteresting for them to be here, and they don't last long. And we aren't state supported, we have no government subsidy, so we can't afford to have deadwood sitting around. We don't have the luxury of one single person who's not really useful. If we can't use them, we don't renew their contract, and we aren't doing *Prince Igor* every Thursday night, you know, where you've got to have them just to have the rows of bodies. In state-supported theatres there are so many people who can't be gotten rid of, and they are a drain on everybody else. So as hard as it is to sometimes make those decisions about a borderline person, it's healthier for the company, it's always better for everybody.

But, for instance, Kent took a huge chance . . . I guess we were both involved in making that decision. He did a ballet called *Silver Lining* to Jerome Kern music for the end of the anniversary season, and, oh, it was heaven, with Ming Cho Lee sets and a new costume designer [David Murin] we'd never worked with before who turned out to be a dream. It was the biggest hit we have ever had, a huge success. Anyway, I asked him if there was any way he could get everybody in. Usually there's somebody left out in case there's an injury, but we didn't have one person who wasn't featured in some way in this ballet. Every one of the 50 dancers was in it, and we just held our breath and said, "Well, nobody can be injured. They just can't be." And they weren't. You can't count on that happening every time, but it was a real occasion and, psychologically, for anybody to be left out would be so terrible.

And they need to dance, of course, to get better—it's a short career. In the beginning we had a few nice dancers, and if they were out we were sunk. Now there's always a layer behind, we have 16-year-old kids who look fantastic. They aren't all ours, they may be from other schools. There's a remarkable school in Pennsylvania—Marcia Dale Weary, Central Pennsylvania Youth Ballet. It is a cuckoo place, completely cuckoo, they dance from morning 'til night, but we have some wonderful young kids from there. They come to us and complete their training and go on into the company.

I'd like our dancers to have the preparation that makes it possible for them to almost forget about technique. That's the ideal. Then all the expressiveness, the emotional content of *Stravinsky Violin Concerto*, for instance, can be vivid for the audience, warm and clear. But the technique has to be a given. We work so hard on it so that it can be really almost forgotten and so that their bodies are so beautifully trained and shaped that they can truly perform. I feel like we're still reaching for that all the time, all the time, reaching beyond. As the dancers get stronger and stronger, it frees them to be more interesting performers. I want their minds and their souls to be engaged as well as their bodies, and you have to give them the freedom to do that and they have to be encouraged to be individuals and to find that in themselves. We demand such strict discipline, the training's so rigorous . . . But to have the discipline so clear and the training so refined and deep, and to allow them all the expressiveness of their individual personalities and encourage that to flourish, if we could accomplish that for every one of them, that would make me very happy. That's what I do all day every day, try to do that.

There are always some who don't trust themselves enough, and that's when I feel like I've failed. They all have the technique to do whatever is required, but when they don't trust themselves and go beyond it, I feel that I've failed in inspiring the self-confidence that they need. They're all different psychologically, but that's the most fascinating thing about teaching. What a good coach does is approach each one differently, give them what they need, threaten or coax or love them or try and hone the competitive edge, whatever it takes to make them get out there and do the absolute most of which they're capable.

They have this long tradition at the Kirov, it's not good or bad, but every role has been danced by a million other people that the dancers have all heard about. They're competing with ghosts, and they're doing the same ballets over and over and over. They've grown up in them, they've seen them, they've learned them in the school. And the volume of people at the Kirov makes it somewhat impersonal, but on the other hand they spend their lives there. They're in the school as children and they're there as coaches and ballet masters in their seventies. It's so different from our system. We're a relatively young company, and our dancers are doing new things all the time, having roles created on them—it's just so different.

The ones who are most thoughtful about what they are doing love hearing an occasional story or something Mr. B said. But I'm trying to give them flavor, not ghosts. I don't let the ghosts hover over them, and I don't think anyone does it intentionally at the Kirov either. But they talk there about great performers of the past, and that's going to happen here too. Everybody here talks about Deborah Hadley from time to time—she was our ballerina who retired five or six years ago—but there's nothing wrong with that. I feel it's a little bit of a weight on the Kirov dancers because they aren't doing anything new in choreography, of their own. Whereas we are—our dancers are getting to create something themselves, so to have a historical context for other ballets they do is a wonderful thing. And when Deborah Hadley came back and coached Linette [Hitchin] in a role she had created here, Linette loved it. It was a point of view from inside the work, it was a different voice, and Deborah was very encouraging—it was a wonderful experience. I like to take advantage of that whenever it's possible.

You know what I was saying about Volkova and Mr. B and the importance of dance and that it's an indispensable part of life? I think the dancers need to feel proud that they're artists. It's not a particularly easy time to be an artist in America, it's not easy at all, and they need to take great pride in what they do and the seriousness with which they do it and the degree of accomplishment that they have. I also always hope that they will be proud of other dancers doing well and that the company doing well as a whole is something that will make their hearts beat faster—that's very important.

And hierarchy is important, because respect is due the dancers who have performed well over time and become soloists and principals. I love the ballet hierarchy. It goes against the grain of our time, I suppose, but I think it's wonderful. If a dancer has worked hard, established a place in the company, achieved a level of success and recognition, they deserve that respect within the company. And who respects them more than other dancers? But that needs to be reinforced from time to time. On the other hand, the last dog [in *A Midsummer Night's Dream*], the newest member of the P.D. [Professional Division] is also deserving of respect, and of course the reason that they get it is that they might be doing Titania in two years. That's the wonderful thing: A ballet company's the most democratic institution in the whole world. With our hierarchy, anything is possible.

In Creation and Revival

$\mathcal{W}$ITH A LACONIC HINT of condescension, legend records that the producer Mike Todd sat through the first act of an out-of-town run-through of *Oklahoma!* and then walked out, muttering, "No legs, no jokes, no chance." Almost 40 years earlier, the hissing, laughter and groans that greeted the premiere of *Madam Butterfly* forced Puccini to withdraw it from La Scala's schedule after its second performance. Can you believe those cretins? We sneer at them now with the wisdom of hindsight, as if only other people make such foolish mistakes. Alexandre Benois certainly did when he decided to skip the opening night of *The Sleeping Beauty*. Although he was living in St. Petersburg and knew all about it, he wasn't particularly interested in either ballet or Russian music, and none of Petipa's work to date had inspired him to change his mind. And anyway, after attending the dress rehearsal his brother had reported "that the new ballet was heavy and unwieldy, that Tchaikovsky's music was muddled, and that many of the artists said it was impossible to dance to."

As an old man, thinking back to the second performance of *Beauty*, which he did attend, Benois recalled that it had left him "in the power of something entirely new, but for which, nevertheless, my soul had been waiting, for a long, long time." Having woefully underestimated the authors and missed the birth of their creation, he rushed back to the ballet again and again, but he never forgot his original misjudgment. The London reviewers who attacked the first production of *Apollo* in 1928 might have caused more lasting damage than Benois inflicted on himself, as Balanchine acknowledged nearly 50 years later: "I could not read English in those days," he said, "so I never knew or cared what the critics wrote. If I *had* been able to read them, I should have committed suicide."

Long before these ballets were enshrined as landmarks of theatrical dance, they provoked every conceivable reaction from ridicule to indifference, and before they reached the point where the public could respond to them at all, they were nothing more than wishful thinking. As formless ideas they might never have scrambled to their feet in the rehearsal studio to begin with, let alone found their way to opening night or onto a pedestal in history. Diaghilev only hired Balanchine to supply divertissements for various operas. He might have taken one look at the young choreographer's unusual style and dispensed with his services. Or he might have gone broke yet again and dissolved his troupe, leaving Balanchine and everyone else in the lurch. Already 68 when he choreographed *Beauty*, Petipa might have decided to retire before Tchaikovsky began its enchanting score; when he accepted the commission, the composer had not written a note for the ballet in more than a decade. So the works we view now as pinnacles of choreographic art might never have existed in the first place, and given the time that has passed, they might just as easily have vanished by now. During Petipa's reign as ballet master of the Maryinsky Theatre he completed 54 new works, 17 reconstructions and dances for 35 operas, nearly all of which are gone, as are the six ballets Balanchine made for Diaghilev before he made *Apollo*.

The years go by, but nothing changes. Making a ballet is a risky business, laced with dangers that never go away. You can begin and never finish or you can finish and never succeed, which is why new choreography unites everyone who knows about it—and that includes the public—in a monumental act of faith. The formal announcement that "Joe Blow's new creation, *Freesia,* will launch the Bloggs Company's spring season" may read like a statement of fact but it actually guarantees nothing. It merely informs a large group of people that a smaller group has begun to prepare a surprise, which, touch wood, everyone will one day be able to enjoy.

Like clamorous children before Christmas, the public provides the primary justification and ultimate focus of all the activity but must always be the last to discover its secrets. Based on their previous exposure to Mr. Blow or the Bloggs Company, first-nighters, thrillseekers, aficionados and well-organized subscribers will rush to the box office and slap down their cash to buy a pig in a poke, hoping it will turn out to be either a creature of inconceivable beauty or a monster so outrageous that it becomes news if not art. While they wonder and guess, the director shuttles between the studio, the costume shop, the marketing department and the boardroom, keeping one eye on ticket sales and the other on the calendar, and the dancers hurl themselves into rehearsal, praying the familiar confusion will eventually cohere into a piece that flatters and challenges them.

The choreographer, on whom the whole venture rests, crosses his fingers and trudges forward, bar by musical bar, trusting that various doses of craft, intuition and chutzpah will help him locate the work that's somewhere in his head and translate it into steps his dancers can execute; he'll settle for seeing the movement exactly as he envisioned it, but if their skill can improve on his imagination, so much the better. An older artist, especially one whose muse is playing hard to get, may lean heavily on his experience, in the hope that the tricks and conceits that have worked in the past will work again. No responsible adult truly believes that luck will save his skin—ask any cardsharp—and only romantics and screenwriters talk about inspiration with a straight face.

Corralled by the published schedule into a process they know may defeat them, many choreographers fear the first rehearsal and approach it reluctantly, trying to keep the new piece at arms' length. In 1978, when she was still relatively unknown and her company was only five years old, Pina Bausch said, "I always panic . . . I keep pushing it away from me as long as I can . . . I find it incredibly difficult taking the first step because . . . because I know they, the dancers, are then going to expect me to tell them what I want." Bob Fosse was older and more experienced when he admitted, "The most difficult thing for me—because I'm slightly shy and inhibited—was to get up in front of people and try to *create* for them. I mean, I was fine when I was alone in a room, with a mirror and a barre. But . . . to be stuck for an idea in front of forty people . . . I found that the most difficult thing of all . . . And you're always *compelled* to come up with something quickly. Otherwise they'll think you're untalented."

Other dancemakers, and Twyla Tharp is one of them, wouldn't mind starting a piece if only they didn't have to finish it. "My greatest fear in working is always the end. Lately I have taken to tricking myself into finishing by leaving a hole in the middle somewhere, then stitching the two pieces together—the Union Pacific approach." Who wouldn't be scared? The act of creation is exhausting, frustrating and totally unreliable, and the art of making dances involves baffling, elusive processes that just happen to take place all the time. A choreographer walks into an empty room and puts one step after another until, weeks later, a new dance exists where nothing existed before. But nobody really understands how it happens. No one knows where dances come from, how they develop or what constitutes their perfect realization. No one's yet figured out how to mass-produce them, so every replica, like every original, has to be painstakingly handmade. And if that weren't bad enough, the nature of choreography renders it almost willfully resistant to reproduction, because no single element of a dance—not a step, not a floor plan, not a note of music—contains all the characteristics that define the whole. You can see a dance and measure it in space and time, but what you see and measure does not constitute the entire dance any more than your sister's curly hair and wide smile constitute your sister.

As an experiment, in 1972 Balanchine asked Alexandra Danilova to stage *Les Sylphides* for New York City Ballet. To emphasize the importance of the score, he called the work by its original title, *Chopiniana*, and replaced the orchestra with a solo piano, for which the music had originally been written. Most startlingly, he banished the familiar moonlit glade and filmy Romantic tutus, requested a blue cyclorama and sent the dancers out onstage in white practice clothes. Since Fokine had been dead for 30 years, he made no comment, and Balanchine's eventual reaction remains a mystery, though the production disappeared after a single season so he couldn't have liked it very much. Some people, however, adored it, claiming it freed the choreography's intrinsic expressivity from the Romantic imagery that had always clouded the movements and muddied the gestures. Others, considerably more of them, complained that the changes damaged the ballet's essential character. Without its original context, they protested, Fokine's work was not gloriously nude but shamefully naked. Although the choreography could be clearly seen, the ballet had disappeared.

But how could one exist without the other? If something was missing, what was it and where had it gone? Can a work of art survive without it? Would you still recognize that work if you met it in the street? Where did its identity reside, and what was it made of? Sartre argued, famously, that Beethoven's Seventh Symphony doesn't exist either in the printed score, which is totally silent, or in any single performance, since none can be called definitive. So it followed logically that if the symphony were to survive at all, it had to be in the imagination. That reasoning might have satisfied Sartre, but choreographers don't have the option of producing philosophy while tired, patient dancers wait for their instructions and grow colder and more irritated every second they stand still. And try raising the curtain on a stage crowded only with imagination and see how long the public will sit in the dark and watch it.

The people who observe creative activity without practicing it themselves have no option but to talk about it. Without your asking, journalists, critics, fans, and academics will tell you anything you want to know about a work's meaning, inspiration, unwritten subtext, and the gap between its material reality and its ineffable aesthetic dimensions. Their elaborate speculation serves a useful purpose on the arts pages and at lectures and dinner parties, where enthusiasts nibble at it thoughtfully, and at international conferences, where theoreticians address only each other. But all the second-guessing and philosophical conjuring occurs in the civilian world where talk is cheap. Out there, everyone can speculate to his heart's content, because no one's argument makes the slightest difference to the creative work that is going on elsewhere. "I think it's a riot hearing them talk," Mark Morris once chortled, "although if you're paranoid enough, you could think of yourself as dead: 'Mr. Morris' work of the late 20th century . . . ' There's a little bit of the chill of the tomb." The critical suppositions annoy Paul Taylor more than they amuse him: "People are always trying to read my private life into my work. There are times when I read things about my pieces that would give me grounds to sue."

The artists themselves, both the generative ones and the interpretive ones, have better things to do than spout theory, and the persistent inquisitors who coax them into verbal corners quickly discover that they'd rather chat about music or the logistics of an upcoming tour than philosophy. Until the work is presented to the public, choreographers are usually more concerned with making it than with some hypothetical distinction between its physical form and metaphysical content. Some dancemakers are perfectly willing to acknowledge that distinction but won't talk about it, any more than they will talk about the emotional source of their work or its meaning, and those who will discuss these subjects leave the highfalutin vocabulary to the outsiders. "Essentially what I care about is working; that's what I feel my job is," Jerome Robbins protested. "I don't want to fall into profundities and artistry and surround everything with whipped cream. I work, only instead of being a plumber, I'm a choreographer." The painter Barnett Newman put it even more bluntly, declaring, "Aesthetics is for artists as ornithology is for the birds."

Until relatively recently, choreographers weren't forced to deal publicly with analysis or aesthetics, because no one wanted their opinions about anything. Invisible within his creation, the choreographer was the artist whose name people often couldn't remember and whose job they didn't comprehend. I'm not exaggerating. Year after year I listen to conversations that stun me with their innocence. Strangers have asked me if the dancers in a plotless work, say, Forsythe's *In the Middle, Somewhat Elevated*, always perform the same steps in the same order. Some people believe that every performance of *Romeo and Juliet* is identical except for the costumes; as far as they know, the steps come straight from history, just like the text of a play. The same goes for *Swan Lake*. However often they have seen it danced, by English National Ballet or San Francisco Ballet or the Paris Opéra Ballet or the Moscow Stanislavsky Ballet, they assume *Swan Lake* means one thing only, certain music and certain steps joined in an invariable unit.

Performers are far easier to understand, and their larger-than-life stage personalities provoke extravagant passions. The die-hard devotees from standing room and the amphitheatre send birthday presents to their favorites and greet them at the stage door with a singular mix of boldness and timidity, conceding their uncertain status with people they scarcely know but long to claim as friends. For the same reason, better-heeled fans send florid bouquets and invite the dancers to dinner. Despite their different methods, both coteries secretly harbor the same wish, that the artists' magic might be contagious, like some intoxicating virus, and that a little of it might infect an ordinary person if, just for a few minutes, he could linger by the artist's side and breathe the same air.

Boundlessly energetic as only observers can be, the most fervent viewers prolong the performance with their enthusiasm—after one Fonteyn-Nureyev *Romeo and Juliet* at the Metropolitan Opera House in New York, the fire curtain was lowered to send the fans home and then, incredibly, raised again as they continued stomping and cheering—and the extraordinary tributes paid to dancers over the centuries have themselves become legendary. When Marie Taglioni left Russia in 1842, her zealous followers bought a pair of her ballet shoes at auction, cooked them in a special sauce and ate them in her honor, and her effect on the art of ballet in Paris was so profound that a verb, *taglioniser*, was coined to describe it. Hats, shoes and soufflés were named after Marie Camargo following her debut at the Paris Opéra in 1726, and 200 years later normally staid Londoners worshiped the stars of Diaghilev's Ballets Russes as adolescents would one day worship the Beatles. For the composer and conductor Leighton Lucas, who was then dancing in the troupe, the memory of that fevered public infatuation never faded. "I saw a girl at Charing Cross Road fall down on her knees and try to kiss Idzikowski's hand . . . ," he recalled. "It was an intense embarrassment to him, I assure you."

Apart from the adulation of the fans and cognoscenti, who naturally represent a tiny minority of viewers, for centuries the general public seemed content to take dance or leave it. The audience that came to the occasional performance and glanced at the photographs in the local paper when the show passed through town knew nothing about the performers' private lives and paid no attention to them offstage. Except for the few hours they might spend in each others' company—the artists behind the footlights, the polite public in neat rows facing them—nobody gave the dancers much thought, or asked them what they thought, until the 1960s, when television crashed into dance like a meteor, reshaping the art as fundamentally as it reshaped politics.

During his televised debates with Richard Nixon before the 1960 presidential election, John Kennedy looked through the glass screen and straight into the viewers' eyes, smiling broadly and chatting like a man leaning on the back fence, and people who had always considered government someone else's concern smiled right back and slid him into the White House. Even before that, during the Bolshoi Ballet's first visit to London in 1956, ten million people watched its abridged second act of *Swan Lake* in a BBC television broadcast. Few viewers knew one dancer from another or would risk their dignity trying to say the Russian names aloud, but the company's arrival in the West had created too much of a stir for a living-room performance to be casually ignored. Roughly ten years later, Nureyev began turning up on late-night talk shows in America, playing unerringly to the camera and sporting platform boots that matched his snakeskin jacket. By the time he was busted at a party in Haight-Ashbury in 1967, along with a handful of guests allegedly smoking marijuana, dentists and ministers and housewives all over the Western world knew his name and could pronounce it properly. Soon the *paparazzi* were snapping ballet dancers at discos and on the beach, gossip columnists began sidling up to them at society balls, and New York taxi drivers were delivering wisecracks on the subject with the gusto of the street sweepers in *The Red Shoes*.

As the commercial promotion of dance gradually gathered speed, dancers became increasingly involved with their own promotion and developed a profitable relationship with industry. In 1971, Rolex used a photograph of Antoinette Sibley as Aurora in advertisements for its watches, highlighting the parallel between one precision instrument and another. A few years later Fonteyn, Nureyev and Martha Graham appeared together in print, swaddled in mink, on behalf of Blackgama, which regularly wrapped celebrities in fur and posed them beneath the slogan "What becomes a legend most?" Wielding the tools of modern technology with the same exacting determination he applied to his body, Nureyev became the first star to shine simultaneously on television, in magazines and even in two cities. One chilly night he left the Met after his curtain calls for the first ballet on the program, climbed into a waiting limo wearing his dance tights, wooden clogs and a fur coat, and reached Washington in time to dance in a second performance the same evening.

So it's easy to date what happened next. Like children idly kicking pebbles down a hill, Nureyev and television between them started an avalanche of general interest in dance that left the rarefied band of cognoscenti in the dust, and every decade added new power to the landslide they had initiated. The '70s brought Natalia Makarova and Mikhail Baryshnikov, whose dramatic defections and subsequent artistic triumphs in the West kept them on the front page. Matchmaker Robert Joffrey introduced the cerebral wackiness of downtown experimentation to the refined elegance of ballet by inviting Twyla Tharp to create a work for his uptown company. The two worlds tied the knot in 1973 and brought forth *Deuce Coupe*, one of the first audacious offspring of mixed marriages in dance. In 1976, the Public Broadcasting System launched a ground-breaking television series called *Dance in America* with a one-hour program on the City Center Joffrey Ballet. To make sure the cameras would keep up with the dancers, the producers hired cameramen who had been shooting ice hockey. Surveying his audience three months later, Joffrey discovered that 45 percent of it had watched the program and 59 percent of the first-time viewers at his performances had bought their tickets because of what they had seen on television.

When dance became hot enough for Hollywood to sit up and take notice, the silver screen began to glow with aspiring young ballerinas and disco disciples. *The Turning Point* and *Saturday Night Fever* were released in 1977, and both the romance of broken hearts and the Cinderella fantasy of boogie nights became mainstream box-office hits. With the '80s came MTV and rock videos, music in hectic, visual frames that made it more colorful and more substantial than sound by itself. Slickly styled and packaged for mass appeal and promoted with calculated hype bred of sophisticated market research, performers like Michael Jackson, Paula Abdul and Toni Basil hooked the younger, hipper members of the music public on dance—Jackson's *Thriller* video came out in '82. Video recorders romped into private homes like hungry pets begging to be fed, and as they became everyday accessories, they justified the transfer to tape of ballet and modern dance for commercial sale. Hawking their wares for the first time in bright cardboard boxes, the dance companies made a little money, their audiences got to take some of the experience home, and if you couldn't afford a ticket or happened to live too far from a theatre, you could tune in anyway. It wasn't the same as a live performance, but you couldn't beat video for price and convenience—you didn't need a baby-sitter and you could enjoy the show and pay your bills at the same time.

Then it was 1993, and—pow!—the World Wide Web emerged from a research laboratory in Geneva like Athena from the forehead of Zeus, armed with unimaginable power and and fully prepared, as she was, to preside over the useful and elegant arts. At a stroke, or at a keystroke, the characteristics of communication, information and distance changed irreversibly as they fused inextricably. Time folded up like an origami flower as soon as news broke everywhere at once, and because they could, outlets for it exploded like popcorn, multiplying faster than anyone could credit. The print media struggled to keep pace with electronic networks and cable television as information flowed across national borders and international time zones. And with so much space waiting to be filled and so many eager reporters and experts and fans competing to fill it, any public figure could become a celebrity, even a chef or a jockey, even a dancer.

Yet the media got much less mileage out of choreographers. Just like Ted Shawn and Doris Humphrey before them, during the 1950s and '60s Cunningham, Taylor, José Limón and Alvin Ailey led their companies onstage as well as off, as did the younger dancemakers who spun away from their influence to establish their own groups. Articulate in motion they had no voice except in their movement. When the Ford Foundation subsidized a modern dance season in New York in 1969, with Graham, Limón, Cunningham, Taylor, Tharp, Erick Hawkins, Yvonne Rainer and Don Redlich as the participating choreographers, the *New York Times* ran a group photograph of the old guard and their artistic offspring but didn't bother to interview any of them. The same cloak of silence enveloped ballet choreographers, most of whom, by the 1950s, had enough professional dancers at their disposal to write themselves out of their creations and abandon performing for good. Traditionally unheard, they became unseen as well. So for many years they went about their work as choreographers always had, discussing it with their friends and colleagues, but seldom expressing themselves anywhere else.

Then performers began to ricochet around the world as if dancing were a giant game of pinball. International stars turned into common currency, and when big-name personalities came two for a penny, even choreographers made good copy. They began turning up at black-tie fund-raisers, not always in black tie but smiling dutifully for the cameras while they pitched for the cash that would see them through the next season. The younger ones played brazenly to the hip new audience that had reached dance through the raucous excesses of pop videos. A few of the bolder young dancemakers obliged this public's taste for insolence by taking off their clothes onstage, and many of those who didn't strip pounced on the opportunity to step out of the shadows and explain their intentions. By the 1980s they had plenty of chances to speak at conferences or to arrange postperformance question-and-answer sessions, and some of them took to writing lengthy program notes to accompany their work.

But this tendency toward revelation, whether of body or motive, is a relatively recent phenomenon, which doesn't actually change either the substance or the quality of the choreography on display. Most 20th-century masterpieces were originally presented to the public without biographical trimming or philosophical rationalization of any kind, however personal the content and however passionately their authors felt about it. No one expected the birds to discourse on ornithology, so they didn't have to and didn't try. It's possible that they preferred to keep themselves to themselves. At 87, the photographer Henri Cartier-Bresson said, "I've trained myself all my life to be unnoticed, in order to see better . . . to be able to concentrate," and when Balthus was asked to contribute some personal information to a catalogue of his work, he replied, "Balthus is a painter about whom nothing is known. Now, let us look at the pictures." Even if a choreographer were bursting to confess his deepest creative secrets, given all the words in the world, how much could he actually explain? He could talk about his inspiration, name his tools and discuss the way he uses them, but that would only account for the icing on the process, not the cake itself.

Anything can pry open the door to a new creation. A character can wander into the choreographer's imagination, carrying a crowbar or a bag of marbles, and stick around until another character shows up. A tune can sneak into a choreographer's thoughts and stubbornly refuse to leave. A photograph could start the wheels turning or a joke or a snatch of conversation. Anyone can make a dance out of anything . . . well, you probably can't, and I know I can't because I once did, with pitiful results, but for an artist the possibilities go on forever. Graham chose to make dances out of Greek myths, and Cranko turned to Shakespeare and Pushkin. According to an 18th-century historian, Jean Dauberval stopped one day to urinate in the street and noticed, in a glazier's window, a colorful print showing a girl in tears, a youth running from a cottage and an angry old woman hurling the boy's hat after him, which in very short order Dauberval transformed into *La Fille Mal Gardée*. More recently, Douglas Dunn canvassed the 1,500 people on his mailing list for ideas and made a dance from the 30 suggestions they sent him.

Spoken aloud, the subject may only resonate with the speaker. The producer David Selznick predicted that the audience would walk out of *Some Like It Hot* in droves. When Agnes de Mille went to Pavel Tchelitchev for advice about a designer for *Rodeo*, he listened to the story she had in mind and then told her, "This is not an interesting plot. It is not fit for a ballet. Let us think of another plot." Not that it mattered. De Mille stuck to her guns, resolutely ignoring anything that would alter her vision or distract her from it, because until a dance is made, no one else has the slightest idea what it will be or how it can become itself. That's why every artist's vision of the work under construction is both inexplicable and unique, and it's also why a dozen choreographers will realize the same subject a dozen different ways. Sitting on a bus one night with nothing to read, I started making a list in my head of dances about dancers. It began *Konservatoriet*, *The Lesson*, *Afternoon of a Faun*, *Etudes*, *Gala Performance*, *Acrobats of God*, *Variations Sérieuses*, *Foyer de Danse*, *Ring Around the Ring*, *Le Concours*, . . . you get the idea. I've probably seen 20 or 30 different *Romeo and Juliet*s, and there are more than 75 versions of *Le Sacre du Printemps* and literally hundreds of *Nutcracker*s, each as individual as the individuals who crafted them.

The choice of music opens just as many doors as the choice of subject, because nothing automatically suits the first eight bars of music though the result may look inevitable to us years later. Anna Sokolow and Peter Martins have used the same music for different creations, as have Massine and Béjart, Arthur Saint-Léon and Roland Petit, Leonid Lavrovsky and Flemming Flindt, and John Neumeier and Richard Alston. Stravinsky's *Le Baiser de la Fée* inspired different responses from Bronislava Nijinska, Balanchine, Ashton and MacMillan, and an incongruous quartet—Mary Wigman, Alvin Ailey, John Butler and David Bintley—have all fallen for Carl Orff's *Carmina Burana*.

OK, so the subject doesn't determine what the artist finally produces and neither does the music, and if you've started thinking about steps, you can stop now. Neutral as Switzerland, steps can't light the way to the center of the creative maze, because they're only the means for shaping something greater than or at least other than themselves. They can't express anything without a context, and every new context can render their names meaningless. The dancers at American Ballet Theatre devised their own verbal shorthand for Tharp's *Push Comes to Shove*: "I gotta spin-spin-sinkdown-bunny," said one. "I gotta spin-bunny-bunny-curtain call," said another.

Some choreographers return to music they have used for one dance and fit entirely new steps to it years later to make another. Or they compose a riddle with steps, repeating the entire text twice, identically, in a single dance, but changing the music or the lighting the second time around. Remy Charlip choreographed his *Air Mail Dances* by filling page after page with drawings of little figures, 20 or 40 of them to a sheet, and leaving their arrangement to the performers. Steve Paxton created *Satisfyin' Lover* for a large group, 22 people originally but sometimes as many as 84 and not necessarily dancers, who realize it completely by walking from one side of a given space to the other, pausing only to stand still or sit down.

How can an artist explain a choice he probably doesn't even understand himself? "I'll make a dance about gangsters" or "I'll make a dance to Satie," simply means, "This is my preference," just as "Cherry, please," means someone else can have the last prune danish. So whatever defines a work's physical presence and ineffable spirit only begins with this piece of music or that string of steps. Beneath the flimflam and labels—intricate scenarios, technological enhancement, postmodern attitudes and deconstructed vocabulary—lie fundamentals that can't be chosen and never change, and once you strip the veneer of personal preference from choreography, what remains is both simpler and more complicated than choice.

The complications derive from the bare facts. It's hard to translate thought into movement in the first place, harder still to insure that everyone will see what you want them to see, note its dramatic value or graphic beauty and understand its purpose. It also takes patience and subtle persuasion to fabricate something that any group of strangers will want to look at, not just once but again and again. Practice doesn't really make perfect: practice makes fluency and skill. Only talent makes perfect, and even perfection is a matter of opinion. In 1872, a certain Prospero Bertani traveled from Reggio Emilia to Parma to hear Verdi's *Aida*, then scarcely six months old. The performance disappointed him so much that he sent the composer a bill for his theatre ticket, his train ticket and his dinner. Amazingly, Verdi agreed to reimburse him for everything except the dinner, which he claimed Bertani would have eaten anyway, but only on the condition that the gentleman never return to his operas again.

Responsible only for its own amusement, the public reacts to its entertainers callously, and it can switch its allegiance as fast as you can snap your fingers. Like some mythical creature that lives forever and assumes a new face every day, it is thoroughly unpredictable and therefore essentially unknowable. It has no obligation to educate itself, to pay attention, to exercise considered judgment or to stick around for the second act. So it pleases only itself, drifting happily from one diversion to the next, and the choreographer who tries to serve it, or woo it, by tailoring his work to satisfy its whims stands no better chance of anticipating them than he does of winning the lottery.

Which only increases the difficulty of making something out of nothing. Rather than wasting their energy trying to predict the reception of anything they might produce, the more experienced artists dig in their heels and go on working. "When I had my first flop," Robbins once remarked, "I realized that the only difference between a flop and a hit is that one ran, the other dropped off the edge of the planet. Otherwise, my efforts and joys were exactly the same." If an artist decides to dump his ideal creation and make a cold-blooded bid for popular acclaim, he may stop dead in his tracks, paralyzed by confusion or waylaid into dead ends. On the other hand, if he puts his own goals first and refuses to worry about an audience he cannot fathom anyway, he may set out to make a masterpiece, and then, as Balanchine used to ask, how will he ever finish it?

Finishing a piece, now, that's where anxiety is born. Chardin proceeded so slowly that the pheasants in his vibrant still lifes rotted before he finished painting them. Flaubert left gaps in his sentences for years while he searched for the words to complete them to his satisfaction. Most choreographers, however, don't enjoy the luxury of working without a deadline, and the timetables that control them have little to do with either their private goals or the public's indefinable appetite. Threatened with the loss of Carolina Rosati, who was already poised on the brink of retirement when he began composing *La Fille du Pharaon* for her, Petipa polished off the opulent three-act spectacle in an incredible six weeks, calling two rehearsals a day in order to schedule the premiere before her contract ended. [Vaslav] Nijinsky struck a better deal for his choreographic debut, but then, he was negotiating with his mentor and lover. To create *L'Après-Midi d'un Faune*, a twelve-minute ballet with a cast of eight, he appropriated about 100 rehearsals.

In a fledgling company that is still searching for its audience, necessity alone can drag a choreographer through weeks of false starts and wilting enthusiasm. Sixty-five years ago, Ninette de Valois hounded Ashton into creating one work after another for the newborn Vic-Wells Ballet, and Michael Somes remembered her declaring, "Now, Fred, I want a romantic ballet at Christmas and then a twenty-minute abstract ballet by Easter." Decades later, she explained that "Fred's main weakness in the very early days was a certain lack of follow-through. You'd find yourself saying 'But you can't finish it like that' and he was quite capable of replying 'Well, I'm tired of it anyway.'" And she could still easily justify the pressure she had applied: "There was no repertoire—there was a vacuum and we practically produced ballets alternately at one time. The work had to be done."

The deeper you dig, the simpler the explanations become. Beneath the padded spur of a contract and the naked whip of necessity, beneath public expectation and private terror, beneath mountains of choice and slivers of chance, the choreographer's needs are incredibly basic. Never mind critical theory and elaborate program notes; they turn up only after the fact, when the hard part is over and the dance exists. Before the fact, when it matters most, all a choreographer needs to create a dance are dancers and some way to communicate with them. What defines the work? Where does its identity reside? The choreographer defines it, and its identity rests wherever he puts it when he delivers his creation to his performers.

Everything else is merely a practical problem waiting for a solution, a question of time or space or money, which in the theatre represent different faces of the same devil. Although Paul Taylor found certain passages of *Byzantium* in a dream and Fokine began and completed *Carnaval* in three rehearsals, most choreographers need all the time and space they can get in rehearsal. Time to investigate, to try and fail, time for second and third and fifth thoughts. Until American unions began protecting dancers' rights during the 1940s, rehearsals were free of the clock and could theoretically continue forever, like baseball games. But time now equals money; in 1997, when Lar Lubovitch claimed a sizable chunk of ABT's preparation period to make his evening-long *Othello*, his rehearsals gobbled up $1 million of the season's budget, in bites of $200,000 per week. As for space, well, to this day the concrete pillars that break the expanse of the big rehearsal studio at the New York City Center haunt the repertory Gerald Arpino made there for the Joffrey company. If you watch carefully, you'll see their ghosts in those dances, occupying two small patches of floor on which no one ever treads.

Established companies with home bases can supposedly stop worrying about work space, but finding it in the first place and maintaining or retaining it over time can daunt even veteran troupes. The leading ballet companies enjoy the security of exclusive premises in New York, London, Paris, St. Petersburg, Moscow and many American cities. In Germany, Switzerland, Sweden, Holland and Italy ballet companies live and work in municipal opera houses that are wholly supported by the state. But for want of a home, the Joffrey Ballet had to leave New York in 1995, and Sadler's Wells Royal Ballet moved to Birmingham and took that city's name in 1990.

Smaller and poorer by comparison, many modern dance companies live like gypsies. Although the Cunningham company is safely ensconced in dedicated space it acquired in 1971, and the

Alvin Ailey American Dance Theater has chosen a site and begun raising funds for a spectacular new home for the primary and junior troupes and the company's school, Trisha Brown lost her lease in 2000, Paul Taylor lost his in 2002, and the Limón company's will expire in 2004. In London, the Rambert company occupies its own premises, Richard Alston's troupe shares studios with students at the Place, and Matthew Bourne has moved into the Old Vic. But respected choreographers like Siobhan Davies, Lloyd Newson and Michael Clark pay what they must for whatever space they can find, as do many of their American colleagues.

Just when it seemed that commerce would evict art completely, in 2000 the New 42nd Street Studios added five floors of gleaming, well-equipped rehearsal space to New York's dwindling stock. Small, low-budget companies could rent the studios for $10 an hour, which can safely be called dirt cheap when the going hourly rate was $45–$55 and a hamburger could set you back $6.50. Dance Theater Workshop broke ground in 2001 for a new performance complex featuring a media laboratory, a black box theatre and two large rehearsal spaces. That same year, the Place in London opened freshly renovated studios that independent artists could hire for the subsidized rate of £11 [nearly $16] per hour, and Edinburgh sprouted a purpose-built Dance Space, the city's first, that rented out its four studios for £20–£45 (about $29–$65) hourly. Cavalierly ignoring Billy Rose's prudent advice, "Never invest in anything that eats or needs repairing," in 2001 Mark Morris moved his company into a permanent home in Brooklyn, designed and built to order. Motivated partly by the desire to supply his less fortunate colleagues in dance with affordable rehearsal space—rates varied from $8 to $15 an hour—he dismissed the suggestion that becoming a landlord would alter his position in the dance world. "I've been big league for years," he laughed. "Only now I'm big league with real estate."

Though every choreographer dreams of the ideal base for his troupe and his talent, the bare essentials of heat, adequate light, showers and a properly sprung floor can often cost more than he can earn or borrow. But a determined dancemaker can pursue his ambition even without a full-time company, a reputation or enough cash to hire a hall. Before he is burdened, like Atlas, with the weight of a roof and a mortgage, he can always write on his own body. What could be easier? He knows the instrument intimately, he owns it free and clear, it's always around when he wants it, it's incredibly willing, pathetically eager to please, and it obeys without an argument. Or it tries to obey, and if it fails to make the shapes that hover somewhere between his imagination and his muscles, it will make other shapes instead, somehow converting the death of one impulse into the birth of another. Like a peddler with his livelihood strapped to his back, this artist can go anywhere, work any time, and there's his body, loyal as Peter Pan's shadow, just waiting for him to unwrap its possibilities and present them to the world.

While he's making solos for himself a choreographer is peculiarly self-sufficient, and he can fiddle with a dance until it satisfies him. Although his personal abilities will both enhance and limit the way a piece develops—"My leg never went up very high," David Gordon admitted, "and turning still makes me vomit"—they will also, always, propel it from mind to body without words or explanations. As long as the artist writes for himself, he can adjust his creation indefinitely without ever compromising it. In those circumstances, the dancer is the dance, and no distinction exists between the two. Having performed with Cunningham's company from 1950–58, Marianne Preger-Simon was convinced that "Merce created this wonderful technique for us to learn that *he* never used because he just *danced*. We learned the technique to approximate what he did intuitively . . . when you saw him dance a solo, it was really different from anything that we did as a group. The solo was this creature, just *being*. We, on the other hand, were *dancing*."

So, as if making dances weren't risky enough, the moment anyone wants to involve a body other than his own, the decision compounds his difficulties instantly. All of a sudden he must articulate and clarify for others what he has only sensed. He must not harm their bones or their dignity—after all, the photographer Eve Arnold pointed out, "If somebody lends you their face, you owe it to them not to savage them." The dancers waiting on his instruction must also be paid for their time, they must be allowed to rest, and they will not be available to try out a new phrase at 3 A.M. Choosing his method instinctively, the same way he chooses his subject and music, every choreographer comes up with a different approach to the inescapable problem of transmission. Petipa prepared by pushing little figurines around on a table at home to map out the groupings before he reached the studio. Massine arrived at rehearsal with books, handwritten notes, diagrams and about five choreographed versions of every 16 bars of music; he would teach them all and make his selection by a process of elimination.

May O'Donnell, who joined Martha Graham's first company in 1932, recalled years later that "she would plan the material . . . We'd all try it. And then she would stop, sort of huddle. She'd just sit with a shawl over her shoulders, and we'd wait, and she'd think the thing through. And then she'd suggest something else and try it. She needed a lot of quietness." Jean-Pierre Bonnefous described another method to me: "Béjart choreographs right in front of you; the music is on and he's doing the steps . . . He needs to do the movements himself to do the choreography, so you just have to imitate what he's doing. But it was done for you, for your body . . . You're a part of it, because if you can't do a step and by not being able to do it you do it another way, that other way catches the eye of the choreographer and it becomes the ballet." Buzz Miller remembered Bob Fosse working along similar lines: "He threw about a million steps at us, and Carol [Haney], who was Bob's link, would pick them up like a magnet. He'd show us something and Carol would go 'uh-uh,' meaning she hated it, or 'ah-ha!'—it works! Bob loved that kind of feedback. He was so good to work with because he really wanted you to be great."

Some choreographers write their ideas down in private hieroglyphics, and others ask the company to improvise or suggest movement or experiment with given sequences or talk about their characters or sing the score. Each author can choose whatever mechanical means suit him to translate his thoughts into someone else's deeds. But regardless of his method, he must give away every dance the moment it is made . . . no, faster than that, while he is making it, and in every instance the dancers must be tempted, threatened, cajoled, provoked, soothed, bullied and praised to the skies to fulfill a vision they cannot discern themselves. When Ralph Lemon made *Tree* in 2000 as part of his *Geography Trilogy*, he intentionally cast nondancers, including drummers and part-time farmers, and asked them to perform in both contemporary and traditional styles, mixing house dancing with Balinese and West African moves. "Eighty-five per cent of what you're seeing," he claimed later, "is a result of mistranslation. Some things I could make happen, and sometimes I just let the misinterpretations become the work." Preferring to create more collaboratively, Lloyd Newson has grown used to fitting his own ideas around his dancers' choices. "For example," he said, "a female dancer asked me . . . why some of the men are naked in the piece, but none of the women are. I explained that the men had offered and the women had not and that I was not going to ask the women to take their clothes off."

Whether the choreographer treats his company as collaborators, plays them like musical instruments or manipulates them like tools, the successful realization of his dance cannot be separated from his ability to transfer it to their bodies. At first the weeks disappear in moving their limbs through the music and arranging the cast in space, because, as the theatre director Peter Brook discovered in rehearsal, "What is achieved determines what is to follow, and you can't just go about things as if you knew all the answers." Then, just when the last step is assigned and it looks as though the dance is finally finished, a little more space or a little less time starts to make a huge difference. In that respect, artifice is exactly like reality. Your new shoes either fit or they pinch, and once you've mailed a letter it's too late to rewrite it. The same movement performed quickly instead of slowly produces an entirely different effect—one is a slap, the other a caress—and it's no different on the stage, except that you need subtler distinctions than speed to get what you want. In rehearsal a terse correction like "Too small" may refer to the force of a gesture, the pace of its execution, its relative value in a longer phrase, the space it occupies, its relation to the music or the mechanics of one person handling another. "Too small" can mean "Move bigger" or "Project more" or even "Wait longer," since choreographic tinkering also involves the stillness within the action. The Japanese, who savor absence in art as well as presence, treasure the pause between words and images; praising the unpainted canvas for *yohaku-no-bi*, literally "the beauty of extra white," they value even those portions of a composition that the artist chose to leave blank. Comedians love that pause too, and the gift of maneuvering it to best effect represents the unlearnable skill they call "comic timing." Shifting deftly into radio as vaudeville began to crumble, Jack Benny established himself as a comic character who was vain, testy and pathologically stingy. His best-known joke condensed his personality into a single hesitation: confronted by a mugger demanding "Your money or your life?" Benny answered, "Well, . . ."

No one knows how to move or how long to pause in a new dance except the choreographer, who holds everything in proper alignment as gravity holds the planets. No one else has the innate authority to say, "That's too fast" or "Lift your chin" or "Stand closer" or "Use the other leg." In all probability, the choreographer won't know the answers to the questions put to him until the moment they are asked, but he'll always answer, if only by instinct, and gradually the verbal and physical responses and the dancers' translation of them will move the dance a little closer to its fulfillment. "It's all already out there," declared the artist Robert Irwin. "With any new situation, all you're trying to do is to tease out something of significance. You're not trying to form it from the outside—you're just trying to tease it out. The whole game is about attending and reasoning."

If all this talk of exploration and evolution makes choreography sound like a game of Simon Says or a sophisticated, intellectual exercise, I've led you astray. Choreography is a slog. Dancemaker David Gordon insists that "what reads as a matter of fact plan achieved with intelligence and foresight is often a network of chance or fate and foolishness and paranoia and alternating aggressiveness and passivity and envy and naivety and good humor and some smarts and time and more time." Frustration, anger and boredom plague every rehearsal, and criticism rubs at dancers like sandpaper, abrasive but essential if they are to appear flawless. Until the dance is made, the maker can't possibly know how his dancers will respond to it. However noble his conception, if they dislike their movements or the music or even their costumes, which is not the most unheard-of thing anyone ever heard of, his difficulties redouble: he will have to push ahead with his idea and overcome their resistance to it at the same time. Diaghilev's dancers shrank from the monotony and exhaustion of Nijinsky's incessant *Faune* rehearsals, and moaned that dancing to Stravinsky's tuneless score for *Le Sacre du Printemps* was like doing arithmetic lessons. Lydia Lopokova remembered the misery of mastering the awkward positions in Massine's *The Good-Humored Ladies*—"the knee was always bent and the arms akimbo—the limbs never in a straight line"—and the shock of finding herself, at the dress rehearsal, in a thickly padded, heavily boned costume. "It was *torture*. We felt like rugby football players dressed as eskimos pretending to be the most elegant and dainty females of the 18th century."

By the time Michael Bennett began work on the musical numbers for *Follies*, he was already known for becoming "a little Auschwitzy" in rehearsal. Years after the original production closed he told a reporter coolly, "While I was waiting for the music for the Follies section to arrive, I had the show girls walk in slow motion eight hours a day." It's not surprising that the girls' comments were not recorded.

Smart dancers keep their thoughts to themselves, because the next new work can always proceed without them. In a lifetime of executing orders instantly and without protest, the occasional chance to contribute something of their own is both the stick that drives them and the carrot they receive for work well done. To lead the choreographer toward his vision they agree to follow him slavishly; by meeting his needs, they satisfy their own. "I've performed eight different versions of the same ballet in as many performances," one dancer said of a Robbins piece, and it's just possible he was bragging rather than complaining. What's the point of all that preparation and fatigue, all the repetition and anxiety and years of practice, if you can't give the choreographer exactly what he wants exactly when he wants it? Alicia Markova once observed that when she was young, Cecchetti instructed her to turn out in class and then Balanchine asked her to turn in when he was choreographing. "I found that rather confusing," she continued. "In which direction do I go? . . . That was the first time it was explained to me that this is the difference between being a dancer and when you start being an artist. To dance you just turn out, but to be an artist, you have got to go in any direction."

Choreographers who share a past with their dancers, in the studio and on the road, refine them automatically for their own purposes. The private language that evolves during the time they spend together allows them to take explanatory shortcuts, and their habitual intimacy develops into a kind of family radar. So for resident choreographers or those leading their own troupe, a new piece and the available personnel represent flip sides of a single coin. You can confidently cram a variation with tiny flickering beats if you're sure your dancers can move like hummingbirds, and the best way to be sure is to train them yourself.

At New York City Ballet, Stephanie Saland recalled Balanchine saying to her, "'Okay, now you've worked on this and this and this. Now I want you only to watch Merrill [Ashley] and Kyra [Nichols] from the knee down.' And for two years he would never look up. He would watch three acts of my *Coppélia* from the knee down. He was that specific." Balanchine's persistence went hand in hand with his patience—"George would just be like a gnat, and annoy you and annoy you," Le Clercq told me—but he believed he had no choice. "God put me here on earth to tell you what is wrong about you," he would say in rehearsal. "You have friends to tell you what is good."

As recently as 1991 Paul Taylor was content for his dancers to absorb his style in rehearsals and repertory performances, and many of them only took the scheduled company class on tour, when they couldn't visit their usual teachers and gyms. Today his long-standing associates teach his technique in the Taylor School, which developed gradually after the company opened the daily class to outsiders in 1968 and began advertising for students 20 years later. Perhaps he considers the school a breeding ground for the type of dancers he favors, "who reveal themselves right down to the bone." Perhaps he has his eye on the future; he has led a troupe for almost 50 years, making the decisions and calling the shots himself, but no one lasts forever and the wise artist is always prepared.

The restlessness that now permeates the air on both sides of the footlights allows the public to snack on the repertory, devouring it like peanuts, and encourages performers to sample whatever opportunities arise, leaving choreography to take care of itself. So dancemakers must deliver more work more rapidly than ever in order to hold the dancers they want and the audience they need, despite knowing that new pieces are just like everything else—they can be good, they can be cheap or they can be fast but not necessarily all three. And every time a dancer retires or wanders away to greener pastures, the process begins again. The choreographer must return to step one, train the new arrival to the standard he desires, and begin to construct a new frame of shared reference.

The repertory grows today as it always has, from choreographers who can sustain a company for their own pieces or thrust themselves into random opportunities or make compelling solos. Each one follows his own path ("Cherry, please") and invents or reinvents the performers he needs. Elizabeth Streb tosses her dancers onto trampolines and through panes of glass, and Martha Clarke turns movement to dramatic purpose. Having tackled Kafka, Hieronymus Bosch, Chekhov, Tan Dun's opera *Marco Polo* and Gluck's *Orfeo*, in 1999 she said, "Conventionally, people think of dance as dance vocabulary, based on either a modern dance or a ballet idiom. In each piece I do, the physical vocabulary is created for that piece and generally doesn't make it to the next one." The founder-director of CandoCo, a British ensemble of abled and disabled performers, Celeste Dandeker broke her back in 1973 and now dances in a wheelchair, which she says is "like roller-skates, or ice-skates: a new element. The creative possibilities are endless."

Year after year, the language with which artists discuss dance changes as radically as the language they employ to make it, but the terms they accept don't change at all. If a dance never reaches the stage, there is nothing to see. Without dancers, it does not exist, and it can only be as good as the dancers who perform it. W. B. Yeats wrote to a friend that "a poem comes right with a click like a closing box," which you could also say of a dance. But dancemaking "isn't like painting or writing or something that can be done in solitude," explained Jack Cole. "The trouble with choreography is you have to get the person out of the way before you can bring out the dancer." That's each person, one by one, and before you can bring out the dance, you have to get yourself and everyone else out of the way too. As architect Frank Gehry put it, "The most difficult thing for . . . a creator is to get your idea through all of the layers of folks that have to touch it before it's finished."

Mark Morris

b. Seattle, 1956. Studied with Verla Flowers and Perry Brunson. Performed with Koleda Balkan Dance Ensemble and the Laura Dean, Hannah Kahn, Eliot Feld and Lar Lubovitch companies before forming the Mark Morris Dance Group in 1980, which he still leads today. Director of dance at the Théâtre Royal de la Monnaie in Brussels 1988–91, and in 1990, with Mikhail Baryshnikov, co-founded the White Oak Dance Project.

*M*Y FIRST DANCERS WERE THE PEOPLE I was working with, with Hannah Kahn or Laura Dean, or who I knew from somewhere, class or whatever. I was just putting on shows whenever I could, which wasn't very frequently, so whoever was free to rehearse on these days was in the show. If you had time off from Lar Lubovitch, you could dance with me, that would be great. Then I also had auditions and picked people from that; like Kraig [Patterson], who joined before Brussels, came from a big audition of men. What I'm looking for—it's always a gamble—is somebody who can do what I want and hear music the way I do. If you can't hear it in a way that corresponds to the way I do, you're wasting your time, because my work is very hard rhythmically and coordination-wise. It doesn't look like virtuosity, but in fact not many people can do it very well. So, I'm careful.

The thing is that the people who I think are fabulous dancers are alike, no matter what form they're trained in. An example is when I auditioned in Brussels. Without knowing it, the people I chose knew each other and had trained at the same place, at the Folkwang

Hochschule in Essen under . . . Pina [Bausch] was running it at that time. They got things right away. You know, if you took barre 20 years ago at Maggie Black's and stood behind Martine van Hamel, you thought, 'Oh, that's fabulous. No wonder you're so good,' because she could make it relatively stressless and clear and lovely.

Mostly the ballet people don't get it. Just because someone looks like a ballet dancer doesn't mean that person is intelligent or articulate as a dancer. I work with ballet companies a lot, and ballet dancers now think that, like, 19th-century style is a joke. They do it fake and they laugh at it. That's fine, I laugh at it too, but I *can* do it and I like it. What's more beautiful and fabulous? Rehearsing at Boston Ballet years ago, I said, "I want this to be more like Taglioni" or something like that, and they all sort of stood there and looked at me. So once I've got them in my company I teach them versatility. Mostly what people don't have is from really bad training. There are so many failed dancers who have become failed teachers or bad teachers, maybe very successful bad teachers, who are afraid to give a correction because that person won't come back the next day and pay ten dollars. So many teachers are so bad that they say, "This is the way this goes," and that's it. You know, "This form of épaulement is the only legitimate one," which is of course not true. Also, their class usually falls apart after the adagio—it's like, 'OK, now we're just doing these moves that we know.' So when I teach I mix things up a lot. I either do very basic, anatomically correct placement things or difficult coordination things with an arm series that doesn't relate to the torso or to what the legs do. I make up what I think is needed for clarity and to prevent injury and to expand the range of possibilities of dancing. I can teach turning and I can teach jumping and nobody does that, most people don't know how to teach them.

I love teaching. When I started, I taught what I knew and I still do, but the classes I teach now are very different from how I taught ten years ago, because I know more and I know how to get information across to different people, because everybody learns differently. I learned about it from my own teachers. A good example is Perry Brunson, who I studied with as a teenager. He was brilliant and vicious and had no idea at all about anatomy, which was injurious, really. It was "Jump higher" and "Do this, or else I throw you out of class." So you worked really hard, sort of pointlessly I learned later on, but you were very strong and very deformed. Everybody had giant thighs and no calves—it was weird. But he was also highly, highly musical and emotional, so everything was full out and phrased beautifully. In every adagio there was a giant story, like a love lost kind of longing. I learned a whole lot about dancing to music from him, balletically speaking, and of course I was learning those things from dancing too. But it took me many years to unlearn muscularly what I'd learned from him. You were so strong that you couldn't do anything. It's fine to be that strong, but it's not particularly expressive.

I learned to teach by breaking things down, like how to shift weight so that you're actually up in the air instead of just kicking and pretending you're up in the air and how to turn musically instead of just going around. I could always turn and jump really well, but I also understand things. I know that men and women have a different kind of arabesque because of structure, and I know how to get both sexes to understand how it works on their bodies. Because they're all built differently it's very hard to get people to understand how joints work and how muscles control joints, and that's the most dangerous thing in dancing.

I always teach class to my company. No—very rarely Tina [Fehlandt] or somebody will teach. But I teach a ballet class with other things in it, like parallel work for alignment, because I think Pilates is a fabulous technique. A lot of my dancers do yoga and some people go to the gym and some people don't take class of any kind ever, and that's fine, as long as they can do my work. Occasionally I suggest that someone come to my class regularly, like, "You need this 'cause you're not getting it elsewhere, so I can help you," but that's as far as I go. But they have to be able to do what I want in my choreography, and to do my stuff as well as I want them to, they do have to come to class. The same principles are in my work as in my class—music, coordination, clarity, versatility, all of that. I don't have many giant lifts or human pyramids or fireworks. I don't do fireworks very much. I'm not interested in injury or extreme force—I don't think that's interesting to watch, I don't like it, and it's inhibiting. So by taking class from me and learning the logic of the way I assemble combinations and structure a class and the progression from the beginning to the end, you also understand better how I work.

It's not just what I do naturally, because my work isn't what I do naturally—it's what I've learned how to do over many years and what I figured out and decide. I want men and women to be able to do everything the other can do, because I need that in my work, and I think it makes everybody better, more versatile. Class is also about style and comportment. Grace. I'm interested in grace. Comportment is behavior, it's the tone in which you do something, the way you hold yourself. It's carriage and approach and dynamics, it's the range of texture. That's why I'll do something in a duple rhythm and then change it to a triple rhythm, which completely changes how something's coordinated. Or I'll do things in fives or sevens. You can't just say, "Here's how a tendu goes," stick your leg out and stay there for a certain amount of time until you close it. That's not it—it's how to get there and how to get back, and how you, as a full body and as a full person, relate dynamically to rhythm and phrasing and style.

My class is very rigorous and very brainy too, I mean, you have to think all the time and you don't take breaks. And we have fun—there are interesting combinations, and Linda [Dowdell], who plays [piano] for my shows, plays class for me all the time, so it all works. You can teach people to hear music, sure, by breaking it down or *not* breaking it down, or repetition or alteration, trying something one way and then making a variation on that, substituting one thing for another and switching rhythms and tempi and quality. It's like, "That's fine. Now mark it—you're doing it too hard. Do it less hard, and that'll be exactly right." Or, "Now that you're killing yourself, don't," or, "Now that you're not killing yourself, kill yourself, because you need to use more effort." It has to be appropriate.

When I'm setting pieces on San Francisco Ballet, and I did it at Les Grands Ballets Canadiens also, I teach company class, and they're always surprised at how I go for what they think is the ease of something. It's very frustrating for them, because they do everything with such force. They lock, so the standing leg is dead, there's no feeling. Hyperextended knees and locking your arms and just moving from your shoulder . . . that's not interesting to watch. Then you have a trunk and some things sticking out of it instead of a full body that has hundreds of little joints in it, which is fascinating. At San Francisco Ballet, there's an hour-and-fifteen-minute class every day for 70 people and the women have to take it on pointe. So I was like, "No, let's do little soft things to start with. This isn't an audition. You don't have to touch your head with your foot, yet. Let's start slowly and work up to this." And I insist that people begin and end when the music does, because most people don't even listen to the music in a class. Generally it's like eight of these, four of these, turn around, and the pianist is dribbling on and nobody's listening. But I value music in a way that a lot of people don't, and they don't understand . . . Harriet Cavalli, this pianist who played for Perry Brunson, was visiting from Switzerland, and she was playing class for me here [in Edinburgh]—Linda took a break. She plays ballet and opera excerpts for class, in the old, sort of loud, octave-doubling, honky-tonk way, with a fabulous sense of rubato and suspension, and everything is exactly right. And it's weird—a lot of the music's really hokey, but it gets people going.

In San Francisco Ballet they have great accompanists, wonderful. But those dancers are warming up in a very short class that's sort of an audition every day—you know, because it's so competitive—and a lot of them are so young, so they don't know about music. I'd say, "No, it actually doesn't start until the downbeat," or "It ends two, three, and that's the end, not 'kind of.' It has to resolve, there has to be tension and resolution within a phrase of dancing." Or I say, "No, listen to what he's playing. This is what you're doing. They're the same thing. So let's cooperate, it'll be a lot easier."

They want me to teach all the time when I'm there, but that's also because I'm going to go away. If I were there all the time I'm sure nobody would come, but as a guest they love it. You know, I give corrections to the principals, and a lot of people won't correct them because they have to work with them all day and they don't want them sulking, like, 'Excuse me, I'm a principal, I know how to point my foot.' So I go, "You know, your foot looks funny. Could you fix that?" and they're very, very grateful, because they're left alone completely and expected to turn in fabulous performances. So it's like, "Oh, thank you, Mark. I've been having trouble with this ankle," and I say, "It's because your alignment's weird, and here's how to fix it. Feel this," and I get on the floor and move their feet.

I occasionally make up a combination and think, 'That would be fabulous in a dance sometime,' but I don't workshop a piece ever, ever. I don't use class that way. My classes are either a concentrated musicality and physical warm-up, just to get yourself engaged, or a real training session. If we're in rehearsal in New York and I'm teaching a full class, hour and a half or two hours, I stop and explain things and give very specific notes and work on things until they get them. But otherwise it's just to get people dancing and thinking together and musically. My biggest note in the theatre is "Unite." I say with my megaphone, "Unite," and then they unite. And then I say,

"Could you please . . . It seems like everything is voice-activated now. If I say 'Unite,' you unite. Could I *not* say it and you do it?"

When I choreograph I make up something. I don't use improvisation very much, and it usually leads to something being set but not always. Like, I'll work on a passage without music, just trying to get something to happen that I think would be nice, and then rhythmicize it or give it a duration. I less and less say, "Step on your right foot and lift your left leg." I show it, but I don't give words to it. It's like an arabesque but it isn't. So don't call it that, don't give it a French name, 'cause that's not what it is. It reminds us of that, but as soon as you identify it as that, you'll turn it into that. And I don't want *that*—I want something that approaches it but isn't. I work very, very fast, and then I throw things out and I change things. Or . . . designing a lift or something, I'll say, "I want her to go up in the air and this happens and then she comes down." Then I let them work out something that's like that, because I'm not going to pick somebody up to show how to do it. So it's "I want this—go," and then I leave them alone and work on something else. Or it's like, "Nobody has this step but Kraig, so Kraig, teach it to them. I don't want to watch it anymore until they've got it." And I can rely on them absolutely. Sure. *They're* doing the dances—I just make 'em up. But they're the ones who are going to be performing it, and it has to look the way I want it to and have the right tone, the right tone of voice.

There are a few parts in a few dances where I never want it to be the same, ever. There are rules, it has to begin at a certain time and end at a certain time, but the rhythm within is completely open. I want those parts never ever to repeat, from one rehearsal to the next or from one performance to the next. You have to feel different, you have to do a different thing, because I want people to have to decide spontaneously. You get a chance to experiment and see. A lot of *Orfeo ed Eurydice* is like that, where you have the option within the gesture catalogue of doing a step or not or which leg or to do it fast or slow or early or late or not do it at all.

Ten Suggestions, which is a very old dance, started out entirely improvised with no decisions made in advance. And then it fixed itself, over years, and now I have the choice of doing what I fixed it as or not. So I decide as I'm dancing what I'm going to do. When Misha [Baryshnikov] does it, he has the choice too, but he's not comfortable doing that. He starts the piece with a double tour en l'air to the ground, and I always like to start with an off-balance pirouette that goes on too long and drops—you know, it's like a fake climax—to nothing. I choreographed it as a bad pirouette, and he said, "Can I do a double tour?" and I said, "Of course you can. Why not? And this step can take you anywhere on the stage, and this is optional, and . . ."

I do that in very small doses in a lot of pieces. The party scene in *The Hard Nut* was very, very difficult to make up, and it started out . . . We'd had the set designs, and I said, "Here's the Christmas tree, here are the drinks, here's the geography of this room." And I decided to make it more difficult—I matched up people as couples. And then I would turn on the music and say, "It's a party," and we would improvise a party for 20 minutes. We knew a few certain things that had to happen, but that's what I did every day. I added things as we went along—you know, "You're bringing presents"— and I choreographed some dance sequences, but everyone started working out these unbelievably complicated scenarios. I remember asking one dancer, "Could you be over here a little bit farther?" and she said, "Well, let me see. No. Because I just had an argument with him, I'm going over to console her, I stop for a drink, I have a nervous breakdown, I'm crying, I don't know where I am, I see somebody . . . So I can't actually . . ." I said, "That's fine. I'll move somebody else." Then when we filmed it for television, we had to set it, so we fixed it exactly. It was still the exact same scene, but it was very precise. And now, doing it again, it doesn't have to be as precise, and it's harder to make it loose. And I have new people going into it and they learn where you go and then what's going on and then why you go there. But it works, because they're smart and interesting.

In other companies, I work with the people that I think will maintain the integrity of my dances when I'm gone. That's why I don't do much for other companies. I could make a million bucks selling my work all over the place, but very often they don't like how it turns out. That's why I only do commissions. I'm making up the choreography specifically for them. It's just a different language. Male and female ballet dancers have a very different technique, different from one another, and I like that. So with them I'm more likely to do things divided by sex than I would in my company. And I work on pointe for ballet companies and I like the way good ballet dancers dance. My dancers would look stupid dancing that way, and they wouldn't do it very well, and vice versa. My dancers can move their thoraxes and their middle backs, and not many people can do that. My company can do a three against four with me just demonstrating it—they're rhythmically brilliant, whether they know what it's called or not.

They teach too, whatever they feel they can teach well. We taught here for awhile, and we taught in Boston for years. Guillermo [Resto] won't teach anything because he doesn't like to. He's pretty much my assistant in many ways. Tina's a really good ballet teacher for people who can already dance, and Mireille [Radwan-Dana] is really good at teaching beginners. Rachel [Murray] and Mireille and Kraig and Charlton [Boyd] are really good with scary, surly teenagers, teaching them dancing or not being scared or, you know, whatever they can to get them more comfortable with one another and with dancing. Joe [Bowie] is great at teaching disabled people and ancient people; he has a fabulous wheelchair class that he does. And Megan [Williams] teaches modern dance, she's a great teacher.

It's good for everybody. It's good to learn what you know by teaching people and learning from them, and it makes people able to watch dancing better and maybe even imagine dancing at some point. And it's good for business, it's good for audience development, and it gives you information you wouldn't have. There's no arts training in most schools in the United States anymore. There's no music . . . I get kids who can't even clap to a beat. I think, 'Oh, great, I can't help too much,' but actually I can. I teach composition to them or technique, ballet, whatever. I like to teach ballet, but I teach a modern class or a sort of choreography-experiment class. And we don't just do it because you don't get grants unless you have an outreach thing—that's not it.

I don't do things I don't like. I love the language of ballet and I love San Francisco Ballet—that's why I work with them all the time, because I think they're great, as a company of individuals. And I know when I go there how much time I have and who's going to be in it. I know everything about a new piece before I go. Usually I cast it, or I do a couple of days of material and watch people do it and cast it from that, sort of like an audition. And that's it. I have those people and I work with them to make up the dance that I'm happy with. That's what I do with my company too. I do that everywhere. I don't always know what I'm going to do. I very often *don't* know what I'm going to do, and I learn it as I go along from the language that I make up as I'm going along. And if someone naturally dances fast and twitchy, I'm just as likely to give that person a beautiful, slow, legato sequence. I want to see how it changes how they dance, and it changes how I make up a dance too. It's much harder to finish a piece than it is to begin one, because by the end I won't allow myself to make up new material. It has to be derived from what exists. The last minute of a dance is much harder than making up the first 15 minutes. I have to make it make sense.

I don't have a dance in my mind. If they can't do it, I change it. I mean, I work on it and work on it and if it doesn't work, sometimes it's just bad choreography. My intention is to give something that can be done beautifully by the people who are doing it. Maybe not the first time, but every show is different, so some things are better or worse than other things from second to second. That's live theatre. I make up a dance that pleases me and I show it, and then it either pleases or displeases people. I can't decide what they're going to like. How could I do that? It's impossible. But one reason we're successful is that people get along with my aesthetic, with my taste and my choices. Otherwise, why would they come? Like, I decided how long and arduous *Behemoth* was, and I haven't changed a thing. It's a big task for an audience to watch that dance—that's why we did it here, because people here have been watching my work for a long time, so I can give them something that's a lot of work for them. And not one person walked out of the theatre. That surprised me—I thought someone would.

What everybody always says is that my dancers look like people, and I always say, "They *are* people, and so is the tiny little girl in the back row of the corps de ballet who's chewing gum and doesn't know even why she exists. She's a person." The fact is that dancers are encouraged not to be people. They're bred to be another sort of species onstage, like it's a different world. But it's not a different world, it's not. You know, my company would do *Sylphides* really well. Maybe it wouldn't look as glamourous or something, but it could be perfectly musical and they would get it, they're great. They're incredibly versatile and imaginative. I can ask my male dancers to do something like a 12-year-old girl, and they will, they're not embarrassed to. And I can ask the women to do it like an old man, and they can. They're not embarrassed about things. They like the richness of possibility in the dances.

My dancers don't lie. I mean, you're lying because you're in a theatre and you're wearing makeup and it's a heightened experience, but it happens in real time and then it's over. And people who work with us, musicians and technical crews, always love my company, and they make friends and they want to work together again. People are very loyal to this organization, because we're not bullshit.

My company is an eighth the size of New York City Ballet and twice the age of those dancers, twice the responsibility, maturity, experience. That's why they can still dance. They menstruate, they don't have stress fractures, they read books, they're interested in the world. They've been allowed outside—they're not kept like veal. My dancers, and modern dancers in general, I think, are more interested in other things than ballet dancers are. You know, Donald York, who conducted my *Hard Nut,* was also conducting at City Ballet, and he said to them, "I can get you tickets. You people should go see it. It's fantastic." "No." "Why not?" "We don't like what he did with the music." Some dancers at City Ballet said this about my company. Whereas all of my dancers can say, "I saw the Balanchine *Nutcracker,*" and we all go to Merce's shows, we love Merce [Cunningham]. Or I'll say, "I saw this fabulous thing. See it now," and some people will and some people won't. But it's important, because you should see as much as you can to know what you hate and love and why.

And also, every one of my dancers knows what's going on everywhere in a piece at all times. They do. They can step into anybody's part, with some time, and they know how things fit together, because I make them know that. And that's much more interesting. You know, you can have the 24 girls in the corps de ballet counting, not even realizing that it's fabulous music. Then you plug in the soloists and the principals, and the corps doesn't know what they're doing or that it's setting them off. And the principals only know, like, "She was in my way." In Paris Opéra Ballet, they're the ones petting their little dogs in the corner while everyone's rehearsing, and then they come in and do their thing and leave. But if you don't know contextually what you're doing, how can it make sense? It's like bringing in Pavarotti for opening night after you've been rehearsing for a month, and he doesn't know the production.

What happens in my company is, people remember dances and we use videotape to bring something back. I don't even go into the studio until it's pretty much put together, by Tina or Guillermo or Ruth [Davidson] or Joe, depending on the dance and on who was around when I made it up and who's doing too much and needs a break from refereeing a dance. So I have them do that, or someone will learn it from the tape. I say, "You saw them do it, now learn it."

So they learn it, and then I talk about imagination and phrasing and the things that make it the specific dance that it is. I give notes after every single rehearsal and after many performances.

Because ballet companies are often doing a whole bunch of different people's work . . . I come back to look at a dance of mine, and it's been "cleaned up" in the wrong way. Like, it's spaced perfectly in a place that I didn't want it to be, or it's been neatened up and become more vertical, generally. There's less sweep to it, it's become more positional. So I say, "Remember the first day when we made this up and you couldn't do it? That's what I want. You have be able to fall down at any moment because you have choices, instead of thinking, 'This is how this goes.'" I always go back or I send whoever helped me set it, my sort of assistant from my company. And to renew a license on a dance you have to have me see it.

But the dance also should change, because on the stage they're different people every time. You're different every day, you dance differently, you hear music differently, you've shed some skin cells, and that's interesting. And to keep something accurate isn't the same as freezing it in amber. That sort of museum point of view won't make a better *Sylphides*. You have to understand the style—and of course that differs all over the place—but if it's moving it doesn't have to be exactly the way I saw it the time I remember it best. Like last time I saw *Agon* at City Ballet was a number of years ago and I thought it was great. I thought, 'Oh, thank God, someone's finally off-balance and a little too far away from the partner, which makes that exciting thing happen in that exquisite dance.' And I talked to a particular critic, who said, "Of course you should have seen it in . . . ," 1907 or something. Well, I didn't, but it's not the end of the world. I've seen it a bunch of times and I thought this was pretty good.

But I don't think there's very much that's very good. Anywhere. In dancing. Every dancer . . . Laura Dean's company was never as good as when I was in it. Which isn't true, but every dancer feels that about every company he or she has been in. And I've said this very pessimistic thing before, that maybe modern dance is a movement and may have the same life span as the Soviet Union or something. Maybe it's just a subset of dancing generally or of classical dancing. Maybe the revolutionary aspect lost steam over a number of years, and then there was postmodernism and then there's Contact Improv, and people are in diapers now when they dance. I prefer bipedal dancing, I prefer two-legged beings instead of four. But I think that's why people aren't making up really fabulous dances very much, and why a lot of people, who would normally maybe, in another time and another situation, be drawn to a career in dancing or choreography, aren't. That's not happening, because it's going away. You know, it's all simultaneous: money, interest, talent . . . It's like 'Why should I become a dancer? There's no such thing as a dancer.'

My dancers don't feel that way, no. They have a very good job and they never leave. That's what I said the other day: "You, Tina, Ruth, you've been here so long I can't even believe it." I mean, we were having fun, but it was like, "Your children are going to be in my shows pretty soon." There are also no other jobs—if they quit, who would they work with? But my company's an island. We've never really been part of this big brotherhood of dance, if there were such a thing, maybe because I think most dance is really boring. Most of it's pretty low-quality, or if it's high-quality it's high technical quality and not high art quality. It's just aerobic or vigorous or something. I mean, I go to shows, I go to see things, I'm friendly with other choreographers and dancers and critics, and it's very interesting to me, but I also have high standards. People say, "How can you ruin a Mozart string quartet? It's such great music." Well, you can play it badly, and then who wants to hear it? It's the same thing with *Sylphides*. They say, "Oh, it's inviolable." No, it's not—it's violable, and that performance was awful. So don't do it, please, or I won't watch it. I'm not interested in watching that. Why would I want to go?

In every dance there's a texture and a tone, it's kinesthetic. I was in the middle of a *Dido and Aeneas* rehearsal with an orchestra that I'd never worked with before. We're going along and everything was on pitch, it was fine. I was dancing but suddenly I just stopped rehearsal and said, "This is really boring and I don't know why. Let's do it again and have it be less boring. That doesn't mean louder or faster . . ." I was talking to the orchestra and the singers, and us too. We were just doing our sewing machine thing, and that's not interesting really. There has to be more power to it, more intention.

Why would anybody want to watch you do something that you're not interested in yourself? How dare you assume that you're going to get a standing ovation? I've said that before *L'Allegro [il Penseroso ed il Moderato]*. In the finale of *L'Allegro*, when people are just going through it, I say, "You're doing this like you're anticipating a standing ovation just because you're so fabulous. And the fact is, it's dull. And here's why it's dull, because it's not right

there and you're not all with it." Everyone is very much less likely
to be automatic when you have live music. You don't know exactly
when the beat will fall, and you have to make it work. You can't
make musicians sound bad: they can make you look stupid. But,
you know, when I think someone's just being stupid or belligerent
or stubborn or not getting something, usually that person is ob-
sessing on something else that is an impediment to getting what I
want. Or he or she is too nervous or going after the wrong idea. I
think, 'Oh, you thought it was *that*? No wonder I hate what you're
doing.' That kind of stuff happens all the time.

I'm not interested in calisthenics, I'm not interested in watching
people just enjoy themselves, like in Contact [Improvisation] or something. I'm sure it's lots of fun to do, but it's not a performing medium
as far as I'm concerned. It's like you're watching the nocturnal house
at the zoo or something. I like the idea of dances being observed. I like
the audience to watch what my company are doing as a company, instead of what you're doing at me to show me that you can do this and
I can't. I love to watch incredibly boring circle dances that go on all
night, but it's more fun to do them. That's why folk dancing doesn't
translate to a theatre medium very well. You have to dress it up and
choreograph it to make it a performing art, which is untrue of other
forms like a lot of Indian or Indonesian dance, Asian dance frankly,
that is either ceremonial or communicative. It's facing in a certain
way, conveying something to people who then get some expression or
information from it, instead of something you look at that is . . .
what's the word? . . . sort of big and loud.

That's why I talk about the keystone of a piece. When I say it's
hardest for me to make up the last minute of something, to drop that
in to support the arch of a piece, I'm talking about classical art of all
kinds, about satisfying the form itself the way I perceive it. So a dance
like *Lovey*, which looks like chaos, is actually structured in a very
strict way. Some of it's improvised, but it has to go in a particular way
with a certain tone or it's ruined, and then it's not satisfying to anybody, dancer, viewer, choreographer. Nobody has to know the crazy
structures and substructures that I've decided on in a particular
dance. I have to know them, the dancers have to know them, but you
don't. I had a reason to do it, and that's the reason—even though you
don't know what it is—that the piece is satisfying. Or else I would be
like Béjart and have 20 pages of program notes with nothing to
watch. Or like Twyla Tharp where, even though every dance is beau-

tifully put together—I admire that about her—I don't like how I feel from watching the pieces. It's too much like 'Fuck you. I can do this, you can't, I'm really smart, and you might be kind of not-dumb.' That's how I feel from her work lately.

Somebody at a press conference said, "How do you top yourself every year?" Well, I don't, I hope I don't. It's fine if you think I do, but I'm not trying to. You know, some people thought how could I ever do anything better than *L'Allegro*? Well, I may not, but I'll certainly do something different from *L'Allegro*, that might be fabulous in a different way. People don't understand how choreographers work. When I do a Q and A after a show . . . I do them quite a bit because I refuse to do a lecture-demonstration, I don't like them at all. But I'll answer questions. I'm very good at working a crowd and funny and sort of friendly and confrontational, whatever is required from the audience. And very often the question starts, "When you visualize a dance, do you . . . ?" and then they give me choices. I say, "Stop, stop, stop, stop, stop. I don't visualize a dance. You do, maybe, but I don't know any choreographers who do." People who are trying to imagine how people make up dances think that I see it with lights and costumes, fully finished, and I just have to teach it, like it already exists. And people think that is genius or something, and the fact is, it is not, it's the opposite.

In Revival

IT'S EASY FOR MORRIS TO TALK. He's not yet 50 and controls his repertory like a benevolent tyrant. Although he frequently leaves home to create a new piece, he will not work for every company that invites him and, with a very few exceptions, he will not allow anyone else to dance the pieces he has made for his own group. As a result, the audiences that sit down in front of each work see exactly what he wants them to see, and as long as he can personally supervise the gap between his intention and its expression, he can prevent the lifeline that connects them from fraying.

A new piece that opens and flops is here today and gone by next season, so no one has to keep it up to scratch. The signature works that a company dances all the time, like Taylor's *Esplanade* or Kylián's *Symphony of Psalms*, don't usually rest long enough to get rusty; limited only by their physical abilities, every dancer can give them the performance they deserve because everyone in the company knows them inside out. If questions arise about the steps, the style, the tempo or the atmosphere and the choreographer is still on the spot, he can answer them himself.

But in between those extremes lie all the dances created a year ago or before the dancers were born or before the company was founded. As time passes, the piercing light choreographers throw on their own creations slowly dims. In place of a single arbiter, memory, passion, hope, guesswork, need, logic and imagination enter the studio arm in arm and take charge of rehearsals, and all of them together can't insure that the work they've gathered to protect will return to the stage as good as new. The choreographer could be teaching in another town or running another troupe. He could be dead. But once he steps away from his creation and shifts his eyes and attention elsewhere, his work becomes intrinsically defenseless and begins, instantly, to deteriorate.

Imagine tying a clothesline around the leg of an upright straight chair and trying to pull it across a room. If the room is empty and the distance short, you'll probably succeed. But if it's a crowded room, say a hotel lobby, dotted with sofas and incidental tables, the chances of the chair crossing it safely diminish fast. The line may tangle or break, the chair is bound to bump into things, and if it topples over, you'd have to drag it. Who cares? It's only a straight chair. But what if it's an exquisitely gilded armchair with a baby nestled in its silk cushions? Would the chair reach its destination intact? The gilding? The baby?

All sorts of people in the dance world worry about the health and safety of its choreographic babies, and their concern has crept into academic circles, where historians dissect every new staging among themselves, and into the press, where journalists air their opinions for the general public. Whenever an existing work returns to the rep or enters it for the first time, the promotion machine immediately grinds into action to pave the way for its reception. Information showers onto the politicians and patrons, ideally to reassure them that their support is justified, and onto the talking heads, who hopefully will buff the work's historical significance to a high gloss and decorate its arrival with social cachet.

Whether the piece is worth staging is a different matter that naturally provokes the question, Worth it to whom? Every company has its reasons for choosing its repertory, and they're all equally valid. Why do you want this work? A director might respond, Because it balances a program. Because this is the anniversary of its premiere or of the choreographer's birth or death. Because the dancers need it. Because the audience will like it. Because I like it. I've heard some version of all those reasons at press conferences, and to the question, How do you plan to revive it? I've also heard directors say, "Don't worry—we've got it on videotape" or "We're working with historians, who have been researching it for years." Both answers are encouraging, but they don't honestly explain the process that lifts an artwork out of tissue paper and restores it to its original condition.

Compared to staging dances, human reproduction is a snap. The cells that become living organisms replicate systematically and function according to their specialized nature—a skin cell is a skin cell from the start and will only generate other skin cells. That's the law of biology: organic matter reproduces itself faithfully and accurately.

Mechanical reproduction is even more reliable. Because any glitch that gums the works can be corrected and eliminated, a machine that manufactures tractors or shoelaces will make copies that are identical or as near as dammit. Trained experts with precision tools will always be able to spot the minuscule discrepancies between one copy and another, but to the naked eye and for ordinary purposes each copy will look and function exactly like the original.

So if biology or technology can manage a specific task, the desired result usually becomes the tangible result. No big deal. But there's another system that introduces variation despite itself, and that system—wouldn't you know it?—governs the reproduction of dances, which cannot govern themselves. Innately frail, the longer they lie unused, the harder it becomes to rouse them. Unable to support their own existence or contribute to their own duplication, they must rely on human intervention for their survival. But as soon as human beings get involved with their reproduction, all hell breaks loose.

In the long parade of continuity's servants, the ballet masters who stage or revive dances differ only in purpose and age from the children at a birthday party who pass a single whispered phrase from one willing ear to the next. Americans call the game Telephone and the British refer to it as Chinese Whispers, but the ridiculously garbled outcome is the same everywhere. Having encountered similar confusion in theatrical rehearsals, Jonathan Miller assigned a simple explanation to it based on the nature of perception: "If you get people to stand in a row in front of you, make a series of gestures and ask the people to copy them, then although they will all see the same thing they will all copy it differently. That's . . . because what they see, and think is being exemplified by what they see, differs from one person to another."

Well, I warned you. The revival process is intrinsically unstable. Along with the material they are demonstrating, the stagers naturally bring to rehearsal their ideas about that material as well, and the dancers respond to what they're shown by replicating what they see or think they see. At the same time, they might filter it through their recollections of the last time they saw it and their impressions of its former interpreters and their notions of its place in history. Every other piece they have ever danced affects them too, and in order not to interrupt the rehearsal's momentum, sometimes they'll guess at what's wanted rather than admit they couldn't hear the correction or see the demonstration or that they weren't paying attention. So the only fixed element in this messy procedure is the choreography itself—no intellect or temperament, no memory— which of course is as precisely fixed as a portrait drawn in sand.

Wait a minute. This is the 21st century. Men have walked on the moon. Scientists have calculated the age of the universe and mapped the genome that defines us as human beings. If we can put bodies into outer space and lifesaving hardware into bodies, surely we can come up with a simple system to sustain the body's art. So what if it's essentially evanescent? Human ingenuity can locate cyberspace, which has no physical existence at all, so why can't it get a grip on dance, whose physical existence is plain to see?

Believe me, it has tried. As a mechanical means of remembering, dance notation has been around since the second half of the 15th century, when the five steps of the popular bassedanse, represented by their initial letters, were written in sequence on a musical score directly beneath the musical notes that accompanied them. Since then, notation systems have grown increasingly complex and numerous—experts assert that on average some new shorthand has appeared every four years since 1928—yet they often introduce unforeseen problems to a process that needs only solutions. Of the two systems most widely used for dance, Benesh notation, which is written horizontally on a five-line musical staff, is relatively easy to write and read but intentionally selective. In an effort to avoid redundancy, its creator, Rudolf Benesh, decided to record only the essential description of each movement and dispense with information that could be taken for granted. Labanotation, on the other hand, which was devised by Rudolf von Laban and is written vertically on a three-line staff, is more analytical and specifically detailed than Benesh but also considerably harder to write and read.

Because both systems do the job they're meant to do, pinning choreography to the page so it can be carried from one studio to another over distance and time, they've become valuable staging tools despite their limitations, and more arcane systems have opened some dusty windows to dance history. Scholars have deciphered Nijinsky's private notation to stage his *L'Après-Midi d'un Faune*, and in 1999 the Kirov Ballet based a spectacular revival of the original *Sleeping Beauty* on scores notated by Nicholas Sergeyev in the now-obscure Stepanov system. To clothe and frame the decoded contents of Sergeyev's notebooks, the Kirov dug into its archives in St. Petersburg and unearthed the production's original designs, the model for Act II, and a batch of photographs, shot onstage after the premiere in 1890. The theatre's museum held drawings, maquettes, light plots, instructions for changing the sets, even some of the original costumes, so the reconstruction brought more history to light than anyone had anticipated.

Few companies in the West can afford to maintain such extensive resources in their own backyard. Instead, historical documentation usually scatters to different countries, where it winds up in museums, private collections, archives and university libraries, depending on the original owner's inclinations and the space and cost required to house it. Simply locating the relevant material for a revival can take awhile, so the search must begin well in advance of rehearsals. Once the dancers reach the studio, however, getting the choreography on its feet becomes the top priority, and companies today regularly choose videotape over notation as their standard tool. Tape is cheap, portable, tireless, and easy to access and store. Whatever it captures, it captures accurately since it can't inadvertently thrust an additional layer of interpretation between itself and the performance. But it can't see through the bodies in the foreground to grab the action behind them and it tends to distort the visible space, especially if the center of the performing area is not clearly marked. Because of a dancer's injury or the shape of the studio, and because editors and videographers make necessary and valuable contributions to the process, every piece that is recorded may pick up minute modifications during its recording and editing, which then live forever on the tape. Unflagged and initially unremarked, they slip silently into the text, and the next time a ballet master pops that video into a machine and asks dancers to learn their roles by watching it, no one is any the wiser.

Transfixed on tape like a pressed flower in a locket, the single performance of a work that the camera captures may eventually become the authoritative performance because it is the only one available for reference. It might not be absolutely accurate, and it certainly will not endure indefinitely, because tape deteriorates. Although video technology has revolutionized the way dance is documented and the way dancers learn, age-old problems plague the tapes themselves; like all archival documents, they require cataloging, housing and proper maintenance. Some of the master tapes for *Dance in America* were disintegrating only 20 years after they were made in the 1970s, and barely 15 percent of the Rambert Dance Company's reel-to-reel tapes, also shot in the '70s, could be used by 1982. Nevertheless, more and more individuals and organizations have shouldered the responsibility for preserving dance and recording the choreographer's intentions as well as his artifacts. Their single-minded efforts have generated an international library of dance from which teachers, dancers, stagers and scholars borrow constantly, yet documentation cannot keep pace with the steady erosion of the material. Preservation amounts to capturing steam in a sieve, and reviving a work that has dropped from sight is like assembling a massive jigsaw puzzle to which different experts hold different pieces. The danger is not that the pieces will not fit together, but that when they do, they will form a recognizable image whose defining spirit has fallen through the cracks.

There are few villains. Those who hold the pieces feel morally compelled to handle them responsibly, especially when the choreographers have left some blueprint as to how the guardians of their work should proceed. Although George Balanchine and Jerome Robbins bequeathed their ballets outright to many different individuals, the George Balanchine Trust and the Robbins Rights Trust license the works' performance on behalf of all those legatees and oversee the stagings, which at least keeps the revivals in a stylistic ballpark of accepted dimensions.

In the absence of a licensed spokesman or approved organization to serve as the final authority on style and leasing, a dance's fate rests with the choreographer's heirs, who naturally have their own ideas about the most responsible way to carry out their duties. Kenneth MacMillan, for example, left his ballets to his wife, a painter, who supervises their revival with the assistance of dancers who knew them well and of a Benesh notator, Monica Parker, who worked closely with MacMillan from the 1960s onward. Deborah

MacMillan is conscious of her obligation to his repertory but refuses to give it all her time. "I have to prepare the next stage: the future of Kenneth's ballets after Monica Parker, and indeed after myself. I haven't rushed at setting up a MacMillan Trust, and I'm glad, because I've been learning about how much is involved. I also have work of my own which I keep doing; I really can't work full time on Kenneth's." No one can predict how MacMillan's works will change while his widow is learning how to administer their survival, but they are more widely performed now than in his lifetime, which alone should help keep them healthy—as doctors say about limbs and muscles, "If you don't use them, you lose them."

More cautious heirs, who try to protect the integrity of their inheritance by imposing tougher licensing conditions or charging higher fees than the market can bear, may wind up on the road to hell—that's the one paved with good intentions—with their solicitude and their legacy right beside them. It's only logical. If no one acquires a piece, fairly soon no one knows how to dance it, and if no one ever sees it, after a while no one cares about seeing it because no one knows it exists. If your daughter always plays by herself without leaving her room, she may never get the measles but she also won't have any friends. Carelessness can cause as much damage as caution: the person who inherited all of Lester Horton's works in 1953 didn't get around to establishing a foundation to supervise their staging until 1999, by which time many dancers and most of the public had probably forgotten both Horton and his innovative creations. Charles Weidman, who founded a pioneering company with Doris Humphrey in 1928, died without a will, and José Limón left a will that made no disposition of his work.

"When I die," Balanchine supposedly told Nureyev, "everything should vanish." If he meant it, nobody believed him, so his ballets still astound and delight audiences today. Between the choreographer's death in 1983 and the year 2000, 273 companies based in 45 countries applied to the Balanchine Trust for the right to stage them, and by February 2002 another 96 companies had joined the list. Tragically, the opposite can also come to pass. After Martha Graham's first solo performance, an acquaintance came backstage, intent on talking some sense into her. "Martha, this is simply dreadful," the woman exclaimed. "How long do you expect to keep this up?" "As long as I've got an audience," Graham replied. And so she did, but the audience she built for her remark-able repertory has recently had to live without it. Emotionally sup-ported for 20 years by a devoted follower named Ron Protas who helped her run and promote her company, Graham anointed him as her associate artistic director; after her death in 1991 he suc-ceeded her as the troupe's artistic director. In her will she be-queathed to him "any rights that I might have" to her repertory of nearly 200 works, none of which had been either copyrighted or notated. The man she chose to lead her artists and nurture her legacy was neither a dancer nor a choreographer, and many felt he was unqualified for the job she had awarded him. After he had agreed and then refused to relinquish his position, in 2000 the board of directors fired him. He responded by withdrawing the right to perform Graham's work from her company, essentially closing it down and forcibly detaching her dancers from the irre-placeable artistic treasure she had entrusted to his care. The dis-pute left her repertory, her dedicated performers and her anxious public equally high and dry, and finally had to be resolved in court.

The Graham company wasn't alone in needing those works—the world needs them too, just as it needs Cézanne's paintings and Mozart's music. It's not as if new masterworks are cropping up every day, and when choreography hit a slump, the established winners from the past became all the more valuable. Back in the '70s, as the audience grew, the companies had beaten the bushes for choreographic innovation and excitement, hoping to keep the curious punters coming back for more. American Ballet Theatre acquired Limón's *The Moor's Pavane* in 1970 and swallowed Twyla Tharp's company whole in 1988. Joffrey invited the mini-malist Laura Dean not only to make her first piece for ballet dancers—that was *Night* in 1980—but to follow it up with two more, and the Royal Ballet latched on to Glen Tetley, adding *Field Figures* and *Laborintus* to the repertory in 1971 and '72 respec-tively. Since 1968, when he gave the Royal Danish Ballet permis-sion to perform *Aureole*, Paul Taylor has leased his dances to more than 65 ballet and modern companies around the world. Among them, Pacific Northwest Ballet in Seattle has also danced Cunning-ham, Limón and Lucinda Childs, and the Paris Opéra Ballet has presented Bausch, Armitage, Maguy Marin and Angelin Preljocaj.

But the fizz that enlivened the '70s gradually bubbled away, leaving behind a residue of grim necessity. The public's taste for discovery hardened into an insatiable appetite for perpetual stimulation, and the fickle audience began treating the dance repertory like Kleenex, using each new piece once or twice for its amusement and then tossing it away and demanding another. Though the companies were willing to gamble on commissions, the glint of a good idea often turned out to be a flash in the pan, and by the 1990s the crossover phenomenon was ancient history. Ballet and modern dance had been hitched for so long that the audience scarcely batted an eye at seeing them together in public. Once considered strange bedfellows, the mingled repertories dropped off the cutting edge and landed on the subscription brochures, and when the revival business exploded, those former novelties were among the bankable assets in constant circulation.

Yet something happens to a dance when it leaves home, even if it's still robust and vibrant and has never languished long enough to need reviving. As a work travels farther and farther from its creation, either in time or in geographic distance, it becomes less supple; though the original dancers inhabited it like their own skin, each new company wears it proudly but carefully, like a new suit. If it must vault from one set of rules to another, from the fundamental precepts of modern dance, say, to those of ballet, some aspect of its natural idiom always fails to make the transition. "Poetry is what is lost in translation," Robert Frost remarked, which is exactly what the performers sense themselves as they acknowledge distinctions of impulse and execution that they know they can't duplicate. When she first saw the Graham company, Margot Fonteyn eloquently compared the dancers to her Royal Ballet colleagues. "We fall like paper bags," she commented, "You fall like silk."

Until dancemakers began weaving film, videotape and computer-generated images into their creations, the only element of a dance that you could actually touch were the bodies that danced it, and for decades the owners of those bodies, and their muscles and memories, represented the best and only tools with which a work could be recreated in the absence of its maker. "I was there and I remember" seemed to cover the bases on authenticity, except for the fact that choreographers so frequently changed their minds. Fokine made *Les Sylphides* for a charity performance in Russia in 1907, rejigged it for another in 1908, revised it again for Diaghilev in Paris in 1909 when it acquired its present form, and staged it for the last time, for Ballet Theatre in New York, in 1940. Balanchine habitually rewrote solo variations to suit the dancers who inherited them from the first cast, and he knocked the original opening off *Apollo* shortly after its 50th birthday.

Critics and historians wrangle endlessly about these variant stagings—Nietzsche claimed that all life is an argument over matters of taste—but even when one version overlaps another or several of them fuse, no one denies that the dance is still itself and still authentic provided the choreography on show came hot from the maker's hands. Its ultimate form is his decision, and sensible interpreters defend his right to do anything he likes with his work, regardless of its age or iconic status. "I see lots of things that have changed," Le Clercq told me, "and it's hard to say they shouldn't have because you don't know if Balanchine has changed them . . . Now, should I say to George, 'I saw it, and she's not doing it the way I did it'? How do I know he hasn't thought, 'Oh, I hated the way Tanny did that step, always hated it, all those years. And now I've gotten rid of her and gotten somebody else who will change the step the way I've always wanted it'? I *don't* know."

So the living links to the dance's making are still considered the most reliable sources when it comes to revival, even though textual discrepancies may exist and even though the validity of memory itself is up for grabs. Scientific research now indicates that years after witnessing the same event, two people will often have completely different recollections of it. As each old memory is dragged from the unconscious and installed in consciousness, the brain apparently takes it apart and modifies it to reflect that person's more recent experience before refiling it, permanently transformed by fresh proteins, in deep storage. Neurobiology is only confirming in the laboratory what empirical evidence has proved in the studio time and again. When the original cast of a piece gets together to try reconstructing it, the dancers usually listen to the music and then start moving and speaking at the same time. "I did this," says one, ". . . uh, something like this . . . in a big curve, and then I stopped on eight, stage left, facing front, and bent over like . . . no, no, that was the second time . . . like this. I had to stare at the calluses on your heel, Pat, because my nose was almost touching it." Then Pat will say, "No, that can't be right, it wasn't my heel, because when the clarinets do that tootle thing, on five and six and seven and eight, I'd be all the way upstage right looking into the wings. Remember that carpenter, the one who drank so much? He always used to shake his belly at me."

Listening in, a civilian observer would laugh at first and then fidget, finally growing as restless as Alice in the Wonderland courtroom of the King and Queen of Hearts, who began the day thinking "I wish they'd get the trial done . . . and hand round the refreshments!" and ended it in despair crying, "You're nothing but a pack of cards!" The push and pull can go on for hours, like an awkward three-way tug of war between memory, music and the body's limits, and each time another hand reaches for a solution, it drags the whole endeavor in a different direction. But the process only seems nonsensical if the outcome doesn't matter to you, and the tugging hands, despite their indecision and backtracking, can still carry a heavier burden than their mechanical assistants. Video and notation may raise a skeleton from obscurity but they won't put the flesh on its bare bones.

What's worse, for something to happen or for nothing to happen? The tangible forms of physical documentation effectively prevent an intangible art from lying dormant, with nothing happening to it at all, which is worth a lot. But transferring steps from the page or the screen to able bodies does not produce a performance that will move an audience, nor does it turn dancers into artists— accuracy, said Matisse, is not truth. Truth is whatever the choreographer intended, not only what he made but what he meant by it, which can only pass between the people who value it enough to take care of it. The baby in the gilded chair can remain surprisingly safe, neither an orphan nor a mass of bruises, as long as capable guardians look after it.

With oblivion lurking just around the corner, the job of preserving a dance's body and spirit can expand into a noble crusade, the theatrical equivalent of saving Grand Central Terminal from the wrecker's ball or cleaning centuries of smoke and grime from Botticelli's *Primavera*. "Every artist's work changes when he dies," warned the philosopher John Berger. "And finally no one remembers what his work was like when he was alive." No arguments there. Everyone agrees, preserving our cultural heritage is an absolute necessity. In the next breath, they also agree that necessity has its limits. How much room—physical room, mental room—

should we allocate for preservation, and which artifacts should we restore? The Film Archives of France railed against Henri Langlois, the founder of the Cinémathèque Française, for daring to show the historic films he had collected, which the Archives claimed were too fragile to be screened. Kyoto's municipal government and chamber of commerce have decided to protect its ancient crafts and business interests at the same time. They are digitizing the designs of traditional textiles and ceramics, both to hide them from copy-cats and to insure their survival if the current manufacturers go bust. The Kirov Opera has called on the U.S. Library of Congress to help it catalogue and microfilm its massive collection of disinte-grating music scores, and the Maryinsky Theatre has built a multi-media recording studio so it can document its own productions without involving commercial firms. At the same time, the British Library has recently cleared out 60,000 volumes of newspapers covering 130 years—almost one-tenth of its entire collection—in order to make room for the next batch; British newspapers alone now increase the collection by more than half a mile of shelf space annually.

Despite the respect and admiration the crusaders earn and clearly deserve, some people believe they're fighting a losing battle, because even if the dances can be rescued, the world and our per-ception of it are evolving too fast for anything old to be new again. The artist Marcel Duchamp claimed that paintings enjoy an active life of about 30 years and that all the wonders of modern restora-tion could not preserve their characteristic aura indefinitely; he re-ferred to the masterworks of the Renaissance as "those miserable frescoes," adding wryly, "we love them for their cracks." The dis-tinguished Russian critic Vera Krasovskaya took a more vehement stand regarding the Kirov's revival of *The Sleeping Beauty* in 1999, arguing, "The idea itself is wrong. Petipa wrote that any ballet, like a human being, is continually changing and developing. I believe that a ballet production can preserve the delicate aroma of the past and its inherent energy but it cannot be fossilised . . . To my mind, it is not worth the pains the company has taken to revive it." And Martha Graham reminded her dancers that "what was powerful in 1930 is going to look deadly today."

Or silly. Or simply dead. Some dances seem destined to die no matter how lovingly they are staged. Reminiscing at a conference about the Polka in Ashton's *Façade*, a role she had created in 1931, Alicia Markova informed a rapt audience that "it was all based on music-hall turns, which he knew and I knew. Recently he said to me, 'I had to change it. The girls don't understand it and I couldn't explain it.'" Peter Wright once pointed out to me that with every revival of *Les Sylphides* the dancers understood it less. Each time it was gently coaxed to its feet after a long rest, it took a bolder leap of their imagination to grasp its ethereal atmosphere, because as the years passed they knew less and less of the ballet's luminous history, had less and less contact with any place resembling a hushed, moonlit glade and didn't care about such things either.

According to Fred Zimmermann, who played double bass for the New York Philharmonic in the 1930s, Toscanini used to insult his musicians mercilessly, calling them jackass, stupid, lazy and *antimusicale*. When they failed to produce the effect he demanded, he accused them of conspiring against the music, which to him represented "a truth to which we had a moral obligation." Reasonable ballet masters probably shy away from outright insults—though Danilova used to chide her pupils for moving like cows on ice—while inwardly sympathizing with Toscanini's impatience and frustration. Since a dance can't revive itself and the most devoted stager on earth can't bring it to life alone, the dancers have to make a constant effort too, but it's an uphill struggle. For every artist like Vladimir Malakhov, who once protested that he could not sprawl on his couch watching television without thinking, "'Is this a good pose for *Bayadère*?'" there is another who flips to automatic pilot as the curtain parts and light floods the stage. For every dancer like James Fayette, who seems to treasure the fact that "you cannot escape history at City Ballet; you look at the score and you read, 'Suzanne jumps,'" there is another who resents the long shadows of the interpreters who preceded him. Artists who are disappointed, overworked, unappreciated, insecure or even too secure inadvertently betray a work's integrity even if they don't mean to, by lending it their limbs but keeping their minds to themselves. In performance they remind me of the statues called acroliths that were created in regions of ancient Greece where high-quality stone was at a premium; sculptors would use whatever stone they could obtain for the visible parts of a figure, the head, hands and feet, and carve the rest in wood, masking the subterfuge with painted draperies.

Dancing to taped music, as many companies now must, drains a little vitality from every piece; the programming around a work casts a reflected glow and changes its overall impact; the public's hunger for pyrotechnics encourages performers to replace nuance with power; and the acid bite of competition burns away their reticence and subtlety. And all the while the repertory must keep expanding, partly to prevent the dancers and their public from dying of boredom as the same pieces whiz past them year in and year out. The crowds on both sides of the footlights need to be shaken up occasionally, and whether they encounter an old piece with a distinguished history or wrestle with a relatively new one, everyone profits from the thrill of discovery. After spending more than a month working with Pina Bausch on her *Le Sacre du Printemps*, a member of the French cast described the rehearsal period as "one of the primordial experiences of my 17 years at the Paris Opéra Ballet." But that thrill doesn't come cheap—discovery has its price. As each repertory swells, the public, the critics and the performers slowly lose contact with certain works they once knew intimately. Since each one rolls around less often, the memories of viewers and participants alike start to blur, and the details they swear they remember clearly . . . after a while the honest ones won't swear to anything.

By comparison, scholars work on Easy Street. The St. Petersburg Conservatory now offers a five-year course in Sources of Dance History. In the first year, the students learn how to learn from dictionaries and encyclopedias, address books, telephone books, and cemetery lists. The second year they turn to the press. The third year they look at diaries, memoirs, letters, the so-called "sources of personal origin." In the fourth year they concentrate on archives and in the fifth they study important Russian dance historians and critics. This academic program introduces them to stable, legible maps, which they will usually be able to study sitting down. Ballet masters, however, do not enjoy such luxuries. They cannot work sitting down, they cannot draw on a vast assortment of permanent records, and they often prepare for their job accidentally, while they are doing something else. It's not enough to have the right temperament for the job—patient, meticulous, good-humored—they must also possess the right tools. Pastry chefs need cool hands. Surgeons and astronauts need keen eyesight and low blood pressure. Ballet masters almost invariably start out as dancers who can learn quickly, dance with the group on the right or the group on the left, replace anyone in any position onstage, reverse a sequence without hesitation, notice the overall pattern, remember the details, and keep track of all the changes. Nature usually endows these artists with a capacious memory, wraparound peripheral vision, and an instinctive preference for order, and it never hurts if they can maintain discipline and crack a joke in the same breath.

They need all that and then some. On their feet in the studio, these ordinary magicians push the ambitious, pull the recalcitrant and watch the clock, the video, the score, the tempo and the spacing, day after day. Having done the job at ABT since 1976, Susan Jones defined it as far more than the sum of its visible parts: "This is not just about my ability to take 24 girls from 24 different schools and say something in a way they'll understand so that they start to move together. This is about giving them the belief that they are the support system of the entire ballet. They have to be encouraged and inspired." The visible authority a ballet master projects derives from complementary responsibilities, to the ideal performance of that dance and to the public, who may not know what to expect when the curtain rises but who come to the theatre anyway and wait, trustingly, to find out. To satisfy those responsibilities, the stager will use anything he can lay his hands on, fully aware that the concrete tools are crude and the living tools are only human, but they're all he's got.

Ultimately, the most pressing concern for the dancers, the stagers, the historians and the audience is the one element no one can name, the quality that makes a dance uniquely itself in any costumes and on any company and with any of its variant texts. Dances don't survive without that quality, even if every step has been documented from every conceivable angle and the original designs have been preserved in perfect archival conditions. Once a dance dwindles to an empty shell, it is too late for anyone to revive it fully, and that means we will never again see it as its author intended or find in its visible shape the invisible part of himself he placed there for our pleasure. "What would an authentic performance be [of a Shakespeare play]?" Jonathan Miller asked rhetorically. "It would be closest to the one that least distressed Shakespeare when he saw it."

Nothing can preserve the interior life of a dance but sustained attention, whether that attention takes the form of continual performance or the thoughtful transfer of the work from body to body and from generation to generation. And nobody shills for a dance. The people who teach it and produce it and perform it fulfill all their obligations to it simply by doing their job. But the public has a hand in its maintenance too. People see a dance and they talk. They tell their friends, they fret, they rave, they stand at bus stops and fling their arms out. They say, "That's the one with the composer and the telegram, and everyone poses for a photograph, right?" or "Then she sort of pulls her dress over her head like a cave—it's amazing. It made me cry." Someone is always seeing a piece for the first time; after the third act of *Swan Lake*, I once heard a man exclaim to his wife, "Say, the black one looks just like the white one." And someone else may peer through tonight's Odette and see last week's Odette and beyond that the Odettes of other seasons or other countries, one superimposed on the other in a weightless, translucent stack of interpretations stretching all the way back to his childhood. All different, yet all alike in their attempt to realize the essence of what Petipa imagined and then made real more than a century ago.

Do you know about the Ise shrine? The most venerated Shinto shrine in Japan, the Grand Shrine of Ise is a complex of about 200 wooden buildings first erected in the third century. In keeping with Shinto tradition, every 20 years the buildings are ceremoniously torn down and rebuilt on an adjacent site. The new buildings are identical to their predecessors and constructed in the identical manner—made entirely of interlocking pieces of wood, they are assembled without nails—which guarantees the preservation of the ancient techniques that produced the originals. The gates at the shrine's entrance are rebuilt with timbers from the dismantled temples, which are also distributed to other holy sites and used for their reconstruction. The process was last repeated in 1993, when the shrine was rebuilt for the 61st time, and there is no reason to believe the cycle of ritual renewal will not continue indefinitely. Every visitor knows full well he is not visiting the original temple, but he has not traveled to Ise for the buildings. The shrine houses divine relics called the Three Sacred Treasures, a sword, a mirror and a jewel, that are so holy no one is permitted to see them. As long as their sacred nature is worshiped and cherished, the structures that house and protect them will be holy places as well.

So for a dance to live and never grow old, the ballet masters must keep its essential nature alive in every vessel that houses it. What's the alternative? "An art in which the spirit of the artist is translated into the body, the dance belongs to the living present in which it moves," wrote Eudora Welty. "In fact, isn't its transience one of its awe-inspiring properties? If the same physical law applied to all the arts, we would need to have lived after 1787 and before 1791, and to have known the right people, and then not to have had a cold on the night of the invitation, to have heard *Don Giovanni* once."

Jean-Pierre Frohlich

b. New York, New York, 1955. Entered the School of American Ballet at 12 and joined New York City Ballet in 1972, having already performed with the company as a student. Promoted to soloist in 1979. Company ballet master since 1990, and now stages Jerome Robbins' ballets worldwide as a ballet master for the Robbins Rights Trust.

I WAS ALWAYS A VERY ENERGETIC CHILD. I liked sports, I was on the swimming team, I've done all that, so to me dance was another aspect of using my physical talent. At SAB I learned a lot from everybody, I got something from each teacher. When I became a professional, I understood more what they were really saying, but when you're a kid, all you really want to do is bounce around the room.

Stanley Williams was an influence, of course, and I used to love when company members taught class. I was watching Edward Villella, more as a goal than a model, and I admired Jacques d'Amboise, but he wasn't someone I looked up to as much as Edward Villella because I was short, so there was that similarity to Villella. Also, I admired John Prinz . . . he was quite fascinating. When I was a kid I didn't realize it, but he had this kind of raw sexuality, very much like a toreador. He was very earthy and he was unpredictable onstage. Sometimes he would be brilliant and sometimes he would not be brilliant, and that kept me interested. I liked him a lot.

I knew I was headed for the company. I was told that the year before I got in, but I wanted it. I knew Balanchine liked me, because to him—I learned this later—I was part of the family, the system, from the school days. Now there are a lot of little boys taking ballet lessons, but when I was at the school there were very few young boys, so he knew who the boys were, so he knew who I was.

Since I grew up in the system, who I saw when I was a child was basically Balanchine. At the time, when I was 11, 12, Jerry [Robbins] wasn't really around, he was doing his Broadway phase. But the minute I got a glimpse of how Jerry was working, I was very much attracted to that, because . . . Jerry was American. Even though I came from a European family, I grew up in New York in the streets, and I remember, before Lincoln Center was built, that whole area where the film of *West Side Story* took place. So I felt very early that I could easily go up to Jerry and talk to him. I was never afraid of him. He was kind of a curious figure, but I saw him . . . He loved to rehearse at the school, so I would see him in the hallways and he would come in and watch men's class for five minutes. And he would come up to students and correct them, he was very open. You know, a lot of the mystique about Jerry was the aura he created, I mean, he created this difficult, demanding persona. Balanchine was demanding too, but Balanchine was a little different. A little different? A lot different in personality from Jerry. Balanchine was more relaxed about things, "Oh, we'll do it tomorrow" or "Don't worry about the steps. I'll change it for you." Jerry would not do that as much. He was more intense and he would be very specific. That was the contrast between Balanchine and Jerry, but they balanced each other. Because they were so different, that's why it worked.

At the school I felt very special, especially when Jerry asked me to do *Watermill*. What happened was . . . He called me to a couple of rehearsals, in the beginning when he was choreographing. Then I went back to the school and he continued with other things, and then he called me back. And then he went to Balanchine and said, "I know Jean-Pierre's not in the company, but I would really like to use him in *Watermill*. Is that OK?" And Balanchine said, "Of course it's OK. He's family." That's where I got "family" from. This is a story Jerry told me. I had the look he was looking for. You know, there's an overall look of all his pieces, he creates a mood, and I was part of that mood, because to him I looked vulnerable. I think there was an innocence. Also I looked a little bit like Eddie [Villella], with my long hair, and in the ballet Villella was on the floor, reminiscing back in time.

When I performed *The Nutcracker* when I was ten years old, I liked that attention. I liked the idea of being around the theatre, it excited me. So I knew right then that it probably was what I was going to do, but *Watermill* is when I really got hooked. I didn't analyze much at the school, I went with instincts a lot, with my gut feeling. You might not trust it but go with it because it's really what you feel you should do, not what someone else wants you to do. It's hard to trust that, I still have problems trusting it, but I always went with being who I was.

But I learned a lot more when I stopped dancing. I really learned how to dance when I became a ballet master, after my career was over. While I was dancing people probably were teaching me things that I wasn't picking up on, or maybe I didn't realize I knew what I knew, because at the time I was not explaining it to anybody. When you're a dancer you're thinking about yourself, about your own performance, your own body, you're taking class and doing it for yourself. You have to take everything in. Sometimes I would get very nervous, when I was supposed to get onstage towards the end, because I wanted that performance to be just as good as the last performance. Sometimes I would do things that I knew could be better . . . I wish I knew then what I know now, to have corrected myself then.

I stopped myself from becoming a principal dancer, from having a real, real career. I got in my own way. I know that for a fact. First of all I got a lot of injuries, and I think that's mental, mind over matter. And Balanchine got disappointed in me. I think he expected me to grasp things very quickly, but I take my time, I go slower. But to be honest with you, the career wasn't as important as what I'm doing now. Now I'm in the right place.

It was my decision to stop dancing. I'll tell you what happened. When Jerry was doing his retrospective in '90, I was having trouble with my back. I had a meeting with Peter [Martins]—also I mentioned this to Rosemary Dunleavy, the ballet mistress—and I said, "I've always wanted to work with Jerry, be an assistant to him." And they said, "I think that's a wonderful idea. I'll talk to him," and then seven, eight months went by, and nothing happened. So I thought, 'Well, I guess I have to take this up on my own.' Jerry was starting preliminary rehearsals, and I met him going into the theatre. I said, "Jerry, listen. I know you're looking for a new person for *Watermill*," because it was 20 years old. "If you need any help with anything . . . I've done so many of your ballets, you've choreographed on me, I would love to help." And he went, "Great. Come to my rehearsal . . .

I have rehearsal right now for *Watermill*." I went, and he was trying a new dancer in something and the guy couldn't figure it out, and I saw right away what Jerry wanted. So I said, "Do this." I didn't even think about the other ballet master in the room—I just kind of said it, because I was thinking, 'This is for the work. It's to get something out for the work.' I knew the answer and I knew I could provide the answer, so I said, "Try it this way." And the guy did it and Jerry went, "That was right." He was a little surprised. I gave like two corrections, and after that rehearsal, he said, "Good work."

Then I just kept on surprising him. In that process of being . . . like an apprentice, you could call it, or interim ballet master, I started to go to all the rehearsals, and he saw that I was very organized. He would test me and I knew it was a test, so I would just do what I had to do. And because everyone was working in different studios, we would try to divide everything up. He said, "Can you rehearse this and this and this and put these together?" and I said, "Sure." "Do you know it?" "Yeah, of course I know it. You'll see." He gave me the confidence, and I did it, and he was really surprised.

I wasn't surprised, because I wanted it. I had the work ethic and I knew what it took to prepare yourself—you had to be one step ahead of Jerry. No one else knew I could do it, but I knew it. I don't mean that as an ego thing, I just had a gut feeling that . . . I was a child that got along with people. When I was young and I used to go to summer camp, sleep-away camp, they wanted me to be a junior counselor, they saw that I had that kind of trait. When I started working as a ballet master, I knew that it was something I wanted to do. And also I knew, ahead of time, that you had to be very organized and you had to do your homework and you had to make sure the dancers weren't sitting around while you tried to figure something out—you had to know it. I watched, I observed all the other ballet masters and mistresses with Jerry, when was it good not to talk or when he expected you to have the answer because he couldn't figure it out. I just saw it instinctively, plus I felt there was something about the connection between us . . . I mean, I don't know if it's because of his upbringing, but I'm half-Jewish—my father was Jewish, my mother was Catholic—and I grew up with a European upbringing also, a very strong, strict family, don't trust people, that whole system, very similar to when he was a child. So it's part of understanding who Jerry was and why he was the way he was. I understood where he was coming from and how much passion he had for his work, and I respected that. That also made it easy for me, because if you respect the person you're working for, I think you do good work.

Working with him as a dancer . . . Well, if he's not under pressure he's very relaxed and very giving. He concentrates on whatever he feels he's not getting out of the dancers at that time. You don't know that until you're in the studio. He loved the dancers, he cared about the dancers, and he was an incredible coach. A lot of people think he was really a tyrant—it's because he expected you to be better than you really were. He wanted you to get to another level, that you thought you were at already but you were not. And he also loved dancers that were very smart, smart in that they did their homework, they came in prepared and ready to work, they thought about it when they left the studio. They'd know their steps, he didn't have to go back and teach the ballet again.

For example, there's a young girl called Alexandra Ansanelli in the company, and she did *The Cage* a few years ago. Jerry was going through his low period, so I cast her but I said to him, "Take a look at it, and if you don't want her to do it, cross it off. But you trust me. Come to rehearsal tomorrow and take a look at it." And I told this girl, "When you see Jerry for the first time, perform it like it's a performance. He wants to see a performance level in that studio. He doesn't want to wait 'til the curtain goes up." And he was wowed. Some of it wasn't right, but she knew what it was supposed to be, and some of it was so interesting and so thought-out in her mind that he couldn't believe it. He said to me afterwards, "She was incredible." He always wanted that performance level in rehearsal. That was part of his wanting to see what he was going to get on that stage. He wanted to see the product, because he wanted to be secure enough himself, in his ballet and in his dancers. Unless he knew the dancer very well and it was a ballet they'd done before, he wanted to make sure. That's why he always used the same dancers, because it was very important for him to feel comfortable in the studio, working with that dancer. Sometimes he would pick a dancer that he liked and he was comfortable with for a certain role that I felt they really were not suited to. I was surprised he would pick them, and I think he did it because it was someone he knew and had a relationship with.

Depending on the ballet, I mean, if it was a ballet that was, say, *Fancy Free, Les Noces, Interplay*, that had a theme, he wanted to know who you were. I think of *Fancy Free* as a play. It's not a ballet, to me anyway, it's a play with all these little nuances, and when you put your leg up or turn your head, those are your lines in the play. So you had to know who you're dancing with and never perform to the audience. He would want you to concentrate on that: "Who are you looking at? Why are you doing this?" About a year before I became ballet master, I started acting lessons and I studied for three years. And for *Fancy Free*, he wanted us to write a scenario, our past lives, who you were, who's sleeping on the top bunk, where's he from, what does he like, what are the ports that you've been to . . . ? He wanted us to create that on our own, for the character to have a life. You have to be someone before you get onstage—it can't just happen once you're there. You have to be that character, and if you have a scenario and you have a past life, it moves onto the stage.

An example is *West Side Story Suite*. He said this in interviews, and it's true. There's a group of dancers in the Dance at the Gym, and no one is a corps de ballet member. If you look at the play—it's not a ballet—everyone has a different color dress, different hairdo, they're all different people. He would stress this constantly: you are not corps de ballet, you are an individual, so each person has his own personality. And many times, to break the ice sometimes . . . Because the dancers got so used to rehearsing and they knew what was next, they would not wait for the question, they would respond before the question, because each dancer knew what he had to do. So Jerry would go to the dancer who was giving the answer and say, "Do something different." He would make them do something different and see if the other dancer that was responding would pick up on it. Sometimes it would throw the other dancer for a loop, because it changed all of a sudden, but Jerry was testing to see if you were really focusing on what's going on.

It's hard for certain dancers. Some dancers like to just go out there and perform, and not go through the process of being around a studio every day rehearsing a lot, which Jerry demanded. He's very specific, he wanted a certain look to it, lunge, low, not placing the arm deliberately, because he wanted things off-balance, he didn't want anything that was so straight, he wanted his dancers to bend their bodies more. You know, he never liked a dancer to be stiff, like something was up their ass. He liked dancers more grounded, with more weight to them, so when you watched them from the audience, you weren't nervous watching it. They were sure of themselves. When a dancer dances straight up all the time, they look a little more nervous, and it makes the audience nervous.

But being lower gives more weight, puts more security in their dancing and gives the audience security too.

So Jerry had a certain look, and when I stage ballets for Jerry I tell them how it's supposed to be. But sometimes, certain dancers—and Jerry allowed me to do this as a dancer—look better doing it a different way. Everyone was always afraid to change things, but Jerry would change it for the dancers many times because it looked better on their body that way. So there will be a different version from the New York City Ballet one in the Paris Opéra, because with that company he wanted to play with it and change little details. So many times before I went staging a ballet without him, I would call him up and say, "What version do you want me to do for these dancers?" He said, "Pick what's best for them."

This legacy is the most important thing in the world to me, because I've seen many things change when someone is not alive. Yes, things have to move on and change, but you've got to keep the wish of a person and their standards. That is very important. You're responsible for giving that work the integrity that was there when he was alive. That is what your job is—to me it's very simple. I know a lot of people would like to be in my position, and it's a hard job to be in, it's not a fun job sometimes. A lot of people like to be the one calling the shots, but are they willing to be in that studio, working with those dancers and getting down on the floor in your sweatpants and sneakers and nurturing them? That's also another job, to nurture the dancers and give them life. You are the one giving them independence. You have this little bud and you're the one that's turning it into the flower. You're the one, you wake it up.

And also, you have to be very willing to say no to somebody. A lot of people are afraid to say no. Let's say a dancer wants to do an outside performance somewhere and they want to do a ballet that they've already danced, but it would be done with taped music or with half a set . . . it won't be done the way it should be done or the way the ballet is intended to be seen as a whole, OK? And you like this dancer and you'd like to let them do it, but you know deep in your heart that this is really something that should not happen, this way. So as a person who's in charge of keeping this legacy, you have to be willing to say no to that person or "You can't do this" or "You're not the right person." And what is it about? Is it about pleasing them, or is it about keeping the standard at a certain level? I mean, right now, Peter [Martins] does not get involved with Jerry's casting, he doesn't do any of it. I do the casting with the other ballet masters, so it's important that I'm able to say no and it's hard. But it's not about authority, and it's not about me. That's what I try to tell people—it's about the work. It's always for the work.

I knew Jerry so well. Sometimes I would know exactly what he would say for a correction, because sometimes I would say it before he did. So this job came easy. I didn't have to really learn very much. I just knew what had to be done for the piece. See, because of Jerry, I had a lot of freedom in New York City Ballet. They allowed me to do what I want, even when Jerry was alive. He gave me that freedom because he trusted me quite a bit, and he was never hard on me, because my timing was very right and he knew— he said this to a friend—that "J-P and I are like this when it comes to the ballets," like my crossed fingers, we're like two the same, meaning we think the same.

On my day off I would work with him; when he choreographed with Misha [Baryshnikov], I *made* free time. And when he was rehearsing *2 & 3 Part Inventions* at the School of American Ballet, he was alone without a ballet master. He needed someone there, I was his main ballet master, I was there. You don't think about it, you just do it. It was my choice, and I made sure it did not interfere with anything at New York City Ballet. Our head ballet mistress felt it was interfering, but I said, "No, this is connected to New York City Ballet." I had some people saying, "Why are you doing this?" and what I said was, "If Balanchine was alive, at that age, I think you would be there also to make sure he had help. Jerry is all alone in the studio—it's not right."

Jerry used to talk a lot to the dancers and I do too, to explain what you need. You teach them the steps, of course, and then you teach them how you want the steps done. Not phrasing, but getting more intensity. Like in *The Cage,* "Thrust your hips more forward. You don't just stand—use more force." The alteration changes the look of the step. See, Jerry demonstrated everything. Every one of his ballets is him, it's his personality, it's what's inside of him, and he always used to tell the dancers, "Watch me. Watch how I do this movement." I'm very good at mimicking, just by watching a videotape, so when I demonstrate I'm really being Jerry. I mean, there's a way of doing every step in his ballets, so I just see how he does it. Like in *The Concert,* he could do those characters better than anyone else because he believed he was each character. So I show them Jerry, but they don't know it's Jerry. *I* know, but I don't really analyze it.

There are a lot of rehearsal tapes with Jerry rehearsing ballets too. They're not open to the public, but we have a lot of tape, records of a particular performance sometimes—a good chunk of performances and all the first performances usually are video'd. But when I'm staging, I don't show videos. I only show a ballet after it's staged and coached—I say, "OK, let's see it now." I don't like people learning it through videos, because if you see a dancer on the video, often you think that's the way it's supposed to be. I mean, I think you can learn from videos, but many times you have a dancer who comes into the studio with a concept from looking at a video, and it's hard to break that concept. Because they don't know who they are yet, they're trying to be like somebody else.

Technically dancers are better now. I've seen some interesting videos of famous dancers, and I was so surprised how they danced—it's just smaller. For that time it was incredible, but they would never be a principal dancer now. Jacques d'Amboise . . . never. Eddie Villella . . . naaah, he'd be a soloist. But for the men there was no other competition at that time. Women were different, there was more competition for the women. And they all had personality. This is why I think videos are not good—a lot of these ballets were taught to people when there were no videos, so they had to create a performance, because they didn't have anyone else to look at. That's why you had more personalities in those days, because they would have their own idea of what a ballet should be.

They're always harder to stage if you didn't dance in them, but with a ballet you haven't performed or danced in, after you've staged it a few times it's not hard at all. I never actually danced *Cage*, but I feel like I know the piece very well, from staging it, from rehearsing it with New York City Ballet, from being in the studio with Jerry. Same thing with *Glass Pieces*. Sometimes it's good to have the dancer that the ballet was created on come in and rehearse. I think it's good for the dancer that's going to dance the role to listen to what that person has to say. It happens occasionally at New York City Ballet, not as often as I think it should, but that could be about a lack of money. It could be about keeping the family happy—if you bring someone in from outside it's like saying to your ballet master, "Maybe they can get a little bit more out of this person," and you don't want your ballet master getting all upset. Everyone has an ego, there's a lot of egos.

You've got to make sure you're not ruffling feathers, but at the same time, as I say, it's not about that—it's about the work.

And sometimes you end up with conflicting responses. There were many times when Jerry did not want help himself when he staged a ballet. If a dancer was in town, let's say in Paris, and we were staging a piece in which this dancer was the original dancer when Jerry choreographed it, when I asked him, "Do you want to have this person here?" he said, "No." Because I think he wanted the dancer learning it not to be confused, and also he wanted that dancer to put a little bit of himself into it. People said Jerry was very controlling and specific, but if a dancer creates a mood that works for that ballet, even though it's a little different, he allows it. If the idea is there and it still looks like his piece, then he's content.

We can preserve the ballets with video, but you still need that person who worked with that creator because there are certain things that the creator said to *get* certain things out of those dancers. My responsibility in staging a ballet is to get the dancers to understand the ballet and get it out of them. You're the heart of that ballet—it's not the dancers. *You* are, the ballet master or the stager, because your job is to get it out of them, to nurture them. They don't have any idea . . . And it's not just about steps. See, with Balanchine, they're learning a style at the school. A dancer can come out of the school and right away fit into a Balanchine ballet, because they already have his style. If they went into a Robbins ballet, it's a whole different . . . That's why he was such a stickler on coaching and having rehearsals. That was his way of teaching them how to move the way he wanted. Balanchine ballets don't look as good to me outside the New York City Ballet, except for certain companies, because there's a certain training that goes along with those ballets. Jerry's ballets look wonderful with the Paris Opéra, they understand them. His ballets work well with San Francisco Ballet—*Glass Pieces* was brilliant, and *The Cage* was danced well there. And Jerry's are more accessible to people. I'm talking about the dancers, but to the public too. That's why people like Jerry's ballets, because they can understand them and relate to them.

Oh, the ballets won't die, not in my lifetime. They *can* be gone. It's very simple to lose them. It depends how they're taught and who goes out there and teaches them. Of course, anyone can stage a ballet, but after the count three and the step on nine, you have to have a passion to go in that studio and work. A lot of people feel nowadays, 'I've got the step on nine, I've taught the ballet, it's finished.' That's just the beginning. That's the skeleton, you've blocked it out, then you have to put the molding and the sheetrock on.

I've seen a lot of ballets staged that I think, 'It could be better,' but sometimes you can't fix certain things. Sometimes you work and work and work, and you can't get it out of the dancer, it's just not there. That happens many times. And also, it depends on the director. Some directors require the dancers to be professional and demand respect from them to choreographers that come in. Certain directors are more relaxed about those things. I think the director sets the example—it always comes from the top. If you set up a very strong example, it finally filters down. But nowadays a lot of board members want a well-known dancer to be a director as a figurehead or because it's a name people know, instant return, but it doesn't mean they're good directors. A lot of positions are filled by dancers or ballet masters that never have created and never have learned the craft of being responsible.

And I think this generation of dancers is different. It's very easy now, it's easier than it was. It has to change, I'm not saying it doesn't, but I remember when I was a student and then I'd got in the company . . . *Nutcracker*—soldier, Chinese, Candy Cane, Hoop, cavalier. It was such a big deal to do each of them, it showed an up-and-coming dancer. Nowadays, after a lot of dancers have done a part for three or four years, they don't want to do it anymore, 'I deserve something else.' I never felt like that, I mean, unless I was doing a part for 12 or 13 years, and I would say, "Let the younger dancers do these things." I would never say, "I am beyond that," but I think because of cable television, changing channels all the time, fast food, it's a very self-satisfying . . . everybody wants everything quick.

I'm worried about the time aspect in general. There's not enough rehearsal time. It's very frustrating. Jerry demanded time because it was his ballets. When I stage a ballet elsewhere I always get the time because I'm a guest. But here [at New York City Ballet] it's harder, because of the repertory, because of circumstances, it's just harder. And I'm worried about that because with Jerry's ballets you do not take someone from the school, plug them in and they fit. Jerry used to let dancers stay in the corps or stay in the back and be an understudy for about a year to get the feeling of a ballet. He would eventually put them in, but he would wait awhile.

He always picked the best dancers, because certain things in his ballets are very simple. Like a small port de bras in *In the Night*, you need to have someone to create an illusion. You can't just have some-one doing any old port de bras, it has to be a way of moving that needs a very talented dancer. There are certain pas de deux that he would teach to people that weren't as experienced and then to some-one else who was experienced, and . . . it's a different ballet. That's why he demanded the best dancers, because he knew they would do something for him. And also, they would love his ballets.

When he was alive . . . When I did *The Concert* in Canada, I went ahead and cast it, and he came two days later and put it on the stage. That was it—I was very fortunate. He said to me afterward, "You're more than an assistant," and I was very touched. He gave me that re-assurance, maybe to make me work harder, but I got a thank-you and that's very important. We all want to be appreciated, and I think it's important that you're told that you're appreciated. A dancer's job is a very hard job because, you know, many times you do a performance and then you go through the down period, all that work and all of a sudden it's over and it's like a letdown. Well, Jerry would come back-stage and correct dancers all the time, and he'd also say, "Thank you very much. It was wonderful. There are a couple of things to talk about, but I'll tell you later." Now, if you want them to work for you, you have to compliment them at the same time that you correct them. They'll give you something back if you give them something—it's human nature. There are times, as a ballet master, when you have to say, "This is what I want," but you can't be a bully all the time and you can't always be someone's friend. It's hard. There's a time to be friendly with people, and there's a time to get down to work.

For example, *The Concert* is a very difficult ballet. It looks very simple, but everything is exactly to a T. And it can be very easy for the dancers to broaden it, it can get overacted, because when they start hearing the laughs, they play to it. So I try not to give that bal-let to a company that I don't know. If they're doing a Robbins for the first time I'd rather give them . . . Not myself, but I ask the Trust or the committee or that director to suggest another ballet. I usually ask them to try to do something else first so I get to know the company, and then maybe do *The Concert* later, because certain dances, like the rain section, are so subtle and a lot of dancers get turned off by the ballet master, myself, being so specific. They think they're doing the movement right and they're not. They like to put a lot of themselves into *The Concert* and ad-lib, so they have a hard time with me say-ing, "No. It's not right. Do it again." And I explain it—I'm incredibly patient. I had some of the Royal Ballet dancers come up to me when I staged it in London and say, "We've never worked like this before. Usually we're allowed to ad-lib a lot more in big productions. So we're not used to someone going, 'No, this is wrong.'" Some of them loved it; some of them, I'm sure, behind my back, felt very squeezed.

Also I've found that certain companies are star companies and certain companies are more repertory companies. OK. In companies that haven't danced Jerry's ballets, some of their principal dancers would like to embellish and do what suits them. They say, "I feel more comfortable doing it this way," but they're changing the choreography. So then I have to be tougher and say, "No. This is what it is. If you want to do it, you have to do it this way." So I have come into conflicts in that respect, but when they know that you are the one that is responsible . . . You know in *Apollo*, just after the male solo, where the fingers touch? Knowledge passes through the finger. Someone gave me a card in Canada many years ago, and they wrote, "You're very blessed to have the knowledge to give to other people."

But you can't just give any of Jerry's ballets to any company. It's a marriage, between the Trust and that company. That ballet has to make the company look good, and the company has to make Jerry's ballets look good at the same time. There's a committee, we all sit and discuss it and we decide. Sometimes I go out and see the company before the decision's made, sometimes we send somebody else. So we know what we're working with. When you put the ballet together, usually I have a ballet master or mistress there who is then responsible to maintain it while you're gone. Right now a company can usually do a piece for about two years. I've been implementing that Jerry's ballet masters have to go back after a year or eight months to look at it, to make sure it's OK. But we also have the option . . . If it doesn't look right on a company in the beginning stages or if for some reason it's not working out, it doesn't happen. You don't want to do that ever, but you have the right to cancel it, to not let them have it. It has never been done . . . except Jerry's done it, he pulled something. The first time the Paris Opéra was supposed to do *Dances at a Gathering*, he started to stage it and then he stopped and said, "Let them do *In the Night* instead."

There's quite a bit of demand for these ballets. For example, everyone wants *Concert*. Because it's a crowd pleaser it's successful no matter where you perform it. The audience likes it, it's funny, it's timeless, everyone wants it. It's a closer, and there are not many successful closing ballets. But you have to be really careful in not saturating the Robbins repertory either, because what happens is . . . A lot of companies have a lot of our repertoire now. So when New York City Ballet goes on tour, maybe a ballet fan might not buy a ticket, because they'll say, "OK, I've seen this ballet with one company, I've seen this other ballet already with another company." That's how I see it—I mean, the Robbins rep has to be out there, but it has to be controlled and maintained, that's the most important thing, because Jerry's ballets are very fragile. They're not like Balanchine that can withstand the test of time more. I think Jerry's are all about the atmosphere and the camaraderie and the relationships that he creates. They're all about who you're dancing with, and that's why you have to rehearse those ballets a lot and why he always was a stickler about rehearsing. He always used to say, "At the premiere, I want it to look like it's your fifth performance."

My work evolves, it goes into different phases. You learn more about people, you learn more about yourself. Right now I'm struggling with the New York City Ballet work and the outside work, to find the balance for my time and to make sure they both are treated equally. How I will change . . . I'm already starting to see a way of allowing the dancer . . . not to change the movement but to put something of themselves in the piece. At one point, you know, you had Jerry behind you. You'd stage a ballet or you might rehearse a dancer and . . . He was moody. He might like it, he might not like it. What is easier now is that you're not worried that much that he's not going to like it, because he's not there. So you're a little bit . . . I mean, I always was relaxed with Jerry, but I just finished putting together *Moves* with the New York City Ballet, and I had the most wonderful time in those rehearsals with those dancers. They're all young, new, some of them have never seen the piece before, and it was a wonderful experience for them because they learned to use a peripheral vision, to watch each other, to be part of a group. And this piece with this cast will probably stay like this for a long time.

I have to tell you, things are going to change. You can't control that. This will go on beyond my lifetime. Like Peter Martins said to me once, he's going to die, I'm going to die . . . I don't know what will happen to the ballets. Hopefully they'll be maintained correctly. Petipa's not being performed now the way it was when it was first created. But there's a torch there that has to be eventually carried. It *has* to be carried to make sure the dancers understand who Jerry is or what Jerry was about. I promised him when he was on his deathbed that I would do the best I can to, you know, maintain his wishes, and part of his wishes is to maintain his work. That was my agreement with him. I got to know him very, very well, I was very close with him, and people were envious because of the relationship, but they didn't understand the relationship. He was more like a father relationship. So when I get upset about something and I see something going in the direction I know he would not want, even though he's not here, I have a hard time with that, and I speak my mind. I don't want him to be taken advantage of. I don't have to hold to my promise, no one does. But when I promise someone something, I go all the way. I mean, that's my personality, I just do it. It's an obligation, and I'm an honorable man.

Shelley Washington

b. Washington, D.C., 1954. Studied at Interlochen Arts Academy and Juilliard School of Music. Danced with the companies of Martha Graham 1974–75 and Twyla Tharp 1975–88 and, from 1988–91, with American Ballet Theatre, where she also became ballet master for Tharp's work. Since retiring in 1991, she has supervised the staging of Tharp's ballets worldwide.

ACTUALLY, MY MOTHER AND FATHER were the greatest inspirations when I started dancing. They wanted to give my sister and me all the things that they didn't have when they were growing up. The respectable thing to do in the early '50s, being black, was to be in the army or a teacher, where you could really have a career, but my parents were actors at Howard University before he was in the army. So ballet class was one of the many things that we did—I was six. I took violin lessons, piano, all those kinds of things.

When I was 14 I went for the summer to the national music camp at Interlochen Arts Academy in Michigan, and there I really fell in love with the idea of being a dancer. It was the first time I had been in a room with people who really wanted to be in the arts. Prior to that I had always been the only one in my school that was a dancer or played the piano—I was sort of singled out. Then all of a sudden I went away to this camp and for the first time I heard live music played for class. It was the first time I ever saw male dancers and the first time I ever had a variety of teachers and different kinds of classes in the same day. It was really a thrilling experience to be surrounded with all of these people who had the same sort of ambitions. I didn't feel so odd anymore.

I begged my parents to be able to go there all year round, so I spent my sophomore, junior and senior year at Interlochen Arts Academy, and during the summers I would go to different summer camps, Jacob's Pillow on a scholarship in '70, Connecticut College in '71 and '72 and American University in '73. A lot of dancers went from Interlochen into Juilliard, and that was really my aspiration, to continue. So I followed the crowd to Juilliard in 1972, and Juilliard was pretty amazing. Alfredo Corvino was teaching then, Hector Zaraspe—it was not unusual for Rudolf Nureyev to come to take Hector Zaraspe's class—Anna Sokolow, Kazuko Hirabayashi, Ethel Winter. Danny Lewis was there, so I had great José Limón teachers and great Graham teachers for my introduction to Graham. Actually, that started earlier, because Helen McGehee and Richard Gain came to Interlochen and choreographed dances for us—I was in both of their pieces. And I still went to summer camps, and at summer camp in 1974 I worked on a piece with Anna Sokolow that I later performed at Juilliard. Someone from the Graham company saw me in that performance . . . I'm not sure if it was Martha or Ron Protas, but I got a phonecall from Martha Graham asking me to come in and audition.

My best friend, Christopher Polofian, and I had done a duet from *Choreographic Offering* at Juilliard—it was the only thing I knew. So I asked him if he'd come with me to my audition, and he and I did that. At 19 years old, very naive and anxious, my audition in front of Martha Graham and Ron Protas was a piece by José Limón. I remember her asking me if I could do Graham and I said, Yes, I had studied at Juilliard for the last two years. So I changed my clothes and came back in, and she offered me a job. Then I had to go back into the school . . . I was finishing my sophomore year at Juilliard, and you had to kind of audition . . . go through a class in front of all your teachers to progress to the next year, and at that point I said I had been invited to join the Graham company.

My mother and I decided that I didn't really want to finish school and wait two years. Who knew if the opportunity would be there again? I went to Martha. I might have stayed with Martha forever. A lot of people did. I stayed one year. Well, when I went to summer camp in '73, I was apprenticing with José Limón to be one of the extras in *Missa Brevis*—because José and Martha and Cunningham were the three techniques offered at Juilliard—and Twyla was also resident choreographer or resident teacher there, along with the

Limón company. I asked her if I could take one of their classes, and every day, for six weeks, I took the late afternoon class. I didn't know her, I'd never heard of her company, and I was terrified at first of her dancers. They were . . . very different dancers, with a different kind of protocol from at Juilliard. They wore baggy clothes, they danced with their hair down—I was still with my hair in a bun—some of them smoked cigarettes or, God forbid, they drank beer.

But I was young and inquisitive and I wanted a change, and I didn't want to be a Tharp dancer—I wanted to be a Limón dancer or a Graham dancer or a Cunningham dancer. So I just wanted to learn from it, and she did amazing things. Every day we learned ten positions, she would add more on, and this went on and on for weeks and weeks. It was like music, I mean, you could dance like music. You could dance not facing the audience, you could dance repetition . . . I guess before that I had only thought of dancing with my heart. I had never really put my head and my heart together. At the time I was just throwing myself into movement, and because I hadn't worked with a lot of choreographers, it didn't occur to me that you could repeat a phrase facing stage right, upstage, stage left, or that by putting these positions in a different order the dance would completely change. Or you could lie down on the floor and do the whole dance lying down. Or you could do the whole dance backwards. Some days we would have an hour class, and you would have to move from position one to position ten . . . how slow could you possibly go? Or sometimes, so fast.

At the end of the summer school, they were doing a lecture-demonstration for the public, and she called me—I didn't even think she knew my name—to come up to the stage. I had to stand by the American flag over on the stage-right corner, and while her company was performing and she was talking, she asked me to go through all the movements we had learned in the six-week course. Which I did, and that was it. Then I went back to Juilliard and then I got into the Graham company in '74, and in 1975 Twyla had auditions and somebody remembered me, "What about that girl? Remember that girl who stood on the stage by the flag and did all those positions?" Someone got my name and called me . . . I swear, my two dancing jobs, calls out of the blue, Martha Graham and Twyla Tharp.

I went to the audition, and four dancers in her company—Kenneth Rinker, Tom Rawe, Jennifer Way and a senior member, Rose, Rose Marie Wright—auditioned me, Twyla was not there. After the audition they said, "Well, we're interested. Would you like to come work with us?" Back in those days it really depended on whether the dancers liked you or wanted to be with you. Certainly if they could work with you, Twyla could work with you. In my early days, when people were coming to audition for Twyla, our whole company—however big it was, six people, seven—would all be a part of it and pick the dancers that we liked. We were as important in our say as Twyla was.

So I called my mom and said, "I really want to do this. I really feel like she's the start of something new. I'm very excited when I see her. I feel like she's going to help me find out who I am." I had a gut feeling that I wanted to do something no one had done before. I can remember saying to my mother, "She'll choreograph something someday that'll be just for me, not me trying to be somebody else." I hadn't quite figured out yet how you could do a repertoire and not try to duplicate another person. I understand that now, but at that age I didn't really get it. I felt a little bit like I was preserving works and not being a part of something that was making a new statement in dance. I had the utmost respect for Graham and the technique, but I just wanted a change.

When I went into Graham, I was the baby and I was very grateful to be where I was. You still had the great dancers there, and there was this huge resurgence . . . this was the year Rudolf Nureyev came and wanted to learn modern technique, and we did *Lucifer.* I learned a tremendous amount and I grew up with Martha and her presence and her incredible stories. I was dancing in *Diversion of Angels* and *Clytemnestra* and *Night Journey* and learning *Appalachian Spring* and *Cave of the Heart.* Martha was not dancing, but Takako Asakawa and Yuriko Kimura and Ross Parkes, Phyllis Gutelius, Diane Gray . . . they were. You could watch these people transform into incredible actors. We would all take class onstage at 6:00, and I would watch Takako. She would slip out of her slippers and go to her little space onstage and warm up. She was always so friendly and so nice, "Hello, Shelley," and then all of a sudden, by the time she came off that stage, you couldn't talk to her. She was not Takako—she was Medea.

I had a paycheck that, to me, coming out of school, was a big check, and I was working 40-something weeks, maybe 48, I was really working. I had a lot of security, plus I was looking at masters, *masters*, and I was learning and learning and learning. And it's not like I had studied at her school for five years and feared Martha: it just happened, and the way it happened was so pleasant. Of course there were days when I was scared of some of the ballet masters or the dancers, because they were tough. There was no such thing as them teaching you a part—you learned it from the ballet master or off of a video. Now dancers come in the room and someone shows them their parts and helps them. Not at the Graham company. No. This was serious stuff.

But I wasn't afraid of her because I didn't even know enough to be afraid. I wasn't doing her roles, I was in the chorus, and she was very kind to me, as was Ron. So I felt pretty secure and I believed in what I was doing. I believed in myself, but really, I believed in Martha and I believed I could do it. I just believed, you know? I really thought, in my naive way, that if you say "Please," somebody will say "Thank you." I believed if you took class every day, no matter how you felt, that you would be a better dancer. I was like that all through my career. When I think about it now, I'm not so sure. I am sure there were days when I was so tired that probably staying in bed would have been better for me than taking class. But then I was determined, pushing, I was going to figure out how to turn these legs out more and point that foot more, and it was all about just saying, "I took class five times this week" and sometimes not paying attention to the rest of my needs.

I left Martha and went to less than half the salary, but I never signed a contract with Twyla and I didn't even know when I got into the company. You're sort of invited in to work and then you're just there. I remember Tom Rawe saying he was there for like a year and a half before he thought, 'I must be in the company now. They haven't sent me home.' I was paid for 52 weeks a year, which was the first time this new company was really getting paid, and we worked for 48 weeks and toured for three—I'm not exaggerating. Maybe there were some vacations in there, but I only went on tour for three weeks that first year and the rest of the time was working in the studio. And it was interesting because by the time our company finished—the company that I started with—we were touring for 40-something weeks and in the city for three or four or five. Each year it progressed more and more, 'til we sort of disbanded in '88, when we were performing all the time.

I didn't go in expecting the world. I just wanted to learn, and I got hooked. On Twyla, Rose, Sara [Rudner], Tom, Jenny, music, dance, working, friends, challenge, repetition, mind, physical challenges and changes in your body. The repertoire was amazing and it was an amazing feeling to work with a team, and the company was so based upon that. It wasn't competitive—it was a group of people working together. It's why I love cycling so much—it's a team effort. Let's say you're the team leader but I'm really good at climbing hills. So I get in front of you and put out all the hard work because my legs can do that. Then right before it's time for you to win the race, I pull off and you go out. But you winning it gives me points, gives our team points, and I like that. Everybody gets a chance and everybody's good at something, but you can have it all, in that team, if you work it and respect it together.

And if you have the same goals, and that's what I sort of coach. People are going to say, "Aw, she's talking a bunch of shit," but if you can get everybody going for the same goal, I promise you they'll look more together than if every finger and every head is in the right shape. This is the challenge, for the coach, dancer, anyone. That's what teaching is and that's what rehearsing is. You get it all going, and then, when you unleash the thing, it's like letting horses out. You lift the fence, and those horses just shoot ahead.

I was scared the first year or two with Twyla. It was a huge change and it was hard. Well, state the obvious: Twyla was probably 30 and Martha was 80-something. One is talking and showing, and the other is up on her feet, going 1,000 miles a minute. We worked hard. We had no union rules. We took breaks when they happened—someone would go off and get water and then the next one would go and then the next one, and we'd sort of stall. Or somebody would get hungry and pick up a sandwich and eat a bite, and I'd go, 'Oh, they're eating, I'll eat.' It wasn't designated, "From 2:00–3:00 we're going to . . ." You just went in and you worked, and I'll tell you, we worked hard but Twyla worked harder. Twyla never, ever asked us to do anything that she couldn't do herself. But we did really work. It wasn't a lot of "Well, shall we try this?" You just . . . did it, just by repetition and rehearsal.

One of the greatest things . . . 1976, *Give and Take*, my first big . . . uh, little solo break. I was not and still am not very turned out and I have a really big jump. So what did she do? She made my first solo on all the things that I could not do well. It was all about turnout—it didn't have a jump in it. Oh, I think it's quite brilliant. Every day she made me work on the things that made me insecure, and I actually found a way to do it and got better at it and got over some inhibitions about not having the legs that every dancer should have. It wasn't a dare. She's not going to put me out there and make a fool of me . . . but maybe she would, who knows? But she gave me something to work on, something for me.

I took over a couple of roles, but for every few of those there were so many more that were new. I did do her part in *The Bix Pieces* and [*Eight*] *Jelly Rolls*, and I did do Sara's part in *Jelly Rolls* and I did do *The Fugue*. But on top of those there was *Give and Take, Country Dances*, then *Baker's Dozen* came in, then *When We Were Very Young* and *Chapters and Verses*. Certainly she did roles for me, but Twyla doesn't really come on to you and say, "You were great tonight" or "This is for you." Martha came to every show and sat in the stage-right wing, and a lot of ballet companies have the same thing; you go back and talk to them right after the show, "Very good show" or whatever. But I can remember Twyla coming from the audience and going across the stage, just walking by, "Good night." I mean, I was very insecure, and everybody wants to be recognized for hard work, for getting better, for trying. Of course she said, "This was good" and "This was better," but it was a different attitude. I need Twyla sometimes in the downstage right wing, but I don't need her there all the time. I don't need anybody all the time. We need to make our own decisions and choices, and one of the things that Twyla said to me was, "Assume you are great until you're told you're not." This is a direct quote, and I repeat it to dancers everywhere I work: "Assume you are great until you're told you're not."

I don't remember asking Twyla a lot of motivational questions or what a piece meant or anything—I just did it, I found my way. I was a maid in *The Catherine Wheel* and Chris Uchida ultimately played a pet, she wore a little furry thing. That came out of . . . Twyla started a piece called *Order and Chaos*, which became eventually the maid and the pet, but for years it was *Order and Chaos*. Chris was Chaos, because Chris was always all over the place, and I was Order. I am the most orderly . . . Everything has to look good, and I just sit in a hard chair so I don't mess anything. For half my life I never even knew you could get back into bed—we made our beds as soon as we got out of them. But all of a sudden in *Catherine Wheel* I was a maid, which all these people had problems with because I was black, and she was this pet and she was Oriental. Not until someone said something did I even think of that, and it wasn't meant that way. I didn't mind wearing a maid's costume, I was comfortable in it, because if somebody else had been Order, they would have been in it.

When Twyla went to ABT, I was 33, 34, and I saw it as an opportunity to shift careers. I had started working side by side with her even then, helping more with the dancers. I was still dancing in her company, in every ballet, every night, eight shows a week. The performances were fun, and we were touring without Twyla, so there was a lot going on. I was coming up in seniority in the company so I was starting to have other responsibilities. When we were in New York, we all went out and took our own ballet classes. When we traveled, which was more than we were in New York, Richard Colton or I taught. That was just a natural way to keep everybody uniform and together when we started bringing in new dancers. When Gil Boggs came to the company for a year, he taught a few classes, and we would rotate among three or four of us. And when we were in Australia for two-and-a-half months, Richard and I were responsible the entire time for the company, responsible for everything—he and I were seniors, but we fell naturally into that role. In every company there's somebody who can stand in front of a room and get respect out of the dancers or they can organize a schedule that works best for everyone.

Going to ABT . . . First of all it was a job, let's be honest, but I'm not going to say it was just a job. I wasn't ready to leave. I wanted to stay with Twyla, I wasn't through dancing, and what an incredible coup, to be a modern dancer and go into Ballet Theatre as a soloist—the year I joined there were 101 dancers in the company. I have always known a lot of the dancers at Ballet Theatre because we rehearsed there, and I took class with them because I'd always taken ballet classes, so it wasn't as if I was going into complete foreign territory. But it was hard, we had to prove ourselves. And to be fair, it's sort of strange to go into a company as a soloist based upon where I'd been with Twyla, when in actuality I couldn't do soloist classical roles and, you know, there are only so many slots. So I was the first to say, "I don't need to be listed as a soloist," and that's kind of when I became a ballet mistress. One day she's sitting there and I'm just taking over, people are asking me and I know the counts and I'm talking to the conductor or the pianist and telling them . . . it just naturally evolved. And I also couldn't . . . I was the only dancer there who didn't wear pointe shoes, and that's quite a difficult thing. So I'm very different—I've had a whole fantastic career off of being different, but now I'm *very* different.

She did [*In the*] *Upper Room*—there was no way I could teach *Upper Room* and dance *Upper Room*. Once a week? Once in a while? So I actually retired early. I just got everybody together and put *Upper Room* on . . . I was fine. I had a great career, I had worked with the people that I wanted to work with, I danced with some of the greatest dancers, Sara and Rose and Tommy. I'd had it all. So I figured it was OK to let it go. I didn't want to have to butcher my body or go through mind games to be in incredible shape, all the time, in order to do one performance a week, with great kids who were dancing three ballets a night. I couldn't do it at 35 . . . I didn't want to do it. I wanted to be one or the other.

Of course when I was standing in front of people at ABT, so was Twyla. But also, I was standing there as someone who had been with Twyla for 13, 14 years. People knew who I was with her, so it wasn't like I just walked out of nowhere. It felt pretty natural, and she and I could . . . You know, before she would even say where to start, I'd already be there. And I'd be able to tell if she wanted to go back 20 times on the CD and the 21st time I would fast-forward because I knew she was going to want to go forward. People would say, "How do you know?" and I don't know, but it had been like 20 years of practice. And I liked that she was going to talk really fast and throw something like this at me and then say, "What did I do?" And I could say, "Well, you talked really fast and you threw something like this at me and said, 'What did I do?'" I'd throw it back a little, but I learned how to do that from her, she's so smart, yeah, she's the best.

Now I am a freelancer. I work for Twyla, all of my work is from her, but she does not pay me, each company employs me. This year I came in for a month in October and did *Mr. Worldly Wise* again [for the Royal Ballet]. Twyla and I did that together in '95. I came in November to Birmingham [Royal Ballet] to work with them for three weeks, for *Upper Room*. I came here [to London] in January to work with Rambert on *The Golden Section*. I went back to Amsterdam to do *Upper Room* last month, which I had staged on them last year, and I was in Australia prior to Amsterdam.

The way I work . . . Well, when I knew Rambert was going to do *The Golden Section*, I'd never seen the company in my life. So when I was working with the Royal I saw a show by Rambert—I just looked. When I came back to start rehearsing I went up to the studio, I sat in the back—they're all expecting me, of course—and Steven Brett, who's my assistant, told me everybody's names, and I cast the ballet, which is all 13 people. I just looked at them in class and immediately I knew, 'OK, the girl in the black is Chris Uchida.' It's different in different places. Sometimes it takes me longer, sometimes I take 15 women and teach them a whole series of something from the ballet and then I choose the six that I need. I don't teach class. At Rambert the company's quite small, so it's not like I had 50 or 60 people and I could only choose 13. If you go into a ballet company and there are 50 or 60 and you're only choosing 13, then one takes time. And not only that, you have to get your second cast. There might be somebody you wanted in the first cast, but because they're so strong you might want them to cover the strongest person. It depends on the piece. In Australia I watched them perform, but I was coming in brand-new, with a new director, and *Upper Room* is a massive piece. So I went for two weeks and watched the company, and taught all the men one day and all the women the next, and sort of picked who I thought would be the ballet movers and who would be more modern movers. And then I went back a month later and set it. Twyla doesn't cast 'cause she's not there.

Sometimes you audition people and you can't make up your mind, so you bring them back again and again. But Twyla says that people walk in the room and she watches how they put their bag down and where they stand, and she knows. You can tell. I mean, we've done auditions with 500 people for the Tharp! group, and when I was the dance captain for *Singin' in the Rain* we had the entire New York come in onstage. So I've gotten very good at auditions. You can just tell—the person who has a great sense of humor, the person who's very afraid, the person who wants the job too much, the person who has no regard for anyone around them or who's trying so hard. I always say to people, "I'm not interested in how high your legs go. I'm interested in how your leg gets to where it is. I've seen high legs. I've seen 12 pirouettes. If you can do two or three and they're beautiful and calm and placed, that's enough." And when someone goes around 12 times I'm also the first to say "Wow," because I've never been able to do that. It's contradictory in a way, but there are as many different aspects of dance as there are of life.

My main responsibility is to Twyla and making sure that all of the steps and the way that I learned them are in place, that the dancers really know where everything is coming from. My obligation has to be to get across the energy, the steps, the rhythms, the musicality, but I never thought of it as an obligation. I feel responsible to Twyla, to the director, to the dancers, to the work, and obviously if it's something that I know like the back of my hand, I need the time to pass on the physicality.

In terms of teaching it, a lot comes down to money and time. Time is money, money is time. There are sections of *Upper Room* that I remember clearly the day that Twyla taught them and her mood and where it came from . . . everything. And I teach it the exact way that I learned it—if I have the time. There's a whole section of *Upper Room*, when Twyla made it she didn't talk for two hours. It was just for Chris and myself, and she never said a word. We had to pick it up from her. She showed over and over and over, but she never said, "It starts on a seven. The arms are doing this, this is turned out, this is a downbeat." She'd turn around and look, and she'd shake her head, no, and she'd point, like 'Watch this the next time.' Over and over.

If I go to a place where there's enough time for me to teach it like that, I wear the same kind of shirt that she had on, which was long-sleeved and drapey and silky, and when she lifted her arms the sleeves would drop back and she would reach up like she was trying to get her hand out of the sleeve. You don't have the same feeling if you have a T-shirt on and I'm saying, "Get your hand out of your sleeve." So I tell people the day before I teach it, "Everybody wear a baggy sweatshirt." And then I come in and Do. the Phrase. Over. and Over. and Over. For like an hour. And then I turn around and say, which Twyla would do, "Just do it."

She's incredible, and she's always on time. I remember at Boston Ballet, she'd start rehearsals at 12:00, and she's dancing and people are putting their shoes on and she's just moving around to the music, and no one gets up because they don't know the rehearsal's started. Well, in fact, the rehearsal *has* started, and she's doing it *slowly*. So they get up slowly, and they go, like, 'Oh my God.' She's started already, and they missed it.

Anyway, that takes time. If I don't have time, then I say, ". . . seven, eight. One, two—this is a yoga position—three, four—and you flip your hands here—and this is six. Remember this is six for when you retrograde. And every time you do it to the right, the right foot is picked up, and when you do it to the left . . ." And then I have to tell them how to retrograde, whereas if I'd just done it, you wouldn't even know I was retrograding. It certainly takes a lot less time to say,

"OK, you wait until five, you plié on six, you stretch your arms as if you have a silk shirt on on seven, eight, you bring them down one, two . . ." In an hour I could teach the whole phrase to 20 people, who will get it because they know every single count.

We don't have time. Who has time to spend eight weeks getting to know something without counts? Twyla can put a thousand steps in a minute, and then they go backwards and do all kinds of inversions. So time is a major factor, because first people have to learn the steps, and then you try to get a style going. It's very hard. It's like a relationship, it takes time to get comfortable with someone, with somebody else's steps, with another choreographer, especially in a repertory company where for two hours a day you're working on a Paul Taylor ballet, for two hours you're working on a ballet ballet in pointe shoes, and then for two hours you're working on Tharp. It takes a while for it all to go in.

I use a lot of video. We actually have a lot of teaching video for some pieces. When we were doing, let's say, *In the Upper Room*, at some point with some of the original cast we would put the whole ballet on videotape, talking each part, not so much during the creation of the piece, but after it had been performed. So it would be me saying, "It starts on my right foot, and I go . . . ," and you'd video it from the front and from the back. Most of *Upper Room* is on teaching tape, and we show all the complicated lifts, from the back, from the side, where everybody's hands are, where you stand. It was sort of a collaborative idea. When you have to start teaching those works, even to other people in Tharp's company, who has the time and the ballet masters to do it? So over the last years when we were a group, we put these tapes together. I take them with me depending on the ballet, but I tend to not like to use video because video is slow. It depends on the company, on the dancer, on the piece. Some people can look at video and not get freaked out by it, can sort of observe the person it was made on or even a second-cast or a third-cast person, get what they need from it and make it their own. Some people can't.

You have to allow for change and for different bodies and different companies and different countries. I mean, just because something is made on someone who can jump really high doesn't mean that everybody has to be able to jump really high. There are other attributes that dancers have and bring to it. And I say to them all the time, "I don't want you to do it like another company. I don't want you to look at a performance of somebody else. You're just starting—do it your way, and a year from now it'll be through the roof." It's about learning and trusting. Yesterday I was watching the Rambert dancers doing some lifts in *The Golden Section*, and a couple of weeks ago they were scared to death to try them. I've seen some bad accidents, so it's up to me to think, 'How do you work them up to not being afraid of this lift?' We get spotters in, or I tell them, "When you do it wrong, it feels like this" or "If you put your hand here it's going to give her a bloody nose." It's like children, when they take the first step in the water, and now the lifts are just incredible.

The work is in the heart, in the soul, probably in being able to know it so well that you can let it go, you know, throw some of the movement away so it doesn't become so calculated. It's like building the foundation of a house, and then you do whatever you want once you have your foundation. *Golden Section* is a very difficult piece; it came at the end of a bigger piece, it's total ecstasy, but it has a throwaway careless feel to it—that's what's so hard about it. There's a release in Twyla's work, energy and trust and a willingness to let it go. But I think people are so hung up on doing everything exactly right that they don't allow themselves to fall and find it. You say, "Run, run, run and swing your arms," and it never goes past what you've shown.

With something like *Upper Room*, it takes me four weeks, six hours a day, two hours with this group, four hours with that group, every day, five days a week, to Teach, The, Steps, and there are so many steps. And you need to know when to turn to the right or turn to the left, which foot is it, how to cover this distance in space, you need to know the art of running backwards, you need to know how to be grounded. The hardest thing to put across is the weight, to get people to drop their weight down, to trust their plié. I say things like, "The floor is your best friend," because when you get nervous or frightened, you pull up instead of relaxing into the plié, using your pelvis. Twyla always said to me, "Sometimes people look like they're dancing in green and they're dancing in red"— like the red light and the green light—"but they haven't got the orange," which is the caution before you stop, that's sort of your lower back. Your weight's not only up or only down, it's how you go into it—you've got to get the yellow light.

And there is an order in which the piece should be taught. I can't just come in and start teaching the second section—it's way too complicated, it's got too many inversions, it goes way off the music, you have to count the whole time. You need four weeks of working with me on the other stuff so that when I slip that one in, it doesn't hurt. There's a way to not make people afraid, to not scare people in lifts you know are frightening, to build people's trust and for people to build trust toward me and towards each other. There's a huge responsibility in knowing who works well together and who doesn't. And a lot of times I don't like to know who's the principal and who's not—I want to come in with fresh eyes and put who I think is right into the parts, with the help of a director, of course.

Obviously if somebody's really not cutting the mustard, you have to take them out and put somebody else in. It doesn't happen often, but it happened to me once. Days before a show it was apparent that someone in the first cast couldn't do it and I had to put on the second cast, and it was horrible for the person that was not in it and horrible for me to have to do it at such a late point. I kept hoping and thinking that the dancer would get it, and it actually didn't happen and I had to make that decision. It's a very fine line, because one becomes so attached to the dancers that it's hard to stay unbiased. You fall in love with all of them, and whether they get to it by opening night, you know where they've come from.

You put your whole life or your whole heart into something for six, seven, eight weeks, you get to know people intimately when you're working in a studio, and it becomes your whole focus and theirs also. It has all kinds of highs and lows in it, and then opening night comes . . . and that's it. It's sort of like having nine months of pregnancy and then somebody else takes the baby. After the opening night, my contract is done. My job is to come in and set the piece to the best of my capability and see it through their opening show, and then another person takes over. None of the bigger problems of the company are my problem. I'm just a guest, so I don't have to get involved with scheduling, politicking, money, broken bones. It's like I'm an aunt. I love my nephews, I can spoil them, I can give them things their parents may not, give them a new insight to this and that, and be lovely and wonderful. But that's it—I'm not putting them through college. I leave. The benefit to me is to work with different dancers and set different ballets, to continue to learn and to spread what I know. The benefit is to work with Christopher Bruce and Anthony Dowell and Kevin McKenzie and Baryshnikov. There are certain companies that I go back to, and I love having that rapport. I love doing what I do because I don't want to be a performer anymore and it's very clear to me where I am in the dance world.

Nobody's going to ask a ballet master who specializes in one choreographer to stay on for a year, it doesn't make sense. I work on something in the studio that I know and believe in, and hopefully I come back to oversee it when it's needed. You want to be able to nurture it. There's sort of a danger if you pass a piece on, and then it gets passed on to a company within the company, and you don't get back to see it. Let's say you keep the original cast for a year and then half of those people leave and seven more people come in, and somebody else, who wasn't there when I was teaching it, teaches it with the help of other people. Steps begin to go, everything . . . not by anyone's fault, just because . . . That's why we have trainers when we work out, that's why we have ballet teachers. You can take a ballet class every day by yourself but you still need someone to say, "You're swaying your back." You still need eyes.

I love work and I love Twyla's work. I love doing something that I know and can do well. I love to give, I love to get back, I love to watch people take a challenge, and I love to be challenged. I do believe there are different ways of working, and that is what being a good coach or a good dancer is all about, adapting and trying and changing. I've learned unbelievable amounts about doing this job. I've learned how to figure out, in the first or second week, if a dancer can't do it. I've learned to put my emotions aside and do what's best for a piece and for a company. I've learned to teach it in the right order. I've learned how to put people in the right places— I very rarely, if ever, cast wrong. But one of my biggest learnings is that if I don't think it's right I know now how to deal with it. There's a point where you give everybody a chance and then there's a point where I stick to my own guns. I've learned when I need to be stubborn and deliberate and when I need to be adaptable. You can't be unapproachable, but you can't be a dancer, you've crossed the line. I never forget what being a dancer is like or how tiring it is, but sometimes we've got to rehearse now because of this or that, and it's not always about the dancers. It can be about who's coming in to watch or the lighting people, the schedule . . . One has to maintain some sort of boundary, not distance but separation.

You know, one of the reasons I like working in London is that I like protocol and the idea of school and continuation and learning from the people before and taking more on. There's a tradition here in England, and there was a tradition and a protocol with Martha Graham. You entered the studio from the back, and when Martha Graham walked in, we all stood up until she sat down in the front, and in rehearsals, when she spoke, no one spoke. You couldn't walk into a Graham studio with holes in your tights, and you wouldn't want to. But that's because she didn't and the people before her didn't. I'm not saying it's bad or good, I'm just saying that was the example in front of me.

I've been in two similar situations, and they've both been extraordinarily creative. In both of the companies that I danced with, there were very, very strong women, choreographers, running their own company, and also it was just their repertoire. There's no question about who was in charge or where the authority lay. There's no question about protocol or seniority, and for me it was extraordinarily valuable. I sat or stood or danced, and I watched and I learned, from the greatest. I grew up in a rank—I didn't come in in the middle, I started at the bottom, and there was no question of where I was supposed to be and where I could go. It just was like climbing a ladder. I started, and I watched the top and admired it and learned it and wanted to go there but step by step. Twyla was the choreographic, creative center in the front of the room, and the same with Martha. So I didn't have other choreographers coming in and saying, "We're going to move our bodies like this."

This is a new change that's been happening to dance companies in the last 20 years, acquiring other companies' ballets. Twenty years ago, the Paris Opéra was not acquiring Twyla's ballets, right? Nobody was taking Martha's ballets. Paul Taylor didn't have ballet masters setting his pieces. So if we are looking to see *The Golden Section* the way we remember it 20 years ago, are we being fair to the people who are trying to learn it now? How long does it take for them to grow into it? You have three weeks to know people you've never worked with before, teach an entire work that probably took that long to be created or maybe longer, and then they have to do it. In fairness, I can't think of a piece that Twyla created in three weeks and the fourth week we were performing it. The thing that would be sad is if you went back to see *The Golden Section* at Rambert two years from now and it hadn't grown, and it was worse than you remember seeing it now.

But how do you find all these different parts of yourself if you're working with so many different choreographers? Think about it. If people come from a studio where they've been wearing pointe shoes to a studio where they're going to be wearing tennis shoes, how long does it take to make that transition? And how do you protect the dancers in tennis shoes—their knees, their thighs, their backs—so they can go back the next day and put on pointe shoes again? That's a major responsibility that all of us—teachers and ballet masters and therapists and dancers—have to take. When I was in Birmingham I had their physical therapist come to my rehearsal and watch what they were doing so she could help them with their therapy, because *Upper Room* puts so much strain on the knees and their legs are parallel. They're running backwards, running forward, with real power, real muscle, and the women have to be as strong as the men—the lifts don't work if the women aren't as strong. They're not just light girls that the men can bend and pick up—the women are coming in with real force. These kids are working five hours a day like this, so in their training therapy and their Pilates and when they take ballet class the next day, they need something that will lengthen them out and deal with that.

But I have never encountered anyone who has not wanted to be in on the working process of a Tharp ballet. You get people saying, "Why didn't you take me?" Or "Can I just stand in the back and learn it for myself?" Or "I don't care if I'm third cast." Of course when you are third cast and you never get to run it, then you do care, but generally, third casts always get on by the law of averages. And these guys can be very cool. Every different evening, every different season, they must have ten different choreographers going, with completely different styles.

But what's your audience? In the '70s, dancers used to go and support other dancers. You could buy tickets, people could afford it. Now . . . look around. Half of the audience is sleeping, they don't want to be there. It's not as educated an audience as it used to be. But are they the same kinds of people as years ago, or are they just people who can afford tickets? What happened to the price of tickets? What happened to dance that could just be dance without gold leaf, rococo settings, and costumes that cost more than a house? Is the public demanding more? It's like the Tour de France. The bike-riders who take the drugs say they're doing it because we, as an audience, demand that they beat records, and if there wasn't such a demand from the public for more and better . . . I'm just using that as an example. But can an audience go and watch people dance in black leotards and pink tights and feel satisfied? Or now do they have to have "Ooooohh" and "Aaahhh"? I don't know if you can charge $50 or $60 a ticket, or however much it costs, and not give something new.

And also, companies got bigger. When I was with Twyla in 1975, there were five dancers, working in a small studio at a very low salary and being able to live. By the time you get 20 dancers in a company and a repertoire with costumes and thises and thats, it's a huge deal. And you can't have a company of 40 people and only use 10 to make a dance on. Then you have 30 very unhappy people, and you've got to find something for those people to do. So you're finding repertory for different parts of your company, because the people that dance Tharp ballets are not always the same people who do the Balanchine ballets.

Maybe we just went through a very lucky and special time. There was nothing like the '70s for dance, and hopefully it will happen again. Things have to evolve and drop down to go up. Maybe we were all part of something very special and it was a mission . . . a community that we all believed in. I never felt that anything was at risk or like I had anything to lose. And maybe to have that feeling you need a solid family foundation, perhaps something like Twyla or Hubbard Street or Ballet Rambert, where your core of dancers lasts for 10, 12, 13 years, so there's some kind of strength in it.

It's harder in a pick-up group, where the dancers just come in, do a show and leave. But you have to do these short-term groups, and people like them. I don't know what people, but those shows sell out, Stars of the Bolshoi or Stars of the Whatever. It's all "Wow! Did you see that guy jump so high?" It's like looking at a woman in a miniskirt—it's all there, you see it, wow—rather than looking at a woman in a pants suit and having to go, 'Hmm, I wonder what's in there.' They're both valid, they both look good, they're just different. But where can you work constantly? Name me a company in the States where you have a 52-week contract. What are you supposed to do if you have an 11-week layoff? And those are ballet companies. Forget what you're supposed to do if you're in a modern dance company that doesn't have insurance or AIDS funding or a theatre or even their own studio. How else can you dance? How many tables can you wait on? How many classes can you teach? And if you're young and you want to start doing something else, how do you do it?

The world has changed. It becomes harder and harder to make a living off of dancing even though there's more money involved in it.

It can become me, me, you know, 'What's in it for me? What am I going to get out of it?' as opposed to when I started, going, 'Oh, I'll do anything, anything.' I don't know why it's changed so much. It's hard, this life. Why would a parent want their kid to be a dancer when they could be a football player, someone making tons of money, a movie star, a model? I chose it, but things are different now. Everything now is about making money and about your kid going into commercials so he can pay his way through college, because colleges now cost $100,000 more than they did 20 years ago. Every kid is now playing golf to be Tiger Woods, but how many kids are taking ballet to be Baryshnikov? A lot of people dance because they need to, but when you're little, do your parents send you to dance school or to soccer or tennis or, if you have a certain look, to acting? Come on, if you can make $15 million in a movie, why not? But life can't become so much about how you look, who you're with and what you wear and where you went and what street you live on and what your job title is. Ultimately those are not the truths. Dancing is deeper than that, it's somewhere in your soul, in your existence.

But also, I think there are so many other things going on. Dancers are doing their knitware and dancers are computering and dancers are taking film courses and dancers are being actors and dancers are having children. Dancers are going to school, building houses, starting their own catering companies. Dancers are not just dancers anymore—they're doing other things. Today you've really got to plan your future, you've got to be thinking 2010. I don't know what the result will be, but I'll tell you one thing about me and about many dancers in the past, I'm sure: you didn't plan your future, you just did your job.

Yuri Fateyev

b. Leningrad, 1964. Trained at Vaganova Academy 1974–82, member of Kirov Ballet 1982–2001. Company teacher since 1995, company ballet master since 1996. Guest teacher and ballet master with Pacific Northwest Ballet, Royal Swedish Ballet and Ballet of Nagoya, Japan.

I THINK MY MOST IMPORTANT TEACHER in St. Petersburg was my last teacher in the school, Simon Kaplan. He was a famous dancer in Russia, he danced in the period with Konstantin Sergeyev, and he was the partner of Ulanova and Marina Semyonova and Natalia Dudinskaya. He was a great partner and he had soft legs and a huge jump, but some people who knew him in this time told me, like a secret, he was a little bit lazy. Because he had flexible legs, flexible body, for him it was very easy. In the time he taught me, he was 70 years old. I was in the last generation of his students. One year after I finished the school in his class, he was dead. I finished the school in 1982 and in January '83 he died.

My first three years in the school—we started at ten—I had a very good teacher for young children, Nadezhda Feyederova. She was so intelligent. She died just three months ago, but she was so old, she had 90 years. Then Kaplan at the end, and between Kaplan and Feyederova, we had a teacher from the Kirov Theatre, a dancer, he still dances in the Kirov, it was Valentin Onoshko. He took us for one year . . . we didn't know it was for one year, we thought he would take us for the whole future, to finish the school, because he was so young. He showed us many pirouettes, he did every jump, and we loved him.

We didn't like Kaplan because before him we had the young man, Onoshko, who did everything. But Kaplan just sat and just told, and he wasn't like Onoshko, he didn't every day have a smile. And I was not a very smart guy in this time—I think I was 14—because I thought and every guy in my class said, "Oh, he's so old. He doesn't show us the steps. He doesn't move in the class, he just sits in the chair. He's so angry with us if we don't understand." We were not happy and we didn't like him at first. But after two years, maybe we had a little bit more age and we were smarter, because we tried to learn his method. He was a very musical man and he gave us the sensibility of the dance and the atmosphere. He said, "I had a great teacher, [Alexei] Pisarev. I will show you just an old step of the Pisarev program." And he showed us the combination with a good continuing from this step to the next step, a continual movement of this step to that step. After we had one year with him we understood better, because we knew him from the year before, and we knew he was the history of Russian dance. He knew many people from before the Russian Revolution . . . before the Soviet revolution, who knew Fokine, who knew Petipa. He studied in the Vaganova . . . it's not the Vaganova now, it's the St. Petersburg Academy school, and before the revolution it was the ballet school of the Maryinsky Theatre. He studied there, he showed us the room where the boys slept in the school, where the church was, because in the Soviet time there was no church in the school. He brought this history into the studio and, between the classes, maybe in the canteen or in other classes.

We started class at 9:00 in the morning, and we finished lessons at 5:30. We had just a one-hour break for lunch. And after 5:30 we had ballet practice, 'til 7:00 or 8:00. This was rehearsal for the performances in the Maryinsky Theatre. Students of the school . . . You saw *The Sleeping Beauty*, the young children in the waltz? I was in this waltz like those young children and in the dance with seven little boys in the last act. So that time after 5:30 was for the students to do repertory for the Kirov productions. If they did *Don Q* [*Don Quixote*], we prepared *Don Q*. If they did *The Sleeping Beauty*, we prepared *The Sleeping Beauty*. We have many dances in the opera, and the children do these dances too. In *Ruslan and Ludmila*, in *Aida*, in *Raymonda*, in *Bayadère*, we had many, many performances where the children appeared.

We had one teacher, it's Woldemar Korneyev, who rehearsed with the children in the school. Kaplan taught us the classical, traditional variations in variation class. If we didn't have a repertory rehearsal with Korneyev, we rehearsed with Kaplan some variation for the school program, because we have a small theatre in the school, named for [Alexander] Shiriayev, a great actor, and we performed in this theatre for the parents and the other students. We tried to learn the variations I think two years before we finished the school, and the repertory class began when we were small. This class started at ten years old. I had just started my learning in September and in November I went with the school to Moscow for a big gala program.

Even then I knew the ballet steps a little bit because two years before the Vaganova school I had gone to . . . in Russia they say the House of the Pioneers, like the Boy Scouts . . . I had gone there and learned dancing. I was eight years old, I started dancing when I was eight years old, because my mother very liked the dance. She was the chemist in an institute and she danced with a small circle there, with the guys who like dancing, and she had performances for the public, but it was not professional dancing.

I think I was 15 years old when we started to go in the theatre, and every evening if we had time we went to see the ballet performance. We knew every dancer in the company, every variation, every adagio in the Kirov repertory. We very liked to go, and we had a ticket for ten people to go upstairs, in the gallery. In this time, in 1978, 1979, I very liked Konstantin Zaklinsky, who was in very good condition, soft legs, a big jump, many pirouettes, he did a very good *Swan Lake*. This was an idol for us, because he was so tall, he had a nice face, he looked like a prince. And I very liked Marat Daukayev on the stage, because he had a very good technique—in *Notre-Dame de Paris* he did Frollo, amazing—and I liked the ballerinas like Galina Mezentseva and Olga Chenchikova.

When I first went into the Kirov Theatre I was just a corps de ballet dancer. I did the dances in the opera and the ballet. It was not so interesting for me, but I knew, because my parents told me every minute from when I was born, you need to work, work, work and work. I knew this from a young age—I needed to be doing something, to have a result. I needed hard work. If I had a performance that was finishing at midnight, some opera maybe that lasts a long time, I would go home after—using the subway it is about one hour and ten minutes to go home. Some guys who went into the theatre with me wouldn't go the next morning to class, but I would go every day to class, at 10:00 or 11:00. I thought I must go to class if I wanted to do something more, to make the progress. And after three years in the theatre, I had a soloist role, the first one was Golden Idol in *Bayadère*. Before that, I just had the Indian dance in *Bayadère*, with the drum, and maybe some character roles. But the Golden Idol . . . this is like a principal classical role, I think. I danced this role for ten years, '85 to '95, and the Jester in *Swan Lake*. In the school it was my dream to do Siegfried in *Swan Lake*, but I think I'm a smart guy—I went into the Kirov Theatre and I knew I wasn't a prince. Zaklinsky looks like a prince—I'm a jester. If you don't have the body for the prince, you need to do a good job as the jester. It was still my dream to do the pas de trois in *Swan Lake*, but I didn't do it, ever. But I did the Peasant pas de deux in *Giselle*, that's close—it was my dream too.

I prepared for about one year to do this Peasant pas de deux on the Kirov stage. I worked in the theatre with a good teacher, Vladilen Semyonov, the husband of Irina Kolpakova. He's such an intelligent guy. I asked Semyonov to prepare it with me, and he said, "OK, I'll work with you," and he also said to me, "I'll work with you for the pas de trois for *Swan Lake*." He prepared with me also *La Vivandière*, and I did the pas de six many times. Everyone does this—they have a conversation with the teacher, and maybe the teacher says, "No, it's not for you." And you need to ask the artistic director, "I would very much like to prepare this piece. What do you think about this?" And he would say, "Maybe yes, maybe no. Go ahead, prepare it, and I will see. Maybe it's good, maybe it's not good." Then I would ask the ballet department to arrange a rehearsal for me, or maybe the teacher would go to the ballet department and tell them, "Give a rehearsal for Fateyev, for half an hour, for preparing the pas de deux." Then it was in the schedule if I didn't have a corps de ballet rehearsal at that time, because the corps de ballet rehearsal was important, it was first. After one year of work, I showed the Peasant pas de deux to the artistic director, now the former artistic director, Oleg Vinogradov. He said, "It's very good. I'll give you a performance," and he didn't. I showed him the Peasant pas de deux I think three times before I did it.

On tour I tried to see more things. If we were in New York . . . We just arrived once in New York and I knew on that day was the last performance of New York City Ballet. So I took my eyes like this, holding them open because the time changed and I was going to sleep, but I wanted to see that—it was *Midsummer Night's Dream*. And we had a tour in Paris, and in the same time Maurice Béjart was giving the Ring of the Nibelung [*Ring Around the Ring*], and I saw that performance. Half the company, maybe more than half the Kirov company, left the theatre after the first act, but I told myself, "You need to see the whole production," because it's interesting. It's difficult but it's interesting. And after that performance, we went at once with Rudi Nureyev in a small room and saw his *Cinderella* production on a video. I hadn't seen Sylvie [Guillem] before, and I heard so many times about her and I wanted to see her, maybe just on the video.

In the Kirov company I was ten years as the Golden Idol and 15 years as the Jester in *Swan Lake*. But when I was in the school, from the time I was a student, I knew that I wanted to teach people for the ballet. Sometimes the teacher was sick . . . not Kaplan, Kaplan was not sick, never, never. But my first teacher was sick sometimes and I would give the class for my friends. I was 11, 12, but I gave the class. I copied her. I did it because I felt like it, I wanted to do it. Sometimes the teacher did not come to the class in the Kirov, and some people asked me, "Yuri, could you give the class?" And when [Makhar] Vaziev became the head of the ballet company—he was a former soloist—he told me, "I want to ask you about you giving the class in the company." So I began then, in 1995.

My first meeting with Balanchine choreography was in 1989, when Francia Russell came to the company and staged *Theme and Variations*, and we did *Scotch Symphony* too, with Suzanne Farrell. I danced the four couples in *Theme*, and Francia told me, "You're the best in the four couples." She so liked me, she said, because I was so smart—I know this is true—and I had discipline. At this time, this was 12 years ago, there was not very good discipline in the company. Some people were not so concentrated in rehearsal, for learning the steps or understanding the counts, and Francia was a little bit nervous about this. I remember one time she put one dancer out of the studio, because he was not concentrating, he was talking with another dancer, he was not doing the steps. But not me, because I was a little bit . . . looking for different . . . for international people like Francia, like American, like French, people from another planet, another world. I don't know why, because this was the Soviet time, and we had a big complex about people from other countries because KGB told us, "Don't talk with these people, because it's a provocation," blah, blah, blah, blah. But I saw these people and I thought, 'It's not true. I'd very much like to have a conversation and connection with these people.'

Before Francia came, I saw videos in the year of Balanchine's death, '83. In St. Petersburg we have a Palace for the People of the Arts in the Nevsky Prospekt. In this palace, at night after the performance, I think it started at midnight, there was the evening of the memory of Balanchine. I was there this night, and we saw *Serenade* and I think *Apollo* on the video and—I didn't understand it—one ballet in white and black, I don't know which one. This was the first I saw of Balanchine, these films, and they were very interesting, but I didn't understand anything about it. Then in 1987, 1988 maybe, some photographer from New York asked me to take a videotape with *Apollo* for Andris Liepa in Moscow. So I took this tape in New York, and I watched it in Leningrad—I put it in the video and tried to see *Apollo* for the first time. I saw five minutes, seven minutes, and I wanted to sleep—it was not interesting for me. I tried to stop it and to go ahead, ahead, ahead, ahead quickly, and the interesting place for me was just in the coda and finale, the horses, because it's fast. Before the evening of memory for Balanchine, *Apollo* was not so interesting for me, I think because it wasn't action, it wasn't a huge jump, it's not a pirouette. I didn't understand the philosophy of this ballet. And I tell you, in 1991, Pat Neary staged *Apollo* in the Kirov. Andris did Apollo and Konstantin Zaklinsky did Apollo, and the ballet was a little bit more interesting for me, just a little bit, not so much. Maybe it was difficult for me to listen to this music of Stravinsky, I didn't understand this music maybe. But Pat Neary staged *Tchai. Pas* [*Tchaikovsky Pas de Deux*] at the same time, and I very much liked *Tchai. Pas*. Why not? It's classical steps, it's pas de deux, adagio, variations, coda. It was easy for my head to understand this one and for my body too.

And *Theme* was much easier for us than *Apollo*. *Theme* is like present classical Russian style. It's not Russian style but it's close, and *Scotch Symphony* was much easier for the company, I think, because it's much closer to *Giselle* or *Les Sylphides*. The first time, we did *Theme* like *Paquita*—it wasn't a Balanchine ballet. The problem was about the Russian teachers. The people who taught us for the Balanchine ballets tried to teach us the American steps. But some teachers, who rehearsed with the dancers after Francia, tried a little bit to correct the steps for the Russian style. It was not completely right, I think, maybe about the arms. To do glissade assemblé, in the Russian school the arms begin from the first position and go to allongé. In the American school, the direction is different. In Russian down and then open, in American up first, over the head, then a big circle in front of you, down and then open. I think it's necessary to do the right steps—in Russian dance like this, in American dance like that, because it's a different school. This is the style, I think, and now when I rehearse any Balanchine ballet, I try to tell the dancers to do the right arms, the right steps, because I think the little pieces make like mosaic. All the little pieces—it's the style.

In 1995 I started to give class in the company, like the official class. I was still a dancer, and it was my first experience. I think that Mr. Vaziev needed to see if it's the right step or not to give me the class. It's a very difficult problem, for the coaches and the teachers and for him too, because he saw, 'Who are the teachers now?' It was just the old people, like . . . Ninel Kurgapkina is a great teacher, I think, but she had maybe 70 years, I don't know, but she was so old, and Olga Moiseyeva too. The artistic director needed the new generation of teachers. It's important for him to make a new generation of coaches and teachers for the young people in the company, because its tradition needed to continue. It was a big problem, because Kolpakova went to the States, Semyonov went to the States, Tatiana Terekhova went to the States. It was the middle generation, between Kurgapkina and me—everyone in the middle left, Natasha [Makarova], Rudolf, Misha [Baryshnikov], you know.

Then because I was giving the class in the company, I asked Mr. Vaziev about taking some boy to teach him a variation, maybe for the pas de trois in *Swan Lake* or some variation of *The Nutcracker*, and he said, "OK, try it." I tried, and he saw my work, and he thought, 'It's not bad.' And he gave me my first experience working with international choreographers—in 1996, I worked with a Spanish choreographer, José Antonio. He was visiting in the company to create the ballet *Goya*, it was a new ballet for the Kirov, for Mr. [Faroukh] Ruzimatov, and I was like the assistant of him. After he left, there was not a long life for this ballet, maybe a couple of performances, but I prepared it. We started to prepare at the end of the season, and Mr. José Antonio was leaving, so I worked with the corps de ballet and soloists to keep this ballet after he left. We started a new season and I continued to rehearse this ballet with the company, because we had a first-night performance in the beginning of the season, and he came just one week before the premiere.

Mr. Vaziev talked with me a lot about the new way of the Kirov Ballet, and he knew that I was a hard worker, and he tried to give me class to teach, and he saw, 'It's good,' everything worked. I didn't ask him—he asked me, "Do you want to teach the company?" and I said, "Yes." I very much wanted to continue my life in the theatre because . . . Six years ago, I had worked 14 years in this theatre, and I thought I needed to continue my life here because I loved this theatre, I loved to work and I loved ballet. And I knew that a ballet dancer's life is so short—it's 20 years. If you want to continue your life in the theatre and in the ballet, you have to do something more. So I tried to learn and to take something new so I could continue.

On the same day, at 11:00 I took the class and at 12:00 I taught the class. I still do that, and it's very difficult, let me tell you, because if you do the class you need to do every step so right, because one hour later you tell the people, "You have to do the step like that and that." So in the hour before if you do the class badly yourself, then they will not listen. If you're still dancing, you need to dance very clearly, because you're teaching many people the same steps in rehearsal and they know. They see you on the stage and they say, "Oh, you didn't do the pirouettes, you didn't jump well."

I think the older dancers didn't like me, because life is life and I'm so young and why am I teaching them? For the young dancers, a new generation of dancers, it's much easier. And now the company is changing, changing and changing. Now in the six years I am teaching, it's a young company. I'm 36, and I'm the old generation in the company now. It changed because some people went to another country, to Germany, to the States, and some people finished dancing because it was time to finish dancing, and we took the new generation from the school. Sometimes we take talented people from another school or from another theatre, like Daniil Korsuntsev from the Moscow Classical Ballet, like Viktor Baranov from the Perm Ballet. We have one Korean girl [Ryu Ji Yeon], but she finished the Vaganova school, and we have one guy, Islom Baimuradov, who is Austrian but he finished the Vaganova school too.

I take the tradition of my teacher, but I teach a little bit different, because I think time goes on. Technique is a little bit different now, legs move faster now. I try to keep the Russian good arms and the good port de bras, flexible body, and the American movement of the legs, speed in the legs. I think my favorite teacher from the States is Stanley Williams. I didn't study with him, but I know his lesson because I saw his class when I was in New York, and Igor

Zelensky told me about his class a lot and he gave me his class—he taught me—and I loved it. I wrote down everything.

We do now the Balanchine ballets, and that is very important for the company. Because we need to prepare for these ballets, I change the class. It is very difficult for us to dance Balanchine, because the body must remember how it feels in these new steps. After the first or second rehearsal of the Balanchine ballets, like *Apollo* or *Serenade*, some dancers told me their body is pain, here, in the back and the middle. Diana Vishneva told me after *Rubies* rehearsal, "I think the person who stays inside of me is in so much pain." She said it like that. She said someone is in her body, and that person is in great pain after *Rubies*. But after doing the Balanchine ballets since 1999, just two years, now it's much easier, and we don't need a long time for the preparation. We needed a long preparation to learn these ballets the first time—not *Scotch* and *Theme* but for *Rubies, Emeralds . . . Jewels*. But now to bring it back is easy. And I don't go back to the old style in class, I keep this style, because I think the class that I teach for the Balanchine ballets is an important class, it's a class for everything. I take a good, high speed from the televideos, but I don't forego the high jumps for the Russian style. Before we did class for just about one hour. Now we have class for one hour and 15 minutes, every day, and we have time for small jumps, for high speed, and for the big jumps too. When we had only one hour, we had just one tendu at the barre. Now we have three different tendus; the first one is so slow, the second one a little bit faster, the third one is so fast. And jeté the same, at the barre. Now I do this all the time. I talked with Mr. Vaziev, some dancers talked with him, and he understands about changing the length of the class.

But it's not only Balanchine. I'm the ballet master of the Roland Petit ballets too. That's a different style. When Francia came with *Serenade* and *Apollo* and *Tchai. Pas* in 1998, at the same time, in the same month, we prepared Roland Petit ballets too—it was *Le Jeune Homme et la Mort* and *Carmen*—and I stayed in the theatre the whole day and the whole night to learn all these ballets. I stayed because I liked the ballets, because it was so interesting for me, because I very much liked to work with international people who know the different styles, different choreography. Because I think I'm so young now for learning—I wanted to learn all this. No one told me to do it. I chose it. I decided just by myself to change my responsibility, and Francia liked me. When she came the second time to the Kirov, in

1998, she told me, "I would very much like to work with you, Yuri, because you understand the Balanchine choreography. I think I want you to assist me for these ballets." She asked Mr. Vaziev to give me to her, as her assistant, for *Serenade, Apollo* and *Tchai. Pas,* and we worked very closely, about one month, to prepare these ballets.

When I am by myself I rehearse with the dancers and I try to keep any small piece that Francia showed us, to keep the ballet in the Balanchine style. I don't have notation—I just have video. I have videos from Pacific Northwest Ballet and from New York City Ballet for *Serenade,* I have a video from the first-night performance of the Kirov in *Serenade.* I have *Apollo* with Peter Martins twice, in 1968 and 1982, both with Suzanne Farrell. For each ballet, I have many, many videos—not just one. But it's not possible to use just the video without explaining something about it, because ballet is very soft material. Also I have a big American book about Balanchine technique in class [*Suki Schorer on Balanchine Technique*]. It's difficult because it's written in the English language, but I try, pages and pages, to read this book. And I saw there the pictures, with the positions of the arms, of the legs, of the feet, of the everything, and at home I can practice them, of course.

But if I work with many dancers *I* learn. Like, for *Diamonds* I worked with Uliana Lopatkina first. In the time that the American people, like Sean Lavery and Karin [von Aroldingen], were in St. Petersburg, Svetlana Zakharova was in Argentina doing *Corsaire.* But it was my dream to teach Svetlana *Diamonds,* and I did teach her, because she came back to St. Petersburg when the American people were leaving. She worked just with me, and I gave her the Balanchine style, and I think Svetlana is the best in *Diamonds* now, it's my opinion. She's so beautiful in adagio, like Lopatkina, but Svetlana is much better in the scherzo, because she has a very good speed and technique, and the scherzo is so fast.

The speed is difficult for us but it's necessary, because the Bizet [*Symphony in C*] is classical but I think Balanchine is classical of the 20th century. We need these Balanchine ballets, because they're very good for keeping the legs in good condition, better for the legs than the old ballets. And they keep the legs in good condition for the classical ballets too—they help. It's very interesting. It's much easier, after the Balanchine ballets, to do the classical ballets, like the Russian repertoire, *The Sleeping Beauty* and *Swan Lake* and *Bayadère,* because the body moves very well and the legs have a nice speed.

For Svetlana . . . and I taught Dasha [Daria] Pavlenko too, for *Diamonds* . . . I tried to give the girls the feeling and the sensitivity of this piece. I saw many times the videotape with Peter Martins and Suzanne Farrell in the *Diamonds* adagio, and I very much liked Suzanne's feeling in the ballet. In the first step—step, step, and pose, with the arm opening—she kept her eyes like this, down. She doesn't see him. I tell the girls, "You're like many, many, many years ago, maybe in Scandinavia, he's like the Scandinavian prince and you're like the princess. You have blue blood and you're so strong, but you don't see him. You see him just here, and if you give the hands, the eyes are down too." Like modesty, not big. I gave the girls this feeling, and I think they do it this way. It's the same in the other ballets. In *Rubies* I tell them to keep the American style, like a jazzy style. The last step for the girls in *Rubies*, I say to Irina Golub, "You are like the typist. You go to the boss in the office, a little jazzy, in high heels, and you bring coffee for the boss."

We asked Francia, "What did Balanchine say about this movement?" and she said, "He told us just to do the steps—nothing more." But I think he had a talk every time with the different dancers, and every time he told a different dancer different words. I can do this too. If I go to rehearse now and I stay in the studio with Svetlana or Dasha or Igor [Kolb] or a different Igor, Igor Zelensky, or somebody else, I love these people at this time, really love them, like a woman and a man. It's not possible for me to stay in the studio and just say, "Keep the elbow like that. Keep the knee straight." It's not interesting for me. I very love these people in this moment and we're doing this ballet together.

Sometimes I work ten hours in a day, without a break, class and rehearsal. Because if you have four casts for the Balanchine program, you know, and three ballets, one hour for each couple, it's ten, twelve hours. It's hard work, but I like it, and it's very interesting to give the class too, because in class I'm preparing them for rehearsal, and rehearsal prepares for the performance. In April we had a premiere of a John Neumeier ballet [*Sounds of an Empty Score*]. I started at 10:00 A.M. and I finished at 12:00 P.M. I stayed to learn and to teach it to the people, because Mr. Vaziev told me, "You must be the assistant of Mr. Neumeier." He knew that I had worked with international people and nobody had told him bad words about me, not Francia, not Sean, not Karin, not the people who worked with the Roland Petit program.

Now, in this season, I've finished dancing. I'm completely finished. I am the only one between the old teachers and the young
dancers. Igor Petrov is also my age, but he just teaches class and rehearses the classical ballets a little bit. For the Balanchine ballets
we have also Elena Evteyeva, who works with the girls for *Emeralds*, because it's so difficult for me—I do *Emeralds* with the boys,
just the boys. But I very much like to rehearse with women . . . like
Mr. B too, I think.

We had *Apollo* with Pat Neary in 1991. We did this *Apollo* for
about one season, and after this we kept it in the wings. With Francia in 1998, we started a new creation of *Apollo*, again, because
Francia made it a little bit different, and we keep this performance
in repertory. I don't forget things, I can't forget it, because I *know*
it. If I forget something I watch the video and then I think, 'Oh yes,
this is my mistake.' But we need to watch the best cast, and I think
different people do it differently because they are different people.
If I take a piece of the Suzanne video, the best arms, like Suzanne
doing the arms in *Diamonds*, it's very good, very dramatic. But it's
not like Suzanne doing the step, it's like Svetlana Zakharova. Svetlana and Dasha do those arms like Dasha and Svetlana, they are
completely different.

After we worked together in '98, Francia told me, "I saw your
class, it's very good, and I want to invite you to Seattle to teach class
in the theatre for my company." The first time I went there, I just
taught class in the school and the company, and I tried to teach a classical variation for the boys and a classical variation for the girls. Francia wanted to try for her company to do a classical ballet, so I taught
them the variations of *The Sleeping Beauty* and the *Bayadère*, for the
man and the principal woman. And in my last visit, in March, I
staged *Corsaire* pas de trois for the big gala. It's very easy for me to
work in Seattle, because I know I have a class in the morning and
three hours for rehearsal to teach the variation for the girls, the variation for the boys, the adagio for the couple. It's easy work, the
schedule is there and the dancers are so talented. Very nice bodies,
good technique, so I just try to give the feeling of the old classical ballet. Just to move the arms, big port de bras of the body, it's a different style. But working with international dancers is easy, because they
have a little bit more discipline in rehearsal for not losing any time.
They do the whole variation, I give the corrections and they repeat

one more time, first section, second section, third section. They don't waste time, time is money. And they're interested.

Francia asked me about going to Seattle next season, to teach class in the school and in the company, and after the next season she wants to have me for staging the last act of *Raymonda*, to teach the mazurka and the Hungarian dance and the grand pas. It's huge work, but Francia has I think 45 or 50 dancers and in the Professional Division from the school about 30 people, so it's a huge company. I have already done a big work like this—I changed the whole cast of the Roland Petit *Carmen* in the Kirov. In 1998 we had one cast, and then two years ago, half the company went on the Australian tour, and I had just the new people who came to the theatre from the school for a new cast. It was easy to do, but I think *Raymonda* is much easier for me. I know the *Carmen* was very good, but I know *Raymonda* from my school days.

It's very important, continuing. We need to keep things, but we need to try and give new life for these old Russian ballets too. I think people need to be in a conversation. We didn't do the Balanchine ballets before, and Francia's company didn't do the classical ballets before. And now we do many Balanchine ballets, Roland Petit ballets and John Neumeier ballets, and Francia does now *Sleeping Beauty* and she wants *Raymonda*. It's interesting for the American people to do the classical ballets, and after the *Corsaire* program, Francia told me by phone, "It's a very huge success, and the public loves this piece." And in St. Petersburg the public loves the Balanchine ballets too, and the dancers love these ballets. The dancers learn these ballets, and the bodies and legs of the dancers practice them and have a good experience.

In the Details

*L*OCKED AWAY FROM THE PEOPLE HE LOVED and the country he would eventually lead, Nelson Mandela lived behind bars for 27 years. Rather than allowing time's emptiness to oppress him, he used it to write his autobiography, tend a garden, pursue his legal studies, and teach a course in political economy to his fellow prisoners.

Harry Houdini designed his own prisons, one after the other, in order to astound the public by escaping from them. He called his first escape "Metamorphosis," though the trick was generally known as "The Substitution Trunk," so that his viewers would begin anticipating some sort of transformation even before it occurred. Houdini was an ordinary guy and briefly a necktie cutter before he became an entertainer whose exploits confounded logic and baffled common sense. He escaped from a straitjacket while hanging upside down over Broadway. He escaped from a zinc-lined piano crate and from a government mail pouch. Wearing shackles on his wrists and legs, he escaped from a sealed iron box while submerged in New York's icy East River. For him, it was good business, great art and a matter of survival to find and make choices no one else could imagine or achieve.

Nobody imposes such terrifying isolation or dangerous restraints on dancers, who come and go as they please when they're not working. All the same, their lives threaten them with chronic imprisonment. Every morning they deposit some of their liberty in their lockers with their street clothes as they return to the routine that simultaneously wears them out and builds them up. Their teachers tell them what to do in class, the schedule tells them where to go at what time, the ballet masters tell them what to do in rehearsal, and the director picks their roles and their partners. Prodded, scrutinized, scolded and corrected, all day they watch themselves and each other obsessively, trying to match their bodies to the mythical ideal each believes someone else will attain more quickly. Immersed in obedience, they follow one another along the shortest, most efficient route to a common goal, and on the way many of them lose track of the reward that will repay all their effort. As long as they are buried in the crowd of the corps de ballet, they must remain anonymous, but if they advance, featured and then leading roles will finally free them to monogram their dancing with their own, private choices.

Several years ago, I took a computer scientist to Scottish Ballet to see *La Sylphide* for the first time; it doesn't turn up in London very often, and I knew he wouldn't find a better cast anywhere than the two Danes, Johan Kobborg as James and Sorella Englund as Madge, who were appearing as guest artists. Having decided not to burden him with background or history that he hadn't requested anyway, I urged him not to feel impatient if the pace seemed slow, and then I sat back to enjoy the evening myself. He sat back too, prepared to accept whatever might occur, and watched Act I with evident pleasure, exactly as I had hoped. "Anything you want to know?" I asked at intermission. "No," he answered, "I'm fine." In fact, he was more than fine, he was hooked, but I didn't know it until James started playing with the scarf. While he waved it gaily over his head, Madge stood quietly by, her face and posture totally relaxed, even disinterested, peering at him from hooded eyes. Stiff as claws and cramped with tension, her hands hung motionless at her waist, but the moment he tucked the lethal scarf into his jacket, her index finger closed around her belt like a steel clamp—I thought I heard it snap shut. In an instant, his fate and her triumph met in a grip so tight that my friend gasped. One finger, moving two inches, made him gasp.

Years earlier, I went to Covent Garden for one of Anthony Dowell's last performances as Albrecht. As she always does, Bathilde emerged from the cottage, discovered her fiancé in disguise and gently took his arm to lead him away. And Giselle thrust herself between them and asked, "What's going on?" as *she* always does. Then, in the split-second pause between her question and its inevitable response, Dowell did something I had never seen anyone do. Recoiling sharply from Bathilde, he threw his hands up in front of her, palms out, and the beseeching look on his face said, "Don't!" As if he could stop her from answering and revealing his betrayal, as if he could protect the girl he suddenly knew he had destroyed. Too late, of course, but I saw him try, I saw his thought.

Impulses like that are not simply tools for telling a story. They shine just as clearly in plotless, abstract works in which narrative plays no part—I'm thinking of Violette Verdy, pivoting on demi-pointe and flipping a foot up behind her at the end of her rapt, contemplative solo in *Dances at a Gathering*. Robbins selected the pivot, the demi-pointe and the little kick, but Verdy transformed the exit into a rueful shrug and a blithe farewell. When Stephanie Saland stepped into the solo, she twisted a thread of promise into that moment, as if inviting us to follow her into the wings so we could chat together a little longer, a little more intimately.

Somehow, naked virtuosity never sticks in my mind the same way, although I can remember Erik Bruhn in *Giselle*, carving Albrecht's mounting exhaustion in Act II into six grands pirouettes à la seconde, each one miraculously slower than the one before. That was more than 30 years ago, and I've never yet seen any man in any role produce anything like it. More recently, as Odile in English National Ballet's gigantic *Swan Lake* "in the round" in London's Royal Albert Hall, Tamara Rojo rattled off the fouettés without an apparent spot, systematically revolving 380 degrees with each turn so that she faced the entire encircling audience section by section. Her casual assurance made me laugh out loud, but it also made me think of Balanchine's comment that it was always a mistake to demand more than two pirouettes, because once the viewers started counting they forgot about the dancing.

No matter how often you repeat it or how you dress it up, a fouetté is always a fouetté, which may be why the moments that return to haunt me can't be defined by numbers. Pushing gently off her partner's hand in *Chaconne* one night, Suzanne Farrell eased into an arabesque pirouette that maintained its momentum all by itself. She didn't expect it to continue any more than we did, and the smile that sailed across her face, shimmering with her delight, is brighter in my memory than the floating turn. Nureyev used to smile that way at the end of his Act III solo in *Sleeping Beauty*. Finishing a blur of chaînés without touching the brakes, he'd lock his feet into fifth position, heel to toe like shoes in a box, and his grin would say, "Isn't this fantastic?" Not meaning "me" or "this step" but "this, this moment, this effect, which I am privileged to show you right now." I always thought of it as his Cheshire-Cat smile, because it lingered in the air even after he had left the stage. An intentional aside that was public and private at once, it allowed us for an instant to understand how proudly the dancer ruled the prince.

While they were entertaining us and almost without our realizing it, performers like those lured us into a state of perpetual alertness, simply by rewarding our attention with moments of extraordinary intimacy in which their personal vision burst out of them like shafts of light. They taught us that anything could happen, even in a context that we thought we already knew well, and that what happened might never happen again and could never be explained, even by them. How could you look away? Why would you? We found in dance the same flashes of intuition and inspired craft that the novelist Joyce Carol Oates noticed in great prizefights, where "so much happens so swiftly and with such heartstopping subtlety that you cannot absorb it." How could you describe what you had seen to someone who had missed it if, as she put it, "it is happening in a place beyond words"?

Leading our thoughts and feelings with a shift of weight or a curling finger, those expressive conjurers were guides for their colleagues as well, especially for the younger dancers, who could observe them in performance or in class without trespassing on the respectful distance imposed by age and rank. "When I went to the Royal Danish Ballet," Bruce Marks told me once, "Henning Kronstam was my ideal because you could never recognize him. You never knew who he was. Is that Henning Kronstam? That handsome man, that old man, that woman, that toreador with the big teeth? . . . Is he not the ideal dance-theatre performer? That's always what I hoped would happen for me."

As long as the physical skill of dancing was its foundation and premise rather than its ultimate purpose, we regularly saw more of the artists we admired than their bodies. In their timing of gestures and their phrasing of familiar variations, we caught glimpses of the discrete minds and personalities that colored and shaded the steps so they became individual to that character in that situation on that night only. Dancers performed with their eyes and their shoulders, with a swift tilt of the head or a languorous hesitation of the arm, exposing the reason for their movement as clearly as its shape, and when they could no longer completely command their muscles, those inflections could still command the stage and our attention, both filling and fulfilling the role.

The greatest dancers, whose emotional responses made every performance a shared journey of surprise and discovery, seemed to create convincing life by instinct. In the ballroom scene of MacMillan's *Romeo and Juliet*, Lynn Seymour would pluck her mandolin more and more slowly as Romeo's seductive solo drew him nearer and nearer, tearing her eyes from him only when modesty reminded her of her manners. Without actually losing the rhythm, her fingers would move on every note, then on every fourth or fifth note, as if distracted by temptation. Exquisitely hesitant, her dancing in those seconds balanced between gesture and stillness, both of which brought us closer to the emotional core of her character. I could never believe she had prepared the effect or practiced it, but then, the theatrical success of those touches lay in their apparent spontaneity. If they didn't arise naturally from the choreographer's text, or at least seem to, they damaged the illusion like a lopsided wig, widening the crack between artifice and reality instead of concealing it.

At the time, nobody paid much attention to Seymour's hands on the mandolin, and it would have been perverse to watch them during her partner's extravagant solo. But if your eyes wandered or you quickly checked to find out how Romeo's provocative come-on was affecting her, those hands laid a tiny stroke of character on your imagination, quick and soft as a brush touching a painting. And whether you chose to look at her deliberately or glanced her way accidentally, you could always see both what she wanted you to see and what she meant by it, as if her body were a pane of glass, polished to a perfect transparency to show off her intentions.

Before television became interested in dance and before video enabled it to cross national borders in padded envelopes, dancers could only display their talents in person. Diaghilev toured Europe repeatedly with his Ballets Russes, and after World War I Anna Pavlova led her company far and wide, scattering ballet into corners of the Far East, India, Africa and Australia like iridescent confetti. Ted Shawn took his Denishawn Dancers to Asia for 15 months in 1925–26—it was the first American troupe to perform there—and during the 1950s, Merce Cunningham's entire company of six, plus two musicians and a lighting designer, traveled around America in a Volkswagen Microbus.

Although *Time* magazine reported in 1936 that ballet was all the rage in 100 American cities, Agnes de Mille's experience in the early '40s swiftly chopped that sweeping statement down to size—only six of them, she declared years later, could guarantee a full house for a whole week. So the companies kept moving. In 1943–44, American Ballet Theatre gave 143 performances on its transcontinental tour, making 73 stops and playing 48 one-night stands. Continually tired and broke, the dancers often couldn't remember which way to walk from the stage door to their hotel or even the name of the town. One night a company might appear in a sports arena, the next night they'd play a Masonic temple or the state fair auditorium—through the 1960s, the Royal Ballet made biennial visits to the Hollywood Bowl—and as a result the dancers had to learn to gauge their efforts accordingly. You could only be sure that the audience in the last row of the highest balcony could read your intentions if you continuously weighed every gesture against the available space, time and music. You couldn't stop to work it out every time you set foot on a new stage—there wasn't time in rehearsal, there often wasn't time *for* a re-hearsal, and in performance you couldn't stop at all—so as you danced you kept adjusting your dancing, calculating the size of each adjustment second by second for the distance it had to travel.

In small theatres, the dancers went through the same process in reverse, scaling passion and physical force down to miniature pro-portions. Valda Setterfield remembers touring with her husband, David Gordon: "We did a chair piece someplace in Pittsburgh where you could barely lift the chair over your head the ceiling was so low . . . And we made it work." Marie Rambert pinned down the dif-ficulty of dancing at London's Mercury Theatre, where the stage, in-cluding the apron, was only 18 feet deep and the proscenium only 18 feet wide. Playing to a grand total of 150 seats, "Absolute sincerity was required from the artist and complete identification with the part, as the smallest pretence would be felt by the audience immedi-ately." Just as too slight a move in the Shrine auditorium was invisi-ble to most of the spectators and therefore completely wasted, too broad a gesture in a small space could destroy the atmosphere as thoroughly as applause in church.

When every dance performance represented a sustained illusion and performers habitually brought musicality and dramatic con-viction as well as refinement to their dancing, I never wondered how they achieved their effects and I never thought about calcu-lated effort, just as I never consciously watched Seymour's fingers. Analysis had no place in the public's enjoyment of dancing because the silken, seamless product we were offered was so enthralling that analysis was beside the point. In retrospect, I wonder if we felt that dissecting the artifice before us would have insulted the artists who created it. But maybe we never took their work apart, because we were too busy taking it in.

While that idyllic era lasted, we in the audience believed that performances would always be absorbing and that artists like Seymour would emerge from every generation. I never heard a whisper of doom or fear or even doubt. No one looked at dancers and wailed, "This is too good to be true," any more than they looked at the troupes in which those dancers performed and cried, "What on earth is this company trying to do?" We had so much jam and there had been so much jam yesterday that we naturally assumed there would be jam tomorrow as well. Like children, we had no reason to ask who made the jam or how it was made as long as it didn't run out and we were free to consume it whenever we wanted. And no one would have dreamed of accusing us of being either greedy or short-sighted, though of course we were both, because our merry assumptions about the future were irrelevant to the future. As observers, we were doing our job if we showed up for performances with our eyes and minds open. It was our privilege to do so, but it was also an obligation we took seriously, because we somehow knew the performers needed us to complete what they began. Dancing was not a tree falling in a deserted forest—we were the noise of it hitting home, and without us there was only silence.

Life was different for the dancers. While we sat before them avidly lapping up their efforts, they had to figure out how to make the gestures that would keep us there, how to enliven familiar material to hold our attention, how to invent themselves night after night as if they'd never done so before. Their behavior may have looked instinctive, but the inner life of well-known roles, the details that make a performance both individual and memorable, can only be found by trial and error, and the search for them often lasts a lifetime.

The artists who create tangible artifacts with film or canvas or video or paper have a little more time to experiment and a little more leeway to test their solutions; they can always request another take or write a second draft. But in a theatre, where performers face the public in real time, every decision must be effective instantly, now or never. Stage actors and stand-up comics endure the same immediate pressure as dancers, and they attack it with the same equipment. "The crucial thing in performing," for the comedian Steve Martin, "is to find a choice that works for a moment and isn't the choice anyone else would have made. It's a discipline: you can't just do *anything*, but you can't do what's expected either."

In dance, however, the artists must split their attention still further and draw a distinction for themselves between this discipline, of choosing, and the adjacent discipline of academic technique, which demands another type of application and yields entirely different results. The daily class that forces a professional through countless tendus and turns and tortuous adagios—on the flat foot, on full pointe, with changing arms, in reverse—serves only two purposes. As the hours and months pass, it gradually renders him more pleasing for the public to watch, according to certain carefully defined standards, and more adaptable as an instrument a choreographer can use. Since the body forgets so easily and rebels so quickly, every dancer subjects himself to daily class even when he's hung over or fighting with his wife. But as he struggles with its exacting demands, he must also acknowledge that the time spent refining those individual movements can only bring them closer to their ideal form—it can never make them intrinsically interesting. Whether the dancer places her arms over her head or behind her back or across her chest, a fouetté is always just a fouetté.

For some, the monumental challenge of eradicating the gulf between themselves and that ideal is the whole point of performing and the sole justification for those years of repetition in the classroom. Packing every shred of strength they possess into a show-stopping 90-second variation that leaves the public roaring its approval, they are content to offer mastery as the only message. Virtuosity allows them to reveal only what they know they can do best, to exhibit themselves on their terms alone. When someone asked the pianist Shura Cherkassky why he played so fast, he responded, "Because I can." But the bravura technique that flares onstage and vanishes in an instant, like fireworks, burns a microscopic layer off the dancer producing it every time the fuse is lit, and the rewards of such scorching displays sometimes pall even before time, age or injury tear them from the artist's control. Two months after winning the gold medal at the prestigious Moscow International Ballet Competition, Julio Bocca accepted an invitation from Mikhail Baryshnikov to join American Ballet Theatre, where his flamboyant virtuosity immediately brought him international acclaim. Eight years later, in 1993 when he was 26, he remarked, "It's very weird, because already all my dreams have come true. I have a name. I dance around the world, with the best partners, the best theaters. I have always good reviews. Well, what is next? What now?"

The viewers who were watching more and more dancers hurtle through space as if gravity were obsolete might have been thinking exactly the same thing by then, because once the ovation had died down, we were left with nothing but sore throats and fiery palms. We couldn't weave fantasies about the prince or the scoundrel who leaped through the dramatic tales, because each character went up in smoke as soon as each virtuoso went up in the air. We couldn't see music perfectly translated into movement, because dancers were using music like a trampoline, tossing their bodies against it tirelessly but clutching their personal responses close to their chests, away from danger and from us, as if our involvement would wreck their fun.

At a certain point about 15 years ago, I started to miss interpretation in performances. If you entered a theatre expecting mystery and illusion, you found the Olympics instead, incredible exhibitions of movement far beyond the range of everyday possibility, rushing by in the fractured, illogical sequence of street life or music videos. The resonance began to evaporate from the classics like perfume drying, and the artists in them, who had always seemed a breed apart from mere mortals, began to look like anyone else. Imperceptible from one month to the next, these evolutionary changes in dance slowly spread in all directions, until one day I realized that a baseball game offered as much suspense, craft, inspiration, physical precision and theatricality as most of the available *Swan Lake*s. Instead of distilling music or laying bare the heart of human nature, dancers had taken to showing us the bodies and attitudes of mannequins, marvelously unblemished and perfectly anonymous. Narrative ballets were fading like photographs left too long in the sun as their dramatic characters lost their singular nuances bit by bit, and abstract works that had once burst from their scores like vines now ran over them like tractors. In New York, Martha Graham's masterpieces turned as hollow and decorative as painted pots even before her death. In London, the delicate charm and caustic humor of Ashton's work grew brittle and then mannered before vanishing completely.

"Forget about bars," Thomas Beecham used to beg his orchestra, "[they] are only the boxes in which the music is packed." But as virtuosity grabbed the spotlight and took over centerstage, some of the elegant guile that distinguishes dance from gymnastics slipped through the structural bars of choreography and disappeared. Suddenly, like the bitter outcome of some evil curse, only a handful of performers anywhere could move you to terror or tears. The rest were serving up a spectacular banquet of Chinese food, which stuffed your mind for an hour but left you ravenous by midnight. In London, a small band of proven 19th-century titles turned up with the dogged persistence of jukebox hits, always reassuringly familiar inside their pristine new productions, and every few seasons new casts added their first tentative scratches of characterization to the historical patina on the leading parts. Few of the dancers, however, animated the roles or roused the public as the packaging did—a chic combination of shiny black dresses and matte black cellphones set tongues wagging about *The Nutcracker* for weeks. As the productions settled into the repertory, the residual grandeur of the works beneath them sagged under the weight of superficial manners and trivial responses. Finally nothing at all remained of the originals' purpose, and even their names sounded commonplace.

New stars appeared in London with a regularity that seemed almost hysterical, and every girl who took on a leading role was hailed as a ballerina. But the noble qualities that distinguished title enshrines—taste, discretion, intelligence, wit, musicality and charm—could scarcely be found in any of them, and the artists I met were all nice young people who made the same impression on the stage as they did in the street. They occupied the same space and presented the same personality in both settings, and they danced as if duty rather than devotion were propelling them. Willingly, almost eagerly, they seemed to be abandoning their single-minded focus without noticing the consequences of that decision.

I don't mean they weren't working hard or applying themselves—lazy dancers quickly disappear from the casting and careless ones end up on the injured list. But instead of enhancing the repertory, the sum total of their efforts was stripping away its vibrancy, leaving the ballets clean and spruce but airless, like birds beneath glass domes. Wearing their characters lightly and dispatching their obligations with studious care, the dancers gave us skillful imitations of their parts which, like canned food, we could immediately recognize but would never mistake for fresh.

A few years ago, the artist David Hockney mentioned that he gave up on movies because he always knew what shot was coming next. When I found I could correctly anticipate how certain dancers would approach and execute every moment of certain roles, I started to worry that the general public would soon abandon dance for the same reason. Once the life had gone out of a particular work, taking with it the risks that keep us alert and the emotions with which we identify, no one would ever need to see that work again. To my alarm, that prospect didn't seem to worry the artists one bit. "Maybe going 50 times is what's strange," Royal Ballet principal Jonathan Cope speculated. "It's like going to see Elton John do the same set every night for a month. If you've never seen the ballet before then maybe you can go once and that's it. Maybe that's enough." How stupid of him, I thought, even to put the idea in anyone's head; when the public stops coming, he'll be out of a job. But my idea of Cope's job and his own perception of it could not have differed more. "Makarova. Or Misha [Baryshnikov]," he said, ". . . [are] very good at expressing the emotional side of it, which is very hard to do with ballet because, um, y'know, it's so silly." His colleague Darcey Bussell, who was elevated to the rank of principal at 20, complained that she couldn't express much when the choreography itself let her down. In Act II of *Sleeping Beauty*, for example, "It would make the role even more interesting," she reasoned, "if Petipa had given Aurora some less obvious steps to dance."

At the same time that some performers were innocently sabotaging their own accomplishments with their own words, something else was happening: dancers everywhere, men and women alike, took to working out regularly in the gym. Goaded by fashion and possibly by the fear that the old methods wouldn't adequately prepare them for the athletic demands of the super-charged new repertory, they applied the same concentration to weights and circuit training as to their daily class and steadily increased their strength. When serious bodybuilders described the muscular definition the dancers were after, they called it "cut" and "ripped," using words more often applied to damage. The performers, however, displayed their sharply honed tools with pride. Boldly costumed for maximum exposure, the women in skin-tight unitards or bare legs, the men often bare-chested, they paraded their chiseled muscles with the studied nonchalance of catwalk models, apparently unaware of how seriously their new look undermined their supposed theatrical goal. Having thrown away their physical individuality with abandon, from out front they all looked increasingly the same. Well, naturally. It couldn't be avoided. The harder dancers worked to develop the one thing they all have in common, which is human anatomy, the easier it became for us to think of them as interchangeable.

These trends careened through the companies I was watching like cars without drivers, and gradually we got used to seeing stronger and stronger instruments expressing less and less. Surely that was not the dancers' intention. But as the 20th century raced to a close, they raced right along with it, dodging emotional modulation, musical inflection and theatrical conviction to maintain a pace they had set for themselves. The headlong rush left some of their spectators, and some of their art, far behind, because the spirit of their work was suffering while their bodies thrived.

All of which pointed to a simple and terrible consequence. If expression was outmoded and artists no longer cared about individual interpretation, everyone would one day not only look alike but also dance alike, both the same as each other and—even worse—the same as themselves, in performance after performance. The joy of seeing different artists illuminate the same steps with their private gifts would disappear, and so would the satisfaction of watching dancers grow in their roles over time, revealing more of themselves and more of the choreography as they discovered more about them both. If no one could sustain a vision of the piece they were dancing, rather than of their own dancing in it, we'd wind up with nothing to watch but technique and decor.

On the outside looking into the profession, I couldn't understand why any of this was happening, why dancers should be indifferent to the past, scornful of the old values, and careless with the repertory I had always assumed they treasured. But as they continued to substitute high gloss and vapid drama for emotional texture and musical nuance, I slowly grew frightened, not that the public would lose interest but that the ballets would, not that the dancers could not survive this shift in their energy and attention but that the dances could not survive it. Without thoughtful interpreters, *Lilac Garden* would dwindle to soap opera, *Petrouchka* to a gaudy cartoon, and *Appalachian Spring* to a billboard. As soon as I realized that the future of those works was being compromised by the artists to whom they were entrusted, Seymour's hands soared out of my memory unbidden, trailing all the questions we had never needed to ask. Had she learned to make each moment count, or did she discover each gesture instinctively, without assistance or guidance? How much assistance could dancers use? How much did they want? Who could blow on the embers of familiar roles to make them burst into flame every night?

Twenty years ago and more, the public ignored the process of maintenance, because it was indistinguishable from the dancing before us. In the course of enchanting us with illusion the dancers seemed to be keeping the repertory alive and fresh all by themselves, as if they knew they would be shooting themselves in the foot if they failed to do so. "I dance for dance's sake," Desmond Kelly told me in 1979. "If I'm going to do *Giselle*, I dance for *Giselle*. If I'm going to do *Prodigal* [*Son*], I dance for the ballet, to make the ballet great, to make it happen for that audience that night." *Giselle* and *Prodigal Son* were safe forever, or so we thought then, because those involved in their performance were committed to keeping them safe. Logic alone dictated that there was no higher priority for a company than the protection of its repertory, because if the ballets were allowed to deteriorate and their fine, defining detail started to go, the audience would go too. Who would want to see great choreography once heroic passions shriveled and musical responses turned mechanical? It would be just as easy, and much cheaper, to go to the movies.

That's what we thought, but what did we know? Anyone can shake their fists and criticize, but as viewers we are outsiders by definition, wishing for the performances we craved while knowing that we were helpless to contribute any more to them than our fervor. Deep down, we also had to admit that our devotion didn't equip us with omniscience. You could no more fathom a company's methods or an artist's motives by watching a performance than you could understand a marriage by looking at a closed bedroom door.

Bored and exhausted by Bournonville's sunny narratives, for decades the dancers of the Royal Danish Ballet fitted obscene words to the lilting music they could never escape and spat them out like poisoned candy as they bounded, smiling, through their variations. And Balanchine, who deflected the solemnity of historical analysis by cheerfully describing his ballets as evanescent, used to pray for the safety of Suzanne Farrell's knees. Out front, we could afford to demand choreographic magic and theatrical illusion; some would argue we had no greater obligation than to make such demands and keep our expectations high. For the dancers, however, life on the unpainted side of the performance was less about magic than about knees and whispered obscenities. But that had always been true for dancers, and we knew it perfectly well. So what had changed? We had to guess.

Maybe, like everyone in the get-ahead, microwave world, they had simply become impatient for results. Or maybe they were longing to find more in the roles and give more of themselves to the public but they couldn't figure out where to find it or how to give it. Maybe they didn't know who to ask, or maybe the act of asking would imply doubt or insecurity that they didn't dare reveal, either to their bosses or their colleagues or themselves. It's hard to stand up and say, "I don't understand this" or "I don't know how to do this," and dancing is already hard enough. Maybe I was holding the wrong end of the stick, and the dancers were not actually the pinnacle of the performance but the single point on which everything else rested, the repertory, the budget, the touring schedule, the patrons' galas, the glorious history and the unknown future of the art, all held aloft and kept in balance by the aching, weary dancers. Maybe the tedium of repetition and the rasp of competition were simply wearing away their confidence and their inclination to take risks. Or maybe they just didn't have time.

Times change. Significance is not eternal. One hundred fifty years ago, the ballerina represented an irresistible vision, floating on pointe in a cloud of gauze as if airborne, but today the elusive Romantic ideal drifts irrelevantly in the romantic past. The imperial splendor that Petipa mirrored in his majestic fables has crumbled to dust, and so has what Verdy calls "the cosy-homey charm, like country bread," of the rustic village life that Bournonville treasured and celebrated in dance. The upright academic carriage and corseted physical restrictions against which Fokine and Isadora Duncan rebelled so fiercely lost the last vestige of their suffocating power nearly 40 years ago, when women burned their bras in public. And postmodernism, which exalts a patchwork of references over consistent style and unified content, has dismissed codified technique as old-fashioned and relegated it to a back burner.

Outside the theatre, the world has discarded and forgotten many objects that at one time were considered necessities. Buttonhooks, for example. Slide rules and skate keys. No one needs these things anymore, so no one misses them. But if you should want or need a buttonhook, you can find one—or at least a picture of one—with relatively little effort, in a book or a museum or on the World Wide Web, along with a detailed description of how to use it. Crammed with information and apparently limitless in their scope, these sources seem to hold the answer to every question worth asking. But they cannot teach you to cast a believable spell over a palace. They cannot capture the dreadful implication of one witch's finger closing in triumph around her belt, or help you convert music into thought or thought into action. How will dancers manage to do those things when no one can remember how to do them? Why should they bother to try if they don't understand what the effort is for? Who reaches for a prize no one values?

Wait, that's not entirely fair. If no one valued an artist's choices, no one would watch dances, look at pictures, listen to music or ever read another book, but so far, happily, the grim prospect of life without imagination belongs only to the realm of science fiction. Cut off from the civilian herd by the work they've chosen and the temperament that keeps them at it, some dancers also live outside the herd they've joined. Resisting the trend for detachment they distinguish themselves with their intelligence as well as their bodies, regardless of the restraints that time, doubt, and society impose on them. Realizing they can only attain their goals by naming them and mapping for themselves the paths they plan to follow, they accept the fact that no one can do their work for them or take the blame if things go wrong, and after a while they discover that their intentions are the only aspect of performing they can completely control.

Initiative burns in these artists like a live coal. Not ambition, which is sustained by public recognition, but initiative, the private urgency that tends itself and continues to glow when no one is looking, even in the face of failure. Initiative commands a dancer to work on his own whenever he has a moment to spare, and along the way to his imagined destination, it may also encourage him to hook up with a wise companion, someone who knows the roads or the lay of the land. With luck he will stumble on a guide who has already completed his own journey and is ready to share his experience. After that, progress is slower and more difficult but also simpler, because between them the artist and the guide can explore a territory into which neither might venture alone.

When a dancer joins the Kirov Ballet, he acquires a coach, by request or assignment, who advises him, rehearses him, gives him notes between the acts of every performance and often shares his curtain calls and his flowers. The coach's responsibility is considered so important that the Rimsky-Korsakov Conservatory, which stands opposite the Maryinsky Theatre, prepares students for it with a five-year course that includes art history and formal pedagogy. More often, coaches come straight from the stage; as they relinquish their own performing careers, they carry their experience into the studio, take a seat in front of the mirror, and begin the long, careful process of applying it to someone else. In ice skating, coaching and teaching are inseparable—the same person teaches you the formal movements and perfects your execution of them. In baseball, different coaches focus on different skills, one on pitching, another on batting, a third on fielding. In dance, coaches concentrate on expressive interpretation, and whether they zoom in on a single reaction or a single step—Martine van Hamel asks for Myrtha's bourrées to be so tight that the space between the dancer's feet becomes invisible—their private conversations with their charges link the expressive threads of an interpretive web that sustains each role.

Treasured for their voluminous memories and judicious eyes, these watchmen must constantly align the choreographer's intent and its actual fate, the night before or the season before, with the dancers in the studio and the ideal performance they might give in the future. A fusion of scrupulous accuracy and penetrating conviction, the results of their manipulations resemble Oriental locks. Smooth and gleaming, each one is all of a piece, and its separate elements fit so closely that the delicate pattern they form as they come together seems deliberately etched on the surface. What you eventually see onstage is a unique creation with its own distinct mechanism, the mysterious product of all the tumblers falling into place in exactly the right order.

Experienced guides invariably say that coaching is a two-way street and that the dancers must want to learn as much as they want to dance or everyone is just spinning their wheels. They concede that halfhearted performers can sometimes develop a whole heart, but the task of fitting it and coaxing it to beat can test a coach's patience and endurance relentlessly. Some dancers, as the Danish teacher Vivi Flindt conceded, may only take the trouble in order to satisfy their own professional pride. "If you have a stone," she told me flatly, "you learn how to carve a stone." But the responsible performer, who chooses to pull his own weight, finds he can escape the concentric prisons that surround him by cutting the keys to his own freedom.

Determined artists advance by knotting themselves, their guides and their intentions into an intricate pattern with no beginning and no end. The pianist Glenn Gould identified Artur Schnabel as one of his first idols because he "seemed to be a person who didn't really care very much about the piano as an instrument. The piano was a means to an end, for him, and the end was to approach Beethoven." Born 50 years before Gould, Schnabel had once declared, "The process of artistic creation is always the same—from inwardness to lucidity." The actor Yoshi Oida repeated to Peter Brook the wisdom of an old Kabuki master: "I can teach a young actor the movement of how to point to the moon. But from his finger-tip to the moon, that's the actor's responsibility." Oida then added, "When I act, what matters is not whether my gesture is beautiful. For me, there is only one question. Did the audience see the moon?" At 51, Baryshnikov was still guarding this responsibility jealously, calling it his attempt "to decode the choreographic thought," and Vladimir Malakhov, who is 20 years his junior, protests that, "It's not a question of how many pirouettes you do but how you do them. The tradition of classical ballet must be saved, just like wild animals."

Every day, older artists offer their hard-earned experience to younger ones in an attempt to preserve what modern life seems intent on destroying, and every day they wait to learn if anyone wants to accept their insights and objectivity. Tom Trebelhorn, who was 45 and coaching for the Chicago Cubs when he was asked about the changes in professional baseball, answered with a question of his own: "Did you ever throw up bottle caps and try to hit them with a broom when you were a kid? I sure did. It's thirty-five years I've been hitting something round with something flat. Too late to stop now."

In 1997, I snuck into the London Coliseum before a performance of *La Bayadère* to peek at Olga Moiseyeva rehearsing for half an hour with that evening's Nikiya, Altynai Asylmuratova. The two women had worked together ever since Asylmuratova joined the Kirov Ballet in 1978. As its leading ballerina, Asylmuratova had been dancing the role of Nikiya for years, and yet 90 minutes before curtain, her coach was reminding her of this musical inflection and that dramatic effect, this mistake she had made previously and the potential trap in that sequence. At the time Moiseyeva was 69 and long retired; her swift rise through the ranks of the Kirov had begun with an acclaimed portrayal of Nikiya in 1949. Watching them watch each other I expected to see the older ballerina guiding the younger one to a more vivid, brilliant realization of herself. Instead, I saw two dancers pummeling Nikiya with impersonal violence to make absolutely sure she was still alive. Like medics working over a body, they slapped her face to bring the blood to her cheeks and stretched her limbs until her muscles took over and spontaneously stretched themselves. As the concentration between them intensified, they both disappeared, along with the thumping piano and the gray wash of the work lights, and only Nikiya remained.

Several years earlier, in a Royal Ballet performance of *Giselle*, Asylmuratova had confronted Bathilde bravely after Albrecht had abandoned his disguise, saying in mime, "He will marry me." Then, for emphasis, she said it again, and by slowing and separating the gestures she made them louder. Louder mime. Incredible. Had the idea come from her? From Moiseyeva? From Moiseyeva's coach? I didn't really care, except in the numerous performances where Giselle went through those motions without the slightest conviction, when I cared a lot. During that *Bayadère* rehearsal I finally understood that dancing *Giselle* by rote, scrupulously executing the steps and neatly adopting the shapes, was exactly the same as propping up a corpse. If coaches could bring that corpse to its feet, then coaches could keep the repertory from dying before our eyes.

In the back of my mind as I watched them work, I kept hearing Jason Robards' gravelly voice in *All the President's Men,* the movie about the Watergate break-in. As Ben Bradlee, then editor of the *Washington Post,* in one scene Robards stands on his front lawn in the middle of the night with the reporters whose investigations are leading them closer and closer to the White House. Weighing the explosive nature of their discoveries, he warns them to proceed with the utmost caution. "Nothing's riding on this," he reminds them, wrapping his alarm in sarcasm, "except the First Amendment of the Constitution, freedom of the press and maybe the future of the country . . . not that any of that matters."

Don't get me wrong. I know the difference. Watergate was real, and *Giselle* is only art. Dancing is not government, and lackluster dancers are not crooked politicians. No one suffers when dancers step back from their work and present a cooler presence than their predecessors or when beautiful bodies in motion have the stage to themselves. Nothing is destroyed at the performances that often fill our theatres, except perhaps history, creativity and imagination. Not that any of that matters.

Sorella Englund

b. Helsinki, 1945. Trained at the Finnish National Opera
ballet school. Joined Royal Danish Ballet 1966, promoted
solodanser (principal) 1970. Retired 1978 due to ill health,
but returned repeatedly to the company as a character
dancer, ballet master and coach. Ballet master Boston Ballet
1996–99, and independent coach worldwide.

I ALWAYS WANTED TO COACH, but I never wanted to teach because I've met very few teachers who were teaching anything
else but technique. Of course they taught about the beauty of the
movement and the arms, the delicacy of the feet and legs, but very
few who talked about the inner motivation or what the ballet was
about—deep, deep, deep—or what one's character was about. I
wanted the inside of things, the acting and the emotions, all that
side. That was the one thing that interested me the most. So I felt
very lonely, always actually, but I had one fantastic chance when I
was 17. Iria Koskinen, who is completely unknown except in Finland, had made a ballet called *Scaramouche*, and she recreated it—
it's very much like *Giselle* in a way, she dances herself insane and
dies—and she really told me about the character of the girl, so I
completely understood who I was. I was so hungry for this. She
said that if you're longing after something unconsciously, if it's
something you want, the physical form of it is not out in the fingers, it's in the whole body. Hands are usually the very last thing,
when you start doing something. Before it gets there, the impulse
is somewhere in your body, and you don't know what to do. She

explained all this to me so clearly, and I have been able to use the things she told me then all my life. They come back all the time.

Then Mme. Volkova was a great teacher, because she was an artist in her heart and she was able to give it further. There are great artists who can't do that, maybe they're not interested in it, but they expect it to happen to other people without too much coaching, like it happens to them. They know somehow the why and the how, but they don't know how to help their students. That needs a special character, I think, to want somebody to flower, not just yourself. You have to put yourself away as a teacher, and she had that. Henning Kronstam also . . . He was one of the greatest artists I have met. In the beginning, when I met him, I was only in my 20s. He didn't say very much ever, not to *La Sylphide* or any part I did, but the strange thing was that his artistic spirit was so strong, even off the stage and in the rehearsal room. There was something in his eyes, him watching you, so you started to do things and you didn't really know why. He was coaching you, not with words but with his spirit, and it's not to understand because it's beyond logical understanding. He was a man who had a natural authority without him even knowing it. So when he came to the room you responded every time, I think mostly because his love and his respect for this profession was so enormous. We saw him onstage and danced with him, so you would feel like, 'I would do anything to be as good as possible,' because he was something you could really look up to.

Henning Kronstam is gone now in Denmark, and he was the last one who was an incredible coach when he got older. He was amazing, you could just cry from what he could talk about. Nikolaj Hübbe, Rose Gad, everybody, all that generation had him and they couldn't have enough of him. I think they can use that the rest of their life. But there wasn't so much coaching in the ballet, not like if you work with actors—that's a completely different way. But what helped so much . . . Every time you learn a Bournonville part, there are lots of *repliks* [lines] for the mime. You say one thing and I answer another thing and so on—when you learn it, that is all said in words. You speak them and the coaches speak them too, but you do them backwards because they are made backwards in their physical form: You, Me, Love, or Go out, I'm angry with you. But then you adapt them, and very often you put your own words, which really mean something to you, so when you do it, it's not just a gesture but there's life in it. Otherwise, it's just empty. For instance, [in *La Sylphide*] when I'm doing the witch, Madge, I have different sentences or meanings for everything, and sometimes I say them to myself when I do it, not out loud but in my head: 'You go to hell. Who do you think I am?' so it doesn't look just like dumb show. And that maybe makes a difference, so if it's really well done, it seems natural. It's not pretending—it's *doing* it.

Usually I had very little coaching, always quite a lot technically and for the style, but very little about the character. For instance, about the Sylphide—I had no idea who she was. So I asked, "I don't know how to go, what path I should take," and they answered, "You'll find out in ten years. That's what the others did." And it's true, I have found out in ten years, but they didn't know what to say. In Denmark today, the dancers are not so much like we were—we would never ask a question. You did exactly as you were told. Today they ask questions and they can also be quite rude, but that's better than that kind of authority where you are completely paralyzed because you're so afraid.

I think there is a huge lack in dancers' education, and has always been, about the acting, how you create a role. So that's why when I stopped dancing I started to study how theatre directors were working, so maybe dance could get inspired. I followed different theatres. I asked if I could just be quiet and watch the whole process, and it was incredibly exciting. I think I found what I already knew, because that was the way I always had worked by myself. But I found a little bit also some ways to work with younger people, how I would approach it. I mean, you just can't say, "Be like that"—there has to be a way: Who is this person? Where was he born? How was the childhood? Who was the mother? Then you get the whole pattern of the person and you understand why he's acting like this—why James is running away [in *La Sylphide*]—so everything is not only by instinct. I hear so often, "A dancer doesn't need to know why," because sometimes they do it right by instinct. But I want dancers to be fed, I want them to develop in their own lives. I did hundreds of roles by instinct, and they said, "It's wonderful." But I had no idea why it worked, so I couldn't use it next time.

I mean, if a theatre director puts on a play, he has his own view of this particular play. But if a ballet director puts on a ballet, *La Sylphide*, Petipa, anything, he doesn't have any addition or any artistic view. Then it's all east and west, one dancer is playing one direction, one is acting the other, one is very sensitive and lyrical, one is moving, moving, moving, completely active and nothing else. And there is no line, no vision of where the focus is or what the performance is about. It is just *Swan Lake,* a production of *Swan Lake,* nice dancing, and if there are great artists, it becomes a great performance only because of them.

I think today we live in a very technical age, and that's why ballets look as they look. We are so taken by technique, any kind of technique, PCs, videos, everything that works by technique. I mean, you just push buttons and you have the Internet. So it happens a little bit the same in dance and sports. We create these machines, your muscles get more and more specialized, so we become a sort of tool, which in an art form should be the tool to tell about what it is to be a human being. I wouldn't call most classical ballet today an art form—I would call it a body form, because there's never any talk about anything but the legs and the feet. Nothing about the arms anymore, which are so interesting—only feet and legs. This is everywhere, and I've really been around. Now, in Scottish Ballet, there are still people from the time when they had another way. They had this great leader, Peter Darrell, and everybody in the company tells me that he gave every corps de ballet dancer a character for every ballet. So everybody was motivated, and dancers are hungry, they want that. They want to be an individual, a person; even if there are thousands of them, each one is important. And that way the works have a life that is wonderful.

The music has always been my reason to dance, most of all the music and the emotions that music creates in you and the unspoken words about life, which is music, where you can't explain why something feels so dramatic or fantastic or so sad. I had quite a tragic childhood, but many people have that so it's nothing special. But I always had this longing, since I was very small, and I didn't know what I was longing after, and I still have it. When I get closest to not having it is when I'm with nature, usually by the sea, and when I'm dancing with music. So that's maybe one part of why I'm dancing. And then, being onstage for me is like such a power, so I'm not me anymore. In the best moments everything disappears. It's this huge power, not only power in a demonic way, but a huge amount of imagination and visions and things, it's a magical world.

When I stopped dancing, I started to study architecture and literature and psychology and everything, because I was so hungry for knowledge. Life as a dancer is so narrow, so I felt so dumb, unknowledged. At the same time I shifted back and forth between these theatre productions. The first year after I stopped dancing I was completely in a black hole. I didn't do anything, I didn't see anybody, I was lost, completely lost. And I was quite young, 33. Then, I started to do jazz, because I was longing after movement. Of course the doctor said, "You cannot move, you have to rest," because of the heart attack I had. But I thought, 'If I start jazz, just start . . . ' and I was absolutely crazy about it, because it was freedom, it was hips, sensual, sexy, and classical ballet's so different, all control.

There was an American black teacher, Doug Crutchfield, a generous, fantastic man, and he made Copenhagen jazz life like it was a fire, I mean, everybody went to jazz. Young kids and older women, up to 60, were doing jazz every day. He was like a sun of warmth and passion for it. He said, "Why don't you teach classical, in my school?" I said, "I don't want to teach classical ballet. I want to try to teach repertoire." So for the two first years, I had five people every Saturday morning. They were sort of half-amateurs, but they missed the opportunity of expressing themselves. We had a fantastic time, because it's a luxury to have so few people. I could coach a person for a half an hour, instead of just "You do this, you do that" and never going to the depth. We had many scenes from *La Sylphide*, lots of Bournonville's repertory, lots of improvisations, and I did some choreography with a little story and a solo where they had to put different moods—it had to be very aggressive or soulless, mindless, or absolutely bored to death. The solo was like day and night with the differences, you couldn't believe it was the same steps. It was a fantastic time to experiment, but they weren't professionals so they wouldn't use it for anything, just for themselves. And for me at that point, that was fine. I didn't want to be famous, not at all. I had enough, it was fine.

And then slowly somehow . . . the Royal [Danish Ballet] asked me if I wanted to go there for mime parts, which I always wanted to do. And then they asked me if I also wanted to teach repertory and also more modern things, not only Bournonville, because the young dancers need things which are from their own time. This was for the *aspirants*, just before they get into the company. It was just once a week, but it was extremely exciting. And then they asked me slowly if I wanted to coach or be an assistant for choreographers, so I then went into that.

There was a different school, outside the Royal, who wanted me to teach classical ballet, just as a class. I explained to them that my interest is mostly in the quality of the movement and the color and the smell and the energy of the movement, and they said, "That's what we want." So I thought, 'Well, I'll try it.' And I decided, 'This is going to be my way. There are brilliant technical teachers all over the world, but it's not so much my passion. Why should I try to do something half-well that I'm really not known for? I'm going to do something that I am known for. Maybe they won't get so much technique, but they will get something on another level, which they can maybe use.' So that's how I've continued.

I never had difficulties with how to do it, because I always wanted to give somehow and I had no trouble in giving. But I was extremely shy, so I had a hard time talking loud enough. Mostly I was extremely insecure about if I had anything special to give, if I was good enough. Always the typical dancer's syndrome: 'I'm not good enough, it's not good enough.' But now I see a huge difference because I'm getting older, and if people don't like my teaching and they think I'm stupid or silly, it doesn't matter so much. When I was young I thought, 'I shouldn't say these things, they think I'm crazy talking about flowers and bees.' Today I don't care if they think I'm silly. I take this seriously—if they don't, it's fine.

In Copenhagen lately, the last three years, it's all about technique and about the dancers in the company, the high, high professionals, wanting to hear about technique. The guest teachers we had looked from the waist and knees down, and the coaches were exactly the same. Good, nice persons, but it was the only thing they were interested in. I mean, I have seen the role of James being coached just by, "You have to be quick with the back leg." That was the coaching for the part, so it has made me sort of back out. I thought, 'I'm in the wrong field. Nobody wants these other things.' But then I went to Boston, and I did my way, thinking, 'Take it or leave it. If you don't like it, it's fine,' and they were hungry, the dancers couldn't get enough. I did it in every class, because I didn't coach so much, and they started to dance like angels—it was so beautiful I felt like crying. And here too, at Scottish Ballet, they *want* it. I haven't been working in Copenhagen for about three years, so I don't know if the interest has started to come back. It certainly wasn't there in Peter Schaufuss' time and in the recent years, not at all.

This problem is all over, everywhere, I think because of this fascination with technique and the competition between different companies' leaders to have these high, high qualified technical dancers.

The demands are so big, so hard, to have that level of blown-up technique, and somehow they lost something fine. Maybe it's from some kind of insecurity. We always want to go along with the stream because it's quite hard to be alone, you think your way is old-fashioned. I'm not going to give up, but I feel sometimes it's really lonely—I don't know any people who are trying to do what I'm trying to do. Oh, maybe a little bit, "You have to smile" or "No, you're angry here," but it's not with the depth. Anybody can say, "You have to smile more," but why? Be angry? Why?

Mime is a little bit different, but it's still very much the role. It comes out of the technique, but I don't think you can coach people how to mime. You can't say, "When you are very surprised, you lift your eyebrows"—that's not the way. You have to give a picture: "You come to this living room, and there's suddenly a man completely covered in blood and you expected only your cat. You open the door, and this man is standing there. What happens?" They respond immediately, and it's their way of being surprised, not because I say, "Be surprised." They do whatever is natural. If you have a motivation you know how to do it, so I think the only way to coach mime is to motivate the person to know what is happening inside.

That's what I'm trying to do, with *La Sylphide*, for instance. I've been coaching Tamara Rojo, who's very young. In five years she'll be fine, but she has everything in her now, so it will come. I just want to make her know who the character is and why she's there, and know the image of her moving, her talking. The character is very passionate, but because she's a sylph and completely opposite to Effie, it's all like . . . to fog the movements. The feeling should be concrete and content but never the movements, and that's the difficulty of *La Sylphide*. So I tell her, "Every time you say, 'You, with me, come to the forest,' it should never be strong, loud, it should be like a whisper." It's so dangerous and so pulling for him. So I try to use lots of images from the dancer's own life, from their own time—How would you act if . . . ? What would happen if . . . ?—so it's not only about something 200 years ago. And they understand it very well, but it takes some time to sink in.

Tamara has been like a sponge, for everything. I only had a week with her, so I said, "Go home and write down all your doubts, all your black places where you don't know why you are there or what is happening. And then come tomorrow and we will talk about it." Usually it's the other way around: I tell her how it could look. She's a very bright girl, so she came with a long paper of different things, and we went through everything. I said, "Is this clear now, or shall we change the approach?" She could also have said, "There's nothing. It's all fine." That's fine too, because she's bright. Of course the solos are like an expression of being so happy, so there I don't coach what it means but just the feeling of it.

With the *aspirants* I would take shorter, easier sequences. I do only very simple, simple, simple things, because sometimes the students have just been in the classroom and they have faces like . . . I used to tell them in Boston, "I don't want to have the fish look." Their eyes sometimes don't see, don't see each other, don't see anything, just blank. The technique very easily becomes a wall, but I don't want to see a façade—I want to see a human being.

Every role develops you, takes you farther, but you also give something to the role. I couldn't have done any role if I didn't use my life experience, taking everything from there but being very aware that it's personal but not private. So when I see somebody who's 20 and who's been leading a safe, nice, good life, I understand very well why there's nothing in their eyes. I'm trying to explain about the despair of losing the person you love most or dying or whatever, and of course, how would they know? They look at me blankly and say, "Yeah, OK." I didn't say that, and I had many colleagues who wouldn't have said that. We had tough lives, and . . . I know that young people have tough lives today, but maybe in a different way. I think they're very unfed, maybe they don't get so much contact, warmth, inspiration, care, in the mental way. Care from toys, cars, money, all that is there, but inside them is maybe more empty, only because they haven't got that sort of food. I don't know.

When I can see that the dancer starts to feel like in a prison of the role, I go quickly the opposite way. I say, "All your arabesques keep completely free. I don't want to see small, tiny arms. Keep free. Open the sky." And then they start finding their own way. Because I give them freedom, they come back to something which is them. But you have to be incredibly aware. If I'm looking at Bournonville I can't just say that the style has to be exactly like in the pictures of the old times. The dancers were small then, they were round, they had curved arms like this, so when they put them up they came close to the head. But today that's going to be comical. Do you want that? So I'm trusting my own eye for what looks beautiful on this dancer—do it.

And also . . . For instance there are two girls in Scottish Ballet now who are going to do *La Sylphide* later sometime, and one is not the type at all. So I thought, 'I have to find a completely different approach for her.' I was talking to this girl and I told her all the different possibilities, or the different possibilities from the thousands of possibilities, from which she could build the part. I said, "There is also this possibility, which is quite exciting—a very, very erotic sylph, not sexual but erotic. So James puts all his fantasies in this erotic thing he can't get." You see, this girl is very erotic and not lyrical one bit. So if she would start doing it the way I would have done it in my time, or like somebody else who has the open sky in their eyes, it's going to be a disaster. She took the idea right away, because she thought, 'Oh yes, this is me.' And that's exciting. And the other girl is completely like air, dreamy, so I said, "You've just got to be a great soul."

Of course, each James has to be aware of what we all are doing together, because otherwise it's like I said in the beginning. If nobody's coaching, and if a sylph finds out she wants to do it erotic and her James is lyrical, he's east and the Sylphide is west and it doesn't go together. But usually if you, as James, get a very erotic sylph, you can't resist—you just go along with her, because she's suddenly coming with something irresistible. It usually happens quite naturally, but I want them to be conscious about things and learn, so I usually talk about it. Not too much, because you can talk things to death.

I have never thought very much about it, it somehow happens without you knowing, but of course I'm passing the things I've learned, which are like gifts. I would be very selfish if I kept them for myself, so I bring them for others. I used to say, "So-and-so person said this" and "So-and-so person told me that," but today it's a mixture of my own ideas and their ideas, so I don't always say, "She said so." And now they don't know about those people. Lots of them haven't even seen me dance. They know very little. I don't know if that comes from these times, where everything is about the media, the fast tempo, the TV . . . We read very little, compared to the old days. Or maybe it's because we are living in a time where everybody is so specialized in one field. You have to be so incredibly good to make it as a dancer, so dancers get more and more limited in their view of other art forms, because—this is just a guess—they may be using more and more hours in practicing, more and more hours going to fitness centers to make their muscles fit, just to be able to make it. So it's not their fault. It's been happening slowly and it's very strange. I don't think I feel this way just because I'm getting older, and I'm not thinking all the time, 'Oh, our time was the only great time.' No, no, it's not that way. I'm just wondering why it's taken a complete different direction.

But maybe also, young people today feel that they can't connect with the old works. So maybe it would make a difference if they dance works with some more of their own time in them, so they *can* connect, 'This is about *my* despair, this is about *our* time.' I don't know, but I sense it. We can't keep on only dancing dead men's work. They are wonderful, we should keep them, but there also has to be something from the people's own time, like we had Cranko and Tudor. In one way, traditional works are always new, it's always for the first time, but it's challenging and interesting to do something that happens right now.

And we have also been, and maybe still, through a period where feelings are always thought sentimental and sort of looked down on. Too much feeling now is embarrassing. All the intellectuals, I mean in Denmark, for the last five or six years . . . Show too much emotion and it's like, "Oh, come on. It's banal." But we all have feelings, we all have emotions, and we will always have them. So to deny it and to try to be technical and held in . . . I think art should go exactly the opposite way. The more technical and speedy everyday life is outside, the more we should talk about how it is to be a human being.

I'm not any . . . how do you say? . . . saint. It's not that I want to put my art on a pedestal and say, "I'm changing the world." No. I'm just trying to do something I believe in. And I don't even know if it's right, but I'm not going to give up, because I believe in it. My goal is in the spirit of the performance and the person. For me, art is about that, and the body is the instrument to tell about what's inside, about the story, about the human being, about life and death. I know that in Copenhagen now, the dancers talk about New York City [Ballet], Darci [Kistler] and most of the principals of New York City [Ballet]. And about Sylvie Guillem, especially the way she was in the beginning, with the technique and the legs. These are their models. But I'm grateful because I had the chance to watch Ulanova in *Giselle,* [Maya] Plisetskaya, [Raisa] Struchkova and all these big dancers when they were young and on the top. They were always guests in Finland. We had a festival every spring and they tried their young stars out. They wouldn't be let out into Europe; the first stop was always Finland, and then they decided in Russia if they could go on a big tour. I was in the corps of *Giselle*, in the first act, when I saw Ulanova. She was 50, with gray hair and just a little bit of lipstick, and we were young and sort of thought, you know, that everybody who was over 20 should be in their graves. And when she started, we were crying in the wings, we could hardly make it through the first act. Unforgettable. She became 14. She didn't have any technique at that point, not the sort of showy, brilliant technique . . . it didn't matter.

When I was young and I saw all these Russians, our biggest goal or our biggest criticism always, whether it was good or not good, was if the person was an artist or not. We didn't care about technique, we really didn't. So when the British ballet sometimes came over, we all preferred the Russians. Some of the British productions were very cool, very elegant, and we couldn't see the quality in that. We wanted feelings and passion. Today when I hear the young people talking, it's all about technique, and for us it was all about artistry, artists. That's what we wanted as an audience, and that was our goal for ourselves, how we wanted to end up. We wanted to have the guts to go into something and feel it fully. We wanted to focus on that instead of focusing on your legs or a wall of control, checked. Those Russian dancers made me feel grateful, and if they didn't I was disappointed.

I was shocked just before I left the Royal, maybe five years ago, because there was no interest about the audience from the dancers or coaches. I said, "Have you forgotten that there are people who need to get the best of the best? This is not your private ego trip, if you get the balance or not. If it looks sour, so what if you strive over and over again? You are the sleeping beauty, and they have to have the most wonderful vision of the sleeping beauty." It didn't interest them at all, but for me the audience is the main thing, more than the critics. I love the public, I love the interaction, and you have to love that. You have to want to share what's in your heart, to give it out. Now they think about technique and the coach who's standing in the wings and the critics, and there's the standard smile. Maybe something more happens, or it starts to happen, but you are on the peak of the emotion already and it hasn't even begun. But nobody looks at that, because the coaches are looking at the legs. So the dancers give you what you ask for. In Boston, the dancers said to me, "Everything that you're saying is something we knew from way back, but we've forgotten it." I said, "I don't think you have forgotten it, but you give the teachers and the coaches what they ask you to give them."

But I also wonder, where are the guts in coaches and directors? Why is there so little interest in the artist's side from them? If they were not coached themselves or if they just found their way instinctively, then go out and try to learn from somewhere else how to help young people. It's not enough just to say, "Do something" or "Feel." That's what they say: "Go alive in the background. Feel something." It makes me *mad*! Feel what? Who, where, how, when? Then of course everyone's overdoing it, so it's all fake and you couldn't believe in any of it. And now that the coaches are so much on the path of technique, if you go to a professional dancer and you start talking about this, they laugh at you. So it takes guts for a coach to keep on doing it. At the Royal Danish, they have . . . not resisted, but they look bored, like, 'Oh, come on.' I have had dancers nearly laughing at me—not anymore—one turned her back when I was talking to her. So it's tough, because you respect something, you believe in it, and then somebody else is laughing at it. She apologized afterwards, but it really makes you . . . I thought, 'I quit. I'm not going to force my ideas on anybody anymore,' because of course one is vulnerable.

When I had no money last year I came to London because I wanted to see Maggie Smith onstage—that gives me inspiration still. If I wouldn't have that, or concerts or people who are inspiring because they do other art forms, I would die. Not die, but die of being alive. I still believe somehow that working with young people you just try to inspire that side all the time. "Go out and see this picture. Read this book." Sometimes you nearly have to take them by the hand. You say, "Do it" or "Let's look at it together." Very few people said to me, "Go out," so probably you have to have that curiosity inside yourself.

Now I don't want to teach too much or coach too much, because when I start to get bored, they get bored. I don't want to teach the same people five months in a row, because they get tired of me, I get tired of them, I get tired of myself. That's why I left Copenhagen, where I was a coach mostly, because people are in the same house all the time. I'm in there 24 hours, the dancers are there 24 hours. There's no time to see other art forms, to read, to do other things at all. So you're completely dried out with inspiration—it's nobody's fault, it just happens. I said the same things to the same people that I said three years before, and I thought, 'Who cares? Who cares about ballet? It's just boring.' And I thought, 'Now is the time to leave, before *they* see that I am burned out.' And I thought it never would come back again. I left and I thought, 'I'm gone now forever.' But after a year I started to work with smaller groups and outside the theatre, and it all came back.

That's why it's so wonderful to be freelance . . . as long as I get work, of course, you never know. But up 'til now I've been really lucky, more than lucky. But the method I'm using . . . I have no idea if it comes true onstage. I have to keep doing it because I believe in it, but I have no idea if after I've been working with them there's a difference from before. I can see the *La Sylphide* things, but I don't know if other people see them, because they may be focused on something completely different. Maybe other people say, "This is just a boring, bad *Sylphide*." I have no idea. I still follow what I believe, but I have no idea if there is any result. But I know that the dancers feel better, they feel good, so that's already something. And Tamara can use those things for the future, not yet but for the future. She's not a born sylph, but she really wanted to learn.

Violette Verdy

b. Pont l'Abbé, Brittany, 1933. Trained by Rousanne Sarkissian and Victor Gsovsky. Danced with Roland Petit's Ballets
des Champs-Elysées and Ballets de Paris and in the movie
Ballerina (1950). Performed with London Festival Ballet,
Ballet Rambert, Royal Ballet, joined American Ballet Theatre
1957, New York City Ballet 1958–76. Artistic director Paris
Opéra Ballet 1977–80, Boston Ballet 1980–84. Teaching Associate with New York City Ballet 1984–95. Professor of
Music (Ballet) at the University of Indiana School of Music
since 1996 and an independent teacher worldwide.

AFTER ROUSANNE, Victor Gsovsky was my second, most important teacher. He's mostly known for *Grand Pas Classique*, which is of course the ballet one remembers. He did many
others, and they were very interesting, some of the choreography
was wonderful. But he was more of a ballet master-choreographer.
Do you know that particular category, that is more ballet-master
related?

Victor was very tall, very thin, quite an alcoholic, unfortunately, mostly beer. He was mildly drunk most of every day, because he had never found peace with what probably was
homosexuality. At the time it was not really mentioned. You did
not insult people of great artistic caliber by analyzing what sort of
sex they were. It wasn't done in those days, and it was more secre-
tive than it is now. But probably that's what it was, and also some
unfulfilled dream, certainly, about himself as an artist. He had been
educated in Russia but slightly outside of the main school, either

because he started too late or physically he didn't qualify to be a regular dancer. But because of that he had studied with more people. I remember him mentioning a Jewish teacher of great importance who was an extraordinary mime teacher, and he might have gone to [Lydia] Nelidova, who was [Vera] Nemtchinova's teacher too. Then he went to Germany and opened in Berlin the first major, important ballet school with his wife, Tatiana Gsovsky. I got to him when he was the ballet master for Roland Petit at Ballets des Champs-Elysées. He was teaching every day, he was choreographing also some things, and generally speaking taking care of some of the more classical excerpts. We had *la divertissement* from *Sleeping Beauty*, we had little classical things, and he would choreograph wonderful little pieces.

Fantastic teacher. Musical phrasing, lyricism . . . I think probably he was a musician. Phrasing of expression and feeling . . . maybe a little too stylized, I realize now, but with a life, a feeling, that is hard to duplicate. He taught me phrasing and he had in his teaching a much more lyrical aspect than Rousanne. They always said [Olga] Spessivtseva was the soul, Pavlova was the heart, Karsavina was the intellect, and Trefilova was the book. [Vera] Trefilova was absolutely academic—proportions, size, measure, the letter, the form. So because of her, Rousanne was the same. Gsovsky was expression, the phantasmagoric, the personal fantasy and creativity and originality, phrasing with little ritards, rubatos and then devastating bursts of speed.

So. One of the great things that happened was that Victor said, "I have some free time. I'm going to take you in a studio with my pianist every day—you can pay the pianist, you don't have to pay me, I'll do it for free—and I'm going to teach you all the classics privately. You won't have a partner, so you won't be able to learn the pas de deux really, but I'll show you some of the things from them." This was after my big movie, *Ballerina*, so I had the money to pay them, and I think I was out of Champs-Elysées by then so I had the time to do it. He offered to do this because, together with Rousanne, they were thinking of my future, what to do with me, not to lose any time. And also they felt that nobody else would be qualified to do it, so they'd better do it and get to it soon.

He did *Coppélia. Sleeping Beauty. Swan Lake.* And most importantly, a *Giselle* with, in particular, a mad scene totally different from anyone else, and I will tell you why. As I said, Victor was a great alcoholic. He had periods of despair when he drank more and periods when he was almost sober—thank God, he was almost sober during those times and he was able to make a little bit more sense. Otherwise, it was very emotional and sometimes very unpleasant, because he would scream and get annoyed and impatient. Having had health problems also, he had somewhere along the line lost one eye. It had like a cataract, very hazy and slightly off-kilter, looking somewhere else. Not completely blind, I don't think—I never dared to ask. It's too late now, they're all gone, but I was paralyzed with respect in those days and you didn't ask.

So anyway. He was a smoker, naturally, besides drinking, and his hand would tremble as he smoked. And he taught me a mad scene which, instead of the usual general agitation that you see, had only moments of agitation but mostly an absolutely catatonic quality. Totally catatonic, like gone into another, internal world and alienated from the outside world. And for this he literally adopted one of the positions he had himself. Instead of being normal, I would have one arm hanging but the other one bent and pulled up tight beside me, with the hand totally abandoned. And some unnatural body position also, and walking totally aimlessly. Just abnormal gestures, and at the same time a little like the positions of people who are a little bit retarded or damaged. It was absolutely incredible, and I remember it very well.

If I had done the movie I was 16 by then, and I completely understood what he was doing with me. And certain things he showed me in *Swan Lake* were also incredible. He would talk about Tchaikovsky . . . Now I understand why he loved Tchaikovsky so much, because there was that story of homosexuality rampant and the idea of some sort of ideal that he tried to reach but never realized. And the perpetual longing and seeking that ends in despair, regret or noble resignation. I can't tell you how much of the Russian spirit I got from these people.

I didn't know then when I would perform those roles. I was doing this work with the same idea that my mother and Mme. Rousanne had always given me: you first do what is right, and then you will be used. You will be found, you will be needed, you will be recognized, you will have your chance, if you are equipped. I was doing my homework, and I've never stopped doing my homework.

I believe that once you learn to work well on even a small role, you know forever that everything deserves to be worked on in great depth. You have to consider all aspects—the style, the content, the values, the contrast—to make it interesting. If you have the music, you consider the musicality of it and how to use instruments in the orchestra for punctuation. Certain gestures, if they are well written on the music, like with Balanchine obviously, will have either the legato aspect of a violin or the more staccato aspect of a piano or the lightness and the delicacy of a lute. You reflect that in your body because you want to cut facets and to scintillate, and you want to . . . like salt and pepper—it's seasonings—paprika, garlic, curry, whatever. So I learned that if you work on everything that is at hand, you begin to develop all aspects in presenting yourself.

Then when I got to the story ballets that I did with Roland Petit, like his *Carmen*, *Le Loup*, *Beautiful Widow*, *Lady in the Ice*, it was wonderful to transform yourself into what you thought that character should be. And also, I needed help and I received it. I'll never forget my mother telling me, "Violette, when you discover that your husband is in fact a beast, a *wolf* of all beasts, you don't just back up lightly, nimbly, like a little girl in a park or a little dancer. That's not the time to do that. Your legs get cemented in the floor, heavy, and you stumble back, because your legs refuse to even move. That's how you do it when you're horrified and terrified." My mother said that. She knew. So everywhere I learned something.

And the wonderful aspects of doing those roles . . . Even with Balanchine I never really had to lose those compositions completely. Only they were reduced to a vitamin pill, in a way. Instead of a meal, with a fork, a knife, and a spoon and a piece of bread to sponge up the sauce, what you ended up with was health pills that you swallowed quickly, by themselves, all crunched down. But symbolically . . . Choreography is nothing other than symbols, and with Balanchine, even if it was more symbolic, it was all there if you knew what it meant. If you had had the full meal, you could tell what the modern meal was. In Balanchine's words, "You put a woman onstage, you already have a drama." It's true. There isn't one minute of exchange with a partner, for instance, or with other dancers that is not in itself already a divine play. It's the dance of Shiva, you know, it's life.

Style is a different question than content, really. Balanchine saw that with the Americans, who did not have as much of a past as the Europeans and are not burdened by habits or prejudice or biased with style. They're more virgin in their energy and more ready to take in and learn, in a way. And he went to town with that, filling them up with anything he wanted to experiment with, and they just went along with it. They didn't interfere with it—they didn't have anything to interfere with. You know, they didn't say, "This is not the style. My teacher says . . . blah, blah." Balanchine used to say, "You can make café and you can make café au lait, but once you've done au lait you can't remove au lait and still have café noir." You can't take them apart again. With dance, in a way he felt that it was better to come in clean, like a page on which you can write.

Style is a fragile question, because style reflects so-called civilization, the fermentation of it, the gaminess or decadence of it sometimes. Style is related to fashion, it's a nice thing to have, but it's not taste. If you don't have taste, I don't know if you can have style. It's more elusive, more temporary, more impermanent, it's more related to trends . . . style is a moving field, moving sand. It can be reproduced but it doesn't always necessarily reflect something that is present or actual, so it has to be done for itself, as a demonstration. It's like yoga. Yoga is not just a collection of exercises—it's a way of considering life.

You can reproduce styles, but it would be nice to put people in the mood of it, like to explain how you go about it and why it became that way. It's nice in context and historically it's interesting, and it can be done. There are enough people who still know it to be able to help with it, and the dancers can learn it. For some people it will strike a chord of recognition somewhere in their souls. We have a lot of old souls sometimes with dancers—you see someone that you think is a modern kid, and all of a sudden they're entrancing in something Romantic.

Of course, the old ballets are still alive, they always will be, in my opinion. The form should change a little bit now, I think. One will have to rediscover what it really is about and make less of a Walt Disney pageant out of it, because they tend with those big ballets, especially *Beauty*, to make a pageant, opulence and the court. Everybody wants to see that because not everybody has it, you know, richer times, maharajahs and kings. But the thing is, that's not only what there is to it. There's also what it really means and the development of the roles. The Lilac Fairy, being the guru, instructs the prince. He doesn't know what he is in for—she knows. And the whole idea of the kiss, which of course enlightens everything, because love is the one light in the world. And you get out of that sleep, which is a funny ignorance, and 100 years, which means eternity—you come out of it, boom. In a way, it could get completely undressed and reconsidered, but then somebody would have to write a new music for it, and I don't know if people are ready to go back to real music to do a real subject like that.

But people still want to see *Swan Lake*, *Giselle* and *Beauty*. And *The Nutcracker* . . . the growing up of Marie, with her good bourgeois parents, and Drosselmeyer, the mystery, a bit dark here and there but not that bad. In fact, he's really good and he knows what he's doing, and he brings her through her dreams to adulthood, represented in its ideal aspect by Sugar Plum Fairy, who is the best possible realization of adulthood when it works. Marie wants to be that grown-up lady, in spite of her wonderful parents, who are lovely and doing a nice job but they can't do that for her. It has to be a Drosselmeyer, who's more of a guru than her parents can be, coming in to do it for her. *Nutcracker* works because of that. Of course it works.

And *Giselle* is about love and the love of dance that overcomes death. Why does *Giselle* work so well? It's not just because of the love of Giselle and Albrecht, who love to dance. The protection they get from their love for each other and their love of dance is bigger than death and bigger than the negative energy and destructive force of the Wilis. Get back to the myths—you get everything you need from that stuff.

It's a shame that I'm not asked to coach, because this is probably my best thing. Of course I'm getting older and it'll be harder later, but I can still do it, especially because I X-ray people so fast when they begin to dance that I know exactly what they need for that role. I love to coach, it's my natural function. And if I would qualify myself as a teacher, I'm as much a coach as I am a teacher. Even with plain teaching I will venture a certain amount of coaching, because it's a deeper relation with the person.

When I came back to New York City Ballet, they asked me to do a little bit of helping with one or two dancers. Those were the days when Kyra Nichols had said, "I want no coaching from anybody. I don't believe in coaching." I never had a chance to talk to her about it and find out why. Apparently she thought that coaching was imposing on you, in spite of who you are, the idea that another person has of the role. But of course coaching is the role and the person and how can the two be made into one achievement, the best possible realization for that person and for that role. That's coaching. The role is there to tell you what's needed, and you take the person in complete consideration, even more than with respect, and you dig out unknown resources to develop with the role.

But anyway, it became a philosophy in the New York City Ballet: no coaching. With me what happened was, 'Oh, she's too much of a perfectionist'—that was another rumor I heard. So I was not allowed to coach there anymore, and nobody was allowed to coach, for that matter. Which is why everybody got so frustrated. So. The ballet mistresses then came to us—because they all are our friends and they're doing a great job—and they said, "Listen, just for the record, just tell me what you used to do here." And then they would go and do it, so they have developed a little more in their coaching because they've really been put in charge. In fact it's nice for them, because they've had to become coaches.

With Balanchine, it was like bel canto, *bella danza*—Mim Rambert said that one day, it's such a beautiful, coined phrase. He wanted the integrity of the choreography and the beautiful execution first and above all. It already spoke for itself if you did that. He always told me, "You can't get rid of people. You cannot. People will never change and they are who they are. And that's very nice, I want that. But I don't want it too soon. I want the steps first." Clean choreography, first the steps. Then he said, "The only thing is, sometimes I can trick people, to show what I really want to see from them. Whether they know it or not, I can trick them. I know how to do it." And then he would allow you more. But once I rehearsed something and I got the point very quickly. I thought, 'Oh, this is divine. I know what this animal is. Oh, là là,' and he said, "Darling, no smooching." Already he could see it coming.

Aurora is the epitome of the role where you can think of doing it that way, steps first. However, Odette? No—being a romantic, extravagant role, that's not enough. But Aurora is very impersonal. The greater it gets, the more impersonal in some ways it gets, I mean, impersonal of the person who is dancing it. That person must not impose her way of dancing. But where she can talk her head off, without interfering personally, is . . . Let's talk about Aurora. Who is Aurora? What does Aurora have to convey? At first, the purity, the happiness of a young, innocent woman, the respect she has for her parents, the way she behaves with princes—because if you are a princess, you don't jump on the guy. You know, you stay at a distance and you're shy. You wait for your orders. There are all those things. In the vision, she suggests what womanhood could be. She is not a seductress, but she makes the prince mad with desire because of the kind of womanhood she represents, as expressed in its platonic achievement, at its best. Then when she becomes a real woman and a real queen and she's married, there is the release and the relaxation and the generosity to her subjects and to the world. If I were coaching Aurora I would say all that. Not only that, I could tell you when in the music some of those things can be seen. If you listen to the score, Aurora is expressed by a violin solo, so you usually have a little concerto for violin when Aurora dances. There is a tenderness, a joy, you have all those delicious ripples of happiness, little laughs, I mean, millions of things you can talk about—it's in the score. But nobody asks me to do this.

Coaching is now a function of politics and money. I go to the Royal Ballet, I stay five or six weeks, I do one little class in the morning. My contract says that I should be available to coach for the company and that I should be available to teach in the school sometimes. Fine. In the company . . . Because there was *Ballet Imperial* and Leanne Benjamin insisted on having me for two rehearsals, I did two rehearsals. Because Viviana [Durante] was doing the Nureyev version of *Sleeping Beauty* in Milan and there was nobody who had time to coach her, I was able to coach her. But the rest of the day, I do one class in the morning and that's it. So it's like another New York City Ballet for me: I'm there and I don't do anything.

In Paris, they use me. They're going to kill me there a little bit, really, because when they ask you to come specifically . . . The French work very hard and very deeply on the roles. They like to know everything about them—they always have and they're still doing it. There's a tradition of coaching at the Paris Opéra, and all the older ballerinas coach. They have people that coach even privately, outside of the regular classes, not only for technique but for the roles. And they prepare. Like when [Dominique] Khalfouni did her first *Giselle*, she went to Chauviré for weeks and learned the whole of it, all the details, everything, the hair, how to do the flowers . . . Chauviré chose the costume for her, the flowers, everything. Like Ulanova and the Russians.

Irina Kolpakova

b. Leningrad, 1933. Studied at Leningrad Choreographic School, one of Vaganova's last pupils, and graduated in 1951 into the Kirov Ballet. Principal ballerina until her retirement in 1987, when she joined American Ballet Theatre as guest teacher and coach. Appointed ballet master ABT in 1990 and now also works with Ballet Internationale in Indianapolis.

WHY DO I CONTINUE WITH DANCING? I don't know what else I can do. There's nothing else I can do. I only know on the stage you can be absolutely free. You never can be free in your life, or in our life in Russia. It's always some pressure . . . We cannot do this, we cannot say this, we cannot go there, you cannot meet somebody. But when I come on the stage, nobody can take me offstage or stop me, nobody.

And for me it wasn't difficult. When the teacher said, "Turn out your leg," I turned out. When she said, "Hold your body stronger," I held. "Jump!"—I jumped. When Vaganova taught us how to make our arms, how to make transitions, I always tried to do it. I understood it and I did it. You couldn't have not understood her, because she wouldn't release you, she wouldn't let you go until you had understood her. And she only said, "That's it." She never said, "Good." I don't remember when she ever said, "Good."

She taught us transitions. She taught us how to live in each movement but to live as if it were real life. We couldn't do only steps—we had to move from one transition to another. We had to feel the phrasing of the music. We could never just do the movement and run away, no. We had to move to another movement, and from that movement to the next. And to finish the phrase and begin it. It was life on the stage and it has to be this way, but everybody understands that it is not always this way with everybody today. We had to feel our entire body, beginning with the tips of our fingers, because we speak with fingers on the stage, together with eyes, neck, with the face and legs as well. How you turn your head. How you hold your torso when you enter as a princess or as Cinderella as opposed to entering as a servant. All of that is important, and that's what she taught us.

And this is why I can't watch classical English ballets. All they do is hold their pose and keep on holding it, and that's it. And nothing moves. I just watched the Kshessinska pas de deux [in *Anastasia*]. What is this Kshessinska pas de deux? Who was [Matilda] Kshessinska? The greatest ballerina, the greatest woman. I came to watch from the wings, because I can't bear to watch the ballet from out front anymore, and Irina Dvorovenko, who danced that pas de deux today, asked me, "How was it?" I said, "Just hold your back better. That was simply your mistake. And I can't tell you anything more—there's nothing more in it." It's impossible to dance—she has no material. I can only imagine how Kshessinska appeared on the stage when the tsar's entire court was in the royal box, how she entered, how she went away, and there isn't the possibility in this choreography to express anything.

I think Dvorovenko knows who Kshessinska was, but not the Americans. There's a book about [Tsar] Nicholas and [Tsarina] Alexandra, with photographs, and all the American ballerinas told me they had read this book. But as for Kshessinska, the question is a little more complicated. They don't have the history of ballet— how could they know? We studied everything. When I was there it was simply the Vaganova school. Now it's the Vaganova Academy—just imagine what they study there . . . unless something's been eliminated. They've already eliminated piano. It's optional now, it used to be a requirement.

I was very lucky. I had wonderful teachers in school and in the theatre. All my teachers were excellent. Everybody knows only Vaganova, but before Vaganova I had the best teachers in the school, Basarova, Nadezhda Pavlovna Basarova, [Lydia] Tuntina . . . All were wonderful, and more than that, they also brought us up. I remember that I was reproved in school . . . I was leaning against the wall, and a teacher was passing by, and I said, "Hello," while still leaning against the wall. I was so reproved—I was told first, "Take your back off the wall, stand on your feet, and then say hello to me." Here, no-body says hello to you. I don't know how they were brought up by their parents. In Indianapolis we now teach all the girls and boys to do a *révérence* to greet someone in school, because they all run like children. When somebody new comes to ABT . . . I take rehearsals, but there are a lot of people who I don't know personally, and you wait to see when they will greet you. When I come in the studio, I al-ways say hello first, but if somebody passes by, he'll never say hello. For me that's strange, but that's not the point. The point is how they enter the stage, how they hold themselves, how they stand onstage. In America you can't touch children, you can't say anything to them, otherwise they will be depressed. But it's all together. You ask why and how, but it all comes from the same thing. It's all together.

When there is no history of ballet . . . Three or four years ago, here at ABT, we did the last act of *Raymonda*, [Fernando] Bujones' production, and somebody asked, "What's the hero's name?" "Jean de Brienne." "Oh, how nice. What a wonderful name." But, "Who was Jean de Brienne? Why is he dressed in this way?" No-body asked this—just "What is his name?" All the movements that he made had no resemblance to a medieval knight, and he was dressed differently in this production. In our Kirov production, he made an entrance in a costume of chain mail, you could immedi-ately understand who he was.

There's just not enough education now. If they're dedicating their lives to ballet, they need to study in a school that will give them a well-rounded education. That includes culture, art, music . . . various arts, not just the history of ballet. At school we had the decorative arts, painting, the history of theatre. And I also graduated from the ballet master faculty of the Leningrad conservatory. I studied there for five years. I don't even understand how I could do it—it was so hard that it's just unbelievable. This was when I was already a balle-rina. I was the oldest student in the conservatory, I graduated when I was 49 years old. Why do it? It was interesting. Do you think you never have to learn more just because you are a ballerina? No, it was interesting because we continued to study history of music and scores . . . I never saw an orchestral score before the conservatory, I never understood how it worked. Then the history of the theatre was so interesting. They taught us history of theatre in school as well, but we were fools and it went in one ear and out the other. This time around we were more conscious of it. And also painting and art, so when we had tours in Italy, in Florence and Venice, we'd have a lecture and then go to the museum. It was absolutely amazing. We saw it with completely different eyes.

At first, when I was in school, we had a wonderful artistic supervisor, Nikolai Pavlovich Ivanovski, and he taught historical dancing, polkas, gavottes, polonaises and so forth. I was probably 12 then. And then, in the graduation performance, we danced acts from *Sleeping Beauty*, and I was Aurora and Florine. As Florine I danced the whole act, and as Aurora part of the act. He called us to his office—this was the artistic supervisor of the school, not the director of the company—and he began to explain to us what *Sleeping Beauty* is. We had studied it in the history of ballet, but he explained Princess Florine, the Bluebird, the Puss in Boots, the Cat, Red Riding Hood and all the characters. And he asked us, "Do you think that all of these characters . . . Are they real? Is it a real cat? Is it a real puss in boots? A real bluebird?" This was before the performance, of course before. After is too late. We were just sitting there listening, with our eyes wide, waiting to hear what he would say. "When you enter the stage in this performance you must never forget that you are members of the court, members of the king's retinue and the princess's, you are her ladies-in-waiting. You are also of high rank yourself, not from the street or from the village. You have made a present for her—you've dressed up, it's like a half-masquerade, and that's your gift for her wedding. You give this wonderful performance in the court—imagine how you must behave and how you must look. The cats . . . they wear costumes, they have tails and animal heads, but these are details. They are still courtiers and they are raised in this way."

When I saw the English *Sleeping Beauty* and someone came out as the Bluebird, flapping her wings desperately . . . oh, my God! Crazy. For me that's not acceptable—she is playing a princess! Why didn't they read the fairy tales? There are wonderful fairy tales about each story. Princess Florine was sitting in the tower and waiting for the Bluebird, who was also an enchanted prince, and he flew to her . . . These are the fairy tales that you have to know, then you will behave differently.

When I was a student I watched everybody and I loved everybody. When anyone came on the stage, I gasped, "Oh, my God." Everything, everybody, was like a miracle in that time. And now . . . it's different now. I will tell you what it was like. When I left the school, then I had other experiences. We were always changing the director of the ballet, but when [Fedor] Lopukhov came was when I could do anything. Then [Konstantin] Sergeyev came. Then Sergeyev left. Then again Lopukhov came for two years, and I was really happy. One day he stopped me in the corridor and asked, "So, Irina, have you already been to the Hermitage? And have you already seen the French art section in the Hermitage?" I held my breath and I said, "I haven't." "But how will you dance? You must see how they were dressed, what poses they had, how they stood. You must go and see the French artists. You have to go." The very next day I ran to the Hermitage. And that's how we were brought up.

Lopukhov said, "You will work with Lukom." Elena Lukom, she was wonderful. I rehearsed with her *Cinderella*, *Sleeping Beauty*, *Raymonda*, all with Lukom, she prepared them with me. The process was wonderful. She had eyes like this, big blue eyes, and . . . To be honest, I was very well prepared at school. After Vaganova I had five, the highest mark. By well prepared I mean classical positions, correct, hands, I felt the poses, how to pose . . . Vaganova, it's Vaganova, all from her. But Lukom . . . Lukom was wonderful, but she was strange, she never taught us really. If on my pirouettes I was falling to the right, her comment would be, "Hold your left side and go forward." She was always telling us how they used to dance in the old days. "The way we used to dance *Sleeping Beauty*, the first entrance, those small, little leaps . . . We entered and we saw our admirers in the audience and we would respond as if we were greeting them. And then for the second diagonal we were already leaping." She used to say, "A small jump and then a greeting, another small jump and another greeting, and then a big jump." And her advice for the variation was, "You make a greeting to one of your suitors, say hello to him, and then turn to the other side and look at your mama, then to the second one and back to the mother." And there is nothing further to be explained. The movements fit together wonderfully.

Lukom was showing it the same way I am, with the head and the eyes and "Look there." I'm not really imitating—I feel her sensation, from how she was showing it and how she was telling about it. You had to see her eyes—it was just incredible. And then she was telling us how much she liked to dance and how much she liked kissing the grand princes, for example after a concert in Pavlovsk, when they were walking with the grand dukes. We thought this was wonderful. This was about her own life, but it is life on the stage too, it is life. And then you begin to realize that this movement belongs to you, you are in it, you perform it. The movement comes to you, and you feel how good it is.

It was good fortune that it was Lukom, and I don't want to think what would have been if it was somebody else. I can tell you about another person, Tatiana Mikhailovna Vicheslova. Do you know this name? Fantastic dancer, very dramatic. Vicheslova and Ulanova studied in the same class. I worked with her on *Giselle* and a lot of modern ballets—there was a very good ballet, Igor Belsky's *The Shore of Hope*—and in [*The Fountain of*] *Bakhchisarai* I also worked with her. She was absolutely different from Lukom. She was really dramatic. She was always telling me that it was not sufficient, and I was always crying in rehearsal. I prepared *Romeo and Juliet* with her, and she said, "Not enough, not dramatic enough." Her eyes were also so expressive. She was completely wonderful, completely different. She drove me to despair. I kept on saying, "I can't stand any more, I can't do any more." "You can. You're dancing for the first row, but you've got to dance for the last row." All I heard was "not enough," so I always had to find something more.

When Grigorovich came . . . I prepared many roles with Lukom, but Grigorovich was the one who wanted me to work with Vicheslova. It was decided very oddly, it was complicated. It's complex and not even important. What's important is the fact that Vicheslova helped me a lot. She made me move—I had the poses, but not the movement. She taught me to feel the entire body, to feel how it all goes. It's very difficult. I prepared *Bakhchisarai* with my husband [Vladilen Semyonov] and with Seva Oukhov, who called his wife [Galina Kirillova] to show me how to cry in the harem, because I didn't feel the freedom of how the gestures should go. When I worked with Vicheslova, we worked on *Stone Flower*, and [the designer, Simon] Virsaladze was there. We went together to museums, we walked along the Neva together . . . We met at Vicheslova's house, discussing, working, discussing, and he showed us old books with pictures. The whole group worked together on that piece, and it was such an interesting time, incredible. Because Grigorovich was directing this ballet, he was also with us. Working together made us closer, united us. It's natural. Of course.

Life is different now, the life of an American company is different. They have a two-month season where they rush like crazy. We danced year-round, and we would prepare a ballet for months. At the same time we were already performing other ballets, and during our free time we would prepare this new one and then sometimes transfer it to the next season. Here, they don't have any free time— they prepare everything at the same time, in one moment, and they dance everything at once. A ballet will disappear and in two or three years it will return again. The dancers will be remembering it and they will be the same as before, because again there is no time, there is no opportunity to live it or to digest it. But we danced something year after year, and gradually something in you became mature and your image of it changed. It's not interesting to appear mechanical, and we were always taught not to be mechanical dolls. If you go on moving mechanically every year, you become a mechanical doll. You will be repeating the same movements in the same way, and they will become mechanized. But you must always feel something or try all the time to bring something different.

In the Kirov Theatre those dancers who danced well before are working now. Moiseyeva and Kurgapkina, the students of Vaganova, still work there. [Gabriela] Komleva, although she wasn't a student of Vaganova, still had a good teacher, [Vera] Kostrovitskaya. Chenchikova and Lubov Kunakova are now starting to rehearse with others. In Russia, I began to coach very early, while I was still dancing all my roles, and I introduced young dancers to all my ballets, and I had a lot of them! I probably started in '71, and I stopped dancing in '87, I stopped quite late. At that time I coached a lot of young people. But it was easier in Russia, because there was more time and it was calmer. I rehearsed with all our leading ballerinas. Why did I do it? Because it was interesting, and because of the circumstances— people needed help, and they asked me for help. And it was easy for me to be in the theatre, because people didn't look at me as if . . . I gave everything to them that I could, and I took their concerns very much to heart. And when they were dancing my parts, they didn't feel that they were taking them away from me. For all of the ballets that I danced, I rehearsed with Chenchikova, Kunakova, with Larissa Lezhnina . . . the latest was [Tatiana] Terekhova.

It's very interesting to do this. *I* would learn from them. They were the next generation. Sometimes they moved differently . . . I learned from many of them, and I could take something for myself from them and they from me. You can't just teach how you did it. You must also look at their individualities and bring that from them. I left the stage quite easily. When I was asked, "Do you want to continue?" I said, "No, it's normal." It was without any tragedy, no drama, nothing, because it was a natural transition. And so when Misha [Baryshnikov] invited me here [to ABT] . . . I don't know about resting. I would probably do it now. But then . . . not yet.

I like the work, but of course it's very difficult, and it's difficult here. The problem here is the school, their schooling, of course. They are missing . . . the cantilena. They don't even know what the word means. No, I think they know, but . . . As we studied the history and the theory of music, we learned about all these things—legato, cantilena, staccato—and we could feel how they go in music and in dance as well. Now the American dancers are better, because at least they don't deny the Russian school. I think it's a big progress. They love us now, because the silhouettes and the movements are natural. A normal human being can't sit still all the time and not move to express himself. In the beginning, when I first came here to ABT, they all turned to the English school, and not just here but in Australia. Arabesque? Straight. But the idea of stretching an arabesque somewhere? Arabesque is the most beautiful thing there can be in ballet and the most impressive. It is aiming incredibly.

My responsibility is that in different ballets they should feel different styles, they should distinguish between one style and another. They must know what is a Romantic ballet, a post-Romantic ballet, and the difference between *La Sylphide* and *Les Sylphides*, in style, and *Giselle* and *Sleeping Beauty* and *Raymonda*. That is my job, and of course the schooling must be good, the cantilena which is present in the Russian school and, as we say, the soul. They must try to express themselves and feel—here, they just mechanically repeat the steps. What I call the school is the gestures, the mime, the poses of the body, the steps—it expresses the state, it expresses the character. Either you will be standing one way or you will be standing another way. And arms—either the arms will be stiff or the arms will be soft. That's also the character.

They are positive toward me, I think, all of them, even those who do not work with me. I can see the influence our school makes on them—not me, not my training, but our school. Not me—it is our school. But it's really difficult. There is never enough time to talk with them, not about only ballet steps but about life around. They're always running, between one studio and another studio, and between a lot of ballets. There's not enough time and not enough studios. Other people need to work. If there are six Giselles, six or seven, and

Bayadère the same number . . . It's not me who chooses who I work with, and I don't know how it is decided—usually it is the director.

Sometimes in the studio you think, 'God, what am I doing?' because you want to see the result immediately, and a good result that everybody would be able to see is the result that you wanted. I always wanted this, because sometimes it's very difficult to watch ballet. I'm doing everything that I can—it doesn't matter how—because I cannot bear to watch dead ballet, wooden ballets and dead ballerinas. If I heard from my teacher, "Never enough," not only from my teacher but from everyone in Leningrad, "Never, never enough," so I want to let these dancers know that it's never enough.

I enjoy Durante in *Giselle*, because she has very piercing lines, and I think it was interesting for her to touch the Russian school a little. It was also very interesting for me to work with her, because she was very responsive and she's not afraid. She had not a lot of rehearsal but she tried, and that's wonderful. And it's always interesting for a normal artist—if you're afraid, you're not an artist. Why be afraid? You can come back and do it again. What's the problem?

The ballet only exists for the audience, so if the audience is happy, then everything's fine! No, not really. But it's not that bad now. If the audience needs to come to the theatre and they're happy being in the theatre, it's not so bad. If it were too bad, they simply wouldn't come. Bad would be if they didn't come, if they didn't need it at all. As for educating the audience, you need a long time.

Now there is not classical ballet only, because there are a lot of talented modern choreographers, their ballets can go together with the classics, and the classics are changing for the better. It's wonderful, because the ballet cannot develop without modern ballets. It would turn into a museum and die. All these modern ballets—*Stone Flower*, *Legend of Love*, all Grigorovich's ballets, and Belsky's, *The Shore of Hope*—they develop dancers, but the classical ballets must keep the classical form. It must all go together, as it goes in American Ballet Theatre, to support the dancers and what's living inside of them. It's a very good company, a great repertoire, Ashton ballets, Tudor ballets, Agnes de Mille ballets, Kylián ballets, Mats Ek, Paul Taylor . . . Since I came here, all of these ballets were here or they came here. I'm always learning. At the ballet I see dancers who work with other people, not with me, and I'm always learning if I see something different. It's not interesting to close your eyes, close your breath and your mind. And I like this company more than New York City Ballet, because the novelties they bring in there do not compare to what Balanchine did, and I'm afraid that Balanchine will wilt in their company.

We went back to Russia, but I don't think we would go back to work with the Kirov Theatre. Because [my husband] Vladek worked there 39 years and I worked in the Kirov Theatre for 36 years, and it's enough. Now I'm coaching in Indiana—it is a very small company—and my husband is teaching class. There are a lot of Russians there and a Russian school. The director of the company, Eldar Aliev, is Russian; he worked with my husband in our theatre. The company's name is Ballet Internationale, because in America if you are Russian you can call it international. I'm doing the same work there and the responsibility is the same, but it's me, my husband, Aliev . . . we have one direction. The dancers like it, and I'm happy there, I don't know why. Somebody tells me, "You're crazy, going to Indianapolis from New York, from ABT," but life is life, and different things happen.

In the Studio

*I*T HAPPENS ALL THE TIME. Someone makes a comment in passing, nothing special, and without warning all the old truths in your head shift like the colored stones in a kaleidoscope and drop into new configurations. It happened to me like this: I was sitting in the canteen of the Royal Theatre in Copenhagen, chatting amiably with a young man from the School of American Ballet who had come to the Royal Danish Ballet for a few weeks as part of a regular student exchange program. He told me he was having a very good time, learning a lot, making friends, and that he was fairly confident a New York City Ballet contract would be waiting for him when he got home.

"Let's say you could take a month off," I suggested, "and do anything you wanted without jeopardizing your health or your future. What would you do?" Before the question was out of my mouth, he answered, "I'd go to Colorado and climb mountains. I really love it out there." The kaleidoscope started to turn, but I ignored it. "What about dancing? Isn't there something new you'd like to try?" "Nope," he grinned. "I'd much rather climb mountains."

His cheerful certainty has bounced around in my mind ever since, and I realize now that whenever I think about it I automatically make excuses for him. 'He wasn't even a professional yet,' I tell myself, 'he was only a kid. And if he could win a contract like that, straight out of SAB, he'd probably done nothing but dance for years. So he needed a break, and he deserved one.' But my soothing, rational arguments don't convince me of anything, and they don't prevent me from replaying the conversation over and over again, almost as if I'm trying to translate it into terms I can understand, because his response gave

367

my notions a serious jolt. Before I talked to him I believed that dancers were insatiable, especially professional dancers, and that they never stopped learning about their art because they never stopped asking about it. After I talked to him, I wasn't so sure. I began to think my long-held conviction was obsolete or that maybe it hadn't been accurate in the first place. Perhaps the avid pursuit of perfection, which I had always assumed went hand in hand with an artist's job, was only a romantic illusion or a pipe dream for outsiders like me.

Not that I believed dancers tucked themselves voluntarily into a Möbius strip of class, rehearsal and performance, and never crawled out. I knew they had children and hobbies, that they listened to jazz and designed hats, and that they felt the same frustration, boredom and fatigue as anyone else who does the same work day after day. I understood that after they'd breathed a silent prayer of gratitude and relaxed into the security of steady employment, dancing wasn't all inspiration and curtain calls. Come ruptured ligaments or transit strikes, it was a job and a contractual obligation, even on the days when ambition was in short supply. But by the time I talked to that student in Denmark I had also talked to a lot of dancers, many of whom I met in class. Initially, around 1967, I went after work to the old Cunningham studio on Third Avenue. When I decided to return to ballet, where I'd started out 20 years earlier, some of Cunningham's dancers suggested I try Richard Thomas, with whom they studied; at his New York School of Ballet I eventually ran into members of Tharp's company, New York City Ballet, American Ballet Theatre and Eliot Feld's first troupe.

All these artists stood at the barre with amateurs like me, doing exactly the same exercises I was doing and hearing exactly the same corrections. That is the definition of an open class—anyone can come. Aside from the fact that I was working for a theatrical agent and dancing for my own satisfaction and they were professionals who danced for their living, there was absolutely no difference between us. We were in that room for the same reason, to learn what we could about dancing by following a certain set of instructions as exactly as possible, and our effort rendered us equal despite the conspicuous discrepancies in our ability. Certainly we were treated as equals, and to their eternal credit, the pros didn't laugh at the rest of us. They might not have noticed us, any more than you would notice a fly on the wall. They had work to do, and no swarm of flies, however ungainly, was likely to distract them.

The rest of us were naturally delighted by their presence and grateful that we didn't have to endure their ridicule—at least that's how I felt—and we scrutinized their every move in order to benefit from their example. Most of them could have gone through their daily ritual of warm-up and preparation by taking company class, free of charge, from a ballet master or the founder-choreographer of their troupe. Instead, for their own reasons, they had decided to come to a private school, which was open to any member of the public who wanted to hand over a few dollars and pull on a pair of tights, to study with a certain teacher.

What surprises me when I think about it now is that I wasn't surprised. I mean, I was surprised to find myself in such classy company, but finding professionals in that studio at 10:30 in the morning was nothing to write home about, because history and experience had already taught me that dancers studied forever. If you hung around after my class, you could see another gang of name performers in the next, more advanced one, which was taught by Thomas' wife, Barbara Fallis. Both teachers had been professional dancers who had sought out private teachers, who themselves had been professional dancers who had sought out private teachers, and back and back it went, in an intricately braided rope of respect and friendship, trust and daring, through all the generations who wanted to learn.

The first dance dictionary I knew and used was compiled single-handedly by a dance-loving scientist named G.B.L. Wilson and originally published in England in 1957. On the assumption that an artist's achievements cannot be separated from his lineage, it lists every dancer's teachers as part of his biography. I used to read the entries at random, and certain names reappeared with hypnotic regularity, tying the international miscellany of performers together like a silver wire binding a bouquet. Before I left the dancing school over the suburban barbershop, I had discovered Enrico Cecchetti and Nikolai Legat, whose influence spread so far during the 20th century that they seemed to represent matching sources of its pedagogic history. Cecchetti was born in the dressing room of an Italian theatre in 1850 and began teaching in 1890 in St. Petersburg's Imperial school, where his pupils included Pavlova, Preobrajenska, Egorova, Karsavina and Kshessinska, the most illustrious ballerinas of the day. After leaving Russia, he taught the entire Diaghilev company and opened a private school in London. Two of Diaghilev's dancers, Ninette de Valois and Marie Rambert, took it upon themselves to establish the art of ballet in

Britain and trained, in their turn, Frederick Ashton and Antony Tudor. Born in 1869, Nikolai Legat began teaching at the Imperial school twenty years later, when he inherited the ballerinas' Class of Perfection from his teacher, Christian Johansson, who had come to St. Petersburg via Stockholm and Copenhagen and introduced Russian dancers to the style of *his* teacher, August Bournonville. Legat's Class of Perfection attracted the cream of the Maryinsky ballet, including all the ballerinas and Nijinsky, as well as Michel Fokine and less-known dancers like Vaganova. As ballet master for Diaghilev, Legat taught Serge Lifar, later director of the Paris Opéra Ballet, and Alexandra Danilova, who for 25 years taught in New York at the School of American Ballet.

Now, follow me carefully. Cecchetti's pupil Lubov Egorova, who was ballerina of the Maryinsky and then of Diaghilev's *Sleeping Princess*, ran her own school in Paris from 1923 to 1968 and taught everyone from Alicia Markova to the *étoiles* of the Paris Opéra Ballet. Cecchetti's pupil Olga Preobrajenska became the director of the St. Petersburg school while still prima ballerina of the Maryinsky—her appointment shattered the rule that prohibited company members from teaching until they had performed for 25 years. Having opened her own school in Paris in 1924, she only closed it in 1960 when financial problems and bad health forced her into retirement. Her students over the decades ranged from Irina Baronova and Tamara Toumanova, the "baby ballerinas" of the 1930s, through Margot Fonteyn, who used to visit her several times a year, to an English dancer named Anna Northcote, whose classes in London drew British and foreign professionals from 1941 until 1980.

Got that? Now, think about Legat. Legat's pupil Agrippina Vaganova retired from the Maryinsky ballet in 1917 and developed into an authoritative pedagogue, who published her teaching method, *Fundamentals of the Classic Dance*, in 1934, only eight years after Cecchetti's method was formally organized and published as *A Manual of the Theory and Practice of Classical Theatrical Dancing*. The leading teacher of the Leningrad ballet school (formerly the St. Petersburg school) from 1919 to 1951, Vaganova molded exceptional ballerinas, Galina Ulanova and Irina Kolpakova among them, as well as lesser artists like Volkova, whose unremarkable performing career ended in 1943 when she began teaching in England. Having established her reputation in London, Volkova transported Vaganova's ideals to Milan and then, in 1952, to Copenhagen where she was named artistic adviser to the Royal Danish Ballet. Universally recognized as one of the most influential teachers in Europe, she made a particular impact on male dancers, from Nureyev, who headed straight for her class the moment he defected, to Erik Bruhn, Henning Kronstam, Peter Martins, Helgi Tomasson and Stanley Williams.

The links between generations and the paths that learning followed were so clear you could draw a map of influence by connecting the dots. A professional in Paris in 1933 could have taken class from Carlotta Brianza, who was the original Aurora in *The Sleeping Beauty*, or Carlotta Zambelli, formerly prima ballerina at the Paris Opéra, or Vera Trefilova, the first Aurora ever seen in England, who was a pupil of both Cecchetti and Legat. By 1929, Adolf Bolm was running a studio in Chicago—he had trained with Legat as a student and with Cecchetti as a professional—and Mikhail Mordkin, formerly Pavlova's partner, was teaching in New York. To provide his students with performing experience, in 1937 Mordkin organized them into a little company which, two years later, formed the nucleus of American Ballet Theatre.

An American friend of mine, once a member of American Ballet Theatre and now the director of a small troupe in France, remembers wandering down the side streets of that map of influence exactly as I had, gradually discovering where the major roads crossed. "I knew all about those dancers and their teachers even before I went to the School of American Ballet," she told me. "I read those books until they fell apart, and I pored over the pictures. We all did, we couldn't get enough of them. Beryl Grey's satin pointe shoes were the most beautiful things I could imagine." Of course, many young dancers couldn't have cared less about pointe shoes and wanted nothing to do with the rigid vocabulary of ballet, either when my friend was first dancing or when Diaghilev's death in 1929 hit that art like a rock hitting a window. As the fragments of the Ballets Russes shot off in all directions, dancers with different goals were studying at the Denishawn School in New York, founded by Ruth St. Denis and Ted Shawn, or signing up for the summer courses in the "Art of the Dance" offered by Doris Humphrey and Charles Weidman, or making their way to Dresden to enroll in Mary Wigman's school.

However, the map of continuity that fascinates me is largely a phenomenon of ballet, not of modern dance. If you switch from one teacher to another in the variegated discipline of modern dance, you ordinarily swap one technique or style for another at the same time. A Graham dancer, who was trained in Graham technique and has spent her life dancing the Graham repertory, will teach Graham technique. If you want to study Cunningham technique you go elsewhere, and the same applies to any vocabulary so specific to its creator's needs and imagination that it has been systematically structured, the better to teach it and to realize the choreography for which it was developed. In ballet, on the other hand, where technique prepares you for anything rather than for one thing, every teacher concentrates on the same basic vocabulary but in a different way. Whether or not a teacher follows a formal syllabus based on the systems devised by Cecchetti, Vaganova or Legat, the discrete elements are the same all over the world. Ask any student for a glissade, and you'll get a gliding transfer of weight from two feet to two feet. So wherever youngsters begin their training and whatever language they speak, by the time they are old enough to work professionally, they will have learned the same steps and achieved enough proficiency to produce them on demand. And that should be that—the dancer who can execute fouettés and soutenus no longer needs to go to class every day to learn how to turn. In any other profession, accounting, say, or law, once you qualify for your degree and hang out your shingle, your schooling is over. If you want to perfect old skills or acquire new ones later on, you do it on the job rather than in the classroom. But it's different for dancers, because going to class is not the same as learning how to dance, and an artist's education doesn't stop when his performing career begins.

The cellist Pablo Casals sat at the piano every morning and played a pair of Bach preludes and fugues, simply to discover something about Bach or about music or about himself as a musician. Long after any civilian would think a dancer has nothing left to learn, that dancer will make time for a certain teacher, either to strengthen his technique or to refine some aspect of his presentation or to weld mechanics and delivery in some way that will enhance his performance as he's never been able to enhance it before. To tune his instrument, he also has to manhandle it; simply maneuvering it through an average day of practice and rehearsal is asking for trouble—an American critic once likened it to Isaac Stern throwing his Stradivarius up in the air and hoping it wouldn't be too badly damaged when it came down. Balancing on the hairline crack between perfect execution and crippling risk, dancers resemble the circus clowns who tumble off galloping horses and lope away laughing. Only the most proficient riders need apply—anyone less capable and confident would probably break his neck. And then to use their instruments for some complex effect beyond bareback trickery, dancers need more than proficiency. Why study if you can already turn? On the day that Peter Martins, Mikhail Baryshnikov, Fernando Bujones, Helgi Tomasson and Rudolf Nureyev dropped into Stanley Williams' advanced men's class at the School of American Ballet, and Baryshnikov ended a friendly competition by whipping off 13 pirouettes, Williams acknowledged them mildly with the comment, "That's very nice, Misha. But you know . . . it's not ballct."

Anecdotes like that tend to fade out on the punch line so I don't know what happened next, but I would guess that all the men, superstars and teenagers alike, probably grinned, nodded and went back to work. Some of them would already have absorbed Williams' distinction, and some would never absorb it. Others would file it for future reference along with all the other comments and suggestions they had heard over the years and hoard it until the instant when their body or temperament needed that exact guidance. In that respect, artists are supremely selfish; if a correction or observation eventually helps you, it doesn't matter that it may not help anyone else, and it also doesn't matter where you got it. Even when the Imperial ballerinas were still alive and holding court in their shabby studios, serious dancers flocked to another group of teachers as well, whose stage careers had been considerably less brilliant and whose names were completely unknown to the public. Volkova probably heads the list, and few outside the dance community would have heard of Vaganova to this day if the St. Petersburg school hadn't changed its name in 1957 to the Vaganova Choreographic Institute. At that time, and even now, the New York audience had never heard of Margaret Craske, Valentina Pereyaslavec or Vladimir Dokoudovsky, who taught in Manhattan week in and week out. Professional dancers in Britain went to Errol Addison, Kathleen Crofton, Anna Northcote, George Goncharov and Phyllis Bedells—Ashton used to say, "Give me footwork, footwork. Go to Phyllis Bedells." Those in France returned faithfully to Mme. Rousanne, Mme. Nora and Serge Peretti; in Denmark, to Volkova.

All over America, tiny private studios were shaping dancers who arrived in New York fully prepared for any work that came their way. "When Royes [Fernandez] came from Leila Haller in New Orleans," Richard Thomas informed me, "he could do eight or ten pirouettes, with his hands curved in like this, like the handles of a sugar bowl—they do that in the French school. Oh, there were wonderful teachers everywhere: Mary Ann Wells in Seattle, Lillian

Cushing, [Marie] Bekefi, Mme. [Alexandra] Baldina in California, Eddie Caton, Edna McRae, Caird Leslie . . ." Dancers on the West Coast went to Theodore Kosloff or Marian Ladré; to Ernest Belcher, who taught Maria Tallchief, Rita Hayworth and Matt Mattox; or to Carmalita Maracci, another Belcher student, whose pupils over the years in Los Angeles included Agnes de Mille, Jerome Robbins, Allegra Kent and Cynthia Gregory. Once a tempestuous solo artist who performed with equally mesmerizing authority in pointe shoes, in bare feet and, for her Spanish choreography, in high heels, Maracci left the stage to teach full-time during the 1950s. According to de Mille, she had "the great pedagogic faculty of helping us each day to do one single thing we had not done before."

When ballet hit the big time in the 1960s and '70s and its stars' biographies reached a wider audience than balletomanes and dance students, the general public ran into the name of Natalia Dudinskaya, who was Natalia Makarova's mentor at the Kirov Ballet, where she taught the Class of Perfection from 1951 to 1970. Gelsey Kirkland's autobiography singled out two private teachers in New York, Maggie Black and David Howard, and every account of Nureyev's life and career focused briefly on Alexander Pushkin, his revered teacher in Leningrad, who also trained Baryshnikov. Now a permanent part of New York City Ballet history and an enigmatic figure in its expanding mythology, Stanley Williams was virtually invisible until the latter years of his life, and even the dancers who regularly attended his class couldn't always explain why he was so special. Many of them claimed they learned a lot from him despite his inherent reticence and the fact that his suggestions completely bewildered them; when a staff member asked him whether a journalist might watch class, Williams responded, "Do I have to talk? I talked yesterday." Every bit as taciturn, Pushkin was said to guide his students with two elementary corrections: "Don't fall" and "Get up." Nevertheless, as Baryshnikov remembered, "He was teaching you . . . how to look at the dance from your own perspective and be responsible and in command of your mind and your body . . . He knew very well you cannot explain. That was his strength."

At the opposite extreme, Volkova peppered her classes with such vivid images that her pupils are still quoting her today, nearly 30 years after her death. "Mme. Volkova was wonderful," Sorella Englund assured me with a smile. "She had the wonderful ability to use . . . sometimes very banal expressions, but still so clear and simple and beautiful. The opening of the hand was like saying 'Hello' and a port de bras backwards was 'Goodbye, my love.' So you had a motivation why you were practicing technique, and technique wasn't only technique—like bones, muscles, feet—but what you would say with it." Allegra Kent wrote that Maracci "called the room's long diagonal 'the bias.' With a word she altered my perception; the floor became fabric." Audrey de Vos, who taught in London in the '40s and '50s, was known for being equally articulate; "If you were on her wavelength," an English critic said to me, "you could benefit enormously from her. Some of her pupils worshiped the ground she walked on."

If a teacher can explain, reveal or inspire, the method he adopts makes no more difference to his students than the color of his shirt, provided they share some fundamental sympathy. The untutored have so much to learn they can learn it from nearly anyone, but for an educated professional the ideal teacher is like a romantic partner or a parent you get to choose yourself. Over the course of time your teacher will have to contend with your moods and care for your body. He will confront you when you are feeling miserable and gleeful, ambitious and bone-lazy. He will judge you leniently at best and fairly at worst, and as long as your intentions are honorable, even if you stumble every day he will always welcome you back, generously pardoning your mistakes and contriving fresh solutions to them. However splendid his reputation and however willingly you present yourself, you cannot make progress together unless you like him, respect him and trust him, because in the studio he is boss, conductor and traffic cop, your best buddy and your implacable enemy, the first to speak and the ultimate authority.

When an emperor still ruled Germany, military discipline was so strict that it was described with the phrase *kadaver gehorsam*, which roughly means "Even your cadaver must obey." For the sake of drama, novels and Hollywood movies give the impression that the same phrase still applies in the studio, though the regimented formality that once dominated companies and classrooms has vanished; most lessons now end with a round of applause rather than a silent ritual of bows and curtseys. Yet in order to clear his ego from the path of instruction, every dancer who enters a class sweeps his right to question, argue, protest or refuse behind the law of instant compliance. In theory, every teacher comes prepared to furnish those swept paths with his own experience and knowledge, and in exchange for obedience he assumes the initiative for everyone in the room. So taking class is like visiting the doctor. If you tell him your symptoms honestly, hiding nothing, and put yourself in his hands, he will examine you and treat whatever he believes is wrong with you as best he can, in an attempt to make you better. Both parties accept a share of the responsibility for the improvement they both crave, and while abject subservience may be as obsolete as chain mail, every teacher is still king in the studio and free to rule exactly as he pleases.

Pushkin gave a barre that lasted 22 minutes, no more, no less. Preobrajenska, who taught in five languages for three hours a day until she was nearly 90, screamed, shouted, stamped the floor and tore her hair to obtain the results she wanted. When she reduced a student to tears, which was not at all unusual, she would acknowledge the outburst by saying only, "Crying is good for you. Now start again." Cecchetti prodded his pupils' muscles and minds with a flexible malacca cane—he would rest it across his extended finger to illustrate the power of equilibrium over the body's balance. He taught for nine straight hours every day in his London studio, lunching on a cup of chocolate and a banana without interrupting the lesson, whistling his accompaniment so he could give corrections without having to stop the pianist, and rapping the floor with his cane to set the tempo. Equally self-sufficient, Christian Johansson accompanied his classes on a little pocket fiddle that he eventually bequeathed to Legat. To confound his students, he would speed or slow the music unexpectedly and drip water on the studio floor to tax them with a slippery surface. Infinitely wary of the surprises lurking in their future, he is said never to have repeated an *enchaînement* during the 30 years of his teaching career.

Errol Addison reigned over a studio so small that he refused to admit more than 21 students at a time; "If you're number 22," he'd say, "don't come in." Hans Brenaa brought a thermos to his private school in Copenhagen and sustained himself during class with occasional nips of scotch or port, and de Mille remembered Maracci chain-smoking while she taught, only stubbing out her cigarette when she stood up to demonstrate. Their students went right on working, because the results those teachers could produce in them easily outweighed all the smoke, curses, sarcasm and cryptic ambiguity.

The inventor of eurythmics, an influential system of rhythm training based on translating sound into movement, Emile Jaques-Dalcroze told jokes to refresh his students when they were running out of steam, and thus, Marie Rambert insisted, "always obtained from us more than we thought we could give." Eventually, Rambert displayed the same talent with her own pupils, as Valda Setterfield discovered first-hand. "There are stories of her saying to me, 'Why did you come down from half-toe?' and I said, 'I wasn't on balance,' and she said, 'The trouble with you is you only believe in what's possible. You have to believe in what's impossible. Look at me and do it.' And one did it . . . Merce [Cunningham] tells the same stories of David Tudor saying, 'Well, this is clearly impossible. Let's do it anyway.'"

The quest for the impossible has its practical side too. The cost and time of a class, the studio's size and location, even the reputation of an accompanist can boost a teacher's popularity—it's useful to have your doctor right on your doorstep. Though studios drift in and out of fashion like diets and beards, celebrity by itself only impresses amateurs. The professionals who need something particular from their lessons, even if they can't quite discern what it is, watch their friends and colleagues, listen to the grapevine, chat in the dressing room and eventually go where their questions might be answered. Well, some do. Not every dancer is out there hunting full-time for perfection. Once refinement, minute adjustment and obsessive alertness have become second nature, many performers take class in the morning reflexively, to warm up for the day ahead and remind their bodies of exactly how to proceed—muscles forget a little even overnight. Playing basketball at Princeton before he turned pro, Bill Bradley often pounded up and down the court alone, repeating to himself hour after hour, "When you are not practicing, remember, someone somewhere is practicing, and when you meet him he will win." Competing against each other, even contented dancers monitor their work ceaselessly, to hold their hard-won ground and protect themselves against laziness, injury, sloppy habits and bitter resignation. "When you have to do the same movement over and over, do not get bored . . . ," Graham used to advise her pupils, "just think of yourself as dancing toward your death."

But certain dancers are drawn to the studio by an addictive blend of desire, confidence and humility, knowing that flawless dancing, dancing in its consummate form, will always stand just beyond the time and strength they can expend to reach it. Harassed by a nagging imagination, they compete mercilessly with themselves, searching for exposure rather than protection, hoping to uncover their finest artistic nature by sheer diligence and unwavering attention. In an ancient Japanese tale, a man sits alone on an empty beach, running his fingers through the sand. When his neighbor encounters him there and asks what he is doing, the man replies, "I have lost my wife. I know she is somewhere, so I must look for her everywhere." Out of longing for their indefinable best, dancers look for it everywhere, refusing to concede that the reward they most covet will invariably elude them. Tanaquil Le Clercq's eyes lit up when she described it to me more than 20 years after she left the stage. "It's a goal that you never reach, to do it beautifully, to be as perfect as . . . to dance like your image of you dancing. You have an idea of how you should look and how it should be done—and you never can do it, ever."

Coining a mantra for the perpetually disappointed, Samuel Beckett wrote, "No matter. Try again. Fail again. Fail better." He should have been a teacher. And Thomas Jefferson could have beat time in the studio next door, repeating daily his conviction that the price of liberty is eternal vigilance. Though teachers don't need his eloquence, they have a hard time keeping their part of the bargain if Jefferson's sentiment leaves them cold. Whatever your private aim as a student, it's easy enough to show up on time, put your hand on the barre and wait to be told what to do. But the teacher who conducts that stark routine of trial and error every day, or twice or three times a day, must have vigilance tattooed on his heart. And patience. And curiosity. And a fascination with his subject that, like the stone soup in the fairy tale, never dwindles and never disappears and thus can nourish as many as need it. When choreographers train their dancers, they whittle the tools they need to realize their own creations. But a teacher is honing tools for someone else to use, so unless he's a saint—unlikely in the theatre—or a confirmed altruist, he must have his own, less obvious agenda.

Less obvious is putting it mildly. To me, the impulse that keeps him at his task, year after year, plié after plié, represents a paradox of devotion and philosophical abstraction, personal intimacy and academic objectivity that defies rational comprehension. In the natural course of his life in the studio, he will never take a bow, never receive a flicker of public recognition, never make any money and regularly lose even his most cherished pupils. Whether they leave town or sustain some injury or give up, one by one they will walk away and never come back. The twin imps of boredom and frustration sneak into each class to tease his students and taunt his efforts, and the insidious monotony of repetition threatens him with a sort of carpal tunnel syndrome of the eyes. Secure in the knowledge that it's not their job to answer back, the students wear impassive faces and never utter a word, so he cannot be sure anyone is listening—perhaps his corrections are dissolving mid-air, like snowflakes—and their progress occurs so slowly that he can exhaust himself waiting to welcome it.

Yet every class also grants him another jab at mediocrity and approximation and a feast of intriguing possibilities that many teachers sample hungrily. If you love something, it's only natural that you want everyone to appreciate its value. If you have something to say, you want the world to shut up and listen while you say it. That's why people join clubs, to share their passion for dogs or quilts with other people who feel passionately about them too. With luck or skillful application, you will express yourself well enough at the monthly meetings that the others will want to listen to your comments, and you'll articulate them clearly enough that anyone who hears you will understand you.

So perhaps the teacher occupies the most enviable position in the classroom. The recognized expert with the sharpest eyesight, the longest memory and the clearest analytic judgment, every day he can perfect his own talent by putting his mark on the bodies before him. Better than blank, they come to him already primed, expressly to receive whatever he may offer, and in the process of marking them, he may discover something as well about himself or his own art. "How do I know what I think 'til I see what I write?" mused Andre Gide. My guess is that a teacher plunges into the labyrinth of daily lessons to solve the same riddle: how can he learn the full extent of what he knows or what he can convey until he tries to teach it? Every question of line, balance, speed and precision demands a reasonable answer, and no one else can ask the question and supply the answer all at once. Standing forever at the head of the class, he opens his mouth and out fly the voices of all the teachers, all the choreographers, all the coaches to whom he listened himself. Billy Wilder kept a sign on his office wall that read, "How would Lubitsch do it?"

What looks to an outsider like a thankless obligation or a spare-time job for Sisyphus may actually represent pure irresistible privilege. Think of Johansson, setting fresh combinations daily for 30 years. Because every lesson exposes a provocative union of two irreconcilable facts, that a dancer's stage life is short and that learning is slow, for the teacher the day's work is both pressing and deliberate. As a performer grows more physically skilled and emotionally subtle, he also grows older and weaker, which means his teacher must rush and wait at the same time, weighing urgency against endurance like a long-distance swimmer. Bolm constantly reminded his pupils that "you must first be realistic, before you can be artistic," and for all we know he repeated the same warning to himself as he entered the studio every day.

Recalling their teachers years later, dancers sweeten their assessments with affection and respect, forgiving as they praise. Released by time from the embarrassment of their own failings, the artists tell you how slow they were to understand, how clumsy, how impatient, and in their anecdotes they are always the supplicants invoking superior wisdom. Karsavina called Cecchetti "the only absolute teacher of the academic dance in our time." Richard Thomas frequently quoted Vincenzo Celli, who used to admonish his students with the same words Cecchetti had used to admonish him. One summer morning, Thomas threw open the studio windows and a white butterfly coasted in and hovered over the piano. "Look," he said, "it's Mr. Oboukhoff, come to watch the end of class." Most of us smiled and stood up straighter. We knew Anatole Oboukhoff had taught in that room and we knew he had danced at the Maryinsky and with Pavlova. Lincoln Kirstein described him lashing out at his students at the School of American Ballet, "as if he were training big cats, horses, or poodles rather than adolescent bipeds. He barked commands and corrections like a drill sergeant," which we may not have known. But he and Celli weren't strangers to us, that's the point, and their presence during our lesson thrust that long bright rope stretching back and back into our hands and tied us to their students, who had struggled just as we did. I always thought the rope supported us too, like the line Alpine climbers clip to their harnesses for mutual protection. Maybe history attracted me as much as dancing, but even as an amateur I grasped that rope eagerly and carried it proudly, and I can't believe I was the only one who felt that way about it. I'm convinced the professional dancers in that studio responded to it too.

Which brings me back to the American student in Copenhagen, the guy who wanted to spend a month in the Colorado mountains. What had I expected him to say, "I'd go to Preobrajenska"? To Addison? To Thomas? Out of the question. Mme. Preo and Addison were dead. Thomas' studio closed in 1985, a casualty of the real-estate boom that priced independent dance teachers out of the market. The building was literally sold from under his feet, and his school was given 30 days to vacate the premises. "We should all be thankful that the Statue of Liberty is not on the Upper West Side," remarked Thomas to a reporter. "She wouldn't stand a chance. No one could save her." Which might have sounded like sour grapes if *Dance Magazine* hadn't counted heads and determined that his was the 17th studio to disappear for roughly the same reason. Gabriela Taub-Darvish said at the time, "In 1977 my rent was $800. It is now $3,000." More recently, David Howard told me that a few years later, "To get a space I had to take a whole floor, so I became a landlord. I had to rent out the space I wasn't using, and by '95 I was paying $31,000 a month in rent."

The new facilities that replaced those single-minded schools catered largely to the passing trade that had jumped aboard the fitness express. Both America and Britain had discovered gentle jogging and full-scale marathons by 1982, and Jane Fonda's plunge into aerobics in 1983 sprayed those classes with Hollywood glamour. The author of a bestseller entitled *The Complete Book of Running*, Jim Fixx died of a heart attack in 1984 while he was out running, which suggested to many joggers that they might be better off in the gym, where chatty professionals could supervise their exercise. By 2000, most New York dance classes inhabited a rabbit warren of studios united by a single reception desk, a phone number and the rent bill. The doors stayed open 12 hours a day to accommodate a schedule listing ballet, modern, jazz and modern jazz, African dance, ballroom/Latin dance, flamenco, Graham-based technique, hip-hop, theatre dance, funk, tango, Irish step dance, yoga, aerobics, belly dancing, stretch, stretch and tone, tumbling, floor barre and Pilates. According to a couple of hoofers I cross-examined before their morning workout, the Broadway Dance Center was considered "*the* place for jazz, and Steps is better for ballet."

The same change crept through London, where I had found fewer choices in the first place. When I arrived in 1981, open auditions, rehearsals and most open classes, predominantly ballet and jazz, took place in clusters of studios called Pineapple, Danceworks and the Dance Centre. Some teachers rented space for evening classes in vocational schools like the Urdang Academy, where teenagers applied themselves to a three-year degree course during the day. I went to one respected teacher who taught several times a week in a converted two-car garage. Unable to afford better quarters, he also couldn't afford a pianist and played a tape, always the same tape for barre, to accompany us—I quit when I couldn't get its jingling rhythm out of my head. Most dancers apparently stuck to their companies for class, and the demand from freelance professionals, either passing through London on tour or working in musicals, must have been minimal, because I rarely saw them in my class and they didn't have that many options. Twenty years later, Pineapple's schedule still leaned heavily on ballet and jazz but also featured American street locking, dynamic flow yoga, yogamotion, flamenco, rhythm tap, commercial dance, street hip-hop, capoeira, salsa and merengue, tai chi and Kundalini yoga. For variety, Danceworks threw in aikido, lambada, boxcircuit, street jam, cardio groove, jujitsu and Xpress Yo'self, and that's just a partial list. A chain of premium health clubs in Britain added ballet to its fitness arsenal in 2001, by which time the Royal Academy of Dance, the Central School of Ballet, the Rambert Dance Company's school and the Place were all advertising open classes for adults.

So the general public was well served when it came to health, self-improvement and leisure activities, but as studios broadened their scope to attract amateur enthusiasts and relieve them of their cash, the choices for professionals seemed to narrow steadily. The legendary Russian ballerinas and their ramshackle temples of dedication were long gone, and so were most of the great dancers they had trained. Their putative successors, the ballerinas of international renown who left the stage during the last two decades, teach only the select few. Suzanne Farrell gives class to her own pick-up troupe and to the students at Florida State University in Tallahassee, where she joined the faculty in 2000. Antoinette Sibley and Lynn Seymour work occasionally with the Royal Ballet and appear at academic conferences, coaching individual artists in individual roles. Natalia Makarova oversees the staging of her own productions. The gifted performers and choreographers who now run the world's ballet companies teach only their own dancers if they can find the time to teach at all—that predominantly male contingent includes Tomasson, Forsythe, Martins, Bintley, McKenzie, Villella, Schaufuss, Malakhov, Bujones, Frank Andersen, Stephen Jefferies and Reid Anderson. And the artists who channel their experience into a company's school or a vocational academy that lacks a professional affiliation are effectively sealed away from everyone else.

Mary Ann Wells, who was Robert Joffrey's teacher, maintained that "when one of my students achieved a workable technique, I always said, ' . . . Now you must go to a teacher who has been a great dancer, and let that teacher put the ruffles on.'" Sound advice, but it makes you wonder who she would suggest today, when the handful of independent teachers who survive often travel like vagabonds to make ends meet. The thought of paying $3,000 in monthly rent in 1985 appalled Taub-Darvish, who couldn't and didn't, but by 2000 that figure would look like a bargain; having held on for 30 years, a rehearsal space on lower Broadway closed that winter when the monthly rent ballooned from $3,750 to $11,200. "We artists take it personally," admitted the studio's manager, "as a sign of being unappreciated or further marginalized." Unable to support studios on their own, freelancers now have no choice but to grow a thick skin, give class where they can and accept whatever terms that privilege dictates. According to one successful teacher, in 2002 umbrella organizations like Broadway Dance and Steps were taking a dollar off the top of each attendance fee and then splitting the balance with the teacher. From his 40 percent share, the teacher had to cover the pianist and his own insurance—commercial businesses did not pay benefits as companies or universities did. It was no different for artistic experts anywhere else. One of the founding curators of the Museum of London lamented that "senior keepers, those with the world-wide knowledge of their subjects, are seen as expensive luxuries," while in St. Petersburg, curators at the Hermitage were paid about $100 a month including bonuses, and the museum's director remarked, "The pay is symbolic. We do not pay our curators; we give them a little money to stay alive." The fact that Russian street cleaners were earning more than music teachers prompted one well-known pianist to say, "We feel that no one needs music today—that culture in general is not needed."

Even those who still felt they needed a little culture in their lives had less time for it as the 20th century ran down, less time to enjoy it, less time to study it. Amazon.com doled out T-shirts at the 1996 company picnic that read "Get Big Fast," and ordinary people got rich quick. Time became a commodity like pork bellies and crude oil—you could trade it for money or power, even for celebrity if you exposed enough of yourself for long enough that the public couldn't help noticing—and patience ceased to be a virtue. The picture-book geishas who beguiled the tourists in Kyoto might well have paid for a makeover at one of the numerous studios that promised to transform any girl into a credible apprentice, or *maiko*, in 40 minutes. Although customers complained about the bad manners and brash behavior of these "pseudo-*maiko*" and senior instructors in the city's pleasure quarters whispered their disapproval behind their paper fans, few young women were willing to sacrifice five years of their youth to studying traditional music, deportment, dialect, etiquette and dancing. Fashion models and personal trainers peddled their stylized skills exactly as geishas did, exhibiting themselves and their gorgeous wrapping with equal determination. Some of them chose to acquire their ideal bodies without waiting, through liposuction and plastic surgery—better the perfect thighs you could buy, all yours in half an hour, than the ones you had to sculpt gradually and maintain yourself. As a successful plastic surgeon in New York pointed out, "It's hard to achieve society's idea of perfection without surgical intervention—or airbrushing."

Well, that's the problem—dancing is hard, no two ways about it, and its painstaking cultivation cannot be hurried. The teachers who find they can't wait don't teach for long or, even worse, they continue forever but go through the motions heartlessly, setting exercises as if their students were automata. The teachers who can wait, those who accept that their effort can only be repaid if they do wait, combat the trends outside the studio as best they can and teach their pupils to embrace patience too. They let the world howl that the results you have to wait for aren't worth possessing, and go right on doing what they have always done, finding new studios, scratching the rent together and pulling that long, precious rope out of the darkness behind them. It's as if Marcus Aurelius, dead these 900 years, were urging them on each morning with one stoic reminder: If you receive a bad augury before a battle, so what? It's still your job to fight.

Four days before her death Vaganova wrote to a friend, "I can't tell you, how I hate the idea of giving up completely." In Washington, D.C., Doris Jones still runs the dance school she opened in 1941, when it was one of the first in the country to accept black children as pupils. A survivor of breast cancer, diabetes and a thyroid condition, at 88 she was teaching at least three times a week, as she had for six decades, fighting for equal rights and artistic excellence at one and the same time and holding a single standard before her students' eyes: "You've got to be so damned good," she encouraged them, "that they can't refuse you." The Russian conductor Ilya Musin, who was Valery Gergiev's teacher, kept the same schedule for more than half a century. On Tuesday, Thursday and Friday he would devote four uninterrupted hours to his conducting classes. On Wednesday and Saturday he would meet his orchestral classes. When a historian probed him for the source of his knowledge, he replied, "For 70 years I have been thinking of nothing else."

Italians describe a teacher with a standard academic honorific, *chiarissimo professore*, most lucid professor. In Japanese, the term of respect for lawyers, doctors and teachers is *sensei*, which means "born before." No such accolade exists in English, which allows for no distinction between a great teacher and a great cup of coffee. And you can't really count on history to celebrate the masters to whom artists entrust their own improvement. A bronze statue of Cecchetti stands in Civitanova Marche, his family's hometown, but no public memorial or plaque bears his name in St. Petersburg, London, Milan or Rome. When the original School of American Ballet occupied fourth-floor studios on Madison Avenue nearly 70 years ago, Sammy's Delicatessen on the ground floor sold a George Balanchine sandwich, honoring the teacher—now, a street sign on one short block of West 63rd Street honors the choreographer. For 26 years, Pushkin's former pupils got together on the anniversary of his death and paid tribute to his memory by arranging his combinations into a commemorative class. The practice was finally abandoned in 1996, when the exercises defeated most of the students.

It's not as if those masters never existed, as long as someone, somewhere, remembers their insights and continues to apply them, but I'm not at all sure that the young man I met in Copenhagen will ever feel about his teachers as they did about theirs. An old tradition recommends that every night, before going to sleep, you should thank the person who led you to your teacher. Will he experience that kind of gratitude? Leighton Lucas recalled that during his years in Diaghilev's corps de ballet, "after a rehearsal or a class . . . the last man out always bowed to the room before we shut the door." Would the young dancer laugh at that old-fashioned image, or would he smile, as we smiled hearing Mr. Oboukhoff's name, and see the empty room in his imagination and briefly dip his head to it in respect?

Years after her death, I had a dream about Barbara Fallis. A few days later, I ran into a friend who had always stood beside me at the barre in the class preceding hers, and I recounted the dream to him. "She was demonstrating pirouettes in her turquoise chiffon skirt," I said, "and when she finished turning she just stood there, on demi-pointe in passé, deciding what to do next. Then she opened her working leg to the corner. That's it, that's the end." As I spoke, we both watched the image that I alone had seen in my sleep, and then he said hopefully, "Did you get it on videotape?"

Margaret Mercier

b. Montreal, 1938. Trained at the Royal Ballet School and joined Sadler's Wells Ballet 1954. Between 1958 and retirement in 1968, danced with Les Grands Ballets Canadiens, Joffrey Ballet and Harkness Ballet. Faculty member Royal Danish Ballet school 1981–94 and its principal teacher 1998–2000. International guest teacher since 1994 and principal teacher of the Swedish Ballet School in Malmö since 2000.

*T*HE WORLD HAS CHANGED A LOT. Today there are many more distractions. I grew up in Canada without television, and I was amazed when I came to England—I was 12—that everybody had a television. The only distraction when I was a child was the radio, and that wasn't distraction in the same way because you really had to use your imagination. And you didn't have to sit still— one sort of tended to, but the important thing was that when you listened to stories on the radio you were using your fantasy all the time. Now you can plunk yourself in front of a television and it's all up there for you, and I think that's a great pity. It's educational to a point, but not as far as your fantasy is concerned. Also, I loved to read and one of my great inspirations was Victor Dandré's book on Pavlova. Somebody gave it to me when I was like nine, and I devoured it. I must have read it 25 times before I was 12, I just read it and read it and read it and read it, and I've still got it. I've never actually seen it again. I don't know if it still exists.

To me dancing was the only thing I wanted to do, that was all there was to it. I left Canada and my family when I was 12 to do it, and as I say, there weren't any distractions. When my parents had a birthday, they sent me money so I could celebrate with them, and my greatest thing was to buy a ticket to Covent Garden. You know, every Saturday the Royal Ballet School got maybe 20 tickets for the students, sometimes standing room, and one of the teachers wanted to take away my standing-room privileges because they heard that I got myself tickets once in a while. But I said, "If I pay for it on my own, it's just extra. I shouldn't be penalized for that."

But that was the way I spent my money; if I got money I got a ticket. All these groups came to London, so I could go and see them. I loved Spanish dancing and I saw Roland Petit's company, and I think I was privileged to grow up with all these people. We were allowed to go to performances on the weekend, we could do anything we wanted on the weekends. We were not allowed to be seen in *any* theatre, not at Covent Garden even, during the week, because we were supposed to be home doing our homework. And we were, because we had so much homework that you weren't about to be going out. But even special occasions . . . I remember when Margot [Fonteyn] recovered from diphtheria and she did *Apparitions* at Covent Garden for her comeback, a sort of quiet comeback so it wasn't too taxing for her, and of course we were just dying to be there. But we weren't allowed to be there, and woe betide you if you were seen by one of the teachers at anything, it didn't matter what it was.

What happened was, people like Margot came to the school for private lessons—she was working in those days with Ailne Phillips—and Moira Shearer sometimes came for private lessons. So we did get to see them, you know, plastered ourselves against the wall as they walked by and sort of held our breath. That was literally what we did: you removed yourself and squeezed yourself into the wall and let these sort of elevated souls pass you, with your eyes lingering after them. I mean, we treated them with such respect. I'm sure the young dancers have idols now, I'm sure the kids at White Lodge are whispering, "Darcey's [Bussell] coming," and I think it's very important that they can put their little nose to the window and see these grown-ups working and doing pliés like they're doing in the morning. It's a shame when that's lost, the contact between the professional theatre and the school, which it is in many cases because they've had to move the schools out of the theatres.

It's very hard to judge, but I don't think the students of today are really as dedicated. Maybe it was a bit too much in our day, I don't know, maybe it was a little too narrow. We had very one-track minds, except that we were very interested in music and we were taken, oh, everywhere by the school. I can remember being taken to the Science Museum and to a wonderful Holbein exhibition at the Royal Academy and to see Vaughan Williams conduct his Seventh Symphony. I can remember the program; it was *Till Eulenspiegel* and I think it was the Seventh Symphony and Vaughan Williams himself conducted it. It was the dress rehearsal for the premiere, it had never been played before. And I remember Haskell—he was principal of the school then—inviting an Indian dancer, a woman, to come to the school and show us her Indian dancing.

And our reading . . . You read because it was going to make you a better dancer. You went to art exhibitions because it was going to make you a better artist, aware. You looked at colors, you listened to music, but you didn't just listen to ballet music and look at art about ballet; you looked at all art, because all this was going to make you a better artist. That's what we were educated to, and thank God. I remember being taught how to use a library, I mean, being taken to the library and taught how you looked up what you wanted to find. Now I don't really like libraries because I love owning books, but it's important to know how to use a library, and part of our education was to learn that.

I think technique has gone forward in the last years, we're more scientific about it now. I'm not sure that the artistic expression of technique has gone forward, unfortunately. Does that make sense? I think it's just the times we're living in. For one thing, to have artistic expression and to absorb things which are artistic you have to be sensitive, and the world today is all about not being sensitive. It's about being tough and getting through and being there and pushing. You know? You're always trying to protect yourself by putting on a sort of hard outer shell to say, 'I'm impervious.' I keep trying to figure out why, what's gone wrong, why do dancers not move me, because often they don't and they don't take my breath away like they used to, and I don't think it's just because I'm getting older and I've seen a lot. Of course, maybe I'm more difficult to please, but I don't think it's impossible to please me. I just think it's in the general way of things. People say they want to be individuals, but they don't really. They all go around in groups and they all wear the same clothes and . . . in a way they tend to take comfort from that, 'Well, if we all wear the same things we're sort of safe. We have to do this, because it's the in thing.'

Unfortunately, technique has become . . . It's starting to turn, but there was a period where technique became *the* thing. You know, it was very important you did seven pirouettes, and if you did two you were nothing. There was a period in America—*not* in New York, I should say, because they were more educated there—when if you did four entrechats quatre in a row, the audience started to applaud. Certainly when I was in England performing and watching performances—I went straight in the company from the junior school, that was a little unusual, I was 16—they were not looking for seven pirouettes because people weren't doing seven pirouettes in those days, anywhere. When I was young they were looking for different things, they were looking for a sort of emotional fulfillment through the performance. They were looking to be entertained or to see something that was extremely beautiful, and that's what they got a lot of the time. But I think that changed, and now I think it's flipping back, because people got sick of . . . I mean, why do people love the Royal Danish Ballet? Because they're not robots doing eight pirouettes. They're people telling stories, maybe not so technically strong as other people but they're more interesting because they're more human and they're more individual.

Do you understand what I mean by this toughness, this tremendous toughness? To be sensitive you have to be quiet sometimes and open to things. And also when you absorb it, it has to get digested and then it comes out into the performance. It's not instant. That's why the great artists and the people who portray 15-year-olds best are usually like 40. I saw Ulanova do *Giselle* and *Romeo and Juliet*, and it was incredible. Her first act *Giselle* I shall never forget. When they came in '56, they wore no makeup and their dress sense was appalling. Ulanova had gold teeth everywhere, she had salt-and-pepper gray hair, she looked like the cleaning woman. Then in the first act of *Giselle*, out of the cottage came this sweet expression and *pretty* face, the braids done up on the top of her head, and she looked 16. And when she hid behind the prince and gathered her dress to hide from mummy, you couldn't believe that she wasn't 16. Second act, OK, it looked old, but when she was acting, when she was being a person, it was absolutely incredible. *Romeo and Juliet*, her first entrance, when she was playing with the nurse . . . incredible. That was when everybody got the bright idea that maybe you could go on dancing longer—before that people retired at 35. In Denmark they went on doing character parts, but this was people going on doing principal parts in classical ballets.

I started teaching . . . When I was a member of the Royal Ballet, it was then Sadler's Wells Ballet, when I would be on tour, especially with a tour to Montreal, I would be asked to teach a guest class for the local dancers. Well, because I came from Montreal and I was now with this famous company, the local people would invite me to teach. OK, that was the very beginning, but what really got me into teaching was Volkova. She used to spend the summer with us, six or eight weeks, at the Harkness company, and she herself was very special. When I knew her I always thought of her as a very gentle person—I heard that when she was younger she was quite tough. First of all she was trained in Leningrad, of course, with Vaganova. She was not known as a dancer, although she did dance with a company. She obviously had a very logical mind, but she had this wonderful way of expressing what she wanted from you, and she taught with pictures. You know, when she did port de bras she would say, "Now there's a bird sitting on your hand, and you have to throw the bird gently away." That's how she got movement from you or even positions. She would say, "You're wearing the tsar's jewels and you want the whole audience to see them, so the chest must be very open." She had, oh, so many images, and I use a lot of her images because they're so perfect. They just stayed, but I wished I had taken them down. When you're young you think you're going to remember everything, and then unfortunately you don't and it's such a pity. I never wrote any of her classes down; some of the steps I remember but I never wrote a class down and I really regret it today. I often tell my students, "Write the combinations down if you like them or if you think they're beneficial. Anything the teacher says, write it down. You will not remember it."

She just had a very great understanding of the body and how it worked, and she taught quality too, the quality of the movement. You can reach a certain number of people with one image, but there are always people you don't reach, so you must find other images for them. I think that's what teaching's all about, really. Just not to be content, not to rest. Don't say, "Well, I say it this way and if they don't understand me, that's tough." It's up to you to make them understand you. So whatever you have to do, if you have to stand on your head and wiggle your toes, then you have to stand on your head.

You can see right away when they understand. It mightn't happen all the time, but you see it happening.

Well, one year, when Volkova had to go back to Copenhagen, the Harkness company didn't really have a teacher lined up to take over. I was pregnant, and she said, "Why don't you let Margaret take over?" So I did. That's how I started teaching. It was really her instigation, strangely enough. She never saw me teach, but at Harkness, she taught company class, and then she took four or five of us and worked separately with us in the afternoon, like a private class. No men—she'd work with the girls separately. It was usually the principals. I mean, it was Brunilda [Ruiz] and Elisabeth Carroll and myself, Esther Fitzgerald sometimes or Marlene [Rizzo]. And probably from the questions I asked, she realized that I was methodical in my thinking about and interested in technique. I used to just ply her with questions, How do you do this and How do you do that and Why is the head this way? I had had Royal Academy [of Dance] and Cecchetti training in England. We worked with Madam's own syllabus in those days at the school. So I had a smattering of those different schools, and with Volkova I had the Russian school, so I was very aware of the differences, stylistically, between the schools. And also, the build-up of steps in the class is slightly different, which steps you learn first, which steps you learn next, how it follows on, and I find that very logical and organized in the Vaganova school.

But when you're a professional dancer and you take over a professional class, you're teaching a level at which you are used to working. And you've done how many hundreds, thousands, of classes with how many hundreds, thousands, of teachers, and you have a very wide vocabulary of combinations, a tremendous . . . library. So when you start to teach at your own level, it's the easiest thing to do. It's not necessarily easiest to do it with your own company, because often they think, 'Oh, she's just one of us and she doesn't really know what she's talking about.' But I had no problems with the Harkness company.

Then Pat Wilde, who was the director at Harkness House, took me as a teacher for the senior students during that same period in 1966, while I was still pregnant. The company was going out on tour in America, so I was sitting in New York by myself, and she said, "This is ridiculous. You should be at the school teaching." I had senior students, so I was teaching very close to my own level. Then I went back to dancing and then I retired, finished my career, had my family, moved to Sweden—there was a gap of nine years when I didn't teach at all. Then when the children started going to school in Sweden, my days were too long. I just wandered around the house thinking it was too quiet and waiting for them to come home. So I thought, 'I must do something,' so in 1975 I started teaching in Malmö, with the company at the Malmö Stadsteatern—by that time I'd been living there five or six years. I didn't want to teach every day . . . I mean, I had the family . . . so I taught three times a week, and that was very interesting because that was the first time that I was teaching professional dancers who hadn't been particularly well trained. It was a very good experience for me, because I thought, 'How do I retrain these people without them really realizing it and without putting them down and saying, "Listen, you can't do anything. We've got to start again"?' It was an excellent learning process for me, because it really made me think about what muscles you used and how you did the steps.

At the same time that I was teaching the professionals, really retraining them, I was also reading a lot about the different schools and about children's training, because I still hadn't really worked with children, which is a whole different kettle of fish. You asked me when I started teaching—it's been going on a long time. Before I ever came to England and the Royal Ballet School and before I was training in Canada myself, I taught a little private class for my girlfriends, when I was about ten. Actually, I did teach some children's classes in Malmö, come to think of it, because there was a school attached to the theatre. So I did teach a few children's classes, not on a regular basis, but I think I tried it once or twice a week. To work with children, it's extremely important that you know the build-up of things— I mean, you don't start with fouettés and go backwards. The quickest way, the easiest way, is to take a syllabus, and the easiest one for me, because it's easy to read, is the Vaganova syllabus. Of course there are nuances to it and details of style, which don't get into the book, but the basic steps, the build-up of the steps, you can read.

So I had five years of teaching in Malmö, and then Elsa-Marianne von Rosen took over the Malmö company, and she lived in Copenhagen. And I thought, 'Well, if she can live in Copenhagen and come to Malmö, I can live in Malmö and go to Copenhagen.' So I wrote Henning [Kronstam, then director of the Royal Danish Ballet] and asked if there would be any interest, and they remembered me, because when Henning and Kirsten [Simone] were in New York they always did class at Joffrey's. So they had met me at Joffrey's and seen me in class. I always wore pink in those days—it was the Fonteyn syndrome, I'm sure—and people remembered me. Harkness had a rule, black leotards and pink tights, and I refused to buy a black leotard. I said, "If they want me to wear a black leotard, they'll have to buy it for me." I hated black, I felt like a spider in black, and the worst thing I knew were black tights, that was anathema to me. So I wore pink. Kirsten said to me, "You were the girl in the pink, weren't you?"

So I went to Copenhagen in 1980, I taught four company classes for Henning, and I was absolutely terrified out of my mind. But at the end of my first class he came up to me and he said, "Beautiful." That's all he said. Then I realized that it was April 1, and I said to my husband, "I wonder if the whole thing was like April Fool's." You know, this was too good to be true. But he invited me back to teach the company on a full-time basis.

Oh, a lot of my teaching comes from my teachers. I wouldn't say it's the content, if you mean by content the actual combinations, because the period is too long, between now and when I trained, to remember the combinations. Of course, some things . . . I can remember Bill Griffith's steps and a couple of Pereyaslavec's steps and a couple of Stanley Williams' things, but it's the quality, I think, that stays with you more. My first teacher at the Royal Ballet School—that was Winifred Edwards—gave me such incredible pictures of how a step should look, how a hand or the feet should look. She had beautiful feet. So I always remember her for pictures, and Ailne Phillips, also at the Royal Ballet School, for arms, I think she's quite famous for arms. And also, when I was in the company, she coached me for various little solos, like in *Swan Lake* and things. She wasn't *my* coach, she coached the younger dancers, and I got a lot of arms from her.

Then when I left the Royal Ballet I went to New York and I started working with Pereyaslavec. That's when I realized that Pereyaslavec was teaching the Russian system. I hadn't thought of it before. I used to love Pereyaslavec, she had a tremendous love, an intensity . . . She used to set adagios, and her little eyes would close with the love of it when she showed the step. And she was very precise . . . of course, she used to scream a lot too. Everybody laughed at Pereyaslavec and her screaming, but she had tremendous energy, tremendous force, and I think that's important when you teach. I don't like quiet, quiet, quiet teachers—it drives me crazy. You have to give energy, and then you get energy back from your class. When you're rehearsing you let them get on with it quietly and then you talk through corrections. But energy in class from a teacher is very important.

So there was Pereyaslavec . . . and [Anatole] Vilzak, I adored Vilzak. They were both in New York. Perey was like for work, so I always went to her first, for 10:00 class, and then you went to Vilzak for style. His sense of style was just incredible, and it was a fun class, you could have fun. He showed everything, and you did sort of slight charactery things too, little mazurka steps. Oh, he was great. I also used to go to his variations class. It would be like the middle of the afternoon, and there would be what I call the professional students, you know, these ladies who just do class. There would be maybe three of them and me, so he would just grab me and coach me like to the little fingernail. It was fabulous. He used to call me Miss Canada, "Here comes Miss Canada," because I was then in Montreal with Les Grands Ballets [Canadiens]. But I used to come down in the summers to New York—summers were a great opportunity.

We had some guest teachers in Montreal too, for example Eddie Caton, who was another very good influence on me. His basic training was Leningrad, and he was a tremendous disciplinarian. We used to laugh, because he'd give a barre, and then he'd say, "Well, that wasn't good enough. We'll do it again." We'd be delighted, because it was so cold out that by the end of the barre we were just starting to get warmed up, so we could really do something the second time around. He had a terrible temper, I mean, ashtrays and chairs used to fly across the room. But it was good, you learned something. Oh, you can find good teachers everywhere and you can find bad teachers everywhere. I don't think it's got anything to do with the country and I don't think it has anything to do with the system you're teaching. If they're RAD teachers or Vaganova teachers, they can be very good and they can be not so good.

I don't need a lot of motivation to teach. I just love what I'm doing. I love to pass it on. Look, I've worked with all these wonderful people. What am I going to do with the knowledge when I'm dead? It's not going to do me any good. Why write it down? Do people read books? I wonder how many ballet students have read that Pavlova book 25 times before they were ten. But there's nothing like getting it firsthand. I learned so much from absorbing Margot. One absorbed her. You looked at her in performance and you ate her. I can still remember her, in *Symphonic Variations*, standing on the side of the stage, not doing anything, standing absolutely still, and it was magic. Magic. I mean, if you stand like this—as I said to the boys this morning—looking like you're waiting for a ticket at the station, forget it. That's not interesting. What makes the magic? It's a certain alertness, a certain electricity.

Martha Graham said that there was no such thing as standing still, that when you stood still you were like a hummingbird, there was this constant vibration through the body. I think that's terrific and I tell all my students that. And I want to see it—I don't want to see you standing there looking comfortable. Or I tell them . . . It's like the animals out in Richmond Park. You know, they're quivering—they're standing still but they're quivering, because they're deer, they're nervous and they're ready to go. And often I'll say to the kids, "Point your ears," and they sort of look at me. But if you point your ears, it's like when you call a dog, and it's things like that, hopefully, that stay in their heads. You can see if your point has gone in. You can't tell if it's going to stay, but you can see if it goes in. You can see on their bodies.

I gave the students a correction in Copenhagen and they said, "Just keep reminding me." That's their attitude, and it's the same in the company. That whole thing about you taking responsibility has been lost. When a teacher gives you a correction, as a pupil or a professional, if you don't understand it you should ask, and then the teacher might have to explain it fully later if they don't have time in the class. But once you understand it, it's up to the pupil, and it could be a professional pupil, to apply it to their body. Everybody's different. I often say to my pupils, "Well, go to the mirror and fix your foot. It's your foot—you fix it. Don't wait for me every day to say, 'That foot is sickled.' You know what it's supposed to look like." Then they must do it physically and think, 'Well, that's the right feeling for that foot, to make it look the way I want it,' and go on from there. You can't rely on the look for too long, because when you're onstage you don't have a mirror, so you have to be physical and feel it. Often I'll put a foot in the right position and then I'll say, "Now close your eyes. What does that feel like? What are the muscles doing? How does it feel? Then try and copy the feeling. Don't look—do your tendu and try and copy the feeling of an unsickled foot."

But to me, the whole sense of responsibility isn't there the way it used to be. I mean, before I ever came to the Royal Ballet School, when I was in Montreal, my first teacher said to me, "If I have to tell you something twice, either you're not listening or you're stupid." It's that simple. Eleanor Moore-Ashton was her name, she's still alive, she's old now. I never forgot that. You certainly didn't want anybody to think you were stupid. And Ben Harkarvy at Juilliard said to me once, "When you give them the correction, your responsibility as a teacher is over." And I said, "Oh, Ben, you've got to be kidding."

Robert Denvers

b. Antwerp, 1942. Studied with Jean Combes, Serge Peretti and Victor Gsovsky. Appeared briefly with Strasbourg Opera Ballet and the Grand Ballet du Marquis de Cuevas, then as a soloist with Maurice Béjart's Ballet of the 20th Century 1963–73. Maintained his own New York studio, the West Side School of Ballet,1979–86. Artistic director Royal Ballet of Flanders since 1987 and an international guest teacher.

J WAS A LATE STARTER, which would not be possible now, and kind of an impossible child also, very energetic but contrary to everything. My father was a bank director, very *bon chic, bon genre*, and he wanted me to go to university, but we were in the Cultural Revolution almost and against a certain kind of tradition. Just to be difficult I didn't want even to learn French—in Belgium you have French and Flemish. So I was a major disappointment to my father, and . . . I was really lost.

At that time my father thought the only way to keep me straight was not giving me anything, so I played poker in the night bars in Antwerp and I made a lot of money. He thought I was stealing it. So he said, "You don't want to go to school. What do you want to do?" and I said, "I want to be a pilot." He said, "Then you have to go to the cadet school. You're 16, you enlist, you do two years in the cadet school, and you become a pilot in the army." This is a nice story, the beginning of my life actually. On the same day that I had to go to Brussels to do my entrance exams for cadet school, there was an entrance exam for the theatre school in Antwerp. So I of course didn't go to Brussels: I went to the national theatre instead. And the letters crossed ten days later, the letter from the cadet school saying to my father that I was not there so of course I was not taken, and the letter from the theatre school that said, "Your son is taken. He can start."

I knew in two or three months that this acting was not going to work because I was going to play angels and benjamins for the next five years—I was 16 but I looked 12. But through the windows I could look in the ballet studio—this was the first time that I came in contact with that—and I saw all those gorgeous girls and all this physical thing, and I said, "What am I doing *here*?" So I stayed for one year in the theatre course and then I started ballet.

My first love was a girl in the ballet of the Flanders Opera, Arlette Van Boven. We became friends and the family took me in, so she started to give me basic ballet classes at her place—we were the same age, but she started at age six—and she took me to her teacher in Antwerp, Tania Tamarova, and I took more classes there. Then [the Grand Ballet du] Marquis de Cuevas came to Antwerp. I went to this performance, and the next day into Tamarova's studio comes Serge Golovine. He just had married Lilian Van de Velde, who danced also with Cuevas, and she was the student of Tamarova and she brought her husband to class to show him off. He had done *Spectre de la Rose*, with this big grand jeté, and he comes in the studio and I was hooked on ballet for life. There I said, "This is what I want to become." He was so nice to me. Jean Combes was in Strasbourg, he came from the school of [Gustave] Ricaux, the French school, like Golovine, and Serge said, "Ricaux and Preobrajenska are the great teachers. I will send you there as an apprentice. You're going to learn your trade."

What was important for me was to catch up. In acting there is no catching up to do. You did a role, you worked with three or four people, while in ballet it's like going in the Olympics. The technique has completely changed between now and then. Then you had to do tours en l'air, entrechat six, you had to jump high and you had to have power. My idol at that time was Jean Babilée, who was the first to dance in naked legs, where the male aspect actually was highlighted. He put in this wonderful athleticism. You would see him in Paris, in the Studio Constant with Peretti. Don't forget, Serge Peretti was one of my teachers. He gave me the love of all the small beats and also a sense of timing as a dancer, phrasing. I was never a good turner, but I had easy jumps, easy *batterie*—it came from Peretti. And Mme. Nora was the fashion-able teacher in Paris at that time, in the Studio Wacker. We saw all the great dancers there. Victor Gsovsky was also teaching there, and I actually took more with Gsovsky. Nora was more fashion-able, but I thought it was a little fake. She knew what she was doing but she controlled everybody and she kept a carrot of some television performances. You had to be committed to her, which, again, was against my grain at the time. With Gsovsky, he gave you an instruction but it's yours, do with it what you want, while with Nora, fuss, fuss, all the time.

This all came much later. This stuff was for people who started at age eight, so at 15 they were already busy trying to become artists. At that time I was desperately trying to catch up on the basic technique just to get a job. I did one year as an apprentice with Strasbourg and one year as corps de ballet, I did some mice and I participated, but I was already 17. Then I went to Paris and joined Cuevas, I did two months with Cuevas and then I went in the army. That was it. By that time I basically had my foundation, just the bare minimum, and I was a very handsome boy. In '62 the Cuevas company folded, so when I came out of the army . . . My dream was to go into Cuevas and do *Sleeping Beauty*. But there was no Cuevas anymore, and in my army company there was a dancer from Béjart who said, "When we are on leave I will take you to Béjart." By the time I came out of the army in '62, that was *the* company, the big splash, and I thought, 'Well, I'm Belgian, and he is in Brussels. Let's go and see him.' It worked like that: I was a pretty Belgian boy and Béjart hired me. And that's where basically my life as a dancer started. Then I started to learn.

I had two teachers who were very important for me there, Ta-tiana Grantzeva, who was a student of Pereyaslavec, and a Cuban woman, Menia Martinez. But Béjart was the sun king, the sun. Everything turned around the sun. So the women were very good teachers with a solid Russian structure, but then they were obliged to adapt that to the taste of Béjart. With Maurice everything was about gravity, weight, power. He loved the classical things, but no decoration, only essence. With Béjart, for the first time probably, we were exposed to silence, because a lot of his choreography was related to the silence or to the spaces between the music.

When I came with Béjart there were great dancers . . . Paolo Bortoluzzi, Vittorio Biagi, Tania Bari, Duska Sifnios . . . I'm talking great in the sense of performance great, not technical great. That is where my values got altered or put up to date, that being nice didn't mean anything when there was not an intent. With Béjart everything was about the intent, the movement was only part of the whole, and so the personality factor became important. Germinal Casado, for instance, Antonio Cano, these were all people who, by the standards of today, would have almost no technique. Béjart's power was to use what you had to offer and then he would create on you the motions that you could perform. And it would look like a million dollars—nobody would know that you couldn't do anything else. They said he was the choreographer with five steps, but the steps, actually, were not important, I mean, they were not the ultimate goal. They were just the chassis to carry what you had to give.

We're not talking about the women at all at this time. Béjart was inspired by men, and I think the dancers that he liked were the marginal ones like me. We were not doing ballet because our parents wanted us to do ballet or because it was fashionable, like the women. No. We were basically not the normal, and he was attracted to these . . . difficult people. That's why I have such patience with difficult people in my company. All the ones who are really doing what I want in class are definitely not always the ones that carry me away when I see them on the stage. But the ones that resist me in class because they have a bad character, because they are lazy, because they would rather do it this way because I asked for that way . . . I'm going to get annoyed with them because they are motherfuckers, but when I have to do my casting I think, 'He has the guts, and the one who did everything the way I wanted, he's a pussycat. So let's put the motherfucker on.'

So he liked the marginal factor of the person that basically is more than a dancer. It was the opposite with Balanchine because he was not interested in exploring your psyche, while Béjart was a great teacher of life also. For him ballet was taught by the teachers, but life was taught by religion, by politics, by reality, by engagement. When he was involved . . . We went through Buddhism and then everybody was vegetarian or macrobiotic, then we went through Hinduism and it was all religion and listening to Indian music because he was making ballets on Indian music. This was up to us—he requested nothing—but we all so needed his attention, his affection . . . He was our god. So we were all the time sneaking and looking, what records was he having, so that if he made us do a cou-

ple of steps on ping, ping, ping, we would know the music already
and he would choose us. The class that we did was, again, like the
wheels of the car, but to be driven by Béjart, having those wheels
was not enough. You had to be in the inner courtyard of Béjart, so
you had to be invited by him to hear him talk, he had to choose you.
We wanted to be chosen and to be loved, it meant opportunity. And
also, it was always blood and tears. Everything was about drama,
the heart, dying and the nonpossibility of communication. That was
the world of Béjart, and that world was quite unique, because in the
same environment you had the world of Roland Petit, who was the
other major French choreographer. We saw Petit from time to time,
but we could not agree. We were the Taliban fighters around Béjart.
We were fanatics that wanted to believe in gods, that wanted to
pray, that wanted to do our rituals, while Roland Petit was about
going out with Yves St. Laurent, cabaret life, facility, good taste, the
beauty of elegance . . . the opposite.

I did this for ten years with Béjart, from '63 to '73, and the
other valuable influence came from Nureyev. Don't forget, I had
met Rudolf before. That summer of '61, Rudolf jumped and I
hated him, because he was destroying the life of my benefactor,
Golovine. When Rudolf came into Cuevas, it was so new, so raw,
so completely different that that was what the public wanted to
see, and that was it—Golovine was out. And this, for me, was terrible. Then of course I got fascinated by this creature that became—for any dancer in the world, I think—the icon or symbol of
everything dance could represent, because he not only did 250 or
300 performances a year, but he was a jet-setter, he was in all the
magazines with the rock stars. So here we had a classical dancer,
one of us, who was actually being wild, being rebellious, saying
anything he wanted, holding up curtains for half an hour, and
being idolized. Rudolf was Taliban in dance—no compromise ever.
There was no one way or another. You had to accept him in his to-
tality, meaning the great side of him that was the dancer and the
horrible side that he showed when he was not onstage. You could
not choose—you had to take the whole thing, because they were
two sides of the coin. The extreme cruelty he could show was part
of the cruelty he had towards himself and his job and his expectations of you—there was no pity.

We became friends, we had such an easy relationship, and at
once my relationship to the whole gay community changed and my

relationship to Béjart changed. I was always fighting with gays, because I said, "Oh, I can't stand them, I can't deal with them." But now in the ballet it allows me to be straightforward. I don't have a problem with somebody that is gay. I have a problem with effeminated gays, and nobody in my company acts gay. Their religion is their religion, but I don't want to see it.

Leaving Béjart . . . So now I am 32 and I wanted to dance. There was never any one moment that I didn't want that. I danced one year at the National Ballet of Canada, and there I got my first bout with illness, my first ulcerative colitis. It was the first time ever that I had gotten any kind of illness, and it was quite severe. That brought me out of Canada into New York, where I died almost. I was carried to the hospital, I lost half of my blood and I stayed four or five months in Mt. Sinai [Hospital]. At once it's the big black hole. I come out of the hospital, I'm handicapped completely. I have no body. I have no hair. I am not pretty little Robert anymore—I am a little old man. But it was the turning point in the life, if that doesn't sound a bit . . . Balanchine always said, "One. One is it. Everything is in one. All the steps are one." And I had become one. The moment that I was dying or that I thought I was dying, I became everything. I became the chair and the floor and the bed . . . A mystic experience, where at once I understood everything. I became the Tower of Babel and all the windows are open, and I could read, I could understand, I could speak all the languages. The best I can explain it is that by getting better all the windows start to close again, but you have had the experience. I cannot talk the languages anymore, I cannot say what I saw, but I remember. That's why I'm so in love with life, with every aspect of everything. It's all the same. It's all related, everything is related, so whatever I do, wherever I go, I don't *have* to do it—I just do it.

After Mt. Sinai I put myself back in shape. It took one year of doing Pilates, hoping that I'm going to still become a dancer. Finished selfishness, finished egoism, thinking, 'Oh my God, I escaped this. Let's become what we have learned.' Don't forget, we went through all the metaphysical stuff with Béjart, but we didn't become it. But here I said, "Let's not talk about the density anymore—let's become gravity. Let's try to use gravity, but still as a dancer." Everyone was saying, "Remarkable! Darling! After one year? Fantastic!" Compared to what I was months before, it was a spectacular recovery. I went to Maggie Black and to David

Howard, I did what I thought was a great class, and I felt, 'I'm back, I'm back.' Stephanie [Saland] was the only one . . . I was with Stephanie at the time and I said, "I think I'm back in shape and I'm going to go to Balanchine and ask if he is going to take me." And she didn't react to that. So I said, "This morning you told me yourself it was great," and she said, "Robert, it was great, but it's not that great. It is great from where you came from, but it is not great if you're going to compare with Peter Martins and Baryshnikov and all those people. Balanchine is not going to take you as a soloist, but even if he would take you, in one year you're back in the hospital. You have learned nothing. You have to accept the fact that you cannot compete with those people." And I said, "You're right. I won't dance anymore."

So I went to Balanchine and said, "I want to learn how you make dancers over all those generations. I am quite in awe of you as a choreographer, but I am not a choreographer. I have never had the needs or the motivation to do it. Everybody says you're a bad teacher, but you have made great dancers . . ." Everybody was complaining all the time about Balanchine as a teacher and everybody went to Maggie Black basically to learn what he was teaching. I said, "It's not like Ballet Theatre where they hire them from everywhere—you made them. And all this clarity, this attack, this energy . . . You are putting that stamp on your dancers, decade after decade, and I want to learn where it comes from." And he said, "OK, come and watch." So I sat for eight months next to the piano.

I was already involved in a book project with Lincoln [Kirstein]—I was watching company class and Stanley [Williams] and [Andrei] Kramarevsky, studying the classes, and I took on the idea of the six classes of [Asaf] Messerer that [Oleg] Briansky did a book about. So I got much closer with Kirstein in the beginning than with Balanchine, because Balanchine ignored me. He did a little bit what the Tibetans would do with aspiring monks—they would let them sit in front of the convent in the snow, for three or four days until they were almost dead, and if they still wanted to come in, they had proven that they were not just there for food. They would have died at the gates, you know. So Balanchine kind of did that with me. He used to come in the studio for company class and say hello to all the ones he liked. He would go around the barre speaking to everybody, then come to me . . . here I'm sitting . . . pass me by, not look at me, say hello to Gordon [Boelzner] at the piano, and then he would start the class. So one day he comes in, he goes to the barre, and he stops right in front of me and says, "You are really interested in what we are doing here." This was after eight months. I said, "Yes, I am." He said, "This man is really interested. Let him be welcome."

What I found so fascinating with Balanchine was his acceleration in time. The essence of his class, for me, was the discovery of how slow versus how fast. He would always say too fast or slow did not exist, because Where do you start from? What is your basic metronome speed? He would go to the extreme slow motion, where you could almost not sustain it, or to the extreme fast one, where you could almost not achieve it. He would have seven or eight simple combinations of battement tendu, and that they were all front or all side—irrelevant. He would start on a metronome speed of, let's say, And, One, And, Two. And the next one would be And-one-and-two. And the next one would be One, One, One, One. The second day, he would start a little faster, but it was the same kind of progression, and the third day more and the fourth day more, all the time in progression.

The speed gives you the possibility to go as fast or slow as you can when you want it. A cheap car on diesel can only go to 100 kilometers an hour in probably 15 seconds. Now, I drive a Porsche—if I really need my speed, in four seconds I can be at 100 kilometers. With Balanchine that was important, that when he said, "Now you go," you *could* go. It was a necessary quality and it became a part of his technique, to go at tremendous speeds but not all the time. What has been taught and misunderstood by everybody that is teaching . . . the speed has become the sine qua non. No. The speed was only one aspect, like épaulement. For the moment, nobody does épaulement anymore. Balanchine exaggerated the épaulement—he wanted it in écarté, in effacé, he wanted the croisé position—because out of every exaggeration comes energy . . . visibility, lisibility, but also energy. When you twist something, you wind and then unwind. With him there was a reason for everything, and so many things are taken out of the context when people teach now. Most of the dancers that are teaching Balanchine are probably teaching the excesses that he was maybe using to illustrate a point. Now I am talking as a teacher. Many times I say to my dancers, "I showed you an exaggeration. I do not want you to do that exaggeration. This is only to let you see, but you're going to do half of what I'm doing." I am trying to train dancers . . . I think Balanchine said this also: when you create chaos, then you can create order. You have to go to an extreme somehow to come back, otherwise you're always lukewarm, in the middle.

After three or four months Balanchine got sick and he didn't come anymore to class. But anyway, you cannot make a book about teaching. You can make a book to create an interest or to highlight certain aspects or the difference between one way of teaching and another way, but you cannot make a book about it because it's all coming from your gut. The exercises are only an illustration of a specific problem that you're dealing with in one moment, and that was what Balanchine was saying all along, that coming in and watching one class didn't mean a thing. You could not come in and sit for half an hour and have an opinion. You could not look at one class and say he's a good teacher or a bad teacher. You could not make six classes and then say, "Through those six classes, this is Balanchine teaching." To me he said many times, "It is with what you know that you can help. It's not the exercises that are going to help the dancers. You are speaking through your exercises towards the dancers, and the only reason the exercise exists is to make him overcome a specific problem." He said that to me the day that I left to go back to Béjart, basically as a teacher.

My first real teaching opportunity came with Béjart after Balanchine. I couldn't find a job. I had to learn and learn and I had to send hundreds of résumés out saying, "Here I am, Robert Denvers from Béjart, studied teaching with Balanchine . . . ." The only two letters that I got back from probably 80 or 90 that I sent . . . One was from Bobby Lindgren, from the North Carolina School of the Arts and the company, and he said, "With your background I would like to meet you. Maybe you can do something with the company." And Loyce Houlton at the Minnesota Dance Theatre said, "Your résumé is interesting, I like your picture and I would like you to come and dance *The Nutcracker*." I said, "No, I want to teach," and she said, "If you want to teach, you will have to dance *The Nutcracker* first." Those were the two answers.

Then Béjart calls me, this was in '77, and he says, "I don't want the big company anymore. I want to tour with my 15 favorite dancers, and the 60 other ones are going to do a big American tour also. I made Daniel Lommel associate director of this bigger group, but I cannot trust him alone. If you would come, the two of you would keep each other in check. You would make it work." And he said, "Of course you teach the company then. You become associate director and you give the classes every day." That was the start of this adventure. I come back, and I am a Béjart ballet master with the Balanchine vision, and I am unbelievably at ease. The first class that I gave was like I have been teaching my whole life.

I always wanted so badly to dance. I made a small, nice career, but I never felt comfortable because I never felt good enough because I always felt a prisoner in my body because I always felt that my mind could not bring my body to do what it expected it to do. That's why I got so sick—my body started eating itself from sheer frustration. Once I am teaching, it's not about me anymore. At once my mind can flow through the talented dancers. At once my students become the body that I never had. So the only thing I had to do was like Balanchine said, find the exercise and find a convincing way of making you, the student, do what I know is right. Balanchine said to me, "Explain—never justify. You know the why—they don't know—and if you try to justify they will be even more confused." So you don't have to make them believe you, but you have to trick them by your truth to make them do what is going to be good for them. You can do it by making your exercises interesting, but like giving your child medicine, you do it any way you can.

I just did it. I took command. I had no doubt, no doubt, because I felt completely secure in myself. Another thing Balanchine said to me before I left, he said, "Today you're still a student, but tomorrow you're going to be a ballet master. You will start that thing very small, but never forget, from tomorrow you're a ballet master and it's up to you to become a great one. You're going to have the talent to make nice exercises or not. But what is important is that you teach them what you know is right, and never, never refer to where you learned it. Never say, 'We did it like that in New York,' because it has developed."

Probably the first five years I taught by the book, which at that time was the Balanchine book. And every time I gave a class I would think, 'My God, if he would walk in now, am I following the gospel? Am I right?' Of course for the dancers the structure, the hardness, the excitement was completely different from all those Russian classes, but they had seen Suzanne [Farrell] with Béjart, and everybody loved Suzanne and this clarity. They had seen the clock and they liked the clock, and here I was actually explaining to them the mechanisms of the clock, so they accepted that and there were great results. When we came back to Brussels for our performance, Béjart and his people were in the audience, and he hadn't seen his own company for four or five months. And it was a disaster, because this was not Béjart anymore. This was complete treason. The whole look of the company had changed, and they couldn't accept it. Béjart came back and he said, "Robert, what are you doing? I want somebody that is doing *my* work." And we split ways. I always left Béjart on good terms, but they still needed the blood and the tears, and I was beyond that.

Then I went back to New York and I started the studio. I really had nothing, I was starting out again, but I got $50,000 together to make my first studio in the Sofia [Warehouse]. You do things when you are young. The Sofia brothers said to me, "What kind of credit do you have?" I said, "I have no credit." So they said, "How are you going to pay the rent?" I said, "I don't know." They said, "No, no, no. We have to see a piece of paper that at least we're going to be paid the first year." And then came this brilliant idea overnight. I went to [Edward] Bigelow [then New York City Ballet's general manager]—they were always looking for space to rehearse—and I said, "If right across the street [from the New York State Theater], I make exactly the same space that you have there, would the City Ballet be interested in renting it from me for rehearsal between 2:00 and 6:00? The floor is going to be like you have, the piano is going to be the same, new dressing rooms . . . You will have the same." And they said, "Yes, we would be interested." I said, "If you would sign me a lease for one or two years, where you say, 'I pay you monthly $2,500 . . . '" which was not much for them, "then you have the space every day for those four hours." And with that piece of paper, I went to the Sofia brothers and said, "Here is your rent. The City Ballet stands behind me. Can I have the lease now?" I'm not stupid. I had a great deal of luck and also a great deal of guts but not stupid. I gave my morning class from 10:00 until 11:30 and then my 12:00 class until 2:00, and the whole City Ballet that was rehearsing at 2:00 would take my class at 12:00.

Everybody came. Before I took that space in '78, I taught at the Melissa Hayden studio on Broadway and 61st. And I got a lot of City Ballet, because I had been there for one year sitting by the piano, I had lots of friendships, I had been in the school with Stanley and Kramarevsky and I had been with Stephanie. But Millie took too much money from me. When I started getting classes of 25 or 30 people and I had to pay half to her and take the pianist off my share, I thought, 'This is really giving a lot of money away, because those are students coming for me.' So I rented the Puerto Rican Dance Theater studios, on 76th and Broadway, where there is now some gymnasium, and there I started alone. That was my first studio, and there I had two adult beginner classes on Saturday and Sunday, and they paid for everything but the pianist. Then I went to Ballet Arts in Carnegie Hall and there I got another crowd, so when I started my own studio, I had already all those people who I had been teaching over two years.

In a sense I was blessed by the situation. The location on 61st Street, between City Ballet and Ballet Theatre, was very important. From the City Ballet side there were dancers who just wanted to take an easy class before they rehearsed. They might have taken Balanchine's class, but everything went very fast and it was only one hour. Every night I went to see the performances, because Stephanie was dancing them. So, like I do with my company now, the next day half the steps in class would be a function of the performance the night before. I got a lot of the younger ones . . . . Stephanie was 18, Lourdes Lopez was 18, this was a whole generation of dancers that became, later on, the first dancers, and they took Pilates in the morning and Balanchine's class and another class and they took my class at 5:00.

From the Ballet Theatre side . . . People went to Maggie or David Howard or Finis Jhung, but there was never anybody who taught an open class on Sunday, and I did that, because that was my only shot at those people that had a fixed teacher. They would come on Sunday, and then I would get lucky, they would come one more time in the week or there would be a substitute for David Howard so they would come to me. So through the Sunday classes and the classes of City Ballet, I got a core of people, and then the word spread. I also was very fortunate that I knew a lot of stars, and somehow they felt comfortable with me. Makarova, Rudolf, Misha [Baryshnikov] . . . I was not teaching them anything, but they liked to follow my classes and they liked to be out of the context of their company. They could have a coffee with me before the class started, they could warm up quietly, and I always made it very clear that people who took my classes had no business with stars. You didn't come to talk to them or to annoy them, you came to ignore them. You came to work for yourself.

I was free, I was not obliged to anybody. In the first couple of years, I was very involved with the Balanchine environment. And then it dawned on me that if Balanchine would walk into my studio and hear me say those things and stick to the letter, he would be dead bored and walk straightaway out. So I thought, 'Robert, you are dumb. Balanchine doesn't want a clone. He doesn't want a bad Balanchine teacher.' You know, Béjart was always asking his dancers to grow in age, not to dance at 30 the way they danced at 20. He would say, "I'm not interested to see you dancing Mercutio in two years as beautiful as it is today. In two years I want to see you dance it the way you are then." And in my mind Balanchine would now be curious to see what I had become, having been his student, and what would excite him is the way that I have come towards something. Not just a clone, not just somebody who is mouthing what he said. So what comes out is . . . What makes me unbelievably happy when I'm in front of a bunch of people is that I don't really know what is going to come out . . . of us, of us together. I give a first exercise, and out of what I see them all do, I'm going to get my inspiration to get them to do it better.

It's a very disappointing thing to say, but people come to you for the open classes because it's convenient. Of course I give a good class, that's not the point. There were ten other good teachers around me. No, people are going to come to me because they can relate to me or feel not inhibited with me or I give them a certain kind of comfort or confidence. It's very subjective. Your real students are maybe only the two or three that already have understood something and are trying to gain something for themself. And you can see them, consistently, progress. Progress doesn't mean they become good. Progress means they show they understand and they do it better. Here we come to the problem, that understanding does not mean that you can perform it. There are a lot of people, the good ones, that come out and do things on the stage they will never do either in a class or in rehearsal. You only get to see that when they are under the lights. And you have the other ones, that do it in class phenomenally and in rehearsal wonderfully and then come onstage and at once it's a shadow of what it was in rehearsal.

After a while you have to accept the fact that you're only a guide. You're not a creator. As a teacher you're only the guide, and you can guide the ones that have the talent to climb Mt. Kilimanjaro, and even if you don't guide them, they are going to get to the top, maybe less easily without your help but they are going to get there anyhow. So as a teacher in the open market, you become a crutch for a lot of people, because you help them achieve something. They trust you and they think you're getting them somewhere, so they pay you. The ones that don't have talent you can guide only as far as they can go, and they pay you because you make them feel good. They're not going to get better but they *feel* better, and they come back and they pay to feel better.

The first lease that I had, for five years, cost me $2,500 a month. Then when I was obliged to quit the Sofia brothers, I got a five-year lease in another building—there were 7,500 square feet for . . . I think it was $3,500. The Sofia brothers evicted everybody, because they made an apartment building from the warehouse. But I said, "No. I have paid. I'm not going to leave here. You will have to buy me out." So I was the last one there, and at one point they came to me, because they had to, and they said, "OK, what do you want?" I said, "I've found a space and I want exactly the same studio in that space. You give me the money that it's going to cost me to do this studio. I invested $50,000 here four years ago. So I want that $50,000 and then I want a salary for one year, because here I paid $2,500 a month and there I'm going to have to pay $3,500. So I want from you this $12,000, in cash, which will allow me to finish my lease, only instead of finishing it here, I'm going to finish it there." And they agreed.

That was the second studio. Then I was told that my lease in that building would go from $3,500 to $13,500, and that's the reason all the teachers lost their studios. If I had to do that, I could not give just two ballet classes. You could not get $13,500 if you didn't put a shop or a fitness center or aerobics or jazz . . . the whole thing. So what happened . . . David Howard was out of a space for the same reason. He came to me and said, "If I can have this whole floor,"—there were 19,000 square feet on this floor—"I can take it with a Boston contemporary dance company. I only need the 7,500 square feet that you have, but they will only make the lease if I have the whole floor. If you give me your studio . . ." And I said, "OK," because I was divorcing and I had so much fame as a teacher then that I started being invited, to the Danes and the Paris Opéra, to the companies. I had done this for one year, so when David came to me I had already been away half the time.

So this studio was basically from '79 until I sold it to David in

'85 or '86. The result of all this was . . . All the regional companies had ballet schools where those teachers, who had to give up their studios, became the faculty. Millie went to the North Carolina School of the Arts. People went to Boston Ballet and to the Philadelphia Ballet. The teachers moved out, and Steps happened, with their 20 studios and jazz and dance and hip-hop and all that. The first two years that I was without a studio, I kind of took residence in Steps and I gave two classes in the summer months, because those were the moneymaker months when everybody came to New York. Then people started *not* to come anymore to New York. Because the schools went away and rents went up and people could not afford the hotels, mothers who brought three daughters would rather go to Boston, it was cheaper.

But if I would say now, "I'm going back to New York to teach in June and July," I'm sure that in three years I would have exactly the same crowds as before. It would take time for the word to spread and for them to find lodgings, but it would work. And I say this, not with pretension, but it would happen in Paris, in London, because . . . You asked me why did it work so well. The dancer has a gift, comes onstage, can have a bad evening, still a wonderful dancer. I can also have classes that are not working out so well, but a teacher remains a teacher. The connection that you have with people, you will always have. The fact that you can make people feel good about themselves, that you can make people get better, is worth a trip for them. I can get angry in the class and I can yell, but the purpose is always that finally I get something out of them, and they realize that.

Now dancing's technique, but I think that 20 or 30 years ago, one was more busy with the personality aspect. We believed we were great because we had personality, and personality meant being recognized by an audience. They recognized Robert and Daniel, they knew us by the front name, and the choreographers allowed that tendency because they needed your soul, your guts. It is true now that if you don't have a certain amount of technique that is so much higher than it was ten or 15 or 20 years ago, you don't get the chance to get in a company. So people are brainwashed to be able to compete. The dancers are not at fault. A lot of the fault is of the guiding element around the dancers. The technical aspect, as important as it is, should always be helped by the organic quality of the body, the awareness that you're dancing for somebody, the generosity in a step. All those things have to be taught also, and I think they are not taught enough. Technique is not just learning by heart the words. Each class should have somehow a complete roundness. The step is the music, the dynamics of the transfer of weight, the acceleration . . . this is all technique. But we only take one little thing, the step, and we want to have the step so perfect that nobody's moving anymore. They come in and audition and they're standing still.

I've been teaching for almost 25 years, so it becomes second skin, but still I will prepare. I do this automatically, half an hour before the class, because the subject is so vast, and you have to start somewhere. If I give an exercise and nobody's giving anything, good or bad, from themselves, where do I go? But from the moment I see a response, OK, now we're on the road. In your own life and in the development in class, for me it follows systematically that what God gave you . . . You only realize it when you're older, but first you have to say, "It's fantastic. I could be misformed. So whatever I am, I can stand in this class. This is already something, so what can I do with what I have?" That's why I insist that the students not struggle so much. Let's accept what you are and try to make that better, instead of always feeling sorry about yourself. Then you lose what you *have*, because you're all the time saying, "But I wish I could do that." On television you sometimes see those contests with two chefs. They get five ingredients from the audience and in ten minutes they have to make something, and the audience will say what came out the best. They say, "I got a carrot and a piece of chicken and two leeks and two onions. Now, what can I make out of this?" instead of saying, "But they didn't give me eggs or cheese." A dancer has this tendency to excuse himself and say, "Yeah, but this is my bad side, this is my short leg. Yeah, but . . ." instead of saying, "OK, here I am. This is it. What am I doing with it?" You have to make them aware that they are not going to be better loved or more admired if they do three pirouettes. What they're going to be admired for is after one year to have progressed from point A to point B. And regardless of how good or how bad you are, everybody's going to say, "Wow, did you see how he got better?" Now, better is like speed—it's like, Better than what? Are we comparing this guy with Rudolf or are we comparing this guy with the worst in the class? No. We are comparing him with himself.

Now I teach my company and professional companies generally. Last year I was teaching in Copenhagen, and the Beijing Ballet came to do *La Sylphide*, and they asked me to teach them one time. It was quite extraordinary, because they are so trained to execute. We are still very individualistic, we all have different teachers, different opinions. In a class, wherever you are, you see 20 people from different backgrounds, and little by little you get them together. But there, they were all one. The concentration was so intense—they watched what I was doing and they just did it. I explained it to them once, and I saw everybody doing it right, because they were trained from very small to concentrate and not to lose time. Here [at English National Ballet School], in one week I will get their attention and then I will lose it, then I will get it back and I will lose it. The biggest fight as a teacher is to keep the concentration on what they are doing. In a school I will give the same exercise 10, 15 times, always the same thing. With professionals I have to go much further. I have to give the same thing without them realizing it's the same thing. So there I have to build combinations that circle around that one problem—otherwise I lose their attention.

Teaching a professional class is a different world from teaching a school. In the school, everybody is still eager to learn, because they have to get a job. Once they have gotten into the company . . . Let's not forget that they are the best of those students we have been teaching, so one out of ten comes into the corps de ballet and now feels, by birthright, that he is already good enough. So the teacher that is asking him for something might first be met by a certain resistance, because 'What is this guy, telling *me*? I have gotten in Ballet Theatre.' There I will basically not tell them anything, maybe for several classes, I'm just going to take them through paces. The moment they ask me something, we're going to have a dialogue. Then they're hooked, they want to know. Then I have to keep their attention.

As a teacher, the greatest responsibility is creating an awareness that they are not puppets doing movements. My biggest responsibility probably is to bring them in touch with themselves and give a feeling that they are not just doing a step because they have been asked to do it. My responsibility is allowing them also to think. That's why I get so annoyed when I don't get a reaction. I want to see in their eyes, not that they can do it, but a click in their minds that will allow them to do it later, maybe in a year or two years. I try to explain the whys, the ins and outs, and then I leave it up to them to eventually apply it. I'm not training a City Ballet dancer or a Danish Ballet dancer—I'm trying to bring the dancer to the essence of what he represents. The style just depends on the moment—today he's in the Royal Ballet, maybe tomorrow he's going to dance in City Ballet. And if there is no personality, it's not all the fake things that you hang around yourself that are going to make it real—you can only pretend them. So first you take all the pretenses away, and then you either have personality and *that* is going to come out and I'm going to like it and it's going to connect to your audience, or you have no true personality, which is still better than the fakeness. I'd rather have you in front of me bland but as you, who I can like, than have you pretending that you're an overexcited bug and actually dreading this moment with me because now for the rest of your life you have to play this overexcited bug. What I ask my dancers is, "Do not pretend anything." That's my responsibility.

We were different as dancers in the sense that we had to work . . . not to work harder technically, but we had to work harder to get things, to find a good studio, a good floor, to have a pianist, to have the money to go to a school. I had to hitchhike to Paris to take some classes, because outside of the one teacher in Antwerp . . . Now there are beautiful studios with pianos everywhere. I'm not talking maybe about the very small schools, but for the dancers here, it's fantastic, everything is done for them. And the effect is that there is less need to go for something. It's all easy. It's much more hamburger than it is sirloin—everything has already been mashed. So people probably would rather have mashed potatoes and minced beef, because they can eat it easily and they can digest it well. But if you put your teeth in a steak and you have to really bite and pull to digest it, probably your whole being is going to be different than when you just munch, munch, munch.

There were fewer of us who decided to dance, and the ones who did had to do so much more to get things, but we definitely were not more talented than this generation of dancers—people dance so well now, technically, compared with what we could do. But we had this tremendous dream. You wanted to go into this company because you wanted to be like so-and-so. We had prototypes, we had choreographers. So we had, let's say, trucks in front of us behind which you could catch up with your bicycle. But now . . . Many times I think, if I were a dancer today, I would probably be in the environment of Forsythe. Just the fact that he has a creative impulse, that he is going to do something unexpected, would be for me a focus of attraction. Going to a classical company, going to the Royal Ballet, which choreographer is going to make me dance something unexpected? All directors today of classical ballet companies have the problem of fishing in the same ponds, because there is no more creative process that brings enough new, interesting classical ballets. There are a lot of modern guys, there's a lot of theatricality, but there are not two or three—and you only need two or three people—that are interested in telling a story for 50 classical dancers and showing me a new aspect, a new dimension of their classical technique. That we don't have.

I think the key is that the person that is directing or choreographing is able to inspire the people that are there. If there is no inspiration you're not going to create energy or expectation. You're going to create a kind of 'OK, we have a job' boredom. As a teacher too, inspire first, explain later and create a momentum. Get them moving towards something, give them hope. My responsibility at the barre is to bring the ship into dock. First I have to get that barre going and, through the exercises, give them a sense of a rhythm. I dictate, I'm the chef, and I love the class each time, because each time it's new. Each day it's different, the timing, the rhythm . . . The battement is just what you see. It's what you don't see that is so exciting for me. When you're sitting watching, you feel the class is getting the rhythm. At once there is a vibration, and as a captain, I have to know that at a certain vibration, I'm going to the next vibration. Then the gears have to lock in, so I get a bigger and a bigger and a bigger motion, or a smaller and a smaller one—this is for the barre. After my barre your instrument is tuned. If you want to play Beethoven or Bach or Shostakovich, it doesn't matter, everything is ready. Now, what are we going to play? Let's take a little piece, because we are talking now about professional dancers, and let's understand every aspect of that piece, let's make that piece become gorgeous.

We cannot deny the fact that we are the link, that what we are today is tied to the 300 years that we have been doing classical ballet. Whatever we are, whatever we pretend, we are a product. Everything I'm teaching . . . Balanchine had gotten it through this and in Paris they had gotten it through that, and we go all the way back. So even if I don't think about it, I am part of the classical ballet society starting 300 years ago, just like I'm white. It's irrelevant if there are many things in classical ballet that I disagree with—I am still the product of that school like I'm still white coming out of white genes. That's what I am, whether I chose it or not, whether I agree or not, even if for the moment I might like modern dance better most of the time because classical ballet is so prissy or so boring. And I'm very proud. I say to the dancers, "This fifth position in which you stand is the best position you can stand in, because it incorporates 300 years. We do it only since Louis XIV. He was standing in fourth position, and now we're standing in fifth. In essence this is 300 years."

For me teaching is like a fish in the water, like breathing. Why would I stop? I love it. This is my connection with youth. I look around and I see all these young people that are looking at me for advice, for knowledge. That keeps me what I am. Otherwise I would die, I would be old, I would die tomorrow.

Violette Verdy

[*See p. 347 for biographical background*]

ZAMBELLI WAS AN AMAZING TEACHER because she had been a devoted, I would say religiously devoted performer. She was a
great dancer, but she didn't have maybe all the understanding that
you need to teach young children, to adapt to their needs and to
break everything down. She was severe, demanding, very scary, very
imposing, and she did a lot of interesting things to limber the body
that I have never seen since. Strangely enough, instead of pliés or tendus, one of the first exercises was tendu plié second position, and
then there was a big sort of flip of the leg and hip, to just get the hip
free and get to the underneath of the thigh.

I had never had a ballet class before her. But, my God, my
mother had a judgment. She was a schoolteacher and she had studied gymnastics very seriously, and because she had studied gymnastics she had a sense of movement and how you construct certain
things physically. And because she was highly educated to become a
teacher, she recognized another good teacher. The reason I ended up,
very soon after Zambelli, in Mme. Rousanne's class was because my
mother noticed one student who had a deportment of such nobility
and such discipline, not frivolous or profane or worldly but something so special that she asked, "Does she study with someone else?"
obvious question. The grandmother said, "Yes, she does. If you were
not so naive I wouldn't tell you, but you really are naive and you are
asking with sincere candor." So she told us about Mme. Rousanne.

We went to Studio Wacker, which had many, many studios, but
we never got to the higher floors where Preobrajenska was and all

419

those great people. We opened a few doors on the first floor, and we saw a woman looking a little bit like Edith Piaf, very small and thin with big eyes and dark circles under her eyes, with hair in the ballerina chignon, a black dress and very high compensated heel shoes, but with something absolutely unbelievable about her. And that was Mme. Rousanne, whose real name was Rousanne Sarkissian; she was an Armenian, the sister of Tamara d'Erlanger, who was director of the school where [Alexandre] Volinine was teaching. Now, Rousanne was exceptional. Danilova told me of meeting Mme. Rousanne at Vera Trefilova, who was her main teacher. Danilova was next to Rousanne at the barre, and she said to Vera Trefilova, "Who's this funny-looking woman? She's obviously not going to be a dancer. What is she doing here?" and Vera said, "Shut up, Choura. She's going to be a great teacher."

Then Rousanne became Mme. Trefilova's assistant, and when Trefilova closed her studio, Rousanne opened her own studio in Studio Wacker, and Preobrajenska was a great supporter of Mme. Rousanne also. People like that can sometimes have more humility and patience with the elementary basics, with the slow process of teaching elements of technique, because they themselves have had to undergo maybe more patient, and maybe more hopeless, work for learning, knowing that they might not really become dancers. Yet they want to learn because they have another purpose, to learn for learning not for performing. That's what happened with Rousanne.

I didn't have long enough with Zambelli to get to the point where I could completely explore what she might have offered me. But certainly, from Mme. Rousanne I learned to work and in some ways that's when I learned to teach, from being so well taught. It is right there. We must also give Rousanne another justice. She was a highly educated woman from an aristocratic family with apparently some wealth in Russia. She had had to leave, but she had a master's in philosophy and letters and she did some translating work, I think, before escaping the revolution and coming to France. So her approach to dance was a highly philosophical one. She would talk to me about the sacred aspect of dance, not just being an important dancer, having money, a high position, big name . . . I never heard that from her. But I heard things that described something related to Russian aristocracy. Like, "If you shoot a common person, they will have some ugly gestures of fear and hatred. If you shoot the tsar, the tsar will stand straight and receive his shot, and die with nobility."

She gave me an idea that there's an aspect of nobility and high spirit in man that you have to cultivate.

She gave me this idea, that it was in you but that you could also find it in working with ballet, that ballet could represent it. She had seen the great dancers and she said what made them great was not just that they were better technically but they also had a deportment, a majesty and a presence. And she always said, "Presence is something that is here, inside of you," right in the plexus, "Presence can be felt if it is truly concentrated there." I was 9, 10, 11, and I understood her, because my mother was also interested in spiritual matters and she was on a spiritual pursuit of her own. She adored Rousanne, and she felt that she had found, with Rousanne, a great teacher, an educator, who would give an approach and an idea to this particular profession. And it fitted with my mother's philosophy. She had the most amazing philosophy, which was, 'Do your work first, and trust that that will be recognized and used'— just the opposite of everybody else—'Spend the money for what is needed, if it is not for a selfish result but for a purpose, and the money will be found miraculously somehow.' And it always was. The family was saying, "You're crazy. You don't have that money to spend to do this." She said, "We know that she is going to be a dancer, she can be a good one, we have to do what's necessary. Let's not worry—the outcome will take care of itself." And it always did. It was miraculous.

By the time I was 11, 12, it had been made clear to me in the most wonderful, sort of hopeful terms that I could become an important dancer and that because I was interested, I was going to have to do that. Therefore, since I was going to do it I was also expected to live up to all expectations, from my mother, Mme. Rousanne and Victor Gsovsky. So I was in the convent from the beginning. I never had anything else but the convent. First I was too shy to enjoy all this—at the very beginning, the first year I was with Rousanne after Zambelli, I hated to get undressed. I had difficulty lifting my legs very high. Compared to other girls I could see from the Conservatoire . . . Jeanne Schwarz was an amazing teacher, and everybody that went to Jeanne Schwarz at the Conservatoire had incredible extensions. Everybody at the Opéra had great extensions. I didn't have them by nature, and also Rousanne did not really give them, because in those days it was not considered so much what you had to do. Outside of the Opéra you didn't do it.

So. I knew I had limitations, but I wanted to please and I was very obedient. I had been brought up with incredible discipline because I had lost my father, and my mother felt she had to be my father and my mother. So I never knew anything else than discipline, and I resented it a lot. I wasn't allowed to play before I'd done my homework, for instance. And sometimes I didn't want to eat and I was forced to eat, and of course I resented that too. I hated the discipline my mother was giving me because I felt she was not a regular chicken-soup mother. She was not a mama—she was a Mother, with a big M, maybe everything in capital letters too.

I had been told in no uncertain terms that you can be as great as whatever and you're still a student until you drop dead. And I saw it when Yvette Chauviré would come and take class with Rousanne—everybody was fainting with expectation and admiration. Or Jean Babilée would come, Roland [Petit], Zizi [Jeanmaire], Colette Marchand, everybody was in class. All the great stars of the Paris Opéra would come, and we saw what students they were. Babilée was mad and not a good student, so we also knew that that wasn't the way to go. The way to go was Yvette Chauviré, her devotion and what she could still do magically onstage, which had no relationship with the difficulties she seemed to have in class. So by looking at those great dancers we began to learn attitude, approach, and the reality of the studio, which is indispensable for the other reality onstage. We were learning already the connection between this realism and the nonreality of the stage, you know, how you transform ordinary reality into something more magic.

When I entered the Paris Opéra . . . Jhanyne Schwarz, the daughter of Jeanne, was an incredible teacher, kind and lovely and logical and transparent, and I loved her class. I've kept an incredible memory of her, because there were one or two little corrections she gave me that Rousanne had not given me, and I never forgot. She was teaching at the Opéra for the people that were going to be examined after three months. We had three months to be analyzed, to be known, and then we would have an exam with a jury to see if we could enter the school. They hadn't been able to see students during the last years of the war, so we were 600 at the beginning, 600 arrived to audition for the three months, and we ended up 85 after the medical exam and physical exam. I was 11, just a little bit past the age, and they tried to eliminate me before, but my mother brought them a splendid letter. Like the grade-school teacher that she was, she knew how to write a formal, absolutely irresistible letter, so they said, "OK, she can come." So they saw me and I made it through, and after we did the three months, we were just and only 25 people.

At the end of it, we went through the jury exam and all of them said to my mother, "She was the best of the lot, and we want her in the school." But Roland Petit had decided to make his company, and after many discussions, Mme. Rousanne said to my mother, "If she goes with Roland, I'll be there, Victor will be there"—Victor was the absolute ballet master and teacher—"we will take care of her and we'll be sure that she has a normal development as a dancer. And you will be there to do her schooling, so we'll be fine. So maybe she can miss going to the Paris Opéra. Maybe she can avoid that." My mother was also worried about the Paris Opéra school, because in those days they didn't have much of an academic schooling. You went to the minimal required exam, which is *Certificat d'Etudes*, and you had no languages, no music, nothing. My mother wanted me to have languages—she was absolutely a visionary. I had already started learning English, with a wonderful old lady, Ella Field, an old maid and a wealthy globe-trotter from Australia, who lived in Bournemouth but was caught in Brittany by the start of the war and she came to live with us. She started teaching me English when I was about seven or eight, and of course I was already doing music. I had started studying violin with the only schoolteacher who could do it then. So my mother felt that we wanted to continue in this way, and she was concerned that the Paris Opéra was not going to offer this. So we made a huge decision, outrageous in those days, and we didn't go.

There I was in Ballets des Champs-Elysées and, you know, I did solo parts before I could be put in the corps de ballet, because I was too small to be even in the line of the smaller girls. When Victor Gsovsky did his beautiful production of *La Sylphide*, with the Schneitzhoeffer music and with Nina Vyroubova and Youly Algaroff and Irène Skorik and Roland Petit, I finally was tall enough to be in the line of the small girls, the real girls, not the sylphs. Before that I was too small, so I was the one who flew. I also got stuck once, in the first performance naturally, at the Théâtre des Champs-Elysées, I got stuck on the wire, and my feet were hanging down. They tried to lift me up but they couldn't, my feet were still down, and I realized that my teacher was out front so I pointed my feet for the whole second act. My teacher was not very emotional;

she said, "You pointed your feet very well," but my mother, of course, thought I was going to die.

And then, at some point I did a huge film with a leading role, *Ballerina*, with Gabrielle Dorziat, Henri Guisol, and of course Nicholas Orloff, Oleg Briansky, Philippe Nicaud, all those wonderful people. That was heaven-sent, because they signed me for three years. They knew perfectly well that they wouldn't use me much, but they said, "As a symbolic gesture, you will be used in another movie at least," which turned out to be *Olivia*. So then I had a monthly salary, which allowed me to pay Mme. Rousanne, practically for the first time. Because we couldn't afford to pay, she was giving me free private classes, and sometimes she was asking some of her wealthy students, who were taking private classes just for their pleasure, to include me in their classes. They liked it, because they liked me and they thought I worked well and it was inspiring and less boring for them. So she would find all sorts of ways to keep me going.

It became clear that I was going to do this film, *Ballerina*, for 80 days, from 12:00 to 8:00 except Sundays, and I wasn't getting my ballet classes. Victor said, "But this is not possible." So Rousanne said to my mother, "You have to speak to the producers, and Victor will give Violette class before she gets her makeup, her costumes, her lunch and starts filming." So at 6:30 every morning I was picked up in my apartment with my mother by the limo. We would go to the studio, which was, of course, empty. We were given the things that they use to hold the high pieces of equipment like the lights, you know, those big . . . battens, that's it. They would be tied to something to make a barre. Victor would give me a full class, with pointe work and everything. Without music, no music. Then I would go upstairs, take a shower, they would make me up, do my hairdos, give me my lunch, and then I would put my costumes on, my toe shoes, and I was ready to film. 80 days. And I was only 15. They then realized that I was getting dark circles under my eyes from when I took my class, and for certain comedy scenes they said, "We'll wait until the end to do those, and don't take your class so your face is more normal." At 15, can you imagine?

So. You asked about teachers and I started telling you about the film. The connection is just and only that it was very necessary for me to have my daily class. After the film, when I started doing some galas and concerts all over the place, I did some work in Strasbourg, where I got a chance to work with a wonderful teacher. His name was Jean Combes, and he gave one of the hardest classes I had ever had. I think he had studied outside of the Paris Opéra, but probably with those people like Gustave Ricaux, who is like a patriarch of the good teachers and the good dancers of France—Mme. Rousanne had the biggest admiration for him. And later on, when I went to Nice for some performances, I took class with a local ballet master who was called Géo, probably for George, Stone. That man was also an incredible teacher. When you did his class, the combinations, especially the jump combinations, always had pirouettes in them as well, which was a challenge. That was devised to give you control of your legs. Once they were sort of vibrating from the jumping, then you had to plant yourself in a preparation and turn in control, which is the kind of thing that happens to you onstage anyway. In the States, in general, we have not been doing that so much lately. You have to isolate certain exercises to make sure that the students do them well enough to finally put them together, and somehow, because the jumping is maybe not ready enough or the turns are not ready enough, we never get to put them together again. I have other needs that I have to address to help students get what they need, and people are not ready to face this.

We knew about all these people, but Mme. Rousanne wouldn't let me go to them, oh, no, no. Rousanne was divine, but like all the other teachers she was jealous of keeping me in her studio, because it was a necessary thing for her too—every teacher guarded her own students, especially if they had a talented one. When I was traveling, she didn't mind at all. So I went to dance in Milan, and I knew [Esmée] Bulness was the main teacher in La Scala. I had heard about Bulness and when I took her class I loved it. It's funny to think that it was probably very Cecchetti, but it didn't have some of the slight shortcomings that one sometimes associates with Cecchetti when it is not given by someone who really can give it in an excellent way, in the way of making the movement large. Sometimes Cecchetti reduces movement a little bit—it boomerangs to the center of the dancer more than going out—but somehow in the way she was doing it, you had all that plus all the extensions needed and the lyricism and the lovely quality.

She was an amazing teacher with a quiet but strong quality. And she was clear, everything had a simplicity, a logic. You always knew the exercise, there was no question, and it was clear when she was giving it to you what you would have to do with it and what it was for. So she was another one of those teachers that instructs you and equips you. I took her like mad. I discovered that she had a students class at 8:30 in the morning, younger dancers but still advanced students, in the same studio, before the company would come in for their 10:00 class before rehearsal. And I wanted to do more with her, so I started taking her 8:30 class. It was unusual to join the students, but I was still young enough and sufficiently natural. I was sincerely interested, so I adapted myself and I never behaved as a . . . taking over. I always was reserved and not making people feel that I was taking their place at the barre. I was watching my step. Usually I would also take the 10:00 class and then I would rehearse . . . You know, I had been made to think that I could do everything and I was trying to do it, devour everything.

[Yurek] Shabelevsky came along with the Maggio Fiorentino of 1951, where I was hired to dance with a *pléiade* of great dancers, and he gave a very good class with some wonderful qualities of speed but a short barre, which of course I wasn't used to, with lots of things in it. You had to be incredibly ready and incredibly with it to catch the combination, because that was it, you went on to another one. That was maybe the first time that I was exposed to very succinct barres and to the idea of the center being the important thing, and I didn't feel comfortable. I wanted to have done more with the barre and I wanted to feel more ready for the center. But I realized that for a lot of professionals, that way is necessary so they can get to the big stuff. So I began to realize that I needed to work alone, and that is when I started doing that, and my friend Xénia Palley, who was a beautiful young dancer of Russian origin, was doing the same thing. She and I had a friendly competition going; she was much more lyrical than me, and I was more perky than her. Everybody would always cast me in soubrette parts but not the big, monumental, majestic, lyrical adagios. So I thought I had shortcomings, obviously, because of the parts I was given. I thought the dimension was maybe missing in me a little bit and I wanted to improve myself, so I started working alone plus taking class plus rehearsing. And I got so thin that my mother—she was with me there—started getting worried, because she thought I was overworked. And I probably was, but I didn't realize it and I felt so good.

Working alone I did regular barres. You were sort of hanging on with a faith in your teachers, thinking, 'I'm going to try to reproduce what they told me to do, what to be careful of.' So I would summon my memories. 'What combinations should I do now? Well, of course I should do rond de jambe. Yes, let's do that. Which one shall I do? What did Bulness give? Oh yes . . . Oh, that was unpleasant. I don't know if I want to do that today or . . . let's see if I can do it maybe a little bit better. Now I should do Victor's fondu—well, I'll imagine a tango to do it.' All of that, in the dark, backstage, with no music— there was no such thing as a tape recorder in those days—no mirror and not much light and people walking by and different things going on. For one hour and a half, two hours, whatever I could do.

And it was hard. Barre was easy. Center was a pain. And I never knew what to start with. I quickly realized that first you have to find your balance. *Bon.* It's a little easier to start with movements for the arms. Then if you don't feel ready to lift your leg, do maybe a battement tendu something. Good. Then you must get to those développés. OK, I'll do a simple one. And change directions, and do arms. Which arm should it be? And then I would try to analyze: 'Do I really know what I'm doing? Am I doing it in the right order? Is this useful to do? Am I picking up bad habits doing this thing?' I began to learn, without knowing it, to teach, because I was teaching myself.

You have to do it. Sometimes Mr. Balanchine gave very short barres, and of course we were very upset, and I'd think, 'Oh my God, I have to do *Theme and Variations* tonight. How am I going to do it without a barre? I can do another barre later, but my legs will be stiff by then.' It was always a problem. He wanted to get to those wonderful things in the center, so you would come early and do a barre. And he would say to us, "You know, dear, if you want more tendus, you can do them yourself. If you want to sweat, you can go to Vic Tanny"—in those days Vic Tanny was the big gymnasium. "I'm not going to make you comfortable. You can go to Maggie Black. If you want to be comfortable, you want to be cosy, go to other teacher. Go next door. Do your own. Why not?"

Before that . . . I went to America when Roland Petit revived Ballets de Paris, and by then René Bon had already begun to give some classes. René Bon was another short dancer like Jean Babilée and even more incredible technically, but without the James Dean, wild, untamed quality of Babilée. He was from the Paris Opéra and completely Ricaux-trained, of course, like all the people of that time, and they became extraordinary teachers, all of them who came from Ricaux. Now, I'm not lying to you . . . Rousanne never closed her studio except for the day of the examination of the Paris Opéra and the 14th of July, and she took her students, a few of us, some were not really interested, to see the examination. So I have wonderful memories from the Paris Opéra from those years, and those boys were all good, you couldn't decide which was the better one. Between 12 and 15 pirouettes, all of them, from fourth but also from second. They started with arms here in second, and as they did seven, eight, nine, ten, the arms closed tighter and tighter. There was nothing they couldn't do, and that was from Ricaux. You know, Jean-Pierre Bonnefoux knows how to teach this. You take the rounded, curved back at the top of an ordinary wooden chair. You put it on the floor—it's almost like a nutshell and it's very wavy, because if you step in the center of it, it's going to rock. He teaches the boys to turn on that piece of equipment—you learn to use your relevé. Eglevsky turned like that also. He sort of swiveled around in his metatarsal continuously.

So. I mentioned René Bon because he's part of Roland Petit, and it's Roland that made me go to the States, absolutely. And of course I immediately went to the School of American Ballet and I was there in time for Oboukhoff, [Pierre] Vladimiroff, Doubrovska, I got them all, Muriel [Stuart], everybody. And I can talk about Balanchine for hours on end, that is a hot subject for forever. I can describe, I can investigate, I can do all sorts of things with him. And it's interesting from my angle, because I came from Europe and I was already prepared, more so than some of the young people that started directly with him. So I had to make a certain amount of changes, mostly in attitude and also physically as much as I could, in spite of my injuries, wanting to dance for him.

You know, with some of the new choreographies now, I look and look and look and look, and it is like, 'What the hell are they doing?' And you say, "I've got to keep awake and watch. Maybe something's going to happen," and nothing does. You're left expecting and not getting. It's movement, energy, aerobics plenty. It's an exploitation of only certain aspects of the dancers. I say exploitation because it's an expenditure and there is no replenishing. You spend only, you use only. You don't gather and you don't invest. When choreographers now use sophisticated violence as a form of energy—because we've also reached that point where everything is very strident—they spend the dancers' energy and they tire them out, and sometimes they go to the point where the body might almost be a little injured or vulnerable. And the dancer, having accomplished that, feels slightly emptied—this is always the case. You feel emptied when you've done a hard ballet, but if the ballet has a content that touches the heart, that uses the head and that gives some sort of a magic to the spirit, you feel spent of the wrong things and invested with the right things. When you spend the energy on disguised violence and clever, smart moves, a little bit negative and tough, you feel tired, shocked, conflicted a little and not really burnt down in a happy way. Nothing comes back. You just count your bones, hoping that everything is still there, and you go to repair. And that's boring, and you put TV on to fill the gap. Dancers now are used, they're exploited and they're not addressed, refilled, augmented, nourished, taken care of, nurtured.

If you made something with Balanchine . . . It was the most precious, jewel-like experience, to have that with him. It was a form of privacy that was *really* privacy, two people in one. When it is that private it's almost like being with a lover. It's where you don't hardly have to talk—you ask from each other and you know. You deliver, you show, you take, you play, you adjust . . . It was like eating a great dinner, a great gourmet experience, with a feeling of, mmmm, *dégustation*, the things you chew on, the things that you lick your chops about. He would go to the piano, play a little and say, "Isn't this a lovely thing here? I love this little dissonance, this chord here is wonderful." Then come back and say, "OK, let's do this thing . . . you move around . . . Show me."

With Balanchine you reached the point where the choreographer wasn't there anymore, the dancers weren't there anymore, so finally what happened was the choreography and the dancing. It was about choreography and dancing it, and Monsieur Balanchine and Mademoiselle Verdy—gone. But with how many people could you go there? You see, he also had the least ego possible about himself then. He was willing to get no glory but to do the work as the work should be done, not to show himself off but to show what the work should be. And you had the least ego possible about yourself too, because you were in his hands, and the work was going to do it to you. And it did.

We're going to get people like that back again, we have to. If Pina Bausch, that I saw yesterday, is that great in what she does, there is no reason why we wouldn't also get a great choreographer in classical ballet again. I've seen some lovely things from Bintley and from Kudelka, and as I said many times, the teachers and the dancers are going to have a coalition of obligation. All we can do is consolidate, get this thing ready, the meal is going to smell so good that the choreographers are going to have to eat it. The dancers will be so ready they will force the choreographers to come through. And the choreographers will come out of the better dancing that we're doing today and the better teaching that we are getting.

Let me talk to you about beginning to teach. It happened, first of all, because I was injured and I had the time, and I must tell you what triggered my interest. When I was a young dancer with Roland Petit's company in the '50s, and we came for the first time to the States, I had gone to investigate the local teachers wherever I was. And then when I was on tour with London Festival Ballet, which was a long tour, 60 cities, sometimes the company didn't have a chance to give us much classwork. So I decided I would take the Yellow Pages in every city and look at all the ballet schools. What I should have done was to write all this down, because historically it was amazing. I quickly learned that a school that was doing tap, baton-twirl and hula was not the kind of studio where we wanted to go to do a good solid barre. But the one that said Imperial Russian school, ex-Diaghilev or ex-Ballet Russe, that was a possibility and even maybe fun to meet them and to take one of their classes. But in any case we knew we would have a good studio with a floor, barres and rosin and probably even a mirror.

Before even the days of the Yellow Pages I had gone to take class in Washington—Lisa Gardiner, the founder, with a very young Mary Day, of the Washington Ballet, was a dear friend of Mme. Rousanne. So I met them, and I observed some students and I discovered Mimi Paul, who was beginning dance in those days. She must have been . . . something between 12 and 15, I'm not quite sure, and she was a mythological nymph and an inspiration for discovering young talent. The wonder of becoming friendly with an extraordinarily gifted and amazingly bright young dancer gave me the idea . . . I thought, 'How divine, to know young dancers.' I was totally charmed and fascinated by the advent of a young dancer that you would be able to encourage and help succeed. Already the interest in young students started in those days.

Now, at the very first choice of people to be scouts [for School of American Ballet], I was not asked to do it. It was Diana Adams and of course people from the school and maybe one or two other people from the [New York City Ballet] company, I'm not sure who. Balanchine had the [Ford Foundation] grant, and he and the School of American Ballet were the administrators of the grant. So he had gone first, with Eugenie Ouroussow, all around the United States, to the obvious teachers that everybody knows—the Kosloffs, the Christensens, Josephine Schwarz in Dayton, Barbara Weisberger, Dorothy Alexander—he had gone to everybody. He'd seen the Russians, the Americans, the English, the Poles . . . there was a great Pole, Stefan Wenta, in California. There were people from all nationalities, Vladimir Marek in San Antonio who's a Czechoslovak, people that had emigrated were all over the place. So he already had a pretty good idea of what was out there. All these people had been contacted, I'm sure, with the possibilities, "This is what we've got. If you're interested, if you would like someone to come down to see you or if you want to send . . ." Some people never asked the School of American Ballet to see them, because they were antagonistic to the Balanchine philosophy or they were jealous, and you know Balanchine never imposed.

I was one of the many people that were eventually sent, because as I got injured and I knew that this was happening, I asked Mme. Ouroussow if by any chance I could be useful, and she said, "Certainly. Why not?" So they assigned me to some of those tours, and on one of them Ouroussow came with me, and she was really there, I knew, to check on me and see how I was operating, because they had let me go by myself. Apparently it was OK, and so for quite a number of years I was asked to do it. I would come back with a complete picture of each school, the kind of ties they might have with the symphony, the community, the resources they used for organizing parents, children, schooling, the different personalities of the people and the way they taught. When I got to the students, I discovered the kind of people they were, like receptive or rebellious but gifted, whatever. The teacher would ask me on the spot, "How can you tell, in one hour, what we have known only after five years?" I said, "It's obvious, I can see it."

I loved doing it, and all my interest brought me to have an incredible memory. The teachers at SAB would say to me, "But how do you even remember those students?" But I said, "I make a lot of notes." I wrote immediately lots of things: "moody but talented" or "resisting, but in the same time only because she's shy." And they said, "Exactly. How did you know?" I just knew. And then, of course, description, "incredible proportions but weak" or "good feet but turned in in the hips." It was like suddenly I got into a sort of laser state. I was working out of some incredibly strongly driven instinct, I cannot call it except instinct, almost like a switch would go in me and I was in that particular state of X-ray. My knowledge as a dancer was only for doing what I had to do, and in the same time I was fascinated by the human beings that were there, and I was absorbing the human being and the possibility of the dancer all in one package deal and writing madly about the two things.

My horoscope says I'm a natural detective, and I have a gift that people have noticed before I almost noticed it myself, for getting people's number. There's also something that has always happened to me: people confess everything to me. I don't know why. They feel comfortable, they feel that I'm not going to interfere too much. And unless they have something very heavy to protect or a tremendous need for privacy, they just tell me more than I even bargain for. They tell me everything, and the teachers did that too, because teachers are always happy to get some help from the outside, and they were welcoming us, when we were scouting, knowing that we were usually bringing good news. They knew we had in our hands the connection with scholarships, recognition, the possibility for the teachers to go to New York to look at classes and study, ask questions, investigate, develop, replenish, recharge the batteries. All this was happening through my time with dancing and my time with injuries, all these things were roughly the same time. So I was the perfect one to send as a guest teacher, because the others at SAB all had their commitments but people like me, who were floating in so many directions with so many qualifications . . . I was perfect to go. By then they figured that I was really interested enough, and Balanchine had already seen me teaching at SAB.

It was by the grace of George Balanchine and his interest in different people from different backgrounds and his desire for a rich picture of different characters that I was at SAB, I'm sure, because in many ways I think I have always been considered as an oddball. They learned a lot from me, they say. Mr. Balanchine one day came to me and said, "How do you work in France? With soft shoes or old toe shoes?" I said, "Always old toe shoes. Past a certain point you have to have the difficulty of a toe shoe. You can't be in those mushy, soggy-bun, soft shoes." He said, "You're absolutely right," and they changed it—this was when they were still up there on

Broadway—and then little by little it went to the real toe shoe at the beginning of class. Anyway, he liked me, he wanted me, and of course I proved that I could live up to a certain amount of things. But I was a little bit injured, I had gotten married and divorced and, you know, I was different. I was assimilated but I was different.

And I've come to the conclusion that Lincoln Kirstein was eager to establish an American history of the School of American Ballet. They had had their foreigners. The first layer of foreigners was those Imperial Russians with . . . border Soviets, pre-Soviet, Tumkovsky, Dudin. Pavlova-English: Muriel Stuart. Danish: Stanley [Williams]. Kramarevsky was Soviet but Messerer-trained so crossing the politics through the good schooling. SAB had had a little bit of French with Jean-Pierre [Bonnefous] and Mireille Briane, who had taught there very successfully, but for some reason I think the French were not really considered stable or reliable in some ways. Or maybe a little too interested in self-gratifications. I don't know. I know I was suspected of that for a long time . . . I've always been suspected of it and probably still am, and I know that Lincoln, in fact, almost was less suspicious of me than most people. But he was busy writing history with all of this operation and I was not part of his plan, because it was too late to be first generation and it was not the direction they wanted to go to maybe establish a second generation. *Now* they're fascinated by what's going on in France, because they realize it's much too good and that they're losing ground a little bit. So all of a sudden they're happy to have me in the school, which is very nice.

When I left and I went to Paris and to Boston, in a way they considered that I had really left the organization. And when I returned to New York with the advent of Peter Martins, they used me a little bit at the school, I did two more years of scouting a little bit, but they had other people doing it, so they really didn't need me that much. They're very good with their people, very loyal. You don't kick somebody out because somebody suddenly returns from somewhere else. So I did a little bit of teaching in the company, for replacements mostly, which I'm not at all vexed about. I will do any teaching, because to me it's not how or why I am asked, it's the teaching that matters. That's the proof of the pudding. But anyway, I think that's all it is—I was not part of the history Lincoln was really eager to write as cleanly as possible. I might have to come in now and help—if they ask me I will let you know.

If you could see the places I have taught you wouldn't believe it!

All over the country, everywhere, little studios, those huge festivals, conferences in the hotel ballrooms . . . Frankly, it was my fate to be a teacher. When I was on tour with Roland Petit, Roland and I alternated giving class to the company, and I started to teach in America, with the Garden State Ballet company in New Jersey, when I was still dancing. It was in 1964 and it was clear that my injury was very serious and that I was stuck, we didn't know what to do to finish it off. I could hardly walk, but I remember going to New Jersey by bus, once or twice a week. And then when Barbara Weisberger wanted me to dance *Sleeping Beauty* and I couldn't do it, she said, "Could you at least come and help, and teach?" So I commuted to Philadelphia twice a week, to do three or four classes every day that I went, sitting . . . well, by then I was able to get up again. And also, I went to Carlisle, [Pa.], to the early days of Marcia Dale Weary.

Those were my first teaching days, and I was loving it. I was teaching very clearly what I had learned. I was passing on, probably without much alteration, exercises from different teachers that I had considered effective, important, useful, essential, unavoidable. I was really reproducing my teachers then, but also, naturally without realizing it, I had to begin to teach my way. Because I was confronted with pianists and because I was facing people, the truth of those people was already taking over in this operation, which meant that I had to fit my teaching to them and not just to what I knew. It's the dancers that bring it out of you, and Stanley Williams always said that too. He said, "Don't ever worry. The people in front of you will take it out of you. They will demand it, and you will have to give it." It's true. In the same time as I was, for security and for form, using exercises that I had been taught, the corrections I was giving were the corrections already for the people I was teaching, not the corrections that had been given me.

There are general corrections that you get for an exercise, because the exercise contains the corrections. The exercise is given with a particular challenge in it that speaks, itself, to you, and if you don't hear your orders from the exercise, the teacher is there to voice them for you. Balanchine would sometimes give you a step, and you would say to him, "Mr. B, do you want this big or small?" and he would say, "Do it, dear, and you will know." He believed that a gesture is meaningful, the gesture teaches you. It's almost like you want to know with your gesture but the gesture can also give the answer back to you.

So when I teach the New York City Ballet or the Royal Ballet, the big companies where the dancers are totally obsessed by their own personal problems, I send telegrams. I give a little lecture and I don't look at anybody specifically. I get involved and I make fun of it, I talk to the air and I just splash it in the air, hoping it will come down on somebody, that they get a few droplets of it. Philosophically also that works for me, because it's a game, taking the horse to the water and not forcing him to drink. You can't—you can never force him to drink. I just suggest, like Balanchine always said.

Another situation is with the students in a school, when they are at an age where they still consider themselves and we consider them as students. I can be very general with the exercise and address all of them, and then I can help a particular student but never unkindly. I'll always try to do it like, "I have a good suggestion for you, you're going to like this. And if you do it, it's going to be so much easier and so much more fun and you'll get there sooner." I try to do it that way, depending what the customer needs. You can tell right away which students really want it, right away. A particular student might totally want it. Another one might want some of it. Another one might have everything it takes to be great, and not really want it that much. So I address myself totally differently to all those people. The one that really wants it, and quick, I give a sign of recognition— 'I know who you are, don't worry, I'm with you. I'm not going to pay that much attention to you because I trust you. I know you're with me'—and I move on. I go to another one and try to get an appetite going, try to get them to salivate a little, to drool a little, be hungry, try to ignite that fire. The one who has the divine body but is not really interested or doesn't know why they're there . . . I try to compliment them on what they have, to say, "My God, you can do anything with those legs and feet. How wonderful to have that. It's going to be much easier for you, so much easier. All you have to do now is to get going with it." I just let them know what they have and what their chances are. You see, the luck I have is that, knowing their numbers so quickly, I can talk a different language to each one. It's like I spoke 26 languages and I can speak any language for that person. And I'm crazy about students. With waves of good students coming up, I go crazy with happiness. I mean, to me it's like madness and joy, absolutely. I just want to push up my sleeves and help, just do it, whatever is needed.

My premise is simple: I want everybody to dance well. That's my idea and that's my presentation as a teacher. We all long for some form of protection somewhere, we all want to be good at something because we all want to be loved and recognized. And celebrated, even maybe, or important in some way or happy. That's my premise, and I let them know by the way I am with them, a form of eagerness and joyous expectation in a way, that we are there to sort of get a good thing going. If they want to rely on themselves, fine. I know immediately who gets the picture and says, 'All right, let's go,' and I can see the one that says, 'I don't really want to be here. She's crazy.' I can tell what's going on. I make note of it, I ignore it. Because of my experience I don't lose much time at all, and I know what I want right away, direct.

We teachers should be able to deal with any kind of approach to any kind of student. They're less submissive today, but that's not bad. They have better bodies than ever. But the desire for this as a life is not as intense as it might have been before. People were more secluded, they had more private lives, less external communication with television and activities in the world, they were more confined in their choices, and there was more importance to everything rather than a kind of a shopping, consuming mentality about what you can do with yourself in life and about life itself.

Life now is a big dish of consumption, waste and dismissal. Before, there was less to choose from, less distraction, there were less divided attention spans because we had more of a family life. We still had some form of authority and guidance. We were brought up with the idea that an older person with the name of parent or teacher knew something better than we did, and we respected that. Parents and teachers were on the way to the church and God. I mean, in the hierarchy of actual authorities on you, as a young person, the parents were first, the teachers higher, and then maybe a priest or a good church and then your god, whichever god you wanted to give a name to. Now it's too much, too soon, and with no guidance. I was shown, with no confusion, by my mother why she thought in some cases that she knew better—she could explain also why and what the consequences might be if I behaved differently. She didn't terrorize me only—she could do that too—but she also showed me the possibilities and the outcomes. Parents now, as we know, are often as confused as the children. They are either divided or torn apart or they don't always have time to take care of the children, and now we know from all those great scientific studies that if you haven't already gotten hold of the child while they're in the womb or before even a few months old, by the age of two it's too late for certain things already, it'll never happen again for that child in the same way. Maybe in some way, but not the same way.

And the teachers are submerged in the schools by the violence that comes in. Because it has not been channeled or spent before it gets into the school, the surplus of energy and confusion, which creates not even a positive energy but a restlessness, is so enormous for the teachers that they're submerged and overwhelmed. And they cannot do a teaching job, at least as a major effort—they have to also do the peripheral organization, trying to captivate the students. You have to do a certain amount of that, absolutely, but I'm willing to try to do it because I have to use my imagination and my creativity. Some of them will answer you and some will not, and also sometimes you don't find the language that might work for a particular person.

You see, we were closer to some mythological idea of dancing. This is what we don't have anymore—we don't have our myths, because we spend our time de-sacralizing cows instead of remembering who the sacred cows are. It's fine that in the *Raiders of the Lost Ark* we still recognize our myths, but when you lose the sacred values, you can't recreate them just like that. And the meaningless trash that you have to absorb, and that you don't remember, has occupied one space in your brain, even going in one ear and coming out the other. Then the real stuff comes in and you sometimes don't see the difference immediately, so the real stuff comes in and goes out too.

We have only one energy and we can either waste it or use it well and turn it into something positive. The teacher has to get that before it's too late and in spite of anything else. You know, like Balanchine used to say about young children, he said, "We get them at 4:00 in the afternoon, full of all the school's studies and the parents and chocolate, and then we have to teach them ballet," deploring that by the time they got to ballet, they were like hopeless already. Isn't that something? We must understand that this is a pursuit that not only wants to give us full knowledge of the richness of life but wants to give us a corset of orders, some sort of spine, a spinal cord of reliance on our craft. In class yesterday I said, "We have a craft here and it holds us in shape and it keeps us modest, because we have to work on it. We're not a great violin or a great piano and then the pianist comes. This is the instrument and it's not perfect."

You know, teaching is like a witch's cauldron, it's Pandora's box. People that tackle it must be prepared for all sorts of amazing things happening to them, sometimes a little bit dangerous, because there is such an energy, such a mixed-issue energy and so many dark things in there. You have to be a student forever, because when you begin to teach that's when you really go to school. Now that I've gotten rid of myself as a dancer, I'm a much better student than I was before, even if I thought I was an obedient student, because I'm much more consenting now. I really have surrendered to it completely. When you're a dancer there are certain little things that you don't completely surrender, because you feel that you still have to be responsible and in charge and autonomous in some way. There are some secret aspects of yourself that you don't entirely surrender, unless you have somebody so great, like Balanchine, that you surrender everything to him. And also when you are through with all your performing, you do not have the care, the nurturing, the tending and the heavy problem of being a dancer—physically it's a huge, complicated burden. Once you've been able to get rid of your body for dancing, your body then becomes only an instrument for teaching, which is much less burden because there are other things you can use to teach. You can speak, you can use your mind, you can limit your gestures to what is needed, so you don't have a huge worry about the body anymore.

None of us should even imagine that we can do anything in life without sooner or later being confronted with the big questions of the human spirit and the human condition. You encounter the biggest, most serious, important questions about life by doing this, by dancing, by teaching, by doing anything. If you live your life properly, you begin to realize that life has a purpose and you want to know what the hell it is. In a way you're freer to do it when you're older, because there's a time for dancing and there's a time for after-dancing, which is more a reflecting time. When you're young, you want to achieve and you need the audience to love you and admire you and respect you. And you want the audience to receive you well and to reverberate to you their love and their appreciation. But that is the one reward that you want to earn the hard way, in an expensive way really. You don't want to get it without doing your best. You have to learn to not want it before it is honestly earned.

You know, I have an overflow of these things, because to keep myself going and to do my personal preparation, I live with these ideas constantly, and in spite of me I hear myself sometimes spill out little things, give little hints of it. I don't mean to, but sometimes instinctively I take a chance and I think, 'Maybe at this moment I could mention it.' And I do, for their imagination, because they should know that you must do this thing with all of your powers, that when you do it well you have invested in it everything that you're made of, everything you have ever understood or ever assimilated that has become you. So *you* is a big package deal and *you* are going to deliver that package deal in your dancing, selected and carefully chosen. All that richness is waiting to be used, and it's going to come out.

Richard Thomas

b. Paintsville, Kentucky, 1926. Studied with Bronislava Nijinska, Vincenzo Celli and Anatole Vilzak. Danced on Broadway and with American Ballet Theatre, Ballet Russe de Monte Carlo, Ballet Alicia Alonso (now National Ballet of Cuba) and New York City Ballet until 1958. With his wife, Barbara Fallis, ran the Thomas-Fallis School, later the New York School of Ballet 1963–85. Since roughly 1990, faculty member at the Ballet Tech School, affiliated with Eliot Feld's company, Ballet Tech.

*Y*OU'RE WRITING ABOUT TEACHERS or you're writing about teaching? It's hard to write about either of them, because teaching has to do with . . . God knows. I don't know what. I have a hard time about the whole business.

First of all, I'm retired. I teach only in this school—I won't teach anywhere else—because I have no attitude here from anybody. When I came here the boys and girls who are now the company were 10 or 11 years old, I started that class. These children that I'm teaching now . . . Fortunately they have not seen anything and unfortunately they have not seen anything. It's a double whammy. They have never had the opportunity to see great dancing, but then, where would you see it anyway? That's what's so upsetting to me.

Now, I was never a very good dancer. I had a certain amount of talent, I'd had a lot of athletic experience as a boy and the wonderful thing for me was I really wasn't a child when I started. So I studied with my mind rather than just visually aping, like young people tend to do when they start out very young. I don't think children should ever go to ballet school 'til they're 11, 12 years old, 13, because it's so repetitive and they just mimic. Well, I was not a child, and I went to the class and I listened and I learned my lessons.

You have to understand, one of the most important things when I started dancing, which was in the '40s, there were no bad teachers in the United States. There may have been some regional people who ran up to Chicago and took ten lessons in ballet and went back and taught in their dancing school, but as far as I'm concerned that was legitimate, because they were bringing something back to town that might inspire a child to leave and go off someplace else. I was a tap dancer when I started out, and my tap-dancing teacher went up to Edna McRae or Harriet Hoctor in Chicago and she'd study for six weeks and come back and teach the routines that she had learned.

So I was lucky. But when I talk about teachers, I'm not talking about little regional dancing schools. I'm talking about Seattle, Los Angeles, Chicago, San Francisco—there, there were no bad teachers. Mary Day was in Washington, Leila Haller was in New Orleans. In New York City, if you couldn't make this class you could go to that class, and you went to a good teacher because there were no bad teachers. I came in on the end of the time of Fokine, who was from the Imperial school, and of Mordkin, who was from Moskva. They were both acceptable schools, but as Danilova would say, "Thanks God, I came from the Imperial school." Did you ever see that wonderful lecture she did years ago? She talked about, "There were two great ballet masters," before her time, actually, "there was Marius Petipa and there was Bournonville. Bournonville went to Denmark, and Petipa, thanks God, came to Russia." And I always thought, 'Yeah, I know right where you're coming from,' because they were both from the French school, but one encompassed the whole art form and the other had his own thing.

All of my schooling . . . the same with my wife . . . our schooling was right out of St. Petersburg, the Maryinsky. The great bulk of the schooling at the Imperial school was Cecchetti, and it was Petipa, and it was Johansson who was Danish [trained], and it was the Legat brothers [Nikolai and Serge]. One taught one thing, another taught another thing. But you have to realize that the Italian school is the only basic intellectual school of ballet. All of the science of ballet technique came from the Italian school, and everybody else took from them. Now, most of the Russians didn't speak very much English, so consequently they didn't teach verbally a great deal, except to make a lot of noise and stomp around . . . and instill in you an attitude about what it was. But they didn't have the vocabulary to really analyze. You know, everybody laughs now when you say "perch turn." Well, those Russians translated piqué as "perch," Fokine taught you to do "perch turns" and "perch arabesque." It wasn't a vaudevillian attitude about ballet—they had no English. And nomenclature is a very interesting thing. I hear that in Australia now everybody has to call everything the same thing—your vocabulary can only be one way. I went to Celli, I went to Vilzak, I went to Oboukhoff, and nobody called anything the same thing. But they all taught the same thing, all of my teachers, everybody. It was presented totally different from one teacher to the next, but in its theory it was the same.

I'm not talking about style. There is no style in teaching classical ballet. A school must never have a style. You can teach styles, but you must never teach a style, because the style of your dancing changes with the choreographer you work for. You must never be schooled in one way of performing, because then you lack scope as a dancer. You have to be able to do whatever, and years ago we were very lucky because we had such sterling choreographers, and every time you danced for one of them it was all different. Fokine had a port de bras—there are a thousand port de bras—and Tudor had almost no port de bras, because he loved the sternum and this wonderful feeling of movement and he wanted to keep your arms out of the way. Makarova could never do the Tudor ballets, because she couldn't get rid of the port de bras and only use the arm as a gesture, for a statement, not for dancing.

So the teachers all presented it differently, but each one gave you a spirit to dance. Mme. Nijinska was wonderful. First of all, she walked into the lesson, and you never knew how it was going to go. She had a set barre, which was the Italian barre, 15 minutes, bip bip bip, and it was over. Then you came into the center floor, and you did all the Cecchetti exercises, forward and back, and she would give a very pretty adagio, and that was it. We had already gone through exercises that *had* to set you up, because then she started to choreograph. She would show her pianist what music she wanted, and then she would go here, go there, you do this, then we jump, entrechat six, soutenu, snap, snap. The class would be over and she'd still teach—I mean, she'd go on giving these things, "You come from this side, and you come from that side, and we all do . . . ." They were adults in her class and most of them were dancers. I was an exception, because . . .

well, I was a teenager but not a dancer by any stretch of the imagination, so I was gasping! She made you hold your arms in a proper
place and she would smack you . . . My dear, she bruised people all
the time. She hauled off and hit me once because I was lazy—I was
doing passé and I had my toe here, leaning on my knee, and she
smacked me so hard my ears rang.

Have you read her memoirs? Isn't it the prettiest thing you ever
read? I saw the manuscripts, because Irina [Nijinska] pulled them out
and showed me. You could have hung the calligraphy on the walls. I
never realized, until we went through all the books and papers, what
a phenomenal education Nijinska had out of that Imperial school, in
literature and art, in music, everything. She was just a fat little
woman who couldn't speak English and screamed and yelled, and
people hated her. Do you know that she was coming to teach for me
on 82nd Street? Irina said, "Mama said she would love to come and
teach, but you would have to give the barre. If you will do the barre
and the first center floor, then she will teach the lesson." And then she
died. It was heartbreaking for me, because I wanted all my kids to see
this woman, who was a paragon. She was Women's Liberation before
there was any such word, and she was one of the most inspiring people I've ever been in the class with, because she was so in love with
what she was showing you and doing and wanting you to do. She
would stand in the middle of the room like a little round ball and take
a preparation and hit second position, relevé turn, relevé turn, relevé
turn, and pirouette, pirouette, pirouette, and she was an old lady. And
what she couldn't do she would come and beat out on your skin.
She'd take her hands like this and mark it on your body and sing the
rhythms. She wanted you to get all the musical nuances out of the
steps, not just pas-de-bour-rée. She and Balanchine had the greatest
understanding of the musical significance of the vocabulary. Of
course she did not teach it like he did, because she didn't have the
words—she choreographed it but she didn't speak it.

When I went to the New York City Ballet, towards the end of
my dancing career, and he was there teaching, for me it was like a
postgraduate study of classical ballet. First of all, he taught just
like everybody else from the same school that I'd always studied
with. But he had the most phenomenal sense of the musical nuance
of every bit of the vocabulary, so that it became a language with
expression, each step had expression. And the wonderful thing . . .
Everybody hated the fact that you'd go to class and he might only

do rond de jambe in the air. After the first few pliés, you'd spend the whole rest of the class doing rond de jambe in the air, one way or another. And everybody would go, "Aggghhh!" but I thought, 'Isn't this wonderful, because I'm learning *thousands* of wonderful things about what this is.' And I always liked to teach that way, which I think is why a lot of people who ended up choreographing used to like to study with me, because it gave them a sense of ballet as a means of expression. You can do anything with the ballet vocabulary, there are so many things that you can tell.

I studied piano when I was a child, because all good little boys in a small town like that would take piano. I was very musical but I had no talent for playing the instrument. And I was lazy, I didn't want to practice, I didn't want to play in recitals, I didn't want anything, and my music teacher finally just said, "Forget it." She was my grandfather's music teacher, my father's music teacher and my music teacher—we all went to Miss Ora Preston, and she threw me out. She was to die for, a great teacher. When I think about it, I was also very lucky, because I was really not interested in learning and that's why she wouldn't have me as a student. I mean, she *taught*— she knew music and she taught the academics of music and musicality. She was teaching it like a science.

At that time and a little later two men came to my hometown to teach. Percy Lewis came, right out of college, when I was in the eighth grade and took over as the band director in my high school. This was the school band, not a marching band. We marched for the ballgames because we had to, but we considered ourselves a musical band and we studied music and did musical concerts. The first year he came, he took us to the state contest and we played a Bach piece—everybody went, "Hunh?"—and won a superior rating, just like that.

I started out on an old C melody saxophone, which was just horrendous, and then when the school bought instruments for the band, I got a French horn, and I played that for four years. So it was great, and he was a brilliant teacher. He was not a very nice person. He was big and tall and Welsh and handsome and the women were all crazy about him, but he was a taskmaster like you would not believe. And, of course, I thought he had been sent from heaven. First of all, he was beautiful to look at and he had attitude. I started, in the eighth grade, wearing a jacket, a shirt and a tie to school every day, because he said that's the way you should appear when you come to your lessons. My mother said, "Well, you don't have to

wear a tie . . . ," but I said, "No," and 'til I graduated I never went
to school without a shirt and tie on. It was not easy but I did it, as
did a bunch of us, because he said, "You're going to your lessons.
How can you just walk in here like that?" So you comb your hair,
you keep your fingernails clean, you play your instrument, you sit
in your chair a certain way. That was a teacher and I learned that
that's about teaching. Then he left and his brother came and replaced him. Norman Lewis was a teacher in a whole different way,
he was a loving, fun-loving man and he brought all this to you.
They were the two faces of teaching, absolutely.

I really didn't start . . . I took some dancing lessons at the University of Kentucky, and it was miserable. The little lady was very
proper, there was nothing wrong with her teaching, now that I think
back on it, but it was in the upstairs of her house and it was a mess.
But then when I went to Seattle . . . I just went to live with my aunt,
whose husband was stationed there at the army base, and to go to
college. And I went to the Moore Theatre one night and I saw the Ballet Russe de Monte Carlo. The first ballet was *Danses Concertantes*,
the *old Danses Concertantes* a hundred years ago, with Alexandra
Danilova and Leon Danielian, and all of a sudden the curtain went
up on that Berman set and that Stravinsky music, and it was like,
"Oh, my goodness!" You just were overcome with the whole thing,
the glamour, the attitude of the dancers on the stage and the exhila-
ration of the performance, it was breathtaking. It was so . . . shock-
ing to me. I had never seen anything like that. I mean, here came this
funny woman with this nose, she walked out on the stage, and you
just fell out of your seat. And Leon Danielian was wonderful, so agile
and quick, and the eyes. And I thought, 'By God, *that's* what I want
to do. I want to be one of *those.*'

I had seen two ballets. I saw Mia Slavenska with the Columbia
Concerts group in Lexington, Kentucky, and fell madly in love with
her—she did Salome, the Dance of the Seven Veils—and I had seen
Patricia Bowman at the St. Louis Municipal Opera outdoor theatre
in 1943, when I was going to visit my uncle in Oklahoma. We
stopped all night and he took me to see *The Great Waltz,* and Patty
Bowman was to die! But seeing a woman dance didn't make me
want to do it. I didn't take dancing seriously, because I always
wanted to be in the circus. The circus was my thing. But when I
saw *Danses Concertantes* I said, "I want to do *that.*" And I'm
looking in the program and there was an ad that said, "Caird

Leslie. Russian-Italian ballet." So the next day I called, and I went out there and this hateful, hideous old man took a look at me and said, "All right," and signed me up. I was 17, I think.

I started with him, and I was very fortunate because he taught right out of the book. It was Cecchetti, Legat, Cecchetti, Legat. The class was two hours, maybe three, depending on if anybody wanted the studio or how interested he got in how you were behaving. In a way it was brutal, because there was no music—he had a tambour with a stick, and it was all Bang, ba-da-da-da-da-dit. We did a long Legat barre, thank God, because being brand-new and not ten years old, it really put me on the right track. And we did all the Cecchetti exercises, *all* of the allegros at the barre, facing the barre, back and forth and back and forth. And then the same thing in the center of the floor, you did the same allegro when you came off the barre. It was an open class like classes were in those days, and you just got through it the best way you could. He taught it and he saw that you did it, that's all.

Now, my teacher, Vincenzo Celli, who was the *étoile* at the Scala . . . After I joined Ballet Russe de Monte Carlo I went primarily to SAB, but when I came to New York back in 1940 and went on-stage in a Broadway show, I took two classes a day with Mr. Celli. Every day at 11:30 and 5:00 I went into that hideous class, and then I realized that this theory is wonderful but it is not sufficient to get me into a position to be able to present it. So every morning I took my theory class in Italian ballet with Maestro Celli and then I went to Anatole Vilzak, and I was working in the same theory but it was totally different. Then I was not getting the Cecchetti class: I was getting the Maryinsky Theatre choreographic school, and there was Irina Baronova and Igor Youskevitch and André Eglevsky, running and flying . . . It was like a bloody circus, and here I was, still standing with these funky Cecchetti arms, and Mr. Vilzak came to me and said, "You only studied with women in your life?" I said, "No. I study with Mr. Celli," and he said, "With women!" It was a big joke between us for many years. He was a wonderful, wonderful teacher.

Let me tell you about teaching. I never thought I would teach until I knew that I wasn't a dancer anymore. First of all, I really wanted to be a dancer and if you want to be a dancer, that's what you want to do with your life. It never occurred to me, Will I be able to pay the rent? Will I be rich? Will I starve to death? Will I have a car? No. I never gave it a thought. I just wanted to be a dancer, and the idea of being a dancer to get famous or to be rich . . . I mean, it didn't enter into it. I wanted to *do* that, I wanted to be Vaslav Nijinsky. A lot of the problem we have today is that most young people are so interested in the fame and fortune side of being a dancer that they're defeated before they start. And, as I tell my children [students] all the time, I never knew a great dancer that was dumb, but I've known a lot of famous ones that were stupid beyond hope. It just depends on what you want: do you want to be a dancer or do you want to be famous?

And teaching is like dancing—there's no point in going into teaching for money. I started teaching back when I was still dancing with the Alonso company, and Fernando [Alonso] was trying to develop a school. He went to an orphanage and took ten little boys, of a certain age with a certain facility, very much like they're doing here. He brought them to the school twice a week to take ballet class, and he put me in charge of teaching them, I guess maybe because of my background. Not that I was any great dancer, but I did have a good background of teachers. I taught them twice a week, and I enjoyed it, because teaching to me was like Norman Lewis, like Percy Lewis, like Ora Preston . . . you know, you had them in there and, 'OK, I'm the teacher, you're the student, and by God, this is the way it's going to be. This is what you're going to do, and this is what you're going to get from it.'

Then I left the Alonso company, came back, joined the New York City Ballet company. And then, when I left City Ballet company in '58 and joined the circus and left the circus and came home, then I really was not working and I wanted to teach. I came from the theatre. I knew something very special that meant a lot to me. Why would I go do anything other than that? When I stopped dancing a lot of people said to me, "You're going to choreograph, aren't you?" and I said, "No." "Well, why not?" I knew I couldn't choreograph—you have to have a talent to choreograph. That's part of the trouble with the choreography today. All these people get to the point where they have to stop, so they start making ballets, which are, you know, noxious and impossible.

Harry Asmus opened a little school off Broadway and 54th Street, and I taught for him. He was at that time teaching at the High School of Performing Arts, and all these kids came up from there. How well taught they were I don't know, but they always had a flair about them and they were a joy to teach. I knew what I was doing because I was just doing what I had been taught all my life. I was never a creator, ever—as a teacher I never created anything—and I didn't try to form my own theories about anything, because there aren't any new theories. There is no "Cecchetti system." Cecchetti was theory. It was stylized because the style he was teaching was the only format for performing at that time, everybody danced like this. But that doesn't mean that when you teach the Cecchetti school, the Italian school, you have to do all this funky stylization—that's not what it's about. The Cecchetti school is about the theory of classical ballet, just what I was teaching today.

After Harry Asmus, I was teaching at June Taylor [Dance School], and that was like being a prostitute. Sol Lerner said, "You go in the room, there's a pianist, you take on all comers. If there's one student or there's 20 students, it doesn't matter. You take 'em." And I did. I found out that you teach whatever comes in the room, and I probably developed security as a teacher at the June Taylor school, because I taught all day long. And on Saturday, I used to get up at 7:00 and hie myself over to Brooklyn. Marjorie Mazia, who is Arlo Guthrie's mother, had a school in Sheepshead Bay, and I used to go over there and teach, from like 9:00 in the morning to 12:00 or so, and get on the subway and run back to June Taylor's and teach from 1:00 until 5:00 or 6:00 at night. That's when Lupe Serrano left Ballet Theatre school and came to study with me, and I was teaching the June Taylor girls, big, hippy, tough ladies, by the same rules, same principles absolutely. Now, if you don't learn something from that, you'll never learn anything.

Then . . . I never wanted to go to the Joffrey school, Joffrey asked me to come and teach. Bob was wonderful, but the Joffrey Ballet to me was always a mediocre company because . . . Bob never left Seattle artistically. He studied with Mary Ann Wells, who was a very fine teacher, but . . . You know, I can be persnickety about a lot of things, but I can also hootchy-kootchy, and Bob couldn't. He couldn't do both and you have to, because, like I tell the children, "You're studying ballet, but the theatre's a gigantic world. It goes on forever." The first time I was to teach a 5:00 class, Eddie Caton was coming out of class and he said, "Dickie! You're gonna hate it! They can't dance on the music." And he was right, they couldn't, it was mind-boggling. John Prinz studied with me at Joffrey's, and I said, "I like having you in class, but you must go to the School of American Ballet, because there is no future here." I told Christine Sarry the same thing, "Go to Ballet Theatre. You gotta get out of here." I sent Eddie Shellman to Dance Theatre of Harlem. Bob Joffrey hated my guts—I threw them all out.

But I stayed until I went with the company to Russia. Bob dragged me off . . . He said, "You have to go with us, because we have no ballet master." I said, "I'm not a ballet master." He said, "Well, it doesn't matter, you have to come, because you can give company class and you can help rehearse the ballets." I said, "I don't like to rehearse ballets," and he said, "Well, you *can*, and I have no one else." When we came back from Russia, I left Joffrey and went to Ballet Theatre and taught the 6:30 advanced beginners class. Of course that didn't make Mme. Pereyaslavec and Bill Griffith and a lot of people happy, because I started out with like seven people and then all of a sudden I had 20 or 30. Then a lot of other people came in just to listen, and it got too crowded and there was no place for me there. And that's when Barbara and I went over to 56th Street and moved into the old Matt Mattox school, and Eliot's [Feld] father did all the paperwork and all the lawyer work to get us going—we didn't have a nickel. We had nothing.

At the same time I was teaching in Philadelphia for Barbara Weisberger at Pennsylvania Ballet. Getting on the train to Philadelphia and teaching all day long, twice a week. When I was in Philadelphia, Barbara taught on 56th Street, and when she was in Philadelphia I taught on 56th Street. How else was I going to make a living? I didn't have enough money to open a school and run it without working, and Philadelphia was paying me pretty well. We wanted a school in the city and I had all these people saying, "Open your own school."

You know, we didn't leave City Ballet under the best circumstances. There was a big blowup fight and we left, and then I started all the teaching business. But when George [Balanchine] was moving to Lincoln Center, Lincoln [Kirstein] sent a message to me saying, "Dickie, do you want the school on 82nd Street and Broadway?" Now, Ballet Theatre was dying to get in there, Joffrey was dying to get a hold of the premises, everybody wanted it. Lincoln wrote me a letter, and said, "Do you want the school? Because if you do, it's yours." And everybody was pea green with envy.

I don't know why they did it. Well . . . George liked me as a teacher. It's not a humble thing to say and I like to feel like I'm a humble man, but I'm probably the only teacher today who teaches what George Balanchine taught. You think SAB would be surprised to hear that? Well, they would, but they don't know what they're doing. No. George expounded to certain people on certain things to enable them. He never gave them an overall . . . It wasn't like when Oboukhoff did this at SAB and Vladimiroff did that and Muriel Stuart did this and Doubrovska did her thing and Balanchine would come in on a Friday or Saturday and do his. That was already really thinning out. And you have to replace those people because they die, and they did die.

So George Balanchine and Lincoln Kirstein gave me that big school, and they said, "We can't just let you walk in there, so you have to pay us $1,800 for what we leave." I said, "I don't have $1,800," and they said, "It doesn't matter—$100 or $200 a month." Not for the lease. I went right in behind them on my own lease, and I just paid them $1,800 as fast as I could. The barres were left, the mirrors were left, the lockers were left, everything was left. Cockroaches forevermore.

And then we were stuck, yes, stuck, because we never had any money. We never had backers. We never had anybody. Which was OK, because I think that's the way to go, frankly, and I'm not a very subservient person. But we had the school and we did some very good work there. There were a lot of good minds and good people and good thoughts, and I have no hard feelings about anything that ever happened up there. We had good children's classes, from the area up there and they sent me a lot of children from the School of American Ballet. They'd say, "No, we can't take you, but you should go up to the New York School of Ballet, because Mr. Thomas will have room for you." All the modern dancers never, ever left my school, and Lupe and Toni [Lander] studied with me until they retired. I was very fortunate at one period to have a class of brilliant dancers who were students. That was Toni and Lupe, Royes [Fernandez], Bruce Marks . . . They didn't come to me just because you have to take class every day—they came and studied with me and listened and tried out things. Maybe they agreed with me, maybe they didn't, but they all came to my class and tried—they all fell down, they all stood up, they could do this, they couldn't do that, and it was a great era in my teaching career. It was probably the most satisfying time of teaching adults, when all those people were there, doing it.

When we moved up there, we had the American Ballet Company, that was another reason to go to 82nd and Broadway. Eliot started that company from my school on 56th Street, and he started out with kids from Philadelphia too. My little company, U.S. Terpsichore, came in after Eliot took his marbles and went to play someplace else. With children from the children's classes, we started out doing performances all over New York City. We did the opening Prelude from *Sylphides*, you know, the three girls and the boy, we did *Pas de Quatre* and some little ballets. There was Bronwyn [Thomas] and a heavenly little black girl . . . I had four little girls and Owen [Sean] Lavery. The schools heard about it and they would write to us and say, "Could you do a presentation at our school?" I've got a stack of letters this high from all the children that saw my kids, and that was before anybody was doing school performances. We didn't get paid for it, we didn't even have sense enough to ask for money. It was for the children to get experience and it was for the audience, who would learn. We went into schools with people shouting and hitting each other, and two minutes into the program they were like, 'Look at that!' We used to start with a little warm-up and explain how they got ready to do this—oh, they looked so pretty—and then they went out and danced like adults, very seriously.

My school closed in 1985, and that was part of the times' change. I have no hard feelings about the school being gone. It was good time for it to close, it was on its last legs because of a lot of things. It was always a big financial hassle. I had a very hard time escalating the price of classes for the student body, because I didn't understand how they could be waiters and pay. The financial situation in New York . . . I would have been paying almost $10,000 a month rent, and I never had the kind of school that could meet that. I had a hard time paying $3,000 and then going up to like $4,500—that was not easy for me. We didn't have schools like Steps when I started, there were no grind houses back then, not at all, no, no, no.

The world has changed. We live in the '90s. Nobody in this world really chooses to analyze anymore who or what they are as a student or as a person or as an artist. Artist is an easy word to bandy about, but I don't really find much artistry around, because it's gone with the '90s. It's a done deal and it's over, and it's kind of sad. It will come back, the phoenix will rise. It always does—it's happened before. When everybody realizes how boring it is, something's got to change. I do not go to the ballet at all. I can't go to see City Ballet and I can't go to see Ballet Theatre for the same reason. I was in both of those companies, I know all the ballets and . . . they change the steps. But also, I cannot go to the ballet because it bores me. The last thing I went to see at Ballet Theatre, I saw a Tudor program, and they did *Dim Lustre*, and I've never been back, because the dancers, whoever they were—not memorable, for certain—I don't think they knew who Proust was. I don't think they ever read Proust or ever knew what the phrase "remembrances of things past" could mean or ever heard that unbelievable music, because they danced the ballet like they were a little embarrassed. And when she runs and she drops her handkerchief and then he comes along and picks it up . . . the audience laughed.

Oh, those ballets are dead. I really and truly feel that we did the last *Les Sylphides* that I'll ever see. Just the tempi alone . . . I sit there now and think, 'It's going to stop.' When you think of the finale of *Sylphides*, it's not andante, it's not pretty. It's a whirling mass, and those nuances have gone. I know the nuances of a lot of wonderful ballets—*Coppélia, Giselle* . . . I know more about *Giselle* than anybody alive, because I watched Alicia Markova night after night after night. I was on the stage in so many *Giselle*s that if I ever wrote down all the ballerinas who I sat and watched go mad . . . Barbara had a wonderful way with coaching steps and stuff—I don't. I can only do it as a teacher. Coaching is a different thing, and companies aren't interested in that anymore. I couldn't be responsible for those ballets unless I had my own company, because as I said, I'm not subservient and people don't put up with me easily, and I need . . . always did . . . a lot of help. So the companies don't want me.

They could take my dancers maybe . . . They don't even want my dancers, because my dancers are too good and they're not persnickety enough. These kids have a hard time with refining themselves for certain things, because unless they see a reason for it, which they don't with Eliot because Eliot's ballets are so contemporary, they see no particular need. Since the first classes here become the company, they want to be in the company. That's their vision of where they're going, and they don't know about Ballet Theatre or anyplace else. They don't know who Greta Garbo is. But if you're talking about teaching, you have to talk about Greta Garbo. You have to talk about Margot Fonteyn. You have to remember that Beryl Grey was one of the most beautiful Lilac Fairies ever. You have to know that that happened. We tell them. We talk about it, and there will be one or two who listen. Somebody listens. I will not teach adults again, but I teach children because . . . Some of it's selfish. I love classical ballet and I love the theory of classical ballet and I get to see them do things that

I know they should do, and that makes me happy. It's also very good for me, because I'm in my seventies and it makes me use my head. I work crossword puzzles on the train, which makes me use my head, I judge dogs all over the country, which makes me use my head, and I teach ballet, which is what I love more than anything in the world, and that makes me use my head. It also makes me use my body, to some degree. I don't try to do anything in class, because it's not nice for a student to see a teacher stumble around. Your age will modify how much you can do and what you can do.

The nicest thing in this school . . . I have never taught any place before where there wasn't one child that I couldn't stand, but there's not a child here that is not captivating in one way or another. See, they come from no place and from no background, which is wonderful, because then you don't have to deal with any background. There are certain other things you have to erase. You have to erase if they want to be "blaaack" or they want to be "Spanish." Whatever they want to be, they can't bring it in my lesson, and I immediately inform them, "Leave your attitude outside my classroom." If you teach, you don't give class—you have to teach a lesson. If you have a lesson, you have x number of students. If you have x number of students, you're responsible, personally, for each one of those little lives. You are responsible for the future behavior of young people on their own, of tomorrow's citizens, and that's an important thing to take into consideration.

I threw out a whole bunch of girls the other day, because I said, "You can't come into my class with those fingernails. I'm teaching an art form here, and you can't dance on the stage with those nails because you'll hurt someone. You have to cut them all the way back and make them nice and rounded, keep them clean, but you can't wear them that way. You may not wear makeup and eye shadow in my class. I won't have it. You cannot wear all that mess. That's not what we're about here." Nobody can teach them to dance—only God. You can only teach technique, and if you're going to teach technique they have to be prepared to cope with technique, which means they have to be as streamlined as a Georg Jensen knife. There can be nothing hanging out. I just want to see you. I don't want to see costumes—that's for the stage. I have a lot of trouble with the boys and the hair. You know, the black kids like all the funky hair, and I tell them how awful and ugly it is and how I hate it. It's like earrings—I tell them, "You can only have one hole in each ear. More than one hole is mutilation, and I'm not into mutilation so you can't do it."

But you see, even if they hate you for it, it implants a seed that will produce sooner or later. You don't just teach jeté battu—you have to teach deportment. You have to teach, "Don't put your elbows on the barre. Don't lounge. Don't yawn in my face, it's rude." Now, in most schools, for instance in Russia or, I'm sure, the Royal Ballet School, no child would ever yawn in class. They certainly didn't when I was in the Soviet Union, but then, they come from a totally different background. They're frightened to lose the place in the school and they are taught manners. They certainly lose them fast enough after they get to the graduating stage. I was there in 1963, and they wore their bathrobes in company class, and when the teacher gave grand plié, some of them faced that way, some faced the other way, some did it with straight legs . . . No. If you go to a lesson, even an adult, even a finished dancer must conform to the classroom, because it's the only thing that saves his hide in the years to come. I know that from Fonteyn, from Danilova, from Markova, I know that from every great dancer I ever saw on the stage. They never came into the lesson and did their own thing. They came into the lesson, no matter who the teacher was, and did what they were told. So I think if you're not born to teach you shouldn't, because it ain't a job. It's not a job because it encompasses too many things. The only reason I teach now is because . . . not because I see a future for the students particularly, but because there is more to it than perch turns.

A lot of things happened. It was a different time, and it all dried up. I remember Lucia's [Chase] son saying, "I can't go see Ballet Theatre. It's like an old, dusty museum." This was in, oh, 1962. I said to him, "What would we do without the Metropolitan Museum of Art? How can you progress if you have no sense of reference? There is no future unless you have reference. Then it's just the day-to-day miasma—you have nothing." And that's what we have. There has to be intellect behind art. Without intellect . . . you know, it's finger painting. Without intellect it's not choreography, it's ring-around-the-rosy. And that's why teaching has to nurture each individual child. There's no point in going into teaching if you're not going to accept that everyone, every child who's there, is an individual. You cannot teach generally, you have to teach individuals. If you have 20 kids in class, you have to teach 20 different children. This child is not going to dance Aurora, but she has a phenomenal sense of musicality, likes to feel her body. That child will find a means of expression as a choreographer.

I don't think anybody saw the value of what we had. Balanchine was a bad son-of-a-gun because he didn't care what happened after he died. If he had cared, he would never have put Peter Martins at the helm [of New York City Ballet]. It's that simple. You have to look at George and know—he wanted it to die without him, because he had an ego that did not want anything to outlast him. Nobody would agree with me, nobody would admit it and nobody would say it out loud. I can be as wrong as the next man, but I believe it. I cannot believe otherwise, because he had such integrity about his own work.

Look what the Royal Ballet did to their own *Sleeping Beauty*. When they came from England the first time, *Sleeping Beauty* was everything that Petipa would have wanted on the stage, with a woman [Margot Fonteyn] who was not in the least bit exaggerated but who created the role to perfection and did the steps to perfection—and those were the steps that Sergeyev brought in his notebook from St. Petersburg. You knew that you were in the presence of a masterpiece. Maybe the English men weren't so great? It didn't matter, they didn't have to be. They fulfilled the position, they did the ballet. Should they have ever changed a fraction of what they had produced? What was the point of a new designer? What was the point of having somebody come in and "redo" *Sleeping Beauty*? They *had* it. What was the point of changing? I don't understand.

I think what happened in Russia—and this is my own feeble opinion—was that they lost their school, they threw out everything from the Imperial school. All the great teachers left. They only had Vaganova, who, God knows, was not a great teacher. I spoke with Kaleria Fedicheva about it. I said, "Kaleria, she was a terrible teacher." She said, "No. She taught what she knew, which may not have been this or that or the other, but she was inspiring." Vaganova made her name as an inspirational presence in that school, but inspiration's not enough—you have to have some theory. I tell my students all the time, "Never work hard. Always work intelligently. Hard work just makes you tired. You can accomplish twice as much, end up with ten times the endurance, by working intelligently." So they threw everything away when the revolution hit and everybody left, and then they could not accept anything external. Nothing. I remember Maria Tallchief, at the height of her . . . We went to a big embassy party in Vienna, and the Russian ambassador was there and he said, "How pleased to meet you. You must come to our country and dance." And of course Maria, stepping right into the bog, said, "Oh, you have such beautiful dancers." He said, "Yes, maybe you could learn something."

I'm talking about teaching. In 1963 in Moscow, Bob [Joffrey] taught a demonstration class at the Bolshoi school, he used Christine Sarry and Lawrence Rhodes, and the Soviets' jaws dropped! They had never seen anybody that could turn, that could jump, that could beat, that could fly around the room, that never made a sound, that had line . . . They were not a happy group. [Sofia] Golovkina, who was then head of the Bolshoi school, was not there, but later she said, "I have to see this demonstration performance. My school is up in arms, they are all wild to see this performance again. I have never heard such talk. You must repeat this class for me." There was no time to do it again, but Golovkina really wanted to know what was going on.

Now, I never knew a great dancer that was pompous. If an artist is not humble before his art, he is not worth a hill of beans, because art is so grandiose and we are so minuscule. That's what ballet is about. Danilova said to me, "I'm telling my girls, 'The love she comes and the love she goes, but the ballet is there forever.'" She was talking about her students with their boyfriends. She told them, "They come and they go, that's perfectly all right, may there be many. But every morning when you wake up, the ballet is there." And that's the difference between a dancer and somebody who dances.

I think George made a terrible mistake with the Ford Foundation [grant] when he auditioned kids from all over the country and brought them to New York. Any of those kids had enough money to come and study anywhere they wanted to, because their daddies were all rich or they couldn't have been taking ballet where they were in the first place. So there was no great . . . how do you call it? . . . giving. You weren't giving opportunity when you brought kids here. *This* school is giving opportunity, because these kids couldn't afford anything. They come out of the ghetto and out of the five boroughs of New York City, they don't have anything. They're just auditioned and judged on the physical, their musicality, mentality . . . The Ford kids wanted to come to New York, but the tragedy about the Ford Foundation scholarships was, How many of those kids came from Paducah to New York, did not get taken, and had to go back to Paducah, after many years of being here? Balanchine doesn't want you, Ballet Theatre doesn't need you because they have their own school, Joffrey has his own school and takes as much as he can from there, so what do you do? You wait tables? You shack up with someone? There was no life after the Ford Foundation for three-quarters of the people.

Sol Hurok said a very funny thing—I loved him, he was so funny. He stood up to receive his Capezio Award and he said, "First I must tell you, there are too many ballet companies. There is no room. You cannot have this many ballet companies and have good ones," and I thought, 'Right on, Sol.' Three-quarters of the regional ballet companies in America, three-quarters or more—and I'm giving them a big, big margin—are no better than the recitals that were presented from the beginning by those schools around the country without any funding . . . because you don't need funding to do a recital when you have a ballet school. Those companies do three or four performances a year, they get subsidy, they get this, they get that—you're creating nothing but chaos. Sol Hurok was right, because all of this was already beginning to take a toll on the three major companies. It was cutting down their touring. The regional companies—Houston, Atlanta—are very happy, but their scope is too small. Nobody wants to pick up and dance in Paducah. A ballet company, especially if it's funded by the United States government, and I'm talking about Ballet Theatre and City Ballet, should have to be seen by every state in the Union, they should go to Alaska. If you're going to get government money, then you have to put out. I'll tell you something and this is a fact: the National Endowment has probably been the worst enemy for art in America, because they allowed the mediocre to rise to the top.

Now, nothing is worth doing if you can't do it yourself. When I first started dancing, if you couldn't sell a ticket you couldn't have the theatre, and Ballet Russe de Monte Carlo had to make its way. Junky [Julius] Fleischmann gave them some money and they had some private donors who liked to be part of the ballet, just like Diaghilev did. But you have to have a vision, and visions don't usually come with grant applications. It's hard. I said to Lincoln once, "I have no money, and I have a hard time asking people for money." He said, "Dickie, if you're going to be in this business you have to have a taste for shit." George never developed it—Lincoln did it for him, which is fine and understandable—and I didn't either, but I know what he was talking about.

When I set up U.S. Terpsichore, I did two tours of the United

States for Columbia Artists Management—they called it the Richard Thomas Theatre Ballet, because they wanted to use my name, which was stupid. But anyway, out of the money Columbia Artists Management paid us to do the tour, I paid the dancers, I paid the bus driver and the travel, I paid the company manager, and there was enough money left over to go into my school coffers so that I could keep the school open. This was in the '70s. Those kids went out and danced, and we did not get one nickel of funding, and I asked, because we were desperate. Never had any money from the New York state arts council, never had a cent from the NEA [National Endowment for the Arts], not one penny. I didn't need it! We had sold-out houses. We had rave reviews everywhere, except for one town in Oregon that said, "It's not fair for you to bring that company here," and my wife said, "Why not?" They said, "Don't you realize that we have an NEA grant and we're working hard, but we cannot produce what you've done? So it makes it very hard for us after you leave."

One tour we did 15 weeks of one-night stands and we did 12, 14 weeks of one-night stands the next tour, with my kids all under 18 years old. Bronwyn Thomas did 32 fouettés every night of her life, and she was . . . 15? Anyway, Bob Joffrey, Ballet Theatre II, all these companies were going out there too. They were getting the same money from Columbia *plus* they were funded by NEA and the New York State Council on the Arts. The only time we ever got any money, the National Endowment for the Arts gave us $1,700 when we did the season at City Center. Which we spent badly— that happens. But I think the National Endowment should support the great artistic triumphs of the country and build theatres and make it possible for a small company to play in a theatre. Every town should have an opera house—that is for the government to do. Jerome Robbins got how many buckets of money from the NEA to do some project and never produced one thing for the American public. He hired all these people, at big salaries, and they worked together for . . . what? A year or so? But it never produced anything beyond giving those people work for that period of time. There was no performance, there was nothing. So we made—and I say "we"—have made a lot of mistakes, and consequently now we are in a very arid time. And it will or it will not change.

For the present, it's over. Now, all of those people that run out there every night for the ballet are not going to agree with that for a minute. That's OK by me too. It's over for me. I got off the planet.

I stepped down, because there's nothing left for me as far as the performing art is concerned. The teaching, nobody can take away from me. That belongs to me, and if I choose to teach, then I will do what I have done all my life. That's mine. But the performing . . . that arm of the art form is gone. I saw the Louisville Ballet do a television program of *Billy the Kid*, and I thought, 'Hey, enough. They don't even have a clue of what's going on. They don't know what Eugene Loring was talking about. They're posturing and . . . ' The posturing and posing is something I don't understand.

I don't think they think anything. I think most people . . . and this also happens because of all the money . . . most people are involved primarily in making a living. That's what it all boils down to. A lot of parents say to their children, "You have to make a living," and then the kids . . . They get there, they want to make a living. I have nothing against that, but that's what dancing amounts to now—dancing is a good job. And I . . . I'm 71 years old, and I don't feel like I ever worked a day in my life.

Postscript

*I*N MY FIRST YEAR OF COLLEGE, I took an English history course for which there was no textbook. The teacher handed us a reading list and announced that he had reserved the relevant titles for us in the library. "The more of them you read," he informed us dryly, "the less you'll know, because every writer will tell you something different. Don't expect history to be clear-cut. You'll have to work out what actually happened for yourself."

This book grew from a short interview I conducted one dark January afternoon solely to discover what it would reveal. I had no fixed agenda, nothing I wanted to prove and no idea where my questions would lead. But I went ahead and asked them anyway, because I was nostalgic for a time when I didn't have to be nostalgic and troubled by a sense of artistic loss and of *mottainai*, which the Japanese dictionary defines as "a regrettable situation in which something is wasted without its value being fully utilized." I thought that professionals could help me understand what had happened to dance at the end of the 20th century and how it had happened, but now, several years and 18 interviews later, I know both more and less than I did before they started talking.

Grace was undoubtedly under pressure when I began this inquiry, and the pressure had maneuvered dance into a state that was driving away long-term supporters, knowledgeable critics, willing patrons and even relative newcomers, who emerged from their initial infatuation with broken hearts. Though I can't give you numbers, I had friends in all those categories who had loved dance and left it, and every one of them could tell you why. For many others, myself included, returning regularly to most of the companies we knew and seeking out unfamiliar ones had become a lot like accepting a succession of blind dates. Though we couldn't be sure exactly what would turn up, the risk was negligible on any given night, and there was always the chance that this time our dreams would come true. On the other hand, thousands of people were walking into dance performances without any expectations at all, simply to enjoy themselves, and leaving the theatre with dreams they had never dreamed before. I've read that roughly 60 percent of the world's population is younger than 25, so in another 20 years the visions we now share by sitting together in the dark, which often seem to me so flawed, will surely have assumed the glow of irretrievable splendor for some of them.

Everything changes—that's the way of the world. The act of passing dance through time changes dance, just as our passage through time changes us, and it would be useless and senseless to deny it. In 1971, as decimalization replaced the old British monetary system of pounds, shillings and pence, one bewildered woman exclaimed, "Why couldn't they have waited to do this until all the old folk were dead?" Dancers laugh at this story and shrug their shoulders eloquently, acknowledging the sentiment while mocking the speaker's naiveté. After a lifetime in a discipline that defines survival in terms of adaptation, they accept change as they accept patience and failure. And if each of them views it from a different perspective . . . well, as my professor warned, reconciling their differences is up to us.

Despite their misgivings, most of the dancers I interviewed tempered their concern for their art with a measure of hope, and even those who fear for its future have not given up on it. The economist John Kenneth Galbraith often declared that belief has no necessary relation to reality, but artists like these disprove him all the time, generating reality out of nothing more substantial than imagination and fortitude. Younger artists do it too—no statute demands that they retire first. Before Mark Morris ever had a company, he went to lunch one day with his friend Barry Alterman, who had recently agreed to be his manager. Insisting they both "wear ties to mark the seriousness of the occasion," Alterman presented the choreographer with two suggestions. "We'll do nothing to further your career," he began. "You hardly have one anyway. We'll only do things that are fun." Then he said, "You have these friends, they are the same people who do your concerts every year. It's a little de facto company. Why don't we say it's a real company?

It doesn't mean anything, just that if things go well, we will live to fight another day, and live as artists."

Those who live as artists after they have left the stage strike me now as even braver than beginners. Having retired the better to advance, they fight for their beliefs by turning away from the mirror and confronting the tantalizing face of possibility instead. By choosing to ignore their own image, they render themselves deeply unfashionable; in an era obsessed with ego and appearance, that particular choice qualifies as 24-karat eccentricity. But it also sets an example that can outlast fashion and reinforce the values that fitful styles perpetually corrupt.

Fat chance, some people will say. Why bother preserving those values? No one cares about them anymore. They could be right, but I think the jury is still out. The evidence that points straight to cultural disaster proclaims that youth is king, experience counts for nothing, and the last word rests on the bottom line. Eminent heart surgeons and distinguished university lecturers whose faculties and skills are perfectly intact are falling victim to ageism. In some American colleges, undergraduates can major in English literature without reading Shakespeare or Milton. School figures have disappeared from figure-skating events and compulsory exercises from gymnastics—after 12 years of debate the gymnastics federation decided they prolonged the competitions unnecessarily and bored the fans. And discipline has come to stand for repression in ordinary schoolrooms everywhere.

Attacked from within their own organizations, responsible artistic directors have lost their authority and then their jobs as their boards force them through hoops that cramp their style and restrict their creativity. In some countries, outsiders besiege the arts as well. British politicians and journalists regularly chastize theatrical dance for being elitist, as if it were a private club managed by wastrels. Demanding universal access to a discipline that already welcomes everyone, the righteous imply that dance deliberately excludes the uninitiated, and that its special vocabulary and distinctive rigors represent a form of snobbery rather than the tools of an expressive trade that speaks democratically to all.

Yet you still find artists who work wherever they can and follow their ideals straight to the future. Some of them have barely gotten started, like the 200 composers who entered a recent competition for new chamber operas or the 20-year-old student who publicly accused his art school of failing to teach him how to paint and draw. Others can't bear to stop. One half of the tap-dancing Nicholas Brothers whose inimitable act brightened Broadway shows, nightclubs and about 60 movies, Fayard Nicholas is still performing, on two artificial hips, at the age of 87. He introduces himself by announcing, "If you think you're gonna see on this stage what my brother and I used to do—forget it. I can't do that any-more. I don't *want* to do that anymore. And I'll tell you why—it hurts!" Then he puts his feet into action and struts his stuff.

Katherine Dunham was teaching class from a wheelchair at 91 and speaking at educational seminars about the Afro-Caribbean technique she had created 60 years earlier. Having left the Graham company and established her own troupe at the age of 39, Mary Anthony was still choreographing and teaching at 84, and Carmen de Lavallade was 68 when she formed a new concert trio with two old friends. In 2000, a troupe called the Silver Belles consisted of five black chorus girls between the ages of 80 and 95, all of whom hailed from the Apollo Theatre's legendary No. 1 Chorus Line, which kicked off in 1934. Boasting of being "the only original member of Ballet Theater who is still dancing professionally," cho-reographer Donald Saddler dusted off his shoes at 81 to appear in a Broadway revival of *Follies;* he partnered Marge Champion, who was only 80 at the time. Choreographers Merce Cunningham and Maurice Béjart still lead the ensembles they founded more than 50 years ago, and the 65-year-old Moiseyev Dance Company remains under the direction of its founder, Igor Moiseyev, who is 96.

And when those artists die, younger artists, who are just as com-mitted, will replace them, quietly stepping into the front line of de-fense against neglect, corroded ideals, disappointment and ennui. I'm not wishing on the moon—just look around. Peter Boal, a principal with New York City Ballet since 1989, joined the School of American Ballet faculty in 1997, and Nikolaj Hübbe, another New York City Ballet principal, has announced that he will return to his native Den-mark as a ballet master for the Royal Danish Ballet. Irek Mukhame-dov has begun to teach and choreograph, and Paris Opéra Ballet stars Marie-Claude Pietragalla and Charles Jude are now running the bal-let companies in Marseille and Bordeaux respectively. In 2002, Susan Jaffe accepted an advisory position with ABT's administration after 22 years of performing with that company. The very same month, Michael O'Hare was appointed assistant ballet master of Birmingham Royal Ballet after 22 years of performing with *that* company. A founding member of Mark Morris' troupe, Tina Fehlandt became the first director of its school in 2001, and Robert Swinston, who has yet to retire from the Cunningham ensemble, is already staging the Cunningham repertory elsewhere.

There are no guarantees. Dance is just as prone to misfortune as dancers, and nothing exempts it from Murphy's Law: Whatever can go wrong, will. But don't forget those tales of the dancers who materialize like rabbits out of hats, just when they're needed, to save the day. One minute they're sitting out front in street clothes, minding their own business and watching the show, and the next minute they're in the wings, racing to warm up as they wriggle into someone else's costume. "No, it's three to the right and two to the left . . . I'll hold you above the elbow . . . Let me pin this . . . The repeat is much faster . . . ," and on they go, as the injured artist they're replacing limps away. It doesn't happen every night, but more often than you might expect a performance turns into a kind of elegant relay race. In order to bring it to a satisfactory conclusion, everyone must run, even the artists who thought they had the night off. History is the same as anecdote, only longer. The race doesn't end when certain artists leave the stage or when selfless artisans abandon the roles we never see them perform unless there's absolutely no one, in the wings or out front or home watching the game, who is prepared to replace them.

It's important that someone appears to grab the baton, but it's more important that someone always appears to grab the baton. Introducing a study of Leonardo da Vinci, Kenneth Clark focused on "the visible expression of grace. Although Renaissance writers left no formal definition of that word," he wrote, "they would all have agreed that it implied a series of smooth transitions . . . An abrupt transition was brutal; the graceful was continuous." The artists who relieve the pressure on dance enter the studio every day and place themselves between the dancers and brutality. With experience and will as their only protection, they rejoin the race at a full sprint, guiding the pack at their heels between custom and daring and between then and now. To smooth the dancers' progress, they drag all the options they can imagine into every relay, shrewdly herding respect against irreverence, amplitude against moderation and nature against artifice so that each brushes the other as they run continuously together.

Time passes. "Everything moves as it goes along," said Robbins philosophically. My friend's child, the one we briefly and hilariously confused with Baryshnikov, has just started law school. When I last stopped in Delhi, a notice taped to the screen door of that little building near the gas station announced, "Baby ballet, age 3–6, Monday, 3:15–4:15." Someone had shoved the mats and weights against the wall to prepare for that class, so the room looked cool and expectant, just like empty dance studios everywhere. And down the street in the luncheonette, the pie was out of this world.

Endnotes

INTRODUCTION

p. 19 "When I was growing up . . . the way they are." *The New Yorker*, 21 June 93, p. 40

IN THE CLASSROOM

p. 25 "I was paid . . . like crazy!" Frank, Rusty. *Tap!* Revised ed., Da Capo Press, New York, 1994, p. 146

p. 26 "a master planner . . . actually was born." "The Williams Story," Jem Productions, 2001. Ch. 4 (U.K.), Broadcast 19 July 01

p. 26 "There's a rush . . . you don't have." Ryan, Joan. *Little Girls in Pretty Boxes*. Warner Books, New York, 1995, p. 151

p. 27 "In Ethiopia . . . his experience." *Independent on Sunday*, 3 September 00.

p. 28 "The art of locomotion . . . philosophy." *Financial Times*, 30 June 00

p. 29 "My parents . . . had ribbons on!'" Newman, Barbara. *Striking a Balance*. Limelight Editions, New York, 1992, p. 280

p. 29 "I am an advocate . . . breeding and virtue." Aldrich, Elizabeth. *From the Ballroom to Hell*. Northwestern University Press, Evanston, Ill., 1991, p. 39

p. 30 "The man doesn't . . . three legs." *New York Times*, 19 June 77

p. 31 "I was too rich . . . the experience." *Ballet News*, May 1982, p. 20

p. 32 "that there wasn't . . . free of charge.'" Tomkins, Calvin. *Ahead of the Game*. Penguin Books, London, 1968, p. 83

p. 33 "You can teach . . . interesting." Newman, op. cit., pp. 171–72

p. 33 "On days of inspection . . . That is all." Brown, Gene. *Show Time*. Macmillan, Inc., New York, 1997, p. 44

p. 34 "lopsided," "a . . . devil." Smakov, Gennady. *The Great Russian Dancers*. Alfred A. Knopf, New York, 1984, p. 65

p. 36 "There was an amazing . . . of those positions." *Dancing Times*, November 1985, p. 124

p. 38 "The windows . . . grew to love." Gregory, John. *Leningrad's Ballet*. Zena Publications, Ltd., Croesor, Wales, 1990, p. 35

p. 43 "We always wanted . . . Shut up.'" *Ballet News*, May 1982, p. 16

pp. 43–55 Author's interviews, June 1995, June 1999

pp. 59–79 Author's interviews, December 2000, February 2001

pp. 83–95 Author's interview, October 2001

pp. 99–108 Author's interview, September 1995

p. 110 "I don't hold auditions . . . the school." *New York Times*, 11 October 75

p. 111 "You just want . . . your friends." *New York Times*, 27 May 01

p. 112 "You may find . . . on again." Lebrecht, Norman. *The Maestro Myth*. Paperback ed., Simon & Schuster Ltd., London, 1992, p. 158

On the Job

p. 114 "new [board] members . . . $50,000." *New York Times*, 5 October 98

pp. 118–19 "one of the problems . . . do now?'" Author's interview, 5 April 01

p. 121 "I suppose . . . hang ourselves." *The Times*, London, 25 September 98

p. 123 "If Fanny Brice . . . *Cinderella*." *New York Times*, 21 May 97

p. 123 "We should . . . will come." *New York Times*, 5 April 99

p. 123 "To be crass . . . box office." *New York Times*, 7 May 00

p. 124 "Ten years ago . . . that I sell." *New York Times*, 6 August 00

p. 125 "S&M . . . gay clubs." *Frank* magazine, December 1997, p. 143

p. 125 "the people . . . novelties." *New York Times*, 21 May 84

p. 125 "We had . . . 50 dancers." *New York Times*, 24 November 96

p. 128 "confined . . . despotic leaders." *The New Yorker*, 19 April 99, p. 58

pp. 128–29 "Look at who's saying . . . for dancers." *New York* magazine, 11 December 95, p. 56

p. 129 "the RSC . . . at all." *The Times*, London, 30 May 01

p. 130 "the Philadelpha . . . me." *The Economist*, 2 March 96, p. 78

p. 130 "Poor things . . . only allowed to." Author's interview, 22 August 95

p. 130 "when to say . . . 'Never.'" Thelen, Lawrence. *The Show Makers*. Routledge, New York, 2000, p. 19

pp. 131–32 "sometimes I did . . . to 6:00." *Dance View*, vol. 11, no. 4 (summer 1994), p. 31

p. 132 "We used to . . . begin again." Author's interview, 2 June 99

pp. 133–34 "The critics . . . can't be fake." Author's interview, 28 February 97

p. 134 "We had wonderful . . . what I know." Author's interview, 5 June 99

p. 135 "companies have . . . save companies." *New York Times*, 28 November 95

p. 135 "Lincoln asked . . . kill us." Reynolds, Nancy. *Repertory in Review*. The Dial Press, New York, 1977, p. 121

p. 135 "The whole concept . . . you're dead." *The New Yorker*, 20 October 97, p. 191

p. 135 "Before they . . . every stage." *The Times*, London, 23 May 97

p. 136 "Power weighs . . . have it." *Financial Times*, 14 October 99

p. 136 "I am in service . . . you are." *New York Times*, 21 April 96

p. 137 "for dancers . . . dance knowledge." Edinburgh International Festival press conference, 15 August 96

p. 137 "when you are . . . live again." Anawalt, Sasha. *The Joffrey Ballet*. Scribner, New York, 1996, pp. 288–89

p. 137 "We have . . . out of her." Crisp, Clement, Anya Sainsbury and Peter Williams, eds., *50 Years of Ballet Rambert*. The Scolar Press, Great Britain, 1976, p. 44

p. 138 "To be . . . do this work." *The New Yorker*, 30 October 65, p. 106

p. 138 "A New Freedom . . . No scum." Wright, Frank Lloyd. *The Living City*. Horizon Press, New York, 1958. Front insert.

p. 139 "Nothing can . . . an elephant." Fellini, Federico. *Fellini on Fellini*. Eyre Methuen Ltd., London, 1976, p. 104

pp. 141–47 Author's interview, January 1995

pp. 147–61 Author's interview, April 2001

pp. 163–77 Author's interview, August 2001

pp. 179–95 Author's interview, September 2001

pp. 197–208 Author's interview, August 1998

In Creation and Revival

p. 209 "that the new ballet . . . dance to it." Benois, Alexandre. *Reminiscences of the Russian Ballet*. Putnam, London, 1941, p. 122

p. 209 "in the power . . . long time." Ibid., p. 124

p. 210 "I could not . . . suicide." Buckle, Richard. *Diaghilev*. Atheneum, New York, 1979, pp. 502–03

p. 211 "I always panic . . . I want." Servos, Norbert. *Pina Bausch—Wuppertal Dance Theater*. Ballett-Bühnen-Verlag, Cologne, 1984, p. 229

p. 211 "The most difficult . . . you're untalented." Kislan, Richard. *Hoofing on Broadway*. Simon & Schuster Ltd., London, 1987, p. 106

p. 211 "My greatest fear . . . Pacific approach." Tharp, Twyla. *Push Comes to Shove*. Linda Grey/Bantam Books, New York, 1992, p. 129

p. 213 "I think . . . of the tomb." *San Francisco* Magazine, November 2000, p. 200

p. 213 "People are . . . grounds to sue." *New York Times*, 4 March 01

pp. 213–14 "Essentially . . . a choreographer." *New York Times* Magazine, 8 December 74, p. 109

p. 214 "Aesthetics . . . the birds." Tomkins, Calvin. *Off the Wall*. Penguin Books, London, 1980, p. 59

p. 215 "I saw . . . assure you." Drummond, John. *Speaking of Diaghilev*. Faber and Faber Ltd., London, 1997, p. 211

p. 219 "I've trained . . . to concentrate." *Financial Times*, 9 March 96

p. 219 "Balthus is . . . the pictures." *The Times*, London, 19 February 01

p. 219 "This is not . . . another plot." De Mille, Agnes. *Dance to the Piper*. Little, Brown and Co., Boston, 1951, p. 211

p. 220 "I gotta spin . . . curtain call." *Village Voice*, 5 January 76

pp. 221–22 "When I had . . . the same." *Daily News* Magazine, 26 February 89

p. 222 "Now, Fred . . . by Easter." Dominic, Zoë and John Selwyn Gilbert. *Frederick Ashton*. Henry Regnery Co., Chicago, 1971, p. 74

p. 222 "Fred's main weakness . . . of it anyway.'" Ibid., p. 66

p. 222 "There was no . . . to be done." Ibid., p. 75

p. 224 "I've been . . . real estate." *Independent*, 5 October 99

p. 225 "My leg . . . makes me vomit." Banes, Sally. *Terpsichore in Sneakers*. Houghton Mifflin Co., Boston, 1980, p. 105

p. 225 "Merce created . . . were *dancing*." Kostelanetz, Richard, ed. *Merce Cunningham: Dancing in Space and Time*. a cappella books, Chicago, 1992, p. 119

p. 225 "If somebody . . . savage them." *Vanity Fair*, January 2001, p. 133

p. 226 "she would plan . . . quietness." *Ballet Review*, vol. 9.1 (spring 1981), p. 80

p. 226 "Béjart choreographs . . . becomes the ballet." Newman, op. cit., p. 337

p. 226 "He threw . . . to be great." Grubb, Kevin Boyd. *Razzle Dazzle*. St. Martin's Press, New York, 1989, p. 42

p. 226 "Eighty-five per cent . . . become the work." *The New Yorker*, 30 October 00, p. 18

pp. 226–27 "For example . . . take their clothes off." *Independent on Sunday*, 27 August 00

p. 227 "What is achieved . . . all the answers." Williams, David, comp. *Peter Brook: A Theatrical Casebook*. Revised ed., Methuen, London, 1992, p. 10

p. 228 "It's all already . . . and reasoning." *The New Yorker*, 7 June 93, p. 87

p. 228 "what reads as . . . and more time." Banes, op. cit., p. 110

p. 228 "the knee was . . . .18th century." Lopokova, Lydia. Unpublished ms. for proposed radio broadcast, c. 1938, Item LLK/3/7, p. 14, n.d. in Collected Papers of John Maynard Keynes and Lydia Lopokova Keynes. King's College Archive, Cambridge University

p. 228 "a little Auschwitzy." Kelly, Kevin. *One Singular Sensation*. Doubleday, New York, 1990, pp. 65–66

p. 228 "While I was waiting . . . hours a day." Zadan, Craig. *Sondheim & Co.* Pavilion Books Ltd., 1987, p. 139

p. 229 "I've performed . . . as many performances." *New York Times Magazine*, 8 December 74, p. 108

p. 229 "I found that . . . in any direction." Drummond, op. cit., p. 251

p. 229 "'Okay, now you've worked . . . that specific." *Ballet Review*, vol. 22.4 (winter 1994), p. 26

p. 229 "George would just . . . annoy you." Newman, op. cit., p. 179

p. 229 "God put me . . . what is good." Maiorano, Robert and Valerie Brooks. *Balanchine's "Mozartiana"*. Freundlich Books, New York, 1985, p. 49

p. 230 "who reveal . . . to the bone." *The Times*, London, 1 November 00

p. 230 "Conventionally . . . the next one." *New York Times*, 12 September 99

p. 230 "like roller-skates . . . endless." *Independent*, 17 June 96

p. 231 "a poem . . . closing box." *Letters on Poetry from W.B. Yeats to Dorothy Wellesley*. Oxford Paperbacks. Oxford University Press, London, 1964, p. 22

p. 231 "isn't like painting . . . out the dancer." Kislan, op. cit., p. 86

p. 231 "The most difficult . . . it's finished." *Independent*, 23 October 00

pp. 233–46 Author's interview, August 1996

p. 249 "If you get . . . person to another." Romain, Michael. *A Profile of Jonathan Miller*. Cambridge University Press, Cambridge, 1992, p. 34

p. 253 "I have to prepare . . . on Kenneth's." *Financial Times*, 13 January 00

p. 253 "When I die . . . vanish." *New York Times*, 5 January 97

p. 253 "Martha, this is . . . an audience." Graham, Martha. *Blood Memory*. Macmillan, London, 1992, p. 113

p. 255 "We fall . . . like silk." Ibid., p. 253

p. 256 "I see lots . . . I *don't* know." Newman, op. cit., p. 163

p. 257 "Every artist's work . . . when he was alive." Berger, John. *About Looking*. Writers and Readers Publishing Cooperative, Ltd., London, 1980, p. 171

p. 258 "those miserable . . . their cracks." Tomkins, Calvin. *Off the Wall*, p. 127

p. 258 "The idea itself . . . to revive it." *Dancing Times*, August 1999, p. 992

p. 258 "what was powerful . . . deadly today." Quoted by Terese Capucilli, Edinburgh International Festival press conference, 16 August 96

p. 259 "it was all . . . explain it." "Following Sir Fred's Steps: Ashton's Legacy." Conference at the Roehampton Institute, London, 12 November 1994

p. 259 "a truth . . . moral obligation." Haggin, B.H. *The Toscanini Musicians Knew*. Horizon Press, New York, 1967, p. 47

p. 259 "'Is this . . . for *Bayadère*?'" *New York Times*, 8 May 95

p. 259 "you cannot escape . . . 'Suzanne jumps.'" *New York Times*, 23 January 00

p. 260 "one of the . . . Paris Opéra Ballet." *New York Times*, 15 June 97

p. 261 "This is not . . . and inspired." *New York Times*, 25 April 99

p. 261 "What would . . . when he saw it." The South Bank Show, ITV (U.K.), Broadcast 12 February 95

p. 263 "An art . . . *Don Giovanni* once." Welty, Eudora. *A Writer's Eye*. McHenry, Pearl, ed. University of Mississippi Press, Jackson, Miss., 1994, pp. 144–45

pp. 265–79 Author's interviews, June 1999, November 2000

pp. 281–99 Author's interviews, April and August 1999

pp. 301–13 Author's interview, July 2001

IN THE DETAILS

p. 317 "so much happens . . . beyond words." Oates, Joyce Carol. *On Boxing*. Pan Books, London, 1988, p. 11

p. 317 "When I went . . . happen for me." Newman, op. cit., p. 222

p. 319 "We did a chair . . . made it work." *Dancing Times*, December 1985, p. 225

p. 319 "Absolute sincerity . . . immediately." Rambert, Marie. *Quicksilver*. Macmillan, London, 1972, p. 137

pp. 320–21 "The crucial thing . . . expected either." *The New Yorker*, 29 September 95, p. 103

p. 321 "Because I can." *The New Yorker*, 1 April 96, p. 50

pp. 321–22 "It's very weird . . . What now?" *New York Times*, 7 May 95

p. 322 "Forget about bars . . . is packed." *New York Times*, 24 March 96

p. 324 "Maybe going 50 times . . . it's so silly." *The Times* Magazine, London, 8 July 95, p. 32

p. 324 "It would make . . . steps to dance." Bussell, Darcey. *Life in Dance*. Century, London, 1998, p. 121

p. 326 "I dance for . . . that night." Newman, op. cit., p. 329

p. 327 "cosy-homey . . . bread." Author's interview, 22 August 1995

p. 329 "If you have . . . a stone." Conversation with author, 28 September 95 pp. 329–30 "seemed to be . . . approach Beethoven." Payzant, Geoffrey. *Glenn Gould: Music and Mind*. Revised ed., Key Porter Books, Toronto, 1992, p. 6

p. 330 "The process . . . to lucidity." Ibid., p. 79

p. 330 "I can teach . . . the moon?" Oida, Yoshi. *An Actor Adrift*. Methuen, London, 1992, p. 10

p. 330 "to decode . . . thought." *New York Times*, 8 August 99

p. 330 "It's not a question . . . wild animals." *New York Times*, 15 May 98

p. 330 "Did you ever . . . to stop now." *The New Yorker*, 3 May 93, p. 62

p. 331 "Nothing's riding . . . that matters." *All the President's Men*. William Goldman, screenplay. Warner Brothers, 1976

pp. 333–45 Author's interview, February 1997

pp. 347–55 Author's interview, August 1995

pp. 357–66 Author's interview, June 1999

IN THE STUDIO

p. 373 "That's very nice . . . not ballet." School of American Ballet newsletter, vol. XXXIII, (spring 1998), p. 3

p. 373 "Give me . . . Bedells." Author's conversation with Mary Clarke, February 2001

pp. 373–74 "When Royes . . . Caird Leslie." Conversation with author, April 1996

p. 374 "the great pedagogic . . . done before." De Mille, op. cit., p. 176

p. 374 "Do I have . . . yesterday." *The New Yorker*, 8 June 92, p. 8

p. 374 "He was teaching . . . his strength." Solway, Diane. *Nureyev*. Weidenfeld and Nicolson, London, 1998, pp. 73, 74

pp. 374–75 "Mme. Volkova . . . say with it." Author's interview, 28 February 97

p. 375 "called the room's . . . became fabric." *Dance Magazine*, January 2001, p. 69

p. 375 "If you were . . . walked on." Author's conversation with Mary Clarke, February 2001

p. 376 "Crying is good . . . start again." *Dance Magazine*, February 1958, p. 48

pp. 376–77 "always obtained . . . we could give." Rambert, op. cit., p. 47

p. 377 "There are stories . . . do it anyway.'" *Dancing Times*, November 1985, p. 125

p. 377 "When you are not . . . will win." McPhee, John. *A Sense of Where You Are*. The Noonday Press, New York, 1989, p. 65

p. 377 "When you have . . . your death." Graham, op. cit., p. 251

p. 378 "It's a goal . . . do it, ever." Newman, op. cit., p. 172

p. 380 "you must first . . . be artistic." *Dance Magazine*, March 1963, p. 50

p. 380 "the only absolute . . . in our time." Karsavina, Tamara. *Theatre Street*. Reader's Union, Constable, London, 1950, p. 180

p. 380 "as if he were . . . drill sergeant." Kirstein, Lincoln. *Thirty Years: The New York City Ballet*. Expanded paperback ed., Alfred A. Knopf, New York, 1978, p. 108

pp. 380–81 "We should all be . . . save her." *New York Times*, 22 August 85

p. 381 "In 1977 . . . now $3,000." Idem.

p. 381 "To get a space . . . in rent." Conversation with author, May 2001

p. 382 "when one of my . . . ruffles on.'" *Dance Magazine*, June 1964, p. 39

p. 383 "We artists . . . further marginalized." *New York Times*, 13 January 01

p. 383 "senior keepers . . . expensive luxuries." *Financial Times*, 6 June 99

p. 383 "The pay is . . . stay alive." *Financial Times*, 24 November 00

p. 383 "We feel that . . . not needed." *Financial Times*, 9 April 01

p. 384 "It's hard . . . or airbrushing." *New York* magazine, 17 April 00, p. 47

p. 384 "I can't tell . . . giving up completely." *Dance and Dancers*, January 1962, p. 18

p. 384 "You've got to be . . . refuse you." *Washington Post*, 18 May 00

p. 384 "For 70 years . . . nothing else." *Independent*, 10 June 99

p. 385 "after a rehearsal . . . shut the door." Drummond, op. cit., p. 209

pp. 387–97 Author's interview, January 1996

pp. 399–418 Author's interview, November 2001

pp. 419–39 Author's interview, August 1995

pp. 441–60 Author's interview, March 1997

Postscript

pp. 462–63 "wear ties . . . live as artists." *New York Times*, 3 February 02

p. 464 "If you think . . . it hurts!" *Washington Post*, 22 April 02

p. 464 "the only original . . . dancing professionally." *New York Times*, 25 March 01

p. 465 "the visible expression . . . was continuous." Clark, Kenneth. *Leonardo da Vinci*. Revised ed., Viking, New York, 1988, p. 38

p. 465 "Everything moves . . . goes along." *New York Times*, 21 May 84

Index